D0301774

Oscar Wilde's Profession

Oscar Wilde's Profession

Writing and the Culture Industry in the Late Nineteenth Century

JOSEPHINE M. GUY
AND
IAN SMALL

OXFORD
UNIVERSITY PRESS

OXFORD
UNIVERSITY PRESS

Great Clarendon Street, Oxford OX2 6DP

Oxford University Press is a department of the University of Oxford.
It furthers the University's objective of excellence in research, scholarship,
and education by publishing worldwide in

Oxford New York

Auckland Bangkok Buenos Aires Cape Town Chennai
Dar es Salaam Delhi Hong Kong Istanbul Karachi Kolkata
Kuala Lumpur Madrid Melbourne Mexico City Mumbai Nairobi
São Paulo Shanghai Singapore Taipei Tokyo Toronto
and an associated company in Berlin

Oxford is a registered trade mark of Oxford University Press
in the UK and in certain other countries

Published in the United States
by Oxford University Press Inc., New York

British Library Cataloguing in Publication Data
Data available

Library of Congress Cataloging in Publication Data
Guy, Josephine M., 1963-   .
Oscar Wilde's profession: writing and the culture industry in the
late 19th century / Josephine M. Guy and Ian Small.
Includes bibliographical references and index.
1. Wilde, Oscar, 1854-1900—Authorship.   2. Wilde, Oscar, 1854-1900—Technique.
3. Wilde, Oscar, 1854-1900—Relations with publishers.   4. Literature publishing—
Great Britain—History—19th century.   5. Literature and society—Great
Britain—History—19th century.   6. Authors and publishers—Great Britain—
History—19th century.   I. Small, Ian.   II. Title.
PR5827.A9 G89 2000   828'.809—dc21   00-044083
ISBN 0-19-818728-9

3 5 7 9 10 8 6 4 2

Typeset in Ehrhardt MT
by Alliance Phototypesetters, Pondicherry, India
Printed in Great Britain
on acid-free paper by
Biddles Ltd.,
Guildford and King's Lynn

Preface

THIS BOOK is an account of a writer's career, but it does not claim to give a complete explanation of Wilde's creativity, nor does it aspire to be a biography (as that term is usually understood). Our ambition is confined to describing an aspect of Wilde's life which persistent attention to his sexuality and nationalism has marginalized or ignored. We piece together the material circumstances of Wilde's literary production—we look at the commissioning, the writing, and the economics of his *oeuvre*, and the power relationships between Wilde, his publishers, and his theatre managers. Alongside the famous celebrity, homosexual, and wit, we reveal a figure who struggled consistently, and not always successfully, to come to terms with far-reaching changes in the culture industry of the late nineteenth century. We study Wilde's habits of composition and revision in relation to these changes, and reveal a pragmatism and worldliness far removed from the aesthetic purist and socialite who put only his talent into his work and his genius into his life. The story of this book is in part one about the commodification of literary culture in late nineteenth-century Britain, and in part about the need for the professional writer to come to terms with an emergent consumerism.

Our motivation for this study derived from and grew out of editorial work for the Oxford English Texts Edition of the *Complete Works* of Wilde. It made us realize how little attention had been paid to the textual condition of many of Wilde's works. The early and uncollected Wilde is rarely mentioned by critics; similarly ignored are his numerous unfinished projects. The *oeuvre* we describe is both larger and differently shaped from that familiar to most readers. What will be most controversial about our study is our claim that a knowledge of the origins and circumstances of many of Wilde's works makes some politicized interpretations of them difficult, if not impossible, to sustain. Our own views of Wilde have changed profoundly in the course of research for this book; when the OET edition is complete, and the full details of his compositional practice are available, the Wilde of the twenty-first century will almost certainly be very different from the Wilde of the late twentieth.

J.M.G.
I.S.

January 2000

Acknowledgements

WE WOULD like to thank Joseph Bristow and Peter Raby for their generosity in sharing research. We would also like to thank Merlin Holland for answering queries about points of detail, for reading and commenting on the manuscript, and for permission to quote from unpublished and copyright material. Wilde's correspondence is reprinted by permission of Fourth Estate Ltd from *The Letters of Oscar Wilde* edited by Merlin Holland and Sir Rupert Hart-Davis. Copyright Letters © the Estate of Oscar Wilde 1962, 1985, 2000. Editorial Matter © Sir Rupert Hart-Davis 1962, 1985, 2000; and from *The Complete Letters of Oscar Wilde* edited by Merlin Holland and Rupert Hart-Davis, © 1962 by Vyvyan Holland, 1990, 1997 by Merlin Holland. Reprinted by permission of Henry Holt and Company, LLC. We are indebted to the staff of the William Andrews Clark Memorial Library at the University of California at Los Angeles, particularly to Peter Reill, Stephen Tabor, Suzanne Tatian, and Bruce Whiteman. We are also grateful for the help received from the staff of Birmingham City Library. Comments by readers for Oxford University Press were particularly useful to us; we would also like to thank Frances Whistler for her sustained interest in this project, and Sophie Goldsworthy for helping to make this book happen. Josephine M. Guy would like to thank the University of Nottingham for research support.

Some of the argument of this book was rehearsed in a series of articles published in *English Literature in Transition*. We would like to thank its editor, Professor Robert Langenfeld, for his encouragement and for supporting the kind of empirical research we have undertaken. The pieces in question include: Ian Small, 'Popular Wilde', *ELT*, 40: 3 (1997), 310–16; Ian Small, 'The Economies of Taste: Literary Markets and Literary Value in the Late Nineteenth Century', *ELT*, 39: 1 (1996), 7–18; Josephine M. Guy, 'Self-Plagiarism, Creativity and Craftsmanship in Oscar Wilde', *ELT*,

41: 1 (1998), 6–23; Josephine M. Guy, 'Aesthetics, Economics and Commodity Culture: Theorizing Value in Late Nineteenth-Century Britain', *ELT*, 42: 2 (1999), 143–71; and Josephine M. Guy and Ian Small, 'How Many "Bags of Red Gold"? The Extent of Wilde's Success as a Dramatist', *ELT*, 42: 3 (1999), 283–97.

Contents

Abbreviations

For convenience we cite Robert Ross's 1908 edition of Wilde's works by his name followed by the short title of the volume in question; for example: Ross, *Reviews*. The following abbreviations are also used:

Ellmann
: Richard Ellmann, *Oscar Wilde* (London: Hamish Hamilton, 1987).

Encyclopedia
: Karl Beckson, *The Oscar Wilde Encyclopedia* (New York: AMS Press, 1998).

Heritage
: Karl Beckson (ed.), *Oscar Wilde: The Critical Heritage* (1970; London: Routledge, 1997).

Letters
: Rupert Hart-Davis (ed.), *The Letters of Oscar Wilde*, (1962; London: Hart-Davis, 1963).

Mason
: Stuart Mason [Christopher Millard], *A Bibliography of Oscar Wilde* (London: T. Werner Laurie, 1914).

More Letters
: Rupert Hart-Davis (ed.), *More Letters of Oscar Wilde* (London: John Murray, 1985).

OWR
: Ian Small, *Oscar Wilde Revalued* (Greensboro, NC: ELT Press, 1993).

We use 'Society Comedies' to refer to Wilde's four plays, *Lady Windermere's Fan*, *A Woman of No Importance*, *An Ideal Husband*, *The Importance of Being Earnest*; and 'society comedies' to refer to the sub-genre. *Salomé* refers to the French-language edition of Wilde's play; *Salome* refers to the English translation.

I

Wilde the Writer

In 1900 the *Pall Mall Gazette*, a paper to which Oscar Wilde had frequently contributed in the 1880s, published an obituary notice of him which claimed that he 'had wonderful cleverness, but no substantiality', and 'nothing that he ever wrote had strength to endure'.[1] The extent of Wilde's celebrity a century later seems totally to controvert this judgement. The past two decades alone have seen numerous revivals of his dramatic works in Britain and Ireland by directors as varied as Steven Berkoff, Peter Hall, Patrick Mason, and Philip Prowse; Wilde has been the subject of a major film and several television documentaries. He has been memorialized in a window in Westminster Abbey, and by sculptures in Merrion Square in Dublin and near St Martin-in-the-Fields in London. Moreover his popularity at the box office seems to be matched by his standing among academics. It is not unusual for modern cultural historians to rank Wilde with Nietzsche as one of the most important figures in the European *fin de siècle*.

Such celebrity, however, is not quite all that it seems, for the Wilde who has outlived the deprecating judgements of the *Pall Mall Gazette* is not principally Wilde the *writer*. Observing the sudden decline in Wilde's fortunes at the end of his life, the nineteenth-century theatre critic and impresario Jacob Grein noted that readers had 'shunned the artist because the man had gone under'.[2] It is undeniable that for much of the twentieth century Wilde's disgrace obstructed any critical reassessment of his work, and the celebrity which Wilde enjoys today has depended to a large extent upon a revaluation (perhaps even a fetishization) of the life. The reclamation of the man as a cultural icon has, however, been achieved at

[1] *Heritage*, 229–30.   [2] Ibid. 233.

some cost—to pick up Grein's metaphor, the writing still remains partly submerged. Or, more exactly, the details of the biography (particularly of Wilde's homosexuality) continue to be the lens through which the literary works are viewed. For example, many recent theatrical productions of Wilde's works, including Rough Magic's *Lady Windermere's Fan* (1994), Nicholas Hytner's staging of *The Importance of Being Earnest* (1993), and Neil Bartlett's dramatization of *The Picture of Dorian Gray* (1994), have exploited alleged gay subtexts in Wilde's *oeuvre*.[3] In a similar way, Brian Gilbert's 1997 film *Wilde* traded upon enacting in explicit detail aspects of Wilde's personal relationship with Alfred Douglas. The fact that it has taken over ninety years for Robert Ross's 1908 edition of Wilde's collected works to be superseded by a full modern edition betrays the persistence of this anxiety about Wilde's literary achievement.[4]

On the whole modern academic critics have been more comfortable with theorizing about Wilde's iconoclasm, and his status as a figure marginal to British culture, than they have been with discussing particularities of his writing career.[5] This preoccupation with the politics of Wilde's life has unsurprisingly resulted in an uneven interest in his work: the early poetry and plays, the lectures, the uncollected journalism, and the short fiction have been largely overlooked, even though collectively they form well over half of his output. This piecemeal treatment in turn has taken its cue from Richard Ellmann's best-selling biography, *Oscar Wilde* (1987). Ellmann's unapologetic revaluation of Wilde's sexuality placed desire at the centre of both his personal and creative life: homosexuality, Ellmann claimed in a memorable phrase which could stand as the watchword for the whole biography, 'fired [Wilde's] mind'.[6]

Ellmann's interpretation of the life consolidated Wilde's rehabilitation as a central figure in late nineteenth-century British culture. Yet in one respect the terms by which Ellmann was judging Wilde's works had hardly changed from those used in the 1890s. Ellmann

3 For discussion of recent productions of Wilde's plays, see Joel H. Kaplan, 'Wilde on the Stage', in Peter Raby (ed.), *The Cambridge Companion to Oscar Wilde* (Cambridge: Cambridge University Press, 1997), 249–75.

4 The Oxford English Texts edition of the *Complete Works of Oscar Wilde* is currently in preparation. The first volume appeared in 2000.

5 There are some studies of Wilde's writing practices but they restrict themselves to one genre, such as the criticism or the plays; as a consequence they typically fail to notice the contradictions in Wilde's writing practices across the *oeuvre*. These studies are discussed in Ch. 7.   6 Ellmann, 265.

consistently employed the work to understand the sexual constitution of the author, although the value that he placed on that sexuality changed. One consequence of this pattern of treatment, as we
have hinted, is that Ellmann's biography overlooked many of the
details often thought to be important to a *writer's* life.[7] The industry which published Wilde's work, the precise details of his contracts and sales, the nature of his composition, and the extent of his
revisions—this kind of information, because it is not in any obvious
way linked either to a sexual identity or to a sexual understanding of
creativity, was largely ignored. In Ellmann's biography whole areas
of Wilde's *oeuvre* (most glaringly the three volumes of short fiction)
are to all intents and purposes erased.

To write a biography of an artist inevitably requires some working definition of creativity. Even if that definition is never made
fully explicit or theorized, it must rely upon a set of assumptions
about the sort of evidence which the biographer is looking for and
which she believes will explain the particular talents or gifts of the
artist in question. Ellmann's biography was not the first study to
emphasize the connections between Wilde's sexuality and his creativity, but it has proved to be the most influential. Later accounts,
by critics such as Ed Cohen, Richard Dellamora, Jonathan
Dollimore, and Alan Sinfield, while frequently at odds with
Ellmann's, are in many ways indebted to him for legitimating the
'gay' Wilde (for want of a better label) as an area of enquiry, so much
so that it has dominated academic and popular interest for the last
twenty years. In what is now virtually a 'master-narrative', Wilde's
sexuality is seen to be expressed through his works at a subtextual or
coded level. For example, the apparent fascination with bourgeois
heterosexual culture in the Society Comedies is seen to be 'subverted' by a homoerotic subtext. Such readings radicalize the works
in ways which make them compatible with the transgressive sexuality of their author—that is, modern critics' prior understanding of
Wilde's sense of (sexual) difference motivates and makes visible the
oppositional politics which they detect and value in his writing.[8]

7 In this respect, there is a striking difference between the conception of a writer's life in,
say, John Sutherland's biography of Mary Ward (*Mrs Humphry Ward: Eminent Victorian,
Pre-Eminent Edwardian* (Oxford: Clarendon Press, 1990)) and the whole tenor of Ellmann's
project.
8 It is worth noting that interest in the politics of Wilde's life (as opposed to the politics
of his work) continues; see e.g. J. Robert Maguire, 'Oscar Wilde and the Dreyfus Affair',
Victorian Studies, 41:1 (Autumn 1997), 1–29.

It is obvious, however, that some of Wilde's works have been more amenable than others to this sort of treatment, hence the disproportionate amount of critical interest in *The Picture of Dorian Gray* and the Society Comedies. There have been attempts to uncover homoerotic elements in other parts of the *oeuvre*, including the short fiction, but these studies have been much less convincing.[9] Alert to the strains in this master-narrative, and its limitations in accounting for the whole of the *oeuvre*, some critics have begun to question its overall validity. Joseph Bristow, for example, has expressed disquiet about the very use of the modern category of the 'homosexual' when it is applied to Wilde's own understanding of himself.[10] Bristow suggests that there may be a discrepancy between Wilde's perception of his sexuality and that ascribed to him by some modern critics. More precisely, he hints that there is no concrete evidence that Wilde had the politicized view of his sexuality typically attributed to him, nor that he saw it as transgressive in the same way as some modern critics do. In their turn these kinds of reservations have profound consequences for how we understand the nature of Wilde's creativity. Clearly they imply that we cannot assume a straightforward relationship between sexual experience and its textual expression. More fundamentally, Bristow casts doubt on the assumption that an oppositional politics is evident in Wilde's (sexual) life, let alone in his works. In a telling comment, he argues that the debate about the nature of Wilde's homosexuality 'begs significant questions about how we can apply ourselves to . . . historical specificity'.[11] Bristow's critique points to new and complex areas of enquiry, in which not only Wilde's conception of his own sexuality is in question, but also the manner in which it affects his creativity. Controversially Melissa Knox has detected a fear of sexual maturity both in Wilde's known sexual relationships and in his representation of the desirable body. This thesis complicates our understanding of Wilde's attitude to the relationships between power and sexuality, and therefore of the nature of the oppositional politics detected in his work.[12]

---

[9] See e.g. Robert K. Martin, 'Oscar Wilde and the Fairy Tale: "The Happy Prince" as Self-Dramatization', *Studies in Short Fiction*, 16 (1979), 74–7; see also Clifton Snider, 'Eros and Logos in Some Fairy Tales by Oscar Wilde: A Jungian Interpretation', *Victorian Newsletter*, 84 (Fall 1993), 1–8.

[10] Joseph Bristow, ' "A complex multiform creature": Wilde's sexual identities', in *The Cambridge Companion*, 195–218.   [11] Ibid. 196.

[12] See Melissa Knox, *Oscar Wilde: A Long and Lovely Suicide* (London: Yale University

While the 'gay' Wilde remains the dominant concern among modern scholars, there has been another putative master-narrative for combining problematic aspects of the life and the work; this retains the antinomian elements of Wilde's writing, but it understands them in the context of his Irish origins, rather than his sexuality. More precisely, Wilde's Irish upbringing and his subsequent interest in Irish nationalism have been seen to determine his allegedly hostile (and 'subversive') attitude to many aspects of British culture. The relative newness of this 'Irish' Wilde necessarily means that it has been subject to less scrutiny than the more familiar story of the 'gay' Wilde. Nevertheless, the research which has been undertaken points to a complexity similar to that now recognized in accounts of Wilde's homosexuality. Jerusha McCormack, for example, comments that:

To say that Wilde is Irish . . . is to define him in terms of a question: what does it mean to be Irish? How many things does it include? And what must it, implicitly or explicitly, exclude? At various stages of his career, Wilde invoked different definitions of Irishness; to some extent, it would be fair to argue . . . that Wilde was inventing Ireland as he proceeded to invent himself.[13]

Davis Coakley, Richard Pine, and Declan Kiberd have all explored the implications of some of these questions. As McCormack herself observes, this work on the 'Irish' Wilde has produced 'complexity' which 'elicits other complexities'.[14] One obvious source of these complexities is the problematic relationship between Irish nationalism, issues of sexual freedom, and the tolerance of sexual difference. The downfall of figures such as Charles Parnell and Kitty O'Shea suggests a definition of political freedom too narrow to encompass the lifestyle chosen by Wilde in the late 1880s and 1890s. A further problem is that a concern with the 'Irish' Wilde has to confront awkward details of his early life, such as his role as an Irish landlord despairing of the low rents his properties yielded; or what was virtually a self-imposed exile from the country of his birth; or

Press, 1994). See also Victoria White, 'Women of No Importance: Misogyny in the Work of Oscar Wilde', in Jerusha McCormack (ed.), *Wilde the Irishman* (London: Yale University Press, 1998), 158–65.

[13] McCormack, *Wilde the Irishman*, 2.

[14] Ibid. 3. See Coakley, *Oscar Wilde: The Importance of Being Irish* (Dublin: Town House, 1994); Kiberd, *Inventing Ireland* (London: Vintage, 1995); and Pine, *The Thief of Reason: Oscar Wilde and Modern Ireland* (Dublin: Gill and Macmillan, 1995).

his need to find success within British culture, to the extent of applying for employment in such quintessentially British institutions as the British civil service.[15] The writers in McCormack's anthology are alert to these difficulties, although they do not always adequately resolve them. McCormack notes that Wilde's life 'demonstrates . . . that to be Irish is to have multiple, and divided, loyalties . . . to inhabit a space where contraries meet and are transvalued into something else, a something which by definition escapes definition'.[16] McCormack's question, 'What difference does it make to read [Wilde] as Irish?', is no less important than the question of his sexuality; but it is difficult to see how it can be answered when her definition of Irishness is so elusive. It also has to be acknowledged that, apart from some early lectures and throwaway asides about the Celt, there are almost no explicit references to Ireland or Irish issues in Wilde's writing, as there are in the work of contemporaries such as Yeats, Shaw, or even Lionel Johnson and William Sharp. Given the enormous interest in the late nineteenth century in a Celtic identity, both in Britain and Ireland, we do need to explain why Wilde chose *not* to engage more with such an obviously topical subject.[17]

Of course we do not wish to deny the importance of Wilde's sensitivity to his Irish nationality, nor that it contributed in some way to the complexities of his dealings with British vested commercial and literary interests. However, the precise nature of Wilde's Irish politics, and the ways in which they find expression in his work and in shaping his literary career, remain questions as unresolved as that of the role of his sexuality. For our purposes, the utility of the paradigm of the 'Irish' Wilde is most severely tested when it is called upon to explain the *material* details of his writing practices. It should be possible to answer McCormack's question, 'What difference does it make to read [Wilde] as Irish?', by applying it in the first place to explain specific career decisions. For example, while it might be the case that Wilde's Irish upbringing contributed to his

[15] In *Inventing Ireland* Kiberd calls Wilde a London exile, a label which itself begs many questions about the nature of exile, especially if self-imposed.

[16] McCormack, *Wilde the Irishman*, 3.

[17] McCormack gives as an example of the importance of reading Wilde in an Irish context Davis Coakley's argument that the *donnée* of 'The Selfish Giant' was Wilde's memory of playing in the private garden of Merrion Square and seeing slum children pressing their faces against the railings (5). Whether or not this is true, it is certainly not a reading which could have been available to general readers for over a century.

initial failure to find acceptance among English literary circles, it does not explain why he chose to edit the *Woman's World*, nor to write for the *Dramatic Review* in the 1880s. Similarly, it might be tempting to explain Wilde's decision to write fairy-tales by reference to his parents' interest in collecting Irish folklore; however that family connection does not explain the decision to direct one collection of stories (*The Happy Prince and Other Tales*) at a popular readership and another (*A House of Pomegranates*) at a connoisseur market, nor why the first was a modest success and the second a complete failure. Finally, it is not easy to see how a knowledge of Wilde's Irish background helps us to understand why theatre managers in London's unashamedly commercial West End consistently refused *The Duchess of Padua* but were willing to stage *Lady Windermere's Fan*, a play which was much more explicitly critical of British social institutions and *mores*.

It is possible to cite many other details about the material circumstances of his writing career which are not adequately explained by either the 'gay' or the 'Irish' Wilde. Nevertheless it is our argument that precisely such mundane minutiae—the pragmatic and often tedious negotiations required of a professional writer at the turn of the century—had at least as much power in shaping Wilde's literary output as his sexuality or his nationality did. One reason for the tendency of some critics to ignore the day-to-day details of his writing career may be that they are rather 'messy', in the sense that they do not comfortably square with the assumption that he was an oppositional writer, one driven by a politics (simple or complex). To put this another way: the expressive qualities which the 'gay' and 'Irish' paradigms attribute to Wilde's works are not always compatible with the material details of their textual histories—of the histories of their composition and publication. This incompatibility in turn suggests that the model of cultural production underlying both the 'gay' and 'Irish' Wilde, although satisfying at an abstract level, is not confirmed by a detailed study of his specific transactions with publishers, printers, and theatre-managers—with what we call the 'culture industry' of the 1880s and 1890s. It is precisely because Wilde's work has been so relentlessly interpreted by reference to his life that we need to be as certain as possible about what that life—as a professional writer as much as a gay man or an Irish national—entailed.

Our concern in this book, then, is with a very different aspect of creativity, one barely addressed by discussions of Wilde's sexuality

or his nationality. Our interest is in Wilde's writing practices understood from a *material*, rather than a sexual, or psychological, or nationalist point of view. Moreover, we understand the term 'material'
not via a traditional Marxist paradigm, implying as it does a particular philosophy of historical determination, but rather in the more
empirical and tangible sense invoked by Jerome J. McGann in his
theorization of the 'textual condition'.

We have taken our lead from McGann's interest in 'the advent of
meaning as a material event', in text as 'embodied phenomena', and
his attempt to change the emphasis of textual studies from a focus
on 'hermeneutics and reading' to a concern with what he calls the
'material . . . levels of text'—that is, 'the physical form of books and
manuscripts (paper, typefaces, layouts) or their prices, advertising
mechanisms, and distribution venues'.[18] In practice, however, our
understanding of the material conditions of literary production
goes beyond that of McGann, for we give more attention than he
does to the role of literary institutions in determining not only literary form, but also questions of literary identity and value. Underlying McGann's account is a desire to give to factors such as
typefaces, inks, layout, or book prices an element of objective constraint or limit to interpretation; it is as if he wants to 'fix' elements
of interpretation in the unambiguous material properties of texts,
rather than in contested issues such as intentionality. In our view
such an ambition is not sufficiently alert to the complex ways in
which those material properties can signify—certainly in the late
nineteenth century—and therefore to the ways in which their signi-
fying power can be manipulated by the institutions of publishing.
Our research confirms McGann's insight that the material embodiments of Wilde's texts determined in some manner how they were
read and valued; but it also shows how decisions about those works'
materiality were often made for non-aesthetic reasons. Equally
importantly these non-aesthetic criteria could contribute in fundamental ways to a work's identity. For example, the choice of illustrator, the quality of paper and binding, and its very high price were all
designed to signal to a buyer that Wilde's *A House of Pomegranates*
was intended principally for adults, and was to be judged (initially at
least) in relation to *their* tastes. This decision appears to have been

---

[18] Jerome J. McGann, *The Textual Condition* (Princeton: Princeton University Press, 1991), 11–13.

based on commercial rather than interpretative considerations: it was first and foremost a marketing decision.

Creativity is a complex phenomenon, and we do not claim that our account of Wilde as a writer will be exhaustive, nor that it will replace other ways of understanding his creativity. However, we do maintain that any writer always operates within certain material constraints, and that these possess a pervasiveness which it is not possible for any individual acting alone to change. These constraints include not only the nature of print materials, but also the constitution of readers and purchasers of books, the economics of leisure, the organization of the publishing industry, printing and distribution technologies, and the fortunes and policies of individual publishing houses (which almost never depended on the reputation of an individual writer). Simple labels for these complex and varied phenomena are the 'market' or, as we have indicated above, 'the culture industry'. Regardless of the nature of Wilde's sexuality or nationality and how they are expressed in his work, all of his writing was—and had to be—negotiated via these institutions and was therefore inevitably affected and informed by them. Any description of Wilde's creativity needs therefore to take them into account.

In recent years, and in keeping with some trends in modern critical theory, these phenomena—the 'market' and 'the culture industry'—have tended to be understood in terms of ideology. For example some critics, most notably perhaps Norman Feltes, have concentrated on providing theoretical models of the power relations of late nineteenth-century literary markets. These models typically hypothesize the emergence of what is termed a consumerist economy, or a 'late capitalist' mode of production, in which works of literature are alleged to have been traded and valued in radically new ways. Put simply, literature was recognized explicitly to be a commodity. Other critics, such as Regenia Gagnier and Jonathan Freedman, have speculated about the hegemonic nature of these new forms of evaluation—what are termed the discourses of consumerism—and their implications for artists and writers. Taken collectively, this body of work has begun to provide a new vocabulary for understanding late nineteenth-century literary culture in which the old Marxist terminology of 'mass' versus 'elite' (popularized by critics such as Robert Altick and Raymond Williams) has been replaced with a new language of 'spectacle', 'the fetishization of the commodity', and 'consumer culture', a language borrowed in turn from the work of theorists of modern consumerism such as Guy Debord, W. F. Haug, and Jean Baudrillard.[19] One consequence of the relative newness of these accounts is that they are largely untested by empirical evidence. Indeed the work of those scholars who have investigated late nineteenth-century literary culture at an empirical level—such as John Sutherland and Simon Eliot, both of whom examine issues like numbers of readers, and numbers, prices, and kinds of books sold—their work has yet to be assimilated into, or overturned by, these new theoretical models.[20]

Our book has been conceived very much in this latter empirical tradition. On the other hand, our findings do confirm that the buying and selling of books had become oppressively important for authors in the late nineteenth century, to the extent that issues of marketing were on occasions inseparable from issues of literary identity and value. Wilde's writing and publishing practices also confirm the suspicion that the late nineteenth-century literary market was ruthlessly competitive and commercial, and that professional writers who needed to earn a living with their pen were in no place to resist or even contest those values. In other words the idea that Wilde was a writer who 'exploited' or 'subverted' consumer culture, as some recent critics have wanted to argue, makes little sense. While we acknowledge the 'modernity' of some aspects of late nineteenth-century literary culture, we resist drawing too close an analogy with the late twentieth century. What is meant by the term 'consumerism' is clearly a vexed question. The differences between what that term implies for the late nineteenth century and what is understood by modern consumerism, produced as it is by modern technologies and global economies, are still much more striking that any similarities. As a consequence we stress the importance of looking back as much as looking forward. For Wilde in the late 1880s and early 1890s, the literary culture in which John Ruskin and Matthew Arnold worked was still familiar and attractive, even if it was in the process of being superseded.

[19]   See Regenia Gagnier, *Idylls of the Marketplace* (Stanford: Stanford University Press, 1986); Jonathan Freedman, *Professions of Taste: Henry James, British Aestheticism and Commodity Culture* (Stanford: Stanford University Press, 1990); Norman Feltes, *Literary Capital and the Late Victorian Novel* (London: University of Wisconsin Press, 1993).

[20]   See Simon Eliot, *Some Patterns and Trends in British Publishing: 1880–1919* (London: Bibliographical Society Occasional Papers, 1993); see also John Sutherland, *Victorian Fiction: Writers, Publishers, Readers* (London: Macmillan, 1995).

There has been a tendency among some recent literary historians to explain late nineteenth-century British institutions in terms of their hegemony—to see a powerful British establishment which oppressed marginal or dissident writers such as Wilde. This sort of explanation—which seems to derive from an Althusserian notion of state apparatuses—is not one confirmed by the work of social historians, who have tended to focus on the regional nature of power in nineteenth-century Britain, on the differences between, say, judicial, political, and social institutions, and the frequent inefficiencies of British bureaucratic structures.[21] Perhaps some literary historians have not been sufficiently attuned to the ways in which Wilde was accepted and 'celebrated' by late Victorian cultural institutions, even if he was prosecuted by a legal one. As we shall indicate in Chapter 6, it is salutary to learn that Wilde was as much in demand as a dramatist after his imprisonment as he was before it. Such an observation shows at the very least that the interests of the culture industry of the 1890s were diverse and were not easily aligned with other sorts of commercial interests or with political institutions.

Nineteenth-century publishing houses, periodical owners and editors, and theatrical managements adopted widely differing practices and policies, and their reasons for accepting or refusing a writer were equally varied. In our view there is no evidence that Wilde was systematically discriminated against by a British entertainment 'establishment' on the grounds of his sexuality, nationality, or politics. He did often find it difficult to place works, he did publish with an unusually large range of houses, and he worked with a number of theatre managers. It was only towards the end of his career that he came close to establishing a relationship with a single publishing house of the kind enjoyed by a writer such as Walter Pater with Macmillan. Wilde never formed a permanent association with any theatre or company. His basic problem, at least during the early part of his career, was that his books did not sell particularly well, and that successive publishers were understandably unwilling to continue to invest in an unsuccessful author. His problems with the theatre were more basic: he found plays difficult to write, and some of the refusals he experienced were caused by his

[21] It is also worth noting that there is disagreement about whether the 'conservatism' of late 19th-cent. Britain was a result of the oppressive nature of British political institutions, or of its very opposite: a flexibility which contained dissent by allowing it to be expressed in a limited way.

constitutional inability to meet contractual deadlines. Importantly, these sorts of disappointments do not seem to have been precipitated by Wilde's 'purist' sense of his artistic integrity or autonomy. Wilde's views did undoubtedly offend some publishers, most notably Alexander Macmillan; on the other hand Wilde nearly always found some publisher willing to accept his work (his unpublished work is invariably his unfinished work). Moreover there is evidence that he was happy to tailor publications to the requirements of particular markets: Wilde was remarkably willing to take account of 'public opinion', even if he was not always successful in pleasing it.

This brief discussion of trends in Wilde scholarship suggests that the figure who emerges from this book will be one uncongenial to some modern critics. Our fundamental claim is that in his attitude towards his career as a writer, Wilde was (to adapt Norbert Kohl's terms) more the conformist than the rebel, much more complicit with, than critical of the commercial interests of late nineteenth-century British literary and theatrical culture.[22] The Wilde of this book is a writer who saw no real disjunction between making and selling his work, between art and its market, despite his frequently expressed contempt for the public's tastes. We suggest that it may be this willingness to engage with public tastes, with the demands of the culture industry, which explains why Wilde has survived so well.

Some of the material which we draw upon in our account of Wilde's writing career has been widely available for many years, but it has often been ignored or marginalized. It includes the many letters between Wilde and his various publishers and employers (several of which, however, were omitted from Rupert Hart-Davis's editions of the letters); there is also the detailed bibliographic information compiled by Stuart Mason (Christopher Millard). In particular, little reference is ever made to Mason's annotated proof copy of his *Bibliography* in the Clark Library which supplements much of the printed information. We have also examined many of Wilde's manuscripts; of particular importance is the corpus of unpublished material. Taking account of it considerably alters our view of the *oeuvre*, of how Wilde composed, of his 'development', and of his own criteria of success.

---

[22] See Norbert Kohl, *Oscar Wilde: The Works of a Conformist Rebel* (Cambridge: Cambridge University Press, 1988).

We also draw on new material such as the financial returns from the productions of Wilde's Society Comedies which allow us to re-construct the details of missing contracts (particularly with George Alexander) and the nature of Wilde's earnings from West End, provincial, and North American theatres. We challenge received wisdom about the extent of Wilde's dramatic success, and in so doing reconceptualize the shape of his career. We examine closely the nature of Wilde's transactions with his publishers, giving details of all the known contracts for his books. We evaluate the success of Wilde's books in the context of the enormous changes that were tak-ing place in the late nineteenth-century culture industry. Most im-portantly, we confirm the suspicions of some critics and theatre historians that Wilde's career was substantially shaped by the hands of other professionals, from theatre managers, book designers and publishers, to the new phenomenon of the literary agent. What emerges from the following chapters is a picture of a writer quite at odds with the image of himself he promoted; it is a picture of a man struggling to come to terms with modernity, rather than defining it.

2

The Journalist

It is no accident that it is Wilde's later works, particularly the Society Comedies, his novel, and the criticism republished in book form, which have received the closest scrutiny from critics interested in his writing career.[1] The underlying assumption is that the material written after 1889 represents the work of the craftsman and the pieces produced before that date are apprentice or journeyman efforts. In other words, the very way in which the works to be analysed are selected tends to take for granted what needs to be demonstrated: that Wilde's writing career is indeed explicable in terms of a simple developmental narrative in which inexperience equates with failure and success only comes with maturity.

The idea that a successful artistic career follows a pattern of maturation is so often taken to be true that it is rarely questioned. Lytton Strachey's celebration of Shakespeare's last plays, or labels like 'the late Yeats' or 'the late James', all carry with them a notion of development from juvenilia to maturity. In the case of Wilde, however, the assumption of progress needs to be tested, and this can be done in a number of ways. Most obviously, we can investigate how precisely a general pattern of failure leading to success squares with the actual composition (rather than the publication) of individual works. For example, *Intentions* (1891) is invariably categorized as one of Wilde's successful works even though parts of it were composed as early as 1885 during what is routinely assumed to be

[1] See e.g. Sos Eltis, *Revising Wilde: Society and Subversion in the Plays of Oscar Wilde* (Oxford: Clarendon Press, 1996); Lawrence Danson, *Wilde's Intentions: The Artist in his Criticism* (Oxford: Clarendon Press, 1997); and Kerry Powell, *Oscar Wilde and the Theatre of the 1890s* (Cambridge: Cambridge University Press, 1990). An exception to this rule is to be found in Bobby Fong, 'The Poetry of Oscar Wilde: A Critical Edition'. Unpublished Ph.D. thesis (University of California, Los Angeles, 1978); and Fong and Karl Beckson (eds.), *Oscar Wilde: Poems and Poems in Prose* (Oxford: Oxford University Press, 2000).

the unsuccessful or journeyman part of his career. Contrariwise, *The Duchess of Padua*, although completed in 1883 and today considered a failure, was still being offered by Wilde to theatre-managers as late as 1891, in the conviction that his play had already been an 'immense success' in the United States. This discrepancy between Wilde's own assessment of his talent and that made by some modern critics should alert us to a larger problem: the extent to which modern definitions of success and failure coincide with those made by Wilde or his contemporaries. It is possible that Wilde's values—and therefore his decisions about the kind of writer he wished to be—were different from those frequently assumed by modern critics.[2]

The understanding of a literary career in terms of a development from initial inexperience to later success can take a number of forms, from one of smooth evolution to what is virtually its opposite, sudden inspiration which transforms a sustained period of disappointment.[3] The usual reading of Wilde's life as a writer combines aspects of these extremes. It assumes that his career had two distinct stages: the first, as we have said, is broadly characterized as a long period of apprenticeship and relative failure, the second as a short five-year burst of success.[4] The watershed between these two stages is assumed to occur at some time around 1890, and is usually explained by Wilde negotiating a transition from what is seen as jobbing journalist to literary artist—the transformation, that is, from a reviewer and occasional essayist to the author of books, and of performed and published plays. For some critics, that transformation involved the development of a subversive political voice: the oppositional politics claimed for Wilde's more mature work, particularly the satire in the Society Comedies, is assumed to be inimical to the bourgeois institutions of Victorian journalism. John Stokes, who has made a detailed study of Wilde's journalism, has become an

[2] Of course, none of this is to deny that modern critics and historians are entitled to make their own judgements about the value of Wilde's works; but care should be taken when using those judgements as explanations of how and why the works were written in the first instance.

[3] The careers of Dickens and Sterne can be taken to exemplify these two different paradigms.

[4] Such a view underlies the selection criteria in many anthologies. See e.g. Anthony Fothergill (ed.), *Oscar Wilde: Plays, Prose Writings and Poems* (London: J. M. Dent, 1996); and Isobel Murray (ed.), *The Oxford Authors: Oscar Wilde* (Oxford: Oxford University Press, 1989). By contrast, Merlin Holland's revised (3rd) edition of *The Complete Works of Oscar Wilde* (Glasgow: HarperCollins, 1994) devotes a whole section to the 'early work'—to 'essays and selected journalism'.

authoritative spokesman for this line of argument. He has commented that the transgressive Wilde whom critics admire today did not fully emerge until he had 'virtually stopped' popular reviewing and was in a position to 'choose titles and adopt attitudes that no professional [journalist] could possibly permit'—until, that is, he had metamorphosed from journeyman to the author of literature.[5]

This shaping of Wilde's career into a story of ordinariness punctuated by disappointment followed by a sudden and brief period of glittering celebrity tends to foreground the following sequence of events. In the 1870s Wilde is seen as a promising poet with some modest publications who had enjoyed a brilliant undergraduate career both at Trinity College, Dublin and then at Oxford. That career at Oxford, however, was concluded with two setbacks, which are perceived to establish a pattern for the next decade: the failure to win the Chancellor's Essay Prize and the failure to secure a fellowship at Magdalen College (and consequently a further failure to win the security of an academic post). There then followed a short and apparently unsuccessful attempt to set himself up as a freelance writer in London: the two main works composed or published during this period, *Vera; or, The Nihilists* and *Poems* (1881), were commercial and critical disappointments. Wilde, in this view, now short of money, was obliged to undertake a lecture tour of North America in 1882, and then a shorter tour of the British Isles in 1883. For the rest of the 1880s he earned a living in popular journalism, writing formulaic and undistinguished pieces. As we have hinted, this dismissal of Wilde's journalism can be seen in the selection criteria which underlie most modern anthologies of his critical writing: it is ironic that Ross's 1908 editions of Wilde's reviews and uncollected writing are still easily the most comprehensive.[6] In this narrative success finally arrives with the publication of *The Picture of Dorian Gray* in 1890, a novel which brought Wilde to the notice of the general reading public. He was then able to exploit his newly-found popularity to produce the profitable four Society Comedies (1892–5). Earnings from these works in turn released Wilde from the

---

5 John Stokes, 'Wilde the Journalist', in Peter Raby (ed.), *The Cambridge Companion to Oscar Wilde* (Cambridge: Cambridge University Press, 1997), 78.

6 This selectivity is to be seen by contrasting Ross's editions of *Reviews* and *Miscellanies* with, say, John Wyse Jackson (ed.), *Aristotle at Afternoon Tea: The Rare Oscar Wilde* (London: Fourth Estate, 1991); and Richard Ellmann (ed.), *The Artist as Critic: Critical Writings of Oscar Wilde* (London: W. H. Allen, 1970).

demands of journalism, allowing a greater freedom of expression both in his writing and in his life. This brief period of celebrity was brought to a dramatic end by the three trials of mid-1895.

Recently some cultural critics have placed a more complex political inflection on this story, one in which early failure and rejection was turned to account by a process of politicization. In this interpretation, undergraduate success at Oxford initially gave Wilde the confidence to identify himself with an English as much as an Irish heritage. In 1877, for example, there is evidence that he was attempting to affiliate himself to a specifically English literary tradition. In a sonnet to be published in the *Irish Monthly* in Dublin he had used the phrase 'our English land'; when the editor, the Revd. Matthew Russell, objected, Wilde defended himself on the grounds that 'it is a noble privilege to count oneself of the same race as Keats or Shakespeare'.[7] In this view, disillusionment with an English tradition set in when Oxford (and then London) rejected him: these rejections stung Wilde into a bitter dislike of the English and resuscitated his sense of national identity. The 1882 American tour is then interpreted as Wilde's need to escape Oxford's (and therefore England's) rebuffs. For critics such as Declan Kiberd and Fintan O'Toole, Wilde's experience of the northern United States, with their traditions of welcoming immigrants and of vigorous republican politics, brought about a kind of liberation in which he could voice his newly-felt political discontents with England.[8] Similarly, Sandra Siegel draws attention to the anti-English themes in some of Wilde's American lectures, and she explicitly links this polemic to the rejection of *Poems* (1881) by the Oxford Union.[9] However, it is not easy to reconcile such a process of political awakening to Wilde's decision, on returning to Britain, to earn his living by journalism, and therefore to make concessions to those popular and middlebrow

[7] *Letters*, 40; Wilde did make the change.

[8] See Declan Kiberd, *Inventing Ireland* (1995; London: Vintage, 1996), 33–50; and Fintan O'Toole, 'Venus in Blue Jeans: Oscar Wilde, Jesse James, Crime and Fame', in Jerusha McCormack (ed.), *Wilde the Irishman* (London: Yale University Press, 1998), 71–81. O'Toole argues that in America Wilde could identify with a code of behaviour in which the outlaw was also a gentleman: 'Wilde may have shot from the lip rather than from the hip, and his duels may have been conducted across a dinner table, rather than at high noon on a dusty and deserted Main Street, but his public persona had all the hauteur and recklessness of the outlaw' (75).

[9] Sandra Siegel, 'Oscar Wilde's Gift and Oxford's "Coarse Impertinence"', in Tadhg Foley and Seán Ryder (eds.), *Ideology and Ireland in the Nineteenth Century* (Dublin: Four Courts Press, 1998), 69–78.

English tastes which America had apparently taught him to reject. In this politicized account, the journalism has to be understood as a kind of interlude in which Wilde is (silently) developing a political consciousness which only finds literary expression when he finally discovers the appropriate voice for his radical politics, that is (once more) in the successful works of the 1890s. As Kiberd argues, that voice involved satirizing English bourgeois manners and commercial power through the appropriation of an Irish tradition of lying where deceit was the only possible form of engagement by a dispossessed nation.[10] In this narrative, the trials become England's revenge on the Irishman who went too far.[11]

This figure of an increasingly politicized and (by implication) sophisticated Wilde is an attractive one. On the other hand it has little to add to our understanding of the role of journalism in his writing career as a whole. At best the journalism remains a kind of unexplained hiatus, and at worst a simple embarrassment.[12] For those, like Kiberd, Siegel, McCormack, or Pine, who wish to see Wilde's life shaped by a growing antipathy to England's colonial and commercial power, it is necessary to explain why he spent so long working for such quintessentially capitalist institutions as the English periodical press.[13] It is not as if Wilde was, like William Morris, writing for radical journals, either for the working classes in the *Commonweal* or the more educated readers of *To-day*. Nor, like some of his fellow-countrymen, was he writing for specifically nationalist titles (the awkward fact is that Wilde had to all intents and purposes stopped publishing in Irish periodicals, and therefore addressing specifically Irish audiences, by 1880—that is, by the time he had settled in London). It is difficult to imagine a part of the

---

[10] Declan Kiberd, 'Oscar Wilde: The Resurgence of Lying', in *The Cambridge Companion*, 276–94.

[11] Such a view is implicit in much Irish writing on Wilde up to the 1970s. See e.g. Brendan Kennelly (ed.), *The Penguin Book of Irish Verse* (Harmondsworth: Penguin Books, 1970), where Kennelly asserts that Wilde wrote '*The Ballad of Reading Gaol* in an English prison' (15).

[12] Julia Prewitt Brown offers a different account of Wilde's development based on his engagement with trends in British and European philosophy. But she, too, has nothing to say about how Wilde's work as a journalist contributed to this career. See Brown, *Cosmopolitan Criticism: Oscar Wilde's Philosophy of Art* (London: University Press of Virginia, 1997).

[13] For representative post-colonialist accounts of Wilde, see McCormack (ed.), *Wilde the Irishman*; and Richard Pine, *The Thief of Reason: Oscar Wilde and Modern Ireland* (Dublin: Gill and Macmillan, 1995). For a list of Wilde's contributions to periodicals see Appendix B.

publishing industry more mired in British bourgeois values than the bubble economy of the popular periodical press in the 1880s. For example, the *Court and Society Review*, to which Wilde contributed regularly in 1887, was a magazine which depended entirely on middle-class aspiration for upper middle-class and aristocratic values (as did most of the West End theatres for whom Wilde would later write). Nothing could be further from the appeal to working-class solidarity which a paper like William Morris's *Commonweal* propagandized at about the same time. Some critics have claimed that Wilde's attitude to the values of the journals for which he wrote was critical and 'subversive'; but if so, it is not an attitude easy to isolate in the writing itself, which for the most part exhibits an urbane and ironic detachment typical of so much journalism of the time. Unpublished correspondence between Robert Ross and Methuen reveals that both publisher and editor were unsure about the literary value of many of Wilde's occasional and unsigned pieces, and this explains both the selectivity of the *Reviews* volume in the 1908 collected works, as well as throwing light on the simple fact that even today it remains extremely difficult to identify the extent of Wilde's unsigned journalism.[14]

If we accept that Wilde's journalism was largely conventional and sometimes banal, a problem of chronology still remains: how do we explain why the allegedly critical or 'subversive' voice emerged from this ordinariness at the moment *when* it is supposed to have done—around 1889–90? As we suggested, John Stokes has argued that Wilde was more liberated and provocative when he was given the opportunity to write for less blatantly commercial publishing institutions—that is, for more serious literary reviews such as the *Nineteenth Century* rather than penny papers like the *Pall Mall Gazette*. Stokes's suggestion might lead us to think that Wilde's career is in some ways comparable to that of one of his old mentors, Walter Pater, in the sense that serious writing required special conditions—tranquillity, a freedom from writing to deadlines, and from the demands of paid work. Pater, it will be recalled, resigned his teaching post at Brasenose in 1883 in order to sustain the intellectual seriousness and complexity of *Marius the Epicurean*. In

[14] Robert Ross's anthology of Wilde's journalism (in *Reviews*) is selective when compared to Mason's more comprehensive listing; but Mason's manuscript notes to his proof copy of his *Bibliography* show that he was aware that even this list was not exhaustive. Critics such as John Stokes have argued for Wilde's authorship of further anonymous pieces.

Wilde's case, however, we do not see any such simple contrast. Giving up popular journalism (principally reviewing) was not, for Wilde, the precondition for more serious work: the so-called serious or politically engaged writing overlaps, and for a number of years, with the apparently more commercial and therefore more orthodox work for the popular press. For example, Wilde was still reviewing for the populist *Pall Mall Gazette* when he was writing the two parts of 'The True Function and Value of Criticism' for the *Nineteenth Century*. Finally, we should be cautious about equating the commercial nature of publishing with simple circulation numbers and cheapness: it is not obvious that the more expensive *Nineteenth Century* was freer from the power of market forces than, say, the cheaper *Court and Society Review*. Likewise we cannot assume that Wilde's attitudes towards these sorts of commission were different; his audiences might have changed, and the particular nature of the commercial constraints under which he operated changed with them, but they were constraints none the less. There is evidence to suggest that even when he was writing what some critics have seen as his most provocative works—the Society Comedies—commercial considerations and the restrictions which they imposed were still uppermost in his mind. As late as 1890 Wilde claimed in a letter to his friend Norman Forbes-Robertson that he was 'always in need of money' and that he therefore had 'to work for certainties'.[15] Rather than looking for distinct phases in Wilde's career, it may be more helpful to highlight patterns of consistency: was there any fundamental difference between being a professional dramatist and a professional reviewer?

It may be tempting to argue for a change in the *grounds* of Wilde's transactions with the commercial elements of publishing in the later part of his career. The recuperation of Wilde's work from the allegations of triviality and populism (made by contemporaries and some commentators since) has often relied on a perception of him as a figure who became so secure in his knowledge of (and adept in his transactions with) the culture industry that he was able to exploit its debased values for his own ends.[16] It is suggested that his commerce with the emerging mass media in the 1880s—the period, that is, of

[15] *Letters*, 276.
[16] Such a view is implicit in Regenia Gagnier's account of Wilde's allegedly subversive relationship with a society of 'spectacle' in her *Idylls of the Marketplace* (Stanford: Stanford University Press, 1986).

his popular journalism—eventually produced a politicized under-standing of literary taste. And this understanding can be glimpsed in the subtle subtexts underlying apparently conventional works such as the Society Comedies. These subtexts allow Wilde to satir-ize for a 'select few' the values and prejudices of the audience that had brought about his popularity, a strategy allowing him both to profit, but also to stand aloof, from commercial success.

This is an attractive line of argument, because it makes Wilde our (post)modern contemporary, and it affiliates him to anxieties about standards in popular taste in the late twentieth century. However, the argument relies on a number of unexamined presuppositions. The first concerns the validity of subtextual or coded interpreta-tions of his work—an issue which we discuss in detail in Chapter 7. The second is that the works in Wilde's later, 'successful' (that is, post-1890) career must have operated in their culture differently from his works in the 1880s, and that his transactions with the pub-lishing industry must also have undergone some kind of sea-change. Over Wilde's career as a whole, it is possible to observe some changes in the ways he published, in the ways in which those publi-cations were marketed, and in the ways in which his work was received. However, as we shall show in the following chapters, col-lectively these do not involve a fundamental realignment in the power-relationships between Wilde and those who produced and published his work. When we examine closely the details of his negotiations with individual publishers, the contracts he signed, the royalties he bargained for, it is not easy to see them in terms of Wilde being in a position to exploit or manipulate market condi-tions. If anything the evidence points in the opposite direction—to a growing willingness on Wilde's part to accommodate himself to market forces. We shall argue for the agency of other figures in the fashioning of Wilde as a successful writer, particularly his actor-managers (Herbert Beerbohm Tree and George Alexander) and Elkin Mathews and John Lane at the Bodley Head, all of whom were key figures in defining the Wildean style and persona which is so well-remembered today. They were also, to a man, tuned to their fingertips to the imperatives of commerce. If we wish to see Wilde's career in terms of a narrative, then its shape is a simple and consist-ent one: Wilde's motives were always in large part commercial, and this commercial imperative placed him in a position of weakness in relation to the demands of publishing and theatrical institutions.

Wilde's need to write for money changed little over his career because the more he earned the more he spent; the deeper he fell into debt, the more urgent his need to earn.

A different kind of explanation for Wilde's apparent burst of creativity in the early 1890s was given, as we suggested in the previous chapter, by Richard Ellmann. Ellmann implied that the meeting with Lord Alfred Douglas and the aristocratic values which he embodied coincided with (and in some sense enabled) Wilde to find the inspiration to rise above the values of commerce and the media in favour of those of art and political satire.[17] Some critics have generalized this argument to suggest that Wilde's coming to terms with his (homo)sexual identity involved a form of politicization congruent with the exclusion experienced by the Irishman, and that this intensification of Wilde's sense of difference promoted a more sophisticated and provocative art.[18] The causality which this argument invokes is seductive, not least because it chimes with attempts by many theorists in the 1980s to link sexuality with textuality. However, in Wilde's case, it is an explanation which is difficult to substantiate. There is, for example, considerable doubt about when exactly Wilde became a practising homosexual and, as we argued in Chapter 1, about what that practice entailed. The popular assumption is that Wilde was 'initiated' into homosexuality by Robert Ross in the late 1880s, a moment that coincides with Wilde's growing confidence in his literary abilities. Such a claim is not only unproven (Ross, the only other witness, was understandably partial), it is difficult to see how it could be proved. Similarly, there is no easy way to link the production of particular works with levels or kinds of sexual experience (even if our knowledge of these experiences were secure). The most tempting connection to make is the relationship between Wilde's affair with Alfred Douglas and the representation of desire in *The Picture of Dorian Gray*. Unfortunately, though, *Dorian Gray* had already been completed before the two men met.

The main limitation of the narratives which we have described is their failure to account adequately for Wilde's journalism—to give

---

[17] It is interesting that Ellmann does not distinguish either between creativity and creative impulses, or between the activity of writing and the institutions in which it occurs. These elisions in turn allow the reification of creativity, so that the relationship between the creative element in sexual experience and literary expression appears wholly unproblematic.

[18] This is essentially the position of Jonathan Dollimore. See e.g. 'Different Desires: Subjectivity and Transgression in Wilde and Gide', *Textual Practice*, 1: 1 (1987), 48–67; and *Sexual Dissidence* (Oxford: Oxford University Press, 1991).

a convincing explanation of its relationship with the later and more celebrated parts of the *oeuvre*. This failure in turn arises, as we have hinted, because the definition of what counts as successful work tends to be taken for granted, even though it is by no means clear that Wilde himself would have agreed with it. If we attempt to historicize Wilde's views of the writer in terms of the value-judgements available to him in the 1880s, then we can see that there is more than one way of interpreting what to modern eyes have invariably appeared to be setbacks. A good place to start is with that moment in which some critics have detected Wilde's first and paradigmatic failure—the rejection by Magdalen College, Oxford of his application for a fellowship despite a distinguished undergraduate career which had culminated in a first and the Newdigate prize.

I

The term 'rejection' is of course value-laden, and carries overtones of psychological damage, for which there is no direct evidence. All that we can say for certain is that Wilde's failure to win a fellowship immediately closed off a particular kind of literary career—that of a scholarly and refined life in which the writer was to some degree insulated by an academic institution from the pressures of the increasing commercialization of authorship and publishing. The protected nature of such a career can be seen in the lives not only of Pater but also of another contemporary, A. E. Housman. At the same time, the fortunes of these two writers also remind us that the career of the writer–don did have a number of drawbacks, particularly for a gay man, and Wilde could hardly have been unaware of them. Just before Wilde came up to Oxford, Pater had found out that conservative forces within the university could exert their own peculiar pressures and controls: sensitivity to his institutional responsibilities, and the informal policing of college life (particularly by Benjamin Jowett at Balliol), had forced Pater into a form of selfcensorship. The potential conflict between the freedom demanded by the artist and the obligations placed on the university lecturer was finally resolved by Pater's withdrawal of part of *The Renaissance* and eventually by his resignation as a college tutor.[19] In the case of

[19] Billie Andrew Inman was the first critic to find concrete evidence that Pater suppressed the conclusion to the second edition of the *Renaissance* following the discovery of his homosexuality. See Inman, 'Estrangement and Connection: Walter Pater, Benjamin Jowett, and

Housman a similar conflict was avoided only by a rigorous suppres-
sion of his homosexual desire, and an equally strict separation of the
roles of academic and artist. (Housman was initially reluctant to
publish *A Shropshire Lad* with its personal and confessional themes,
and only did so under the protection of anonymity.)[20] More prosaically, the life of a don did not leave much time for creative writing.
As we have said, in 1883 Pater gave up his tutorship at Brasenose in
order to finish *Marius*, and Housman published only four slim volumes of poetry, two of which appeared in the last years of his life.[21]
For Wilde Oxford, far from being a nurturing and protecting environment, must have represented an intellectual and cultural value-
system with very ambiguous attractions for an Englishman as much
as an Irishman.[22] It is possible that its most unequivocal value for
him in the late 1870s was also its most banal: fundamentally a fellowship offered Wilde financial security, and his failure to gain it denied him one—but not necessarily the ideal—sort of career. We also
need to be aware that another type of career, one made possible by
the possession of independent means, and exemplified by figures
such as John Ruskin, was equally unavailable to Wilde.[23]

In the last half of the nineteenth century there was, however, a
further option for the aspiring Oxford-educated writer without private means—one which combined, and was compatible with, certain types of public office. Such a career is represented by Matthew
Arnold's dual roles of a School Inspector and distinguished poet
and critic, or W. J. Courthope's employment as a senior Civil

William M. Hardinge', in Laurel Brake and Ian Small (eds.), *Pater in the 1990s* (Greensboro,
NC: ELT Press, 1991), 1–20.

[20] Evidence of Housman's sensitivities about his reputation is to be found in his witty reaction to A. J. A. Symons's request that he be allowed to include some of Housman's work
in an anthology of 1890s verse. He wrote to Grant Richards: 'Mr Symons . . . may be con-
soled, and also amused, if you tell him that to include me in an anthology of the Nineties
would be just as technically correct, and just as essentially inappropriate, as to include Lot in
a book on the Sodomites.' See Henry Maas (ed.), *The Letters of A. E. Housman* (London:
Rupert Hart-Davis, 1971), 271.

[21] Housman's publications of poetry included: *A Shropshire Lad* (1896), *Last Poems*
(1922), *Three Poems* (1935), and *More Poems* (1936); in addition he published a critical work,
The Name and Nature of Poetry (1933). The vast majority of the published *oeuvre*, however,
concerns his work on classical topics.

[22] Wilde could not have been unaware of the Pater–Hardinge scandal, for he knew
Hardinge, and took part with him in John Ruskin's famous road-building project in 1876.
See Inman, 'Estrangement and Connection', 2–3.

[23] In July 1878 Wilde wrote to William Ward complaining that his disappointing
inheritance from his father, coupled with the failure of a lawsuit attempting to recover family property, meant 'doing some horrid work to earn bread' (*Letters*, 52).

Service Commissioner which he combined with editing the work of Pope and producing a six-volume history of English poetry.[24] The sense that it was quite acceptable to combine a literary career with holding public office is further confirmed by the fact that both Arnold and Courthope were elected to the Professorship of Poetry at Oxford.[25] There is evidence that in the late 1870s and early 1880s Wilde tried, albeit unsuccessfully, to use what connections he had to find himself a public position similar to that of Arnold. In a letter to Oscar Browning, requesting a testimonial for a School Inspectorship, he complained that rents from his family's property in Ireland were 'extinct . . . as the dodo or moly', and declared himself willing to undertake 'any Education work' which promised 'an assured income'.[26] Wilde's application was not successful, and in any case, the life of the writer–civil servant, like that of the writer–don, was also less than ideal. Anthony Trollope's enormously productive career as a novelist, which he combined with working in the Post Office, seems to have been the exception and is moreover one which belongs to an earlier period. After the Civil Service was reformed, occupations in its junior offices were often hard work and not particularly well paid. Arnold constantly complained of poverty and of the ways in which the demands of his job compromised his writing.[27]

Given these limitations, what is revealing is not that Wilde failed to find acceptance in these conservative intellectual milieux, but the fact that he seriously applied to them in the first instance, that he initially thought about a writing career in such conventional and conservative terms. The idea of Wilde as a university don, with all the quasi-parental responsibilities which such a post entailed at that

[24] Courthope produced (in 5 vols.) an edition of Pope's work which included a *Life of Alexander Pope* (London: John Murray, 1889); he also published a six-volume *History of English Poetry* (London: Macmillan, 1895–1910), together with several volumes of his own poetry and several volumes of criticism. Finally for five years he was co-editor with Alfred Austin of the *National Review*.

[25] The Professorship of Poetry at Oxford was—and is—not a conventional teaching post, and does not involve the same institutional responsibilities or financial remuneration.

[26] *Letters*, 63. The choice of Browning as a reference indicates some naivety on Wilde's part, for Browning had recently been involved in a scandal at Eton. For an account of Browning's reputation, see Michael Levey, *The Case of Walter Pater* (London: Thames and Hudson, 1978).

[27] See Cecil Y. Lang (ed.), *The Letters of Matthew Arnold*, ii (London: University Press of Virginia, 1997); many letters document the pressures and financial anxieties Arnold experienced as a School Inspector.

time, fits uneasily with the image of the flamboyant young aesthete which he had cultivated when he was an undergraduate.[28] It is even harder to imagine Wilde as that kind of Philistine figure of public authority, such as an Inspector of Schools, which he later mocks in the Society Comedies; state education in general, and examinations and examiners in particular, would become a persistent target for his humour.[29] Yet both these career paths clearly represented serious (and for Wilde, the best) options for a Newdigate Prize winner with a first in *Literae Humaniores* who had honourable ambitions to be a writer, but who had no adequate means of financial support. We ought also to remember that the only practicable alternative to these conventional routes was an even more compromised one, to write specifically for money, and therefore to accept the even more rigid constraints which writing for popular taste entailed. This is the one option which it seems that (initially at least) the Oxford–educated Wilde *did* wish to avoid, and for understandable reasons. Equally, we should also note that the apparent rejection of him by institutions of English power does not seem to have politicized Wilde to the extent of leading him down the path of the oppositional or avant-garde writer, a path that was becoming increasingly fashionable in the late nineteenth century. According to Ellmann, when Wilde met Paul Verlaine a little later (in the spring of 1883), he was disturbed by the poet's seedy appearance: the life of the *poète maudit* clearly had a limited appeal.[30] In practice Wilde's immediate response to 'rejection' was to set himself up in London in some style with the money released from the sale of family property in Ireland. Even Lady Wilde, who had been widowed in 1876 and had resettled in London in 1879, saw this move in wholly positive terms: despite her long history of nationalist sympathies, she envisaged for her son a highly conventional career in yet another conservative British institution. She wrote to him (and apparently without irony) in November 1883: 'I would like you to have a small house in London and live the

[28] Wilde's comments about a mock academy he set up with the classical scholar Campbell Dodgson and Alfred Douglas in the house of Lady Mount-Temple in Babbacombe Cliff are relevant here. Wilde observed that he had 'succeeded in combining the advantages of a public school with those of a private lunatic asylum' (*Letters*, 333). Campbell Dodgson, who was the 'second master', wrote to Lionel Johnson that 'our life is lazy and luxurious; our moral principles are lax. . . . Oscar implores me, with outspread arms and tears in his eyes, to let my soul alone and cultivate my body for six weeks. Bosie is beautiful and fascinating, but quite wicked' (*Letters*, 868).

[29] See e.g. Ian Small (ed.), *Oscar Wilde: A Woman of No Importance*, (London: A & C Black, 1993), III, 8–10.　　　　　　　　　　　　　　　　　　[30] Ellmann, 216.

literary life and teach Constance to correct proofs and eventually go into parliament.'[31]

The life Wilde led during his brief interlude in London (from the autumn of 1879 to the end of 1881) does not give the impression of a disappointed man. Perhaps the opposite: Wilde was energetically socializing, making all kinds of contacts which would stand him in good stead in later life. Of particular significance were his attempts to insinuate himself into journalistic circles and London theatrical society, activities which suggest that he had very quickly (and not particularly reluctantly) come to terms with the fact that his career would have to involve some element of commercial writing. Wilde's entry into journalism also begins to look very different when we place it in the context of the development of his mother's and brother's careers following their move from Dublin to London in 1879. In London the need for all members of the Wilde family to find paid employment was urgent, and Lady Jane and Willie Wilde both looked to the popular press. Lady Jane wrote for the *Pall Mall Gazette*, *Queen* (which included a column addressed to 'The Upper Ten Thousand'), the *Burlington Magazine*, as well as the *St James's Magazine*, *Tinsley's Magazine*, and the *Lady's Pictorial*. None of these titles could be described as serious or the 'higher' journalism. They are better characterized as periodicals concerned with, and dependent on, the expanding and increasingly wealthy social group who identified with and aspired to fashionable London society. Certainly this audience was a world away from the readers of Lady Wilde's earlier contributions to the Irish *Nation* in the 1840s, a journal that had been suppressed for sedition by the British government following the publication in 1848 of her inflammatory leader inciting the Irish population to an uprising.[32] Willie Wilde had written in Ireland for *Kottabos*, the Trinity College magazine, and had begun working for the *World*, which was edited by his friend Edmund Yates (who is often credited with introducing an American style of journalism, with an emphasis on 'personality' and interviews, into Britain).[33] In 1879 Willie was given the job of chief

[31] Joy Melville, *Mother of Oscar* (London: John Murray, 1994), 181.

[32] Ibid. 36. It is worth noting that Lady Wilde dropped her pen-name of 'Speranza' when she wrote for the English periodical press; instead she traded explicitly on her connections with the aristocracy.

[33] See Peter D. McDonald, *British Literary Culture and Publishing Practice: 1880–1914* (Cambridge: Cambridge University Press, 1997), 8.

correspondent and leader writer for the *Daily Telegraph*, a conservative paper; one of his contemporaries claimed that Willie Wilde's style had become 'the type for society journalism'.[34] It would be strange if Oscar had not been influenced by his mother's and brother's success in writing for the popular periodical press: he would go on to write for magazines where a family connection had already been established, including the *World* and the *Pall Mall Gazette*. There is also some evidence that Wilde was attracted to professional journalism because of the easy living it seemed to promise. Robert Sherard reported Wilde's observation that:

There is a great fascination in journalism. It is so quick, so swift. Willie goes to a Duchess's ball, he slips out before midnight, is away for an hour or two, returns, and as he is driving home in the morning, can buy the paper containing a full account of the party he has just left.[35]

At the same time as Wilde was being attracted to the life of the journalist, he was also assiduously cultivating a number of useful theatrical friendships: with leading actresses and actors, including Ellen Terry, Lillie Langtry, Genevieve Ward, Norman Forbes-Robertson, and Hermann Vezin; with dramatists and critics, such as Clement Scott (who later would ironically side against him in a hostile review of *Lady Windermere's Fan*); and with theatrical impresarios, such as Sir Squire and Lady Bancroft. At this time Wilde attempted (as Ellmann says) to launch his first play, *Vera*, with 'fanfare', 'loftily' submitting it 'to the chief theatrical personages in London'.[36] As we explain in Chapter 4, *Vera* did, of course, prove an expensive failure: the planned London performance never materialized, and only a small number of copies printed specifically for a private production were ever made. Yet *Vera*'s lack of success is not really the point. Of greater consequence is what the decision to write the play, and the simultaneous foray into journalism, tell us about Wilde's attitude towards his career in 1879–80, for even at this early date it seems that he was measuring success—at least in part— in explicitly commercial terms, and viewing the life of the artist as implicating him in a certain kind of leisured and bourgeois lifestyle, one to which he was immensely attracted, but one which, as he also recognized, cost money. He put matters succinctly in October 1880 in another letter to the actor Norman Forbes-Robertson:

34 Melville, *Mother of Oscar*, 148.   35 Quoted in ibid. 150.
36 Ellmann, 115 and 119.

I have not yet finished furnishing my room, and have spent all my money over it already, so if no manager gives me gold for *The Nihilists* I don't know what I shall do; but then I couldn't really have anything but Chippendale and satinwood. I shouldn't have been able to write.[37]

The use of the term 'gold' is interesting; it occurs on more than one occasion when Wilde measures the value of his own work. When he became more famous (and his debts more extravagant), his measure of success would shift to a different form of bullion, to '*red gold*'.[38] What remains constant, however, was a pragmatic realization that the artist lived in a material world, and this enjoined real costs. There would therefore have to be some form of accommodation between commercial and aesthetic values, between art and the market-place. In practice Wilde never fully achieved such an accommodation, in that he never became a writer with a high literary reputation who also sold in large numbers, as Tennyson and Eliot had done, and as Hardy was about to do. Moreover, as his career moved on, and he became financially successful, money became more not less important to him: he was later willing to acknowledge that non-commercial writing, what he called 'speculative work', was a luxury he was not prepared to afford. In Wilde's decision, made as early as 1880, to write for the West End theatre (one of the most constrained and conservative art-forms in the late nineteenth century) we see evidence that almost from the start his conception of a literary career had a strong pragmatic element to it. It is precisely this pragmatism which may in turn explain why it is difficult to find concrete evidence of him in the early 1880s as a figure who was chastened or politicized by 'rejection'. There is little indication that Wilde himself interpreted the failure of *Vera* as an extension of Oxonian (or English) hostility to an Irishman. He seems to have recognized that the fault lay in part with himself—not as an Irish national, but as a writer with no experience of the stage. Drafts of *Vera* had been sent to Hermann Vezin and Dion Boucicault (both experienced men of the theatre) for advice. Boucicault (a fellow-Irishman) told Wilde that he had 'dramatic powers' but had 'not shaped [his] subject perfectly before beginning it'; Wilde admitted ruefully to Vezin that he was finding out 'what a difficult craft playwriting is'.[39]

---

[37] *Letters*, 71.
[38] Wilde's references to writing for 'red gold' occur frequently in letters written in the summer and autumn of 1894: see e.g. letters to Charles Spurrier Mason (*Letters*, 364) and George Alexander (*OWR*, 67).   [39] *OWR*, 96, and *Letters*, 71.

This admission of personal inadequacy, as opposed to blaming institutional (or political) discrimination, may explain why Wilde decided it was worth continuing to write for the theatre (and why too he would continue with journalism). He began the scenario of his next play, *The Duchess of Padua*, in late 1882. He had publicly announced as early as August 1880 in the *Biograph and Review* that he was writing a blank verse tragedy.[40] In that same notice, Wilde had also advertised a forthcoming 'collection of poems'. Like *Vera*, this volume—*Poems* (1881)—proved a disappointment: sales were slow and most reviewers were unappreciative, with some openly hostile. Furthermore, and as we have noted, Wilde had to suffer the ignominy of the volume being rejected by the Oxford Union. The reception of *Poems* was undoubtedly vexatious, and Wilde's acerbic letter to the Union secretary suggests that he was particularly stung by the *ad hominem* nature of the Union's slight. At the same time, the extent to which this insult *was* personal is a reminder that *Poems* represented a failure of a very different sort from that of *Vera*, not least because the kind of artist Wilde represented himself as being in *Poems* was quite unlike that of the aspiring dramatic author writing *The Nihilists* principally for 'gold'.

The announcement which appeared in the *Biograph and Review* is worth quoting fully: 'At the coming Christmas Mr Wilde purposes bringing out a blank verse tragedy in four acts, some essays on Greek art, and a collection of poems.' In this piece of self-advertisement, there is an obvious sense of continuity between the essayist on classical art, the author of blank verse drama, and the poet. All were 'high' art forms valorized by Wilde's Oxford experience; all suggest a writing persona rather different from the Wilde who produced *Vera*, with its unapologetic exploitation of popular romance, melodramatic devices, and topical issues. Importantly, Wilde's decision to take advantage of the commercial potential of the West End theatre (together with his attraction to journalism) more or less coincides with an attempt to launch himself in the *Biograph and Review* and in *Poems* (1881) as the rarefied writer he envisaged when he had published poetry as an undergraduate. It is as if in the late 1870s and early 1880s Wilde entertained the possibility of different but concurrent kinds of writing careers: it does not seem to be the case that either Oxford's double rejection of a fellowship and his volume of poetry, or his need to earn money with

---

[40] Mason, 5.

his pen, wholly closed off for Wilde the idea that he could still be a serious writer. Rather Wilde pursued these different ways of 'being' a writer as if there was no necessary incongruity or tension between them. The poet, the popular dramatist, the journalist, and the putative translator of Greek literature—these are all aspects of the same Wilde of 1879 and 1880.[41]

Accepting that the activities of journalist, popular dramatist, poet, and classicist are not necessarily incompatible does require us to relinquish certain Romantic ideologies of creativity that define the integrity of an artist's work in relation to the sort of life he or she leads. These ideologies were alive and well in the late nineteenth century, propagandized as they had been by writers such as John Ruskin, and lived out by some of Wilde's Decadent contemporaries. Moreover Wilde himself was clearly attracted to them, for on many occasions he celebrated as exemplary artistic lives the careers of Keats and Rossetti, both of whom, according to Wilde, were prepared to suffer for their art. As Wilde put it in an 1887 review, Rossetti 'never trafficked with the merchants for his soul, nor brought his wares into the market-place for the idle to gape at'.[42] On the other hand, Wilde was also honest enough to acknowledge (privately at least) that these values did not represent the ideals by which he could live his own life. Yet we do not need to see his resistance to these models solely in terms of a lack of self-discipline. It is possible to understand his conception of what it meant to be a writer more positively, as a recognition of, and a readiness to respond to, recent changes in the literary market-place. That is, the apparent inconsistencies in the ways he advertised himself as a writer can be seen in terms of his complex reactions to modernity, when modernity is defined in terms of the reality of mass readerships and mass culture. Such a perception in turn places Wilde's writing in a very different tradition from that reactionary elitism associated with some modernist writers, particularly T. S. Eliot and Virginia Woolf, whose textual strategies have, on occasions, been associated with those developed by Wilde.[43]

[41] As we describe in Ch. 3, Wilde was approached by George Macmillan in 1879 to undertake translations of Herodotus and Euripides for the family firm: in the event he never took up the offer.

[42] Oscar Wilde, 'A Cheap Edition of a Great Man', *Pall Mall Gazette* (18 April 1887); repr. in Ross, *Reviews*, 151.

[43] In earlier studies the present authors both stressed the continuities between Wilde and modernist authors; research for this book has led us to revise these views. See Ian Small,

Whatever value the modern reader places on Wilde's strategies, the plural nature of his literary ambition complicates judgements about what is to count as success and failure for him in the late 1870s and 1880s. The event that provides the most useful illustration of this problem is perhaps the American tour, or more precisely the tendency to interpret Wilde's decision of late 1881 to go to America in terms of a political act—as the Irishman's desire to escape from England's rejection. Wilde's motives for the trip must have been largely financial: America may have represented a new politics, but first and foremost it was a new market and, as we show in Chapter 4, one potentially larger than that in Britain. That market was also relatively young and therefore open to the tastes and fashions of which audiences in England had already tired. It is worth reminding ourselves that cultural transfer between Europe and America in the second half of the nineteenth century was largely into America; as Henry James repeatedly observed, European values could become the mark of civilization and cultivation in North America, particularly in New York and the East Coast states.[44] On the other hand, the very strength of that trade in European art suggests that the culture industry in America was no less commercial than in Britain. Wilde's attitude towards his American tour could have been no less cynical or less commercially motivated than that of other promoters of British cultural goods abroad, including his employer Richard D'Oyly Carte, whose touring production of Gilbert and Sullivan's comic opera, *Patience*, provided the occasion for Wilde's trip. It is easy to see D'Oyly Carte in terms of a cultural entrepreneur and exporter; if so, there is no obvious reason to suppose that Wilde's interests would have been radically different from his.

Some details of the trip suggest that commercial considerations were often paramount. Wilde's lecture tour was very long, often arduous, and involved a considerable number of repeat performances in which he was obliged to represent himself to America as the pattern Aesthete—that pattern, as it were, which the opera parodied and which was already out of date in England. The

Conditions for Criticism (Oxford: Clarendon Press, 1991) and Josephine M. Guy, *The British Avant-Garde: The Theory and Politics of Tradition* (Hemel Hempstead: Harvester-Wheatsheaf, 1991).

44 The values attached to European art in late 19th-cent. America were complex, for while being prized, it could also be seen as a source of decadence and therefore of potential corruption of American values. See Sarah Burns, *Inventing the Modern Artist* (New Haven: Yale University Press, 1996).

self-consciousness with which Wilde took on that role can be seen in
his adoption of a costume that he had worn occasionally in Britain
(velvet coat and knee-breeches, soft-collared shirt and cravat) as the
image that he used with the help of the portraits taken at Napoleon
Sarony's studio in New York to define himself in the United
States.[45] Moreover, the financial success of the tour suggests that
the image had worked.[46] Lecturing had demonstrated to Wilde that
there was money to be made out of art, but it required certain compromises, the most important of which was probably a willingness
to sell himself in a way more visible, explicit (and therefore, to the
critical eye, vulgar) than either his aesthetic posing at Oxford or the
socializing he had undertaken to promote himself in London.
Nevertheless, the difference in these activities is one of degree, and
not of kind. The American tour merely emphasized a lesson which
Wilde already partly knew: for the popular writer to retain an identity as an artist involved a certain self-dramatization or pose, as
much as simple hard work. The sheer number of Wilde's engagements in North America testifies to these dual imperatives: we see in
his itinerary both a recognition of the need and the ability to perform wherever and whenever the opportunity presented itself.
Ellmann cites a punishing schedule in which twenty lectures a
month in different places was not unusual.[47] It is tempting to see the
Wilde who speaks on the renaissance of English art in a lecture hall
in Rockford, Illinois or in Boyd's Opera House in Omaha as a far cry
from the poet haunting his dreamy Magdalen walks in Oxford. But
the contrast is not that stark. The fact that Wilde's American fancy-
dress costume was revived from Oxford should remind us that
his undergraduate days too had had a large element of exhibitionism
in them—that Wilde, in some sense, had always been performing
the part of 'Wilde'. The real difference, perhaps, is that America
taught him how to stage a successful performance for a paying
audience.

45 Fintan O'Toole has commented that Wilde 'arrived [in America] as an advertisement',
and that the 'theatrical exaggeration of himself' which he performed was 'capable of almost
infinite and mechanical reproduction' (O'Toole, 72).
46 Ellmann calculates Wilde's earnings for the whole tour as a 'half share' of '$11,210.63'
(Ellmann, 182).
47 Ellmann shows that in any one week (for example, from 1 March to 7 March) Wilde
could travel to seven different towns in four different states (see Ellmann, 178). See also
Lloyd Lewis and Henry Justin Smith, *Oscar Wilde Discovers America* (New York: Harcourt
Brace, 1936).

Evidence from contemporary correspondence confirms this idea
that financial issues were uppermost in Wilde's mind during his
tour of America. A letter from Dion Boucicault to Mrs George
Lewis suggests that in Boston an anxious Wilde had sought advice
from Boucicault about his business affairs. Boucicault commented
that

Oscar is helpless, because he is not a practical man of business, so when I
advised him to throw over Carte, and offered to see him through financially
if he did so, he felt afraid. I offered him a thousand pounds or two if he required it, but he says he will play out his contract till April . . . There is a
future for him here, but he *wants management*.[48]

The 'future' to which Boucicault alludes, together with the amount
he was willing to invest in it—£1–2,000 (a lot of money in the
1880s)—is further proof that American markets did offer Wilde
significant financial opportunities, perhaps greater than those available in Britain.[49] On the other hand, the Wilde whom Boucicault
paints may seem naive; he is a figure familiar from those later portraits by Robert Sherard and Frank Harris, a man torn between a
sense of personal loyalty and an intuition that such loyalty allowed
him to be exploited. This tension between friendship and professionalism is not unlike the conflict between art and the market, and
it recurs at various points in Wilde's life. However, it would be misleading to interpret it as evidence either of a lack of worldliness on
Wilde's part, or his unwillingness to become involved in the business aspects of selling art. On the contrary, Wilde's very approach to
Boucicault in mid-tour is better seen as his realization of the pressing need to acquaint himself with such matters. Furthermore, there
is evidence that Wilde learned very quickly, for by the end of the
American tour his business sense had distinctly sharpened. As we
show in Chapter 4, he worked hard to negotiate terms for the staging of his two plays, *The Duchess of Padua* and *Vera*, in the United
States. The actress Mary Anderson was impressed enough to offer
$1,000 advance and backing for a long run of *The Duchess of Padua*.

[48] *Letters*, 92 n.
[49] The importance of American markets to British writers in the late 19th and early 20th
cents. is confirmed by the career of D. H. Lawrence; John Worthen has argued that
Lawrence's 'break into the American market' initiated his 'most successful' period as 'a professional writer'. See Worthen, 'D. H. Lawrence and the "Expensive Edition Business" ', in
Ian Willison, Warwick Gould, and Warren Chernaik (eds.), *Modern Writers and the
Marketplace* (Basingstoke: Macmillan, 1996), 105–32.

Similarly, after three months of negotiation, another actress, Marie Prescott, offered Wilde a down payment of $1,000 for *Vera*, followed by $50 per performance. In the event the sums which Wilde agreed failed to materialize, but the negotiations themselves are evidence that the selling of his work had become as important to Wilde as its writing. To put this more generally: there is evidence that Wilde was learning that it was important to know one's market when putting pen to paper—an attitude which his friend Boucicault, who had become famous in the theatrical world for his commercial acumen, must have welcomed.

The American tour was not all successes; there were also a number of disadvantages and disappointments. The caricaturing and hostility which Wilde had experienced from some quarters in Britain in the late 1870s were repeated in North America. Once more he was lampooned for his 'unmanly' Aesthetic posing and for his Irishness which was typically identified with primitivism; on one occasion Wilde was memorably pictured as 'Borneo man'.[50] We cannot assume, however, that this mockery politicized Wilde in America any more than it seems to have done in Britain. It is possible that in America Wilde learned how to turn to commercial advantage the publicity which adverse criticism inevitably brought. Wilde did, after all, self-consciously cultivate an image that he knew would be provocative, just as he chose to lecture on exactly the sorts of topics—such as dress, house design, and the Irish famine—that would be most likely to confirm prejudices about the effeminate Irish Aesthete. There need not be any tension between the Wilde who identified with republicanism and attacked British colonization of Ireland, and the successful lecturer willing to market himself as a cultural product. However, in order to make these positions compatible we must be prepared to see Wilde's politics in partly cynical terms—that he was commodifying a form (or brand) of Irishness and Aestheticism that he knew would sell to his American audience.[51] This view of the North American tour may seem unsympathetic and is certainly unromantic; but it is in accord with Wilde's

[50] For recent accounts of this caricaturing, see O'Toole, 'Venus in Blue Jeans', and Burns, *Inventing the Modern Artist*.

[51] Sandra Siegel (in a paper delivered in Los Angeles at a conference entitled *Wilde and the Culture of the Fin de Siècle*) drew attention to the considerable ethnic prejudice which Wilde endured during his American tour. However, in distinction to Burns and O'Toole, she did not concede the possibility that Wilde may have been willing to incur, or even to have invited, a certain amount of caricaturing on the grounds that any publicity was good publicity.

willingness on his return to Britain to commit himself to a profession already renowned for its lack of integrity and to advertise himself by explicitly promoting a cult of insincerity. Put another way,
the inconsistency and cultivated insouciance that came to characterize Wilde's journalistic voice, and that was later elevated in his
critical essays to a defence of lying, may initially have been commercially rather than politically motivated.

Direct evidence of Wilde's reactions to his American audiences,
like his reactions to his Oxford failures, remains limited and we
should perhaps be cautious about the type of conclusions we come
to. Wilde's attention on his tour to the pragmatic and quotidian is
striking: the American experience can only have focused rather than
precipitated his realization that if he were to pursue a career as a
writer, then he ought (as Boucicault had observed) to become more
professional, and this in turn meant taking seriously the professional writer's need to cater to popular taste. Our interpretation of
the American tour, then, is one which emphasizes continuity rather
than change: we see it consolidating a pattern of activity which
began at Oxford in the late 1870s and which continued until Wilde's
death. In it Wilde became increasingly implicated in the selling of
his art and in the construction of a media personality—roles which
had a large degree of overlap. On returning to England from
America (via a three-month trip to Paris), Wilde embarked on another, but less rewarding and more intermittent lecture tour, this
time of Britain and Ireland. The itinerary was equally relentless and
the locations equally unglamorous. Many lectures took place in
Mechanics Institutions, and prophetically, if ironically, one was
scheduled for Wandsworth Prison (where Wilde was later to be in-
carcerated). Ellmann quotes Otho Lloyd, Wilde's future brother-
in-law, describing Wilde 'going from town to town, but in the
funniest way, one day he is at Brighton, the next he will be at
Edinburgh, the next at Penzance in Cornwall, the next in Dublin.'[52]
Agreeing to give a talk on 'Dress' at the Tyneside Sunday Lecture
Society, in the company of other lecturers such as Mrs F. Fenwick
Miller describing 'Our Puritan Forefathers', or one Commander
Cameron talking about journeys 'Across Africa', gives some insight
into the ways in which Wilde's career was developing, and the kind
of compromises which writing for money entailed.[53]

[52] Quoted, with no source, in Ellmann, 229.
[53] These details are taken from a pamphlet advertising a series of lectures for the

That willingness to compromise is in turn exemplified in Wilde's regular employment, from late 1884, as a reviewer for the populist *Pall Mall Gazette*. By necessity his pieces were short and reductive, and required (in a manner similar to his lecturing) that topics such as dress reform and dinner dishes should be given the same space and attention as a translation of Homer or a collection of German poetry. On the other hand, and more in keeping with his intellectual ambitions, in 1885 Wilde also undertook a rather different type of journalism for the newly-established and avant-garde *Dramatic Review*.54 In line with an editorial policy decision, and in contrast to the *Pall Mall Gazette*, Wilde's work for the *Dramatic Review* appeared under signature. Interestingly, his second contribution was a poem, 'The Harlot's House', a work of pronounced decadent and avant-garde themes, and which had been written as early as the spring of 1883. In fact Wilde continued to write and publish poetry, although on a smaller scale, throughout the 1880s, and his longest poem, *The Sphinx*, seems to have been on his mind on and off through the whole of that decade. 1885 also saw Wilde placing a long critical essay, 'Shakespeare and Stage-Costume' in the prestigious *Nineteenth Century* (the piece had first appeared in a different form and with a different title in the *Dramatic Review*, and was later substantially revised for *Intentions* (1891)). In 1887 he placed another piece in a heavyweight periodical: a translation of Turgenev's short story 'A Fire At Sea' appeared in *Macmillan's Magazine*. None the less he continued throughout this period to review for the *Pall Mall Gazette*; his last anonymous review appeared, according to Stuart Mason, as late as May 1890. We can see from these details that the typical dismissal of the 1880s as the period of Wilde's popular journalism is rather misleading, for the critic and poet continued to coexist, albeit under some pressure, alongside the reviewer. It is true that most of Wilde's energy was spent on reviewing work which paid immediately and regularly, but a reason for this is to be found in the mundane details of his domestic life. Marriage (in 1884), and the birth of his two sons in the next two years, gave him pressing financial responsibilities.

Tyneside Sunday Lecture Society; we are grateful to Peter Raby for drawing our attention to this information which he found while researching in the Wallace family papers.

54 The first issue of the *Dramatic Review* appeared in Feb. 1885. Wilde contributed ten pieces, including two poems, between March 1885 and May 1886.

II

If we set aside our modern assumptions about what counted as success and failure—if, that is, we acknowledge the importance for Wilde to earn money—then it is possible to reconstruct the early years of his writing career in positive terms. By the middle of the 1880s he had achieved a reputation of sorts, insofar as his name was public property; he was also widely published on a variety of subjects and in a variety of periodicals, from the *Burlington Magazine* and *Court and Society Review* to the *Nineteenth Century* and *Macmillan's Magazine*. He was also earning a relatively comfortable living, and he was of sufficient stature (when he was just 33) to be invited in 1887 to take over the editorship of the London periodical which was to become the *Woman's World*. Wilde was employed by its owner, Cassell and Co., to refashion it. It was not uncommon at that time to install a new editor with a distinctive public profile to rescue a magazine with falling sales. Sometimes the tactic worked, most memorably (if temporarily) with Frank Harris's editorship of the *Fortnightly Review* from 1886 until the end of 1894. The fact that Wilde was chosen for this kind of task thus speaks to some kind of distinction which was more than the possession of a name and which was not necessarily undermined by his ultimate failure to make the journal profitable. In practice Wilde tried many of the tactics that worked so well for Harris: recruiting a new generation and a new type of contributor, and modernizing the journal's identity by changing its title and the balance of its contents.[55] The period at the *Woman's World* can be seen as evidence that Wilde was coming to terms with the priorities of the new journalism; more prosaically, it conferred on him an identity more serious and substantial than that of the Aesthete of *Punch*, the flamboyant performer on the lecture circuit, or the anonymous reviewer. It also gave him renewed access to parts of 'high' London society, and the many form letters which Wilde wrote at this time to persuade society ladies or aspiring young writers to contribute to the *Woman's World* functioned to promote himself as much as his magazine.[56] As with his attempts to sell *Vera*

---

[55] For a recent attempt to revalue Wilde's role as editor of *Woman's World*, see Catherine Ksinan, 'Wilde as Editor of *Woman's World*', *English Literature in Transition*, 41: 4 (1998), 408–26.

[56] For examples of this kind of correspondence see *Letters*, 200–5, 207, 210, 220; and *OWR*, 41–3.

in 1881, Wilde was aware of an intimate interconnection between social networking and literary prestige.

For a writer who, as we have argued, consistently sought to achieve commercial as well as artistic success, these activities in the early and mid-1880s do not seem to add up to failure or disappointment. Here it is perhaps worth reconsidering the career patterns available to Wilde, and the extent to which they could have permitted him to achieve his twin goals. We have suggested that in the late nineteenth century there were different kinds of careers which (in principle, if not in practice) Wilde could have adopted, and which were not of equal value. In fact the picture is more muddied than this, because not only were these career patterns themselves in the process of change, but so too were the values which attached to them. So the types of writing careers epitomized by Ruskin, Arnold, and Pater—figures whom we have taken to be representative of the independent writer, the amateur, and the don respectively—were becoming anachronistic even as Wilde was contemplating them. As we have indicated, the quiet lives of the academic and the civil servant were being transformed by an inexorable move towards the professionalization of universities and government departments. Moreover, the role and authority of the independent writer, and more precisely of the critic who was not attached to any institution, were also changing under the self-same pressures; so the tradition of belletrist writing, associated with the relaxed grace and urbanity of the amateur or gentleman, had already begun to lose prestige to the newly professionalized academic, and therefore to lose also a clear sense of what its 'educated' readership would be.[57] A further pressure came from the commercial and economic changes in literary and publishing culture.

In the final decades of the century literary markets and readerships expanded enormously, and simultaneously underwent a process of diversification and fragmentation. In early and mid-Victorian Britain it is possible to make a relatively simple equation between literary success, class interest, and what constituted literary culture. Decisions about (and definitions of) cultural value were

[57] There is a large literature devoted to the discussion of the processes involved in the professionalization of knowledge in the late 19th cent. We list this work, and examine some of the issues involved in Guy and Small, *Politics and Value in English Studies* (Cambridge: Cambridge University Press, 1993); and 'The British "Man of Letters" and the Rise of the Professional', in Lawrence Rainey (ed.), *The Cambridge History of Literary Criticism*, vii (forthcoming).

under the control of a relatively small and homogeneous group, and marginal voices were excluded by a range of social disadvantages which were difficult to overcome. These disadvantages included not simply the obvious prejudices of gender and class, but the more basic issue of money, resources, and leisure.[58] By contrast, in the late nineteenth century, these marginal groups were for the first time empowered to participate in decisions about culture: technological, economic, and educational changes began to erode the class basis of cultural power.[59] As a result, we begin to see the emergence of different sorts of reading communities, with different, and sometimes competing, definitions of literary value, and therefore competing definitions of artistic and literary success. Cultural historians have located in these processes both the beginnings of an opposition between mass and high culture, and—more importantly—the onset of a debate about the very nature of culture itself. It is difficult to overestimate the scope of these changes and their consequences for the day-to-day decisions which writers and artists had to make about their careers. Most obviously, the relationship between commercial and cultural success became a vexed one, as did the issue of a writer's intended readership or market.

In the middle decades of the nineteenth century, when the three-decker novel and the quarterlies were at their height, there was no necessary disjunction between popularity and literary worth. Rather the opposite: 'difficult' or 'obscure' writers such as Robert Browning or George Meredith were routinely criticized for their lack of appeal to the 'common' reader, when 'common' still meant a relatively small, privileged, and educated group.[60] By the late nineteenth century, however, the social phenomenon of the common reader had become rather different, and certainly more 'common': 'common' now embraced a much larger social group and as a result a wider range of occupations, social types, and therefore of tastes. For that elite, which had been accustomed to a monopoly on

[58] There were exceptions to this general pattern; for example, writers such as Thomas Carlyle came from very modest backgrounds. There were also significant traditions of working-class writing, including that produced by Chartists in the 1840s. However, the fact that these *were* exceptions merely reinforces our sense of the hegemony of middle-class values.

[59] A useful account of the changes in printing and publishing technology in the 19th cent. is given by Allan C. Dooley, *Author and Printer in Victorian England* (London: University Press of Virginia, 1992).

[60] For an account of the debates about literary obscurity and its political implications in the 19th cent. see Guy, *The British Avant-Garde*.

cultural power and taste, the concept of the common reader began to acquire powerfully negative overtones, ranging from Algernon Swinburne's condescending attitude to what he labelled the 'ready reader' to Joseph Conrad's 'beastly bourgeois'.[61] Furthermore, in circumstances where 'common' readers began to be equated with the 'mass', popularity was no longer so easily or unproblematically aligned with literary merit. There was a persistent anxiety in the late nineteenth century in some quarters that increased numbers and new kinds of readers posed a threat to traditional literary culture— that new forms of 'common' taste, recently economically empowered, were a pollutant to traditional literary taste and literary values, a kind of nineteenth-century dumbing-down. This anxiety was perhaps best exemplified by Edmund Gosse in articles in the conservative *Contemporary Review* and *New Review* on 'The Influence of Democracy on Literature', and W. E. Henley's strident condemnation in the *Scots Observer* of the increasing conflation of literary and bourgeois values.[62]

For writers privileged with private means, or those supported by other occupations, it was possible to engage with (and sometimes to resist) these developments of mass culture and mass readerships. So as late as 1889 in *Appreciations* Pater could redefine literary taste in terms of 'the scholar writing for the scholarly', safe in the knowledge that he did not have to depend for a living on how many of those scholars existed or, indeed, how many of them were actual buyers of his books.[63] Wilde, coming from exclusive and excluding institutions such as Trinity College, Dublin and Magdalen College, Oxford, clearly had sympathy with these sentiments; his first serious publications were poems freighted with classical allusions, which in some ways exhibited his aspirations to be associated with an intellectual elite. His first commercially published book, *Poems* (1881), was explicitly addressed to a minority readership, and sold

---

[61] Swinburne's comments on the 'ready reader' are to be found in his digression on obscurity and Robert Browning in *George Chapman* (London: Macmillan, 1875); Conrad's reference to the 'beastly bourgeois' appears in a letter; it is quoted in McDonald, *British Literary Culture and Publishing Practice*, 22.

[62] For an account of this debate see McDonald; see also John Carey, *The Intellectuals and the Masses* (London: Faber, 1992), and Allon White, *The Uses of Obscurity* (London: Routledge and Kegan Paul, 1981).

[63] For an account of Pater's attempts to resist mass culture, see Josephine M. Guy, 'Aesthetics, Economics and Commodity Culture: Theorizing Value in Late Nineteenth-Century Britain', *English Literature in Transition* 42: 2 (1999), 143–71. Ironically, and as we show in Ch. 3, *Appreciations* did sell well—almost twice as many copies as Wilde's *Intentions*.

only in hundreds. For Wilde, however, the limited commercial success of that volume gave Paterian refinement a rather different, and certainly more ambiguous, inflection. In the 1880s, whether or not he wanted to, Wilde could not afford to divorce success from financial security even if it demanded an appeal to popular taste; this had been particularly so when he had been required to underwrite the production costs of his volume of poems.[64] It is no accident that, as we show in the following chapter, his next published book, *The Happy Prince* (1888), was printed in larger numbers, priced much more modestly, and was quite obviously intended for a market very different from that of *Poems* (1881).

An exaggerated, but nevertheless instructive example of the complexities involved in defining writerly success is, of course, to be found in the *locus classicus* of the late nineteenth-century writer's plight, George Gissing's *New Grub Street* (1891). The novel charts the contrasting careers of the professional 'new journalist', Jasper Milvain, and the Romantic idealist, Edward Reardon: neither career is presented as wholly desirable, but by the same token, neither career is easily judged in terms of success or failure, integrity or compromise. Gissing's novel is fiction, and relies on simplification and caricature, but it does document a dilemma not that dissimilar from the one which Wilde faced, although the problem for Wilde was not choosing between careers, but trying to combine them. The date of the novel's publication (1891) is also significant, because it described conditions which were only just becoming visible enough to be analysed. It is surely not a coincidence that by precisely that time, too, Wilde seems to have reached a much more solid understanding of new market conditions, and had fixed on a literary product—the society comedy—which he would sell with success for the next four years. By contrast, in 1882, the year in which Gissing's novel opens and when Wilde was contemplating the failure of *Poems* (1881), market conditions were not so settled, and certainly not so easily understood or as available for analysis.

Wilde was establishing his career—those years of so-called 'failure'—precisely during this period of transition as a mass market was developing and consolidating. It should be hardly surprising therefore that it seemed to be his ambition from the outset to

[64] The details of Wilde's contract with David Bogue, the publisher of *Poems* (1881), are discussed in Ch. 3.

combine traditional with more contemporary definitions of success, and that there were virtually no models from whom he could learn. Changes in literary culture in the 1880s were perhaps too close and too much part of Wilde's environment for him (or for anyone else) to understand their implications fully, let alone to be in a position to manipulate or exploit them. It is not as if Wilde was born into a world wholly different from that of Arnold or Ruskin. Rather, their writerly world was still visible (and, as we have shown, for Wilde certainly attractive) at the very time when a new set of writing and publishing conditions was beginning to emerge. As Gissing documents in *New Grub Street*, in 1882 the careers of the popular reviewer and the serious novelist or critic were both viable options; but by 1886, when Gissing's novel closes, both Reardon (the novelist) and Alfred Yule (the 'battered man of letters') are dead, and Milvain's success is marked by the offer of an editorship of a popular review, *The Current*. In the spring of 1887 Wilde too would see a measure of security and advancement in taking up the editorship of a magazine—the *Woman's World*.

Milvain's career choices in *New Grub Street* are represented as cynical and pragmatic, but he is not a lazy character. The trade of the late nineteenth-century journalist demanded attention to mundane and prosaic work that was often without signature or acknowledgement, and was therefore of little consequence in establishing a writer's name. We need to bear in mind that although he was beginning to publish criticism, Wilde's main occupation in the 1880s was as a reviewer, not a critic, and that these were quite distinct roles. The whole *raison d'être* of the reviewer was to provide a service for the reader in the sense that the reviewer's personal taste was much less important than the ability to judge on behalf of his readers by anticipating *their* tastes. Moreover the choice of material to be reviewed also had to be governed by editorial judgements about readers' interests. Here, as we have already indicated, the sheer eclecticism of Wilde's reviewing is instructive: he turns his hand to lectures, plays, exhibitions, contemporary fashion, and of course, to books on all kinds of subjects, from history to fiction, to bookbinding, travel, and marriage. All of these were hardly Wilde's interests, but as a professional reviewer, he had to be prepared to write on any subject for which he received a commission, so much so that he would often review several books and events a week. As Milvain comments to his sister in *New Grub Street*: '[i]t is my business to know something about every subject.'[65] In this professionalism we can see a continuity with the lecturer on the American and British circuits. The same demands to write to deadlines would later come from theatre-managers. We should not, then, overemphasize a distinction between how Wilde wrote when he was a journalist and how he wrote when he was an author of performed and published plays. In both occupations he was writing for money: the fact that the sums involved in the theatre were considerably larger, and the tastes of the audience more difficult to satisfy, only made the commercial pressures heavier. As we show in Chapter 4, there is evidence that Wilde always found writing plays difficult, and was attracted to the theatre principally because the earnings from it were potentially so great.

It is also worth remembering that for such a busy journalist, Wilde did manage to produce a significant body of non-journalistic work, however we are predisposed to value it: taken as a whole, the 1880s saw a volume of poems, two plays, and a volume of short stories. In addition, as we have shown, Wilde continued writing individual poems, some of which appeared individually in periodicals, but some not until after his death; and he undertook serious critical writing. Most of these works have been judged by modern critics to be failures: *The Duchess of Padua* is seen as an embarrassment; *Vera; or, The Nihilists* as a crude and dramatically misjudged amalgam of melodrama, politics, and wit; *Poems* (1881), carefully shepherded through what to the untutored eye seem to be five 'editions', but which in reality (as we have said) sold in only hundreds, is at best seen as a very modest, and certainly a highly derivative, achievement. The short fiction (*The Happy Prince and Other Tales* (1888)) is compromised by the insignificance of the genre in which Wilde was working. Furthermore the very eclecticism of this body of work is also sometimes taken to count against Wilde: he is seen to be trying his hand with too many different styles and in too many different genres in order to establish any significant voice.

As with the occasional journalism, though, there is another way of viewing these undertakings in the 1880s. If we concentrate on Wilde's ambitions rather than his achievement, eclecticism can be seen as versatility, as evidence of an imitative and synthesizing talent

---

[65] George Gissing, *New Grub Street* (1891; Harmondsworth: Penguin, 1987), 66. For examples of the eclecticism of Wilde's review topics, see Mason, 160, and Appendix B.

which he exploited more successfully a few years later (and which is entirely compatible with the skills needed to be a successful journalist). More importantly if, as we have suggested, the relationship between types of audience, numbers of readers, and notions of success was changing, then Wilde's apparent flitting from one genre to another can be seen more positively—as an attempt to explore or 'keep up' with rapidly changing market conditions. Put another way, what appears to be dilettantism may be the very opposite, a kind of dogged professionalism. If a writer was aware that markets were diversifying, and that criteria of literary success were changing, then versatility makes good sense. Only if authenticity is equated with a Romantic idea of a consistent subjectivity or expressivity will versatility be judged negatively; but this kind of position is in turn only possible if a writer *and* his publisher are able to ignore market conditions. In reality, such an idealized world has probably only ever existed for a tiny minority of writers; in the 1880s and 1890s, and certainly for someone in Wilde's position, it was all but impossible.

In the second place, it is not necessarily the case that the kind of writing which succeeds as popular journalism is inimical to 'serious' writing. As markets expanded and diversified, so *all* literature became implicated in selling and advertising, in the sense that readerships had to be actively identified. *New Grub Street* again provides us with a register of these changes. Milvain comments that literary success is no longer a matter of 'genius', but rather of being able to create what he terms a 'marketable literary work'. He goes on: '[t]he quantity turned out is so great that there's no hope for the special attention of the public unless one can afford to advertise hugely.'[66] In such conditions an apprenticeship in journalism could be an important schooling for an understanding of taste. Many contemporaries, including George Bernard Shaw and Rudyard Kipling, learned their craft in the same school as Wilde, and it is not an accident that their successful careers (and subsequent distinguished reputations) centred on their ability to appeal to 'popular' and to 'high' tastes simultaneously. It may be that the techniques of journalism could be used to promote rather than hinder a literary career, certainly as it was being redefined in the late nineteenth century. This in turn suggests that a clichéd opposition between high and

---

[66] *New Grub Street*, 60.

mass culture (or between what Peter D. McDonald calls 'purist' and 'profiteer' tastes) may be imprecise for two quite distinct reasons.[67] First, the career of a writer like Kipling, who could earn the fabled 'dollar a word', as well as the praise of a critic as fastidious as Lionel Johnson, suggests that late nineteenth-century markets might not have divided themselves into such simple and mutually exclusive categories as 'mass' and 'elite'. Second, the pejorative evaluation of 'mass' versus 'elite' may be more a product of polemic than practice, when practice means actual commerce with the publishing industry: elite literature was no less self-consciously a product than that which was manufactured for 'mass' taste. Indeed recent research shows quite strikingly that early twentieth-century modernist writers were fully implicated in the commercial practices which they affected to disdain, and that contempt for the mass was a product of modernist anxiety rather than the realities of modernist publishing. It has been argued that modernists, far from opposing their late Victorian predecessors, were actually the beneficiaries of the lessons they had learned.[68]

Questions about the value of the particular pieces which Wilde produced in the 1880s should perhaps be separated from questions about the value of journalism itself to Wilde's career as a whole. As we have shown, there were many positive aspects to Wilde's employment by the popular periodical press, not the least of which was a certain financial security. Moreover throughout his period as a reviewer Wilde did manage to place some work in the big monthly and fortnightly periodicals, and by the end of the decade he had more or less transformed himself from a reviewer into a critic. In 1889, for example, 'Pen, Pencil, and Poison' appeared in the *Fortnightly Review*, 'The Decay of Lying' in the *Nineteenth Century*, and 'The Portrait of Mr W. H.' in *Blackwoods Edinburgh Magazine*. Nevertheless these concurrent successes in 1889 did not mark a dramatic turning-point in Wilde's fortunes. Wilde had not suddenly been taken up by the more serious press. As we have noted, 'The Truth of Masks' had appeared in the *Nineteenth Century* as early as May 1885, and *Macmillan's Magazine* had published his translation of Turgenev's 'A Fire at Sea' in May 1886. If we also take account of his editorship of the *Woman's World* in 1887 and 1888, then Wilde's

---

[67] See McDonald, *British Literary Culture and Publishing Practice*, 14.

[68] This argument is the burden of the essays in Willison, *et al.*, *Modernist Writers and the Marketplace*.

rise to prominence over the decade seems more gradual and unremarkable. It seems to have been an earned progression rather than a sudden change of fortune or metamorphosis.

What may be more significant, though, is the apparent consolidation of this upward trend by the appearance of another series of major works, beginning with the publication of 'The Picture of Dorian Gray' in July 1890 in *Lippincott's Monthly Magazine*. In fact *Lippincott's* devoted a whole number to 'Dorian Gray': it was thus Wilde's name that was selling the issue. *Lippincott's* 'Dorian Gray' was followed by the two parts of 'The True Function and Value of Criticism' in the *Nineteenth Century* in July and September 1890. These solid and substantial publications on provocative topics cumulatively brought Wilde to public notice as a writer with a style as distinctive as his personality had proved to be seven years earlier. As Frank Harris commented in the summer of 1890, Wilde had become a '*chef-de-file* . . . of the generation now growing to manhood': he was now sought-after as a contributor and could afford to begin to be selective about the work he undertook.[69] In February 1891, 'The Soul of Man Under Socialism', which had been commissioned by Harris, appeared in the *Fortnightly Review*; the preface to *Dorian Gray* was printed in the same journal in March 1891. Close on its heels came the book version of *Dorian Gray* in April, *Intentions* in May, *Lord Arthur Savile's Crime and Other Stories* in June (the stories had in fact appeared in the *Court and Society Review* and the *World* in 1887), and *A House of Pomegranates* (two stories of which had appeared in 1888 and 1889 in the *Lady's Pictorial* and the *Paris Illustré*) in November. 1892 saw the first production of *Lady Windermere's Fan* and the beginnings of his successful career as a dramatist. Despite what appears to be an impressive run of sudden successes, the dates of these publications once again do not bear out a narrative of a sudden leap into literary celebrity; instead they indicate a gradually increasing success. Many of the items published in 1891—that year which Richard Ellmann terms Wilde's '*annus mirabilis*'—reprint work that first appeared as early as 1885, 1887, 1888, and 1889.[70] In fact, of the five works which appeared in 1891, only one—an essay—was wholly new, and only one of the books, *A House of Pomegranates*, contained any significantly new material.

---

[69] Letter from Harris to Wilde, quoted in Maggs Catalogue, item 1139; see Ellmann, 309.
[70] Ellmann, 290.

Undoubtedly Wilde was becoming better known between 1889 and 1891 in the sense that he was publishing more substantial and longer pieces of work in more weighty journals; furthermore, the fact that some of his book publications were reworkings of his journalism is itself a tangible sign of the success and popularity of that journalism. On the other hand, and as we show in the next chapter, Wilde did not earn much money from these enterprises: sales from his books at this time were modest, and some were commercial failures. Paradoxically, then, the moment which modern critics generally identify as marking the beginning of Wilde's run of success could have appeared to him, at least in part, as a sequence of disappointments: Wilde's transformation from occasional reviewer into a critic and author of books did not bring about any striking transformation in his finances. If there is a formative point in Wilde's career, a change in his confidence, then a much better claim can be made for a later moment, from the winter of 1892 until the winter of 1893, when he for the first time achieved his dual goals of financial and literary success. He made considerable sums of money from the West End productions of *Lady Windermere's Fan* and *A Woman of No Importance* and saw a number of his works produced under the imprint of the Bodley Head with elegant designs by Charles Ricketts.

The highlighting of this later period points to a new understanding of the factors and circumstances which motivate Wilde's career. Changes in Wilde's style, a growing artistic maturity, and a sense of freedom brought about by his relationship with Douglas are important. But so too are the ways in which Wilde was marketed and in his attitude towards the commercial elements of publishing. Our use of the passive voice is important, because the agency of Wilde in these sorts of changes was fairly minimal. In 1892–3 we do not witness Wilde suddenly learning to exploit a market. In fact, as we shall show in the following chapter, he is as restricted by contracts and publishers' agreements as he was ten years earlier. The difference is that he was now fortunate in finding publishers and actor-managers who realized *how* his work might be more successfully advertised and promoted, and who were also in a position to bring that success about. In this argument Wilde becomes complicit with, and actively encourages, the marketing of himself and his work: in Boucicault's terms, he agreed (if sometimes reluctantly) to be 'managed', even with his 'high' art. The roles played by Elkin Mathews and John Lane (at the Bodley Head) or George Alexander (at the St James's) and Herbert Beerbohm Tree (at the Haymarket) were no different in principle from that played by David Bogue, who published *Poems* (1881), or that by Colonel W. F. Morse, the manager of Wilde's American lecture tour. In practice, however, the marketing strategies of Mathews and Lane, or Alexander and Tree, were more successful, and that success owed as much to *their* commercial acumen, and *their* exploitation of changes in literary and theatrical culture as to anything which Wilde did. In contrast to the more usual view of Wilde, in which maturity gives him the confidence to expose the limitations and debased values of British publishing and the West End theatre, we shall argue that it was precisely the commercial nature of these institutions that gave him in 1893, and for the first time, a real taste of success, as he himself had defined it. In this way, the 'narrative' of Wilde's literary career that we shall present in the following chapters is one of a growing acceptance of, and concessions to, the actualities of market forces: it is arguable that Wilde was far more deeply immersed in commerce at the end of his career than he ever was in the United States or when reviewing for the *Pall Mall Gazette*.

3

'Of Making Many Books'

The last chapter made two proposals about how we might begin to recharacterize Oscar Wilde's career as a writer. We suggested that throughout his adult life he was driven by a need to earn money as well as critical approbation; the corollary of this claim is that there is no obvious disjunction between Wilde's period of journeyman writing (including his journalism) in the 1880s and his period of celebrity in the 1890s. More precisely, there is no evidence that Wilde's attitude towards his career, or that his fundamental ambitions for himself as a writer, underwent any dramatic change. Our second suggestion was that the trajectory of Wilde's career was dependent upon the intervention of other professionals who were far better attuned than he was to the unpredictability of the new culture industry: in particular, George Alexander and Herbert Beerbohm Tree, and John Lane and Elkin Mathews took a large measure of responsibility for fashioning Wilde into that commercially successful writer who also enjoyed a measure of literary prestige. We intend to explore in this chapter exactly this assertion that Wilde's celebrity did indeed come about because he acknowledged what Boucicault had observed, that he 'wanted management'.

One of the most dramatic illustrations of the arrival of that 'management' is to be found in the decision by Elkin Mathews, shortly before he entered into partnership with John Lane in 1892 (as the Bodley Head), to buy up the unsold sheets of Wilde's first book, *Poems*, and to reissue them. As we noted in the previous chapter, the adverse critical reception of *Poems* (1881), together with its relatively poor sales, have invariably been taken as the pattern of Wilde's failure to establish himself as a distinctive voice among London's literary elite. However those critics (both contemporary and modern) who have habitually dismissed Wilde's gifts as a poet have rarely taken the trouble to explain the contrasting fate of *Poems* (1892). That volume, textually identical to David Bogue's final editions, sold out within days. (To be precise, the Bodley Head edition was identical to the 1882 revised edition, which Bogue had called the fourth and fifth editions, but which a modern bibliographer would understand to be the second, a detail which we explain below.) Why should a work which sold only modestly when it first appeared become a sought-after item just ten years later?

It is tempting to explain the success of the Bodley Head reissue in terms of Wilde's social celebrity in 1892, and to conclude that it was principally his personality which was selling the book. There is some truth in this suggestion because the Bodley Head edition was issued in May 1892, just a few months after the first production of *Lady Windermere's Fan*, which was to put Wilde's name firmly before the public as a successful dramatist. On the other hand, at the time when Mathews made the decision to reissue the volume, and when he planned his strategies to market it, Wilde's reputation was much less secure, and certainly less proven. The contract with Mathews was signed on 24 October 1891—that is, just a week or so after George Alexander had reached an agreement with Wilde to accept *Lady Windermere's Fan* for the St James's Theatre.[1] Designs for the cover of *Poems* (and thus decisions about the basic appearance of the book) were already completed by the time *Lady Windermere's Fan* received its first performance on 20 February 1892.[2] These dates are important: as we shall show, it is no coincidence that Wilde agreed to Mathews's proposition for a limited edition of his poetry just weeks after negotiating with Alexander terms that had the potential to bring an income considerably larger than his earnings from journalism.

[1] For the contract with Mathews, see 149 below; part of it is printed in Mason, 322. According to Ellmann Wilde finished *Lady Windermere's Fan* by October, and immediately made an appointment to read it to Alexander; Ellmann uses an account of Wilde's meeting with William Heinemann on 16 Oct. as evidence that the agreement had been signed by then (Ellmann, 315).

[2] Mason prints a letter from Mathews to Wilde, dated 25 Feb. 1892 which begins: 'I hope by the time this letter reaches you that Mr Ricketts will have received specimen cases. I saw one to-day done up in the darker cloth, and the gold design looked splendid. I would strongly urge you to select this cloth . . . as it is distressing to see pale coloured bindings get dirty after very little use' (Mason, 322). The proof of the pale coloured cover survives in the Clark Library; the design is identical (except of course for the binding) to the cover which was finally decided upon. It is clear then that decisions about marketing the book were finalized before Wilde's success with *Lady Windermere's Fan*.

On reading the play, Alexander claimed to have offered Wilde £1,000.[3] This claim, made seventeen years after the event, and when Alexander was near the end of his life, may be an exaggeration; moreover, there is evidence (as we discuss in Chapter 7) that Alexander had no immediate plans to stage the work, even though he wanted it in his repertoire. What matters is the confidence that the signing of the agreement inspired in Wilde. It seems likely that it allowed him to believe that the commercial success for which he was so keen was finally about to arrive; and this same expectation of financial security may well have persuaded him of the wisdom of Mathews's decision to market his literary work to a limited or coterie readership. In other words, the fate of *Poems* (1892) was intimately related to the fate of *Lady Windermere's Fan*, but not quite in the manner which has usually been assumed. Paradoxically, the very breadth of appeal represented by a play in the West End may have made the idea of restricted sales for a volume of poetry seem attractive. Put another way, the anticipated success of *Lady Windermere's Fan* gave Wilde the luxury of appealing to exactly the kind of elite market of 'refined' tastes which he had always admired, but from which had been unable to earn sufficient money. In this sense the 'discovery' of Wilde by Mathews (and then Lane) on the one hand, and by Alexander (and then Tree) on the other, turned out to be pure serendipity: the two forms of success they promised and later delivered to Wilde fed each other.

I

To return, however, to that moment in the autumn of 1891, before the production of *Lady Windermere's Fan* and the publication of *Poems* (1892). Wilde, at this time, was probably best known as a writer of short fiction: that is, of two volumes of fairy-tales (*The Happy Prince and Other Tales* and *A House of Pomegranates*), a volume of short stories (*Lord Arthur Savile's Crime and Other Stories*); and of a short, one-volume novel, *The Picture of Dorian Gray*. The close relationship between this concentration on short fiction and Wilde's work as a journalist and reviewer has been overlooked, mainly because of a tendency to see his book publications as

[3] The claim is made in a letter from Alexander to Ross dated 1 Dec. 1908 and printed in Margery Ross, *Robert Ross: Friend of Friends* (London: Jonathan Cape, 1952), 151–2. It was repeated a few years later in a 1913 newspaper interview cited by Ellmann (315).

marking a point of departure from his journalist work. In practice, however, and as we have suggested in the previous chapter, most of the material published in these early books had first appeared in cheap magazines, and was explicitly designed to appeal to a popular market. It is likely that the principal objective of the collections of short fiction, like the journalism, was financial. And by the late 1880s, there was considerable money to be earned from popular fiction. For example, between July 1888 and September 1889 Mary (Mrs Humphry) Ward earned around £2,375 on sales of 38,000 of the popular 6s. (one-volume) edition of *Robert Elsmere* (sales of the three-decker version had earned her a further £950).[4] Of course Mary Ward's success was exceptional; but the very publicity it generated demonstrated the opportunities open to writers of fiction. In public Wilde was scathing about her achievements; in 'The Decay of Lying' he referred to *Robert Elsmere* as 'a masterpiece of the "genre ennuyeux" '. Privately, though, he must have been much less dismissive, for most of his own fiction was priced to appeal to exactly the same 6s. market.

Many literary historians have considered the first of Wilde's books of short fiction, *The Happy Prince* (1888), to have been reasonably successful: the first edition of 1,000 copies (priced at 5s.) sold out in less than a year, prompting its publisher, the firm of David Nutt, to bring out a second and cheaper edition (at 3s. 6d.) in January 1889. Furthermore, Nutt had also produced a limited large-paper edition, numbered and signed by the publisher; at £1 1s. it was expensive and only sixty-five copies were put on sale.[5] Nutt was a well-established but specialist house which concentrated on finely produced books; in the 1880s it was probably best known for publishing the Tudor Translations series. Wilde's dealings were with the son, Alfred, who had entered the firm in 1878. The trade magazine, *The Bookman*, ran a feature on the house of Nutt some years later in January 1893. It described how Alfred's personal connections with the Folk-Lore Society and the Honorary Society of Cymmrodorion had been influential in determining the nature of the firm's publishing. It singled out in particular Alfred's establishing (in conjunction with Andrew Lang) of the 'Bibliotèques de Carabas', a collection of monographs on folklore; his series of 'Waifs

---

[4] John Sutherland, *Mrs Humphry Ward: Eminent Victorian, Pre-Eminent Edwardian* (Oxford: Clarendon Press, 1990), 130.   [5] Mason, 331–6.

and Strays of Celtic tradition', which had been set up with the help of Lord Archibald Campbell; and his collaboration with Joseph Jacobs on a series of fairy-tales. The 'distinguishing mark' of the firm, according to *The Bookman*, was 'the issue of choice and beautiful books for the bibliophile and the scholar'. The piece ended by noting that 'Mr Nutt has had the honour of introducing to the public at large Mr W. E. Henley as poet and essayist, Mr Oscar Wilde as a story-teller for children, and Mr Norman Gale as a poet'.[6] Given that Nutt only ever published one of Wilde's works (and in relatively small numbers), the mention of his name may seem odd, until we remember that by January 1893 Wilde had become something of a celebrity, following the successful runs of *Lady Windermere's Fan* in the spring and autumn of 1892: Nutt obviously saw an advantage in advertising their association with such an up-and-coming name. Back in 1888, however, Wilde was much less successful, and Nutt's acceptance of *The Happy Prince* represented something of a gamble (as we describe later, the volume had already been turned down by at least one publisher). When the book appeared Wilde received a number of private but glowing tributes from friends and fellow-writers; the most pleasing probably came from Walter Pater, who claimed (in a letter dated 12 June 1888) that Wilde's 'delightful' characters had 'been consoling' him while he was laid up with gout.[7] The press, however, barely noticed the book: a brief announcement in the *Athenaeum* praised its delicacy and charm, but the majority of serious journals ignored it, no doubt because its intended readership was children.[8]

This decision to launch himself as a children's author is difficult to account for if we are disposed to see Wilde's career in terms of the development of a social celebrity or a politically motivated satirist. The most tempting explanation for his decision to publish *The Happy Prince* is personal: that the contents, as Ellmann tries to argue, were partly shaped by Wilde's experience as a father.[9] However, Cyril and Vyvyan, aged two and a half and one and a half

[6] *The Bookman*, III, no. 16 (Jan. 1893), 121.   [7] Quoted in Mason, 334.

[8] Two other reviews appeared, one in the *Saturday Review* by Alexander Galt Ross (the elder brother of Robbie), and the other in the *Universal Review* by Harry Quilter. Alexander Ross knew Wilde well: Margery Ross (356) prints a letter to him from W. E. Henley dated 15 Oct. 1888 inviting him to supper with 'le bel Oscar'. Quilter also knew Wilde personally, and it is therefore probable that there was an element of log-rolling in their notices.

[9] Ellmann, 253. Brian Gilbert's film *Wilde* also connects the book with Wilde's experience of fatherhood.

respectively, would have been far too young to have understood the stories in their father's volume. A much more likely explanation for *The Happy Prince* is a purely commercial one. By the 1880s, the market for children's books was well established and potentially very lucrative. It is worth remembering that in *New Grub Street*, Jasper Milvain advises his sisters that the easiest way for them to earn a living from their pens is by writing children's fiction. The sorts of sums which could be earned can be seen in the career of Kate Greenaway. Her first children's book, *Under the Window*, published by Routledge in 1878 and priced at 6s., had an initial print-run of 20,000. To the evident relief of Routledge (who had apparently not been consulted by the printer, Edmund Evans, over the size of the print-run) the edition sold out almost immediately—a circumstance even more remarkable when we recall that Greenaway was a comparatively unknown writer and illustrator at the time. *Under the Window* went on to sell some 70,000 copies, and at the peak of her popularity Greenaway claimed to be earning around £2,000 a year. Similarly impressive sales were achieved by Lewis Carroll's *Alice* books; by the time Charles Dodgson (Carroll) died in 1898, around 156,000 copies of *Alice in Wonderland* (1865–6) and 107,000 copies of *Through the Looking-Glass* (1872) had been sold.[10] Interestingly Mary Ward's very first venture into fiction was also a book for children; entitled *Milly and Olly* it was published by Macmillan in December 1881, with an initial print-run of 3,000. Ward had campaigned hard for Greenaway to be the illustrator but had had to settle for her friend, Mrs Laura Alma-Tadema (the wife of the more famous artist); presumably by 1880–1, Greenaway was much too expensive.[11]

The fact that Nutt's first print-run for *The Happy Prince* was only 1,000 copies may indicate a degree of caution about its sales prospects. This kind of number was more appropriate to the economics of the three-decker novel which was priced at 10s. 6d. per volume; *The Happy Prince* was to sell at only 5s. There is evidence that Wilde was very anxious to maximize sales. In a letter to Nutt, dated 13 June 1888, he reported that he had been trying to arrange a public reading of the stories by the actress Ellen Terry, then at the

[10] See Percy Muir, *English Children's Books: 1600 to 1900* (London: B. T. Batsford Ltd., 1954), 184, 189, and 142.
[11] In fact the book sold poorly, and 900 copies were still unsold by 1888. See Sutherland, *Mrs Humphry Ward*, 74 and 384.

height of her fame; he also exhorted Nutt to have a 'card' printed for 'booksellers to hang in their shops'. Wilde went on: 'It may show Crane's frontispiece as well as the title etc. of the book. And is it not time for a few advertisements? *Punch* and the *World* are capital papers to advertise in—*once*.'[12] The suggestion that attention should be drawn to Crane's artwork was astute, for children's literature sold as much on illustrations as narrative; moreover by 1888, Crane already had a reputation as a children's illustrator, earned largely from the highly successful series of sixpenny 'toy books' published by Routledge in the late 1860s.[13] The successful careers of figures such as Greenaway and Dodgson go some way towards explaining Wilde's decision in 1888 to write children's fiction; more importantly, though, they put into context those modest initial sales of only 1,000 copies. For children's literature, such figures could hardly be counted as success. Furthermore, there is evidence that both Wilde and his publisher shared this judgement. The decision to print a second edition of *The Happy Prince* priced at 3s. 6d. suggests an attempt to boost sales; but the edition sold poorly. We do not know exactly how many copies Nutt printed, but Wilde reported to John Lane in September 1894 that Nutt's 'average yearly sale of *The Happy Prince* is about 150!'—a figure which he thought 'really absurd', and which could hardly have been economic for the cheaper edition.[14]

Unlike *The Happy Prince*, *Dorian Gray* attracted enormous attention, and it sold (in its periodical form) in large numbers. That said, most reviews were very hostile, and W. H. Smith refused to stock the book version on the grounds that it was 'filthy'. As the *Scots Observer*, then edited by the arch-conservative W. E. Henley, put it in a phrase which reverberated through Wilde's trials, *Dorian Gray* was suitable only for 'perverted telegraph boys'.[15] It might be

[12] *Letters*, 219.

[13] See Muir, *English Children's Books*, 185–6.

[14] *More Letters*, 127. Earlier evidence that Wilde's fairy-tales might not be wholly successful can be found in a letter dated Jan. 1889 from Wilde to George Macmillan. In it Wilde reports how he sent 'The Happy Prince' to the *English Illustrated Magazine* (which was published by Macmillan), and how he demanded the story be returned to him because eighteen months had passed without a decision about publication (*More Letters*, 80–1).

[15] See Ellmann, 305; *Heritage*, 75. Critics have generally explained the hostile reaction to *Dorian Gray* in Britain in terms of recent publicity surrounding the Cleveland Street scandal which had involved the discovery of a male brothel operating near the Houses of Parliament. Donald Lawler has suggested that the more generous reception afforded to Wilde's story in America might be explained by the fact that events in Cleveland Street were not widely

thought that the publicity which surrounded the magazine version would have generated a demand for the book; in the case of George Moore's *Esther Waters* (1894), controversy actually stimulated sales. Moore's novel too was banned by the circulating library of Smith and Mudie because of its treatment of illegitimacy; yet it sold over 20,000 copies by the time of his death. By contrast, five years after the book-version of *Dorian Gray* first appeared, Ward, Lock still had stock from the original printing of 1,000 small-paper copies (priced at 6s.).[16] (Again we should note that the print-run indicates modest ambitions for the book's prospects.)

The extent of those disappointing sales can be seen in the deal that Wilde negotiated for the book. He had received a handsome sum of £200 from Lippincott as an 'honorarium' for the original story.[17] For the book version, though, Wilde was to receive only £125 on account of a 10 per cent royalty. Unhappy with this offer, he complained to Coulson Kernahan, a literary adviser to Ward, Lock (the British publisher of Lippincott) that his naivety—'not knowing the proper price of books'—had allowed George Lock to take advantage of him.[18] In fact the opposite proved to be the case. First, a 10 per cent royalty was not unreasonable. It was the standard amount later offered by John Lane at the Bodley Head, a house considered to be generous in its dealings with writers; only successful and proven authors could negotiate higher sums. For example, the sales of the three-decker edition of *Robert Elsmere* allowed Mary Ward to negotiate a royalty of 1s. 3d.—that is, around 25 per cent of the net price—on sales of the 6s. edition.[19] Second, to earn Wilde's advance, Ward, Lock would need to have sold all 250 large-paper copies (at £1 1s.) and well over 3,000 small-paper copies. *Dorian Gray* clearly fell short of these expectations. It seems likely that the wide circulation of the periodical version, which was priced at only one shilling, had exhausted much of the demand. Significantly in

reported there. See Donald Lawler (ed.), *Oscar Wilde: The Picture of Dorian Gray* (New York: W. W. Norton, 1988).

[16] See Stuart Mason, *Oscar Wilde: Art and Morality: A Defence of 'The Picture of Dorian Gray'* (London: J. Jacobs, 1908), 22. There were plans to issue a new edition of *Dorian Gray* towards the end of 1894. Mason reports that the volume was probably not ready until March 1895, and that Wilde's arrest made it inadvisable to bring it out. The volume finally appeared in Oct. 1895; a year later the edition was remaindered.

[17] In a letter dated 17 Dec. 1889, Wilde asked Stoddart for 'half the honorarium in advance—£100—as I have a great many offers of work, and having been idle for four months require some money' (*More Letters*, 87).

[18] *Letters*, 295.   [19] Sutherland, *Mrs Humphry Ward*, 130.

the winter of 1890 three specially bound numbers of the periodical had been produced, each containing selected portions from the previous six months' issues: in all three *Dorian Gray* appeared as the first and therefore the 'lead' item.[20]

The Lippincott version had clearly been trading on Wilde's personality: as we have mentioned, the first publication of *Dorian Gray* took up an entire issue. J. M. Stoddart, who had originally met Wilde during his American tour in 1882, and who had commissioned the piece in 1889, seems to have been prompted by the perception that Wilde, like Arthur Conan Doyle (whom Stoddart had also approached), was by this time a promising prospect. Interestingly, there is evidence that Wilde himself was slightly embarrassed by Lippincott's aggressive advertising techniques. He wrote to Ward, Lock in June 1890 asking 'Messrs Lippincott' to cease sending out their 'puff' of his novel, that 'puff' being a fulsome advertisement. He wrote at the same time to the editor of the *St James's Gazette* to dissociate himself from his publisher's hype, believing that it would damage his potential reputation among serious critics.[21] Such ambivalence suggests that Wilde was sensitive to the ways in which the relationship between literary value and popularity had become vexed. On the other hand, and as we have shown in the case of *The Happy Prince*, Wilde was certainly well disposed to what he considered to be the right sort of advertising—that is, advertising which he could orchestrate himself. In May 1891 he wrote to W. L. Courtney, the literary editor and drama critic of the *Daily Telegraph*, asking whether the book version of *Dorian Gray* could 'be noticed in the paper'. Wilde went on to explain his reason:

when it first appeared it was very grossly and foolishly assailed as an immoral book, and I am anxious to have it treated purely from the art-standpoint: from the standpoint of style, plot, construction, psychology, and the like. From this standpoint much, no doubt, may be urged against it. Every true critic has his own temperament by whose laws he abides, and I may candidly admit that I admire my own work far too much to ask other people to praise it. But one does want, especially in England, to have one's work treated from the proper point of view.[22]

As Hart-Davis comments, Courtney 'obliged' with a brief notice which appeared on 15 June 1891.

[20] Mason, *Bibliography*, 108–9.   [21] *Letters*, 261.   [22] *More Letters*, 96–7.

Correspondence between Wilde and George Lock, about a year earlier (in July 1890), indicates that there had been other anxieties about selling the book version of *Dorian Gray*; this time they concerned justifying its 'value'—that is, its price of 6s. George Lock wrote to Wilde suggesting that he 'add to the story so as to counteract any damage [that] may be done by it being always on sale at 1/- as it first appeared in Lippincott'.[23] It has been usual to explain the six chapters added to the book version of *Dorian Gray* in terms of Wilde's attempt to tone down the homoerotic elements of the original—that is, in terms of self-censorship. While there may be some truth in this interpretation, and while there were disagreements over the precise nature of the new material, it seems that the initial reason for expanding the novel (rather than the particular form which that expansion took) was a straightforward commercial one: purchasers of the book version had to be given something more for their extra five shillings. The disappointing sales of the six-shilling *Dorian Gray* in turn suggests that they were not given enough.[24] It is hard to avoid the conclusion that the failure of the book version of *Dorian Gray* was principally a failure to understand the market for which it was intended. The usual strategy behind a cheap six-shilling novel was either to exploit the potential for a large run of an original work, or to make available to a larger readership a novel which had previously been successful in the expensive three-decker format. Oddly, the publishing history of *Dorian Gray* reversed this strategy: the cheap market had already been saturated by the time a popular book version was being contemplated, a circumstance which gives a much more prosaic explanation of why so many British publishers had turned it down.

Wilde's next book was *Intentions*, which appeared in July 1891, just a month after *Dorian Gray*. It was priced at 7s. 6d. with a print run of 1,500, of which 600 were for sale in America.[25] Given the controversy that had greeted his novel, it was not perhaps the most propitious time for Wilde to try to launch himself as a serious critic.

[23] Mason, 105.
[24] Ibid. George Lock suggested that Wilde change the ending of the novel—'Could you not make Dorian live longer with the face of the picture transferred to himself, and depict the misery in which he ends his days by suicide or repents and becomes a better character. Lord Henry too goes off the scene very quickly. Could not he also have a little longer and you could make an excellent contrast between the deaths of the two men.' Wilde of course rejected these conservative suggestions; but Lock was in no sense forcing his views on Wilde. As he said, 'it is for you to decide'.   [25] Mason, 355.

On the other hand, *Intentions* might be evidence that Wilde was uncertain about (or perhaps dissatisfied with) the kind of reputation he might achieve as a writer of popular fiction alone. It is worth remembering that with *Intentions* Wilde was doing business with a third publisher—the new firm of Osgood, McIlvaine—in less than three years. That he had failed, up to this point, to establish a loyal relationship with a single house can be explained partly in terms of the range of genres in which he was writing; but it also points to the difficulties that he and his prospective publishers experienced in marketing his work. Wilde did not yet present himself, in the manner of Arnold or Pater, as a writer with a distinctive style and range who appealed to a readily identifiable group of readers, and who could therefore be relied upon by publishers.

Reviewers of *Intentions* were perplexed by it. Prepared to admit that it possessed 'cleverness' and 'wit', they nevertheless condemned its superficiality. In the words of the *Pall Mall Gazette* (a magazine for which, ironically, Wilde was still reviewing), there was too much that was 'the result of a facile formula, a process of word-shuffling'; more damagingly, *Intentions* assumed a 'familiarity with a coterie-speech—not to say a jargon—current only on the highest heights of culture'. The *Athenaeum* was equally troubled by the book's intended market: Wilde was accused of vulgarity, of resorting to 'the tricks of the smart advertiser in order to attract attention to his wares', while at the same time being contemptuous of 'ordinary people'.[26] Both reviewers highlight an uncertainty about the book's intended readership: it satisfied neither popular nor serious markets. One of the more favourable notices, that by Richard Le Gallienne (at this time a close friend and perhaps a sometime lover of Wilde), was also the most perceptive, in that it identified exactly the problem with Wilde's reputation in the early summer of 1891:

[S]ince 'The Decay of Lying', which is here reprinted, Mr Wilde has become quite newly significant. One hardly knows yet what to expect of him, but we may be quite sure that these essays and *Dorian Gray* are but preludes. At present a delicate literary affectation, which is probably irritating to most, but rather a charm to those who know what it means, a suggestion of insincerity, a refusal to commit himself . . . makes him somewhat of a riddle.[27]

[26] *Heritage*, 90–1 and 92–3.   [27] Ibid. 102.

Wilde's reputation in the autumn of 1891 certainly was a riddle: how could the image of the children's author (published by David Nutt) be compatible with the man who allegedly wrote for perverted telegraph boys? And how did either of these personas square with that of the cultural critic advertised by Osgood, McIlvaine? To whom could this cultural critic in good faith address himself? To 'ordinary people' with their appetite for popular subgenres, such as detective and sensation fiction? Or to the more rarefied tastes of the literary 'coterie' identified by the reviewer for the *Pall Mall Gazette*, who appreciated (and would pay for) fine books? This discrepancy between writer, market, and work seems the most troubling aspect of Wilde's early career as an author of books.

Osgood, McIlvaine's decision to follow *Intentions* very quickly with two volumes of short stories may indicate a growing confidence in Wilde. *Lord Arthur Savile's Crime and Other Stories* appeared in July 1891, priced at a modest 2s., with a print-run of 2,000. Its marketing suggests that Wilde and Osgood, McIlvaine had learned from the slow sales of the book version of *Dorian Gray*, for *Lord Arthur Savile's Crime* was priced in the same range as the one-shilling Lippincott version. At the same time, and like Wilde's first collection of stories (*The Happy Prince*), *Lord Arthur Savile's Crime* failed to generate much interest among critics.[28] Given the publicity that had surrounded *Dorian Gray*, the lack of curiosity over Wilde's next work of fiction may seem surprising, until we recall that all the stories in the volume had appeared before—as long ago as 1887, in the *World* and the *Court and Society Review* (both sold at 6d., a price in keeping with the 2s. asked for the book). The decision by both Wilde and Osgood, McIlvaine to reissue them as a collection was probably designed to capitalize on what they thought was Wilde's growing celebrity, but if so the strategy was not wholly successful, for there was no second printing. Here it is worth recalling some simple economic facts, that profits on a book selling at 2s. with a print-run of 2,000 are significantly less than one selling at 6s. with a print-run of 1,000. The sales of *Robert Elsmere* again give us a useful yardstick: between January and December 1890, Smith sold some 20,000 copies of the 2s. 6d. edition, the cheapest he issued.[29]

[28] There were only three English reviews, in the *Graphic*, *Academy*, and *Athenaeum* (Mason, 362); in addition there were reviews in the *Nation* and *United Ireland*.
[29] Sutherland, *Mrs Humphry Ward*, 131.

It is tempting to see the decision by Osgood, McIlvaine to go ahead with a further volume of Wilde's tales, *A House of Pomegranates*, as evidence of their continued faith in him. However, a contradictory explanation may be more accurate, for the way in which the work was marketed represented a dramatic change of strategy. The book appeared in November 1891 in an edition of 1,000 copies priced at £1 1s.—a figure nearer to that of a three-decker novel. When decisions were being made about the pricing and format of *A House of Pomegranates*, it must have been apparent that Wilde's earlier volume of stories, *Lord Arthur Savile's Crime*, was not going to be a popular success. Osgood, McIlvaine would also have been aware that *Intentions* had not been selling particularly quickly; a second and cheaper edition (priced at 3s. 6d.) was not issued until 1894. Of course even the most successful literary criticism did not approach the sorts of sales achieved by fiction. Even so, comparisons with the fortunes of Arnold's or Pater's collections of essays suggest that *Intentions* was at best only a modest success. *Essays in Criticism* (first series) had run to four English and American editions in four years, and twelve by the time of Arnold's death in 1888. Pater's *Appreciations* (which was more contemporary with *Intentions*) was issued by Macmillan on 15 November 1889 in an edition of 1,000 copies priced at 8s. 6d. George Macmillan (Alexander Macmillan's son) wrote to Pater just over a month later on 23 December to inform him that only 120 copies were left, and that a reprint should be prepared 'without undue delay'. A second edition of 1,500 copies appeared in May 1890 (later than Macmillan hoped because Pater had lingered over proofs); in July a further 1,000 copies were printed for sale in America.[30] The demand for *Appreciations* (a volume which had also received mixed reviews) was clearly much healthier than for Wilde's work.

Unfortunately, the decision to direct *A House of Pomegranates* at a connoisseur market proved to be an expensive mistake—the most

[30] See Robert M. Seiler, *The Book Beautiful: Walter Pater and the House of Macmillan* (London: Athlone Press, 1999), 48 and 103–4. The copies of *Appreciations* printed for the American market were not actually dispatched until December. Interestingly, the American branch of Macmillan had also placed orders for other works by Pater, a circumstance which adds weight to our suggestion in Ch. 2 that American markets were becoming an increasingly important source of income for late 19th-cent. British writers and publishers. In July, along with the request for copies of *Appreciations*, there was an order for 1,000 copies of *The Renaissance*; this was followed in August with a further order of 1,000 copies of *Marius*. George Macmillan wrote to Pater in December that 'our people in New York want the book [i.e., *Marius*] badly'. (Seiler, *The Book Beautiful*, 106–7.)

costly by far of all Osgood, McIlvaine's marketing strategies for Wilde's books. Stock from the first edition was still being remaindered as late as 1904, and for just a few shillings.[31] The book also received very poor reviews. Critics who were expecting to find the same delicacy and charm of Wilde's earlier fairy-tales were signally unimpressed by what was termed the ' "fleshly" style' and 'ultra-aestheticism' of the illustrations. The *Saturday Review* went so far as to wonder whether the point of *A House of Pomegranates* was simply a 'deliberate provocation to the *bourgeois au front glabre*'—a reference to intellectual pretension.[32] It is perhaps relevant that Osgood, McIlvaine was a new publishing house, one established only in 1891, and clearly in need of authors.[33] James Osgood no doubt had a feeling that Wilde 'should' sell—a hunch which he shared with other publishers of the time, including Stoddart and George Lock. Frank Harris, too, had written in the summer of 1890 that he was confident of Wilde's prospects. It seems, though, that Osgood, McIlvaine simply did not know how to turn that potential into sales, even though they tried a number of different strategies to promote Wilde's work.

After the failure of *A House of Pomegranates*, Wilde unsurprisingly published no new work with Osgood, McIlvaine. It is not clear whether he dropped the firm, or whether they dropped him. Interestingly Wilde had been making approaches to other publishing houses as early as the summer of 1891, when he sent William Heinemann (another new publisher who had set up business only in 1890, and who went on to establish a successful list) *Intentions* for his 'English Library' series. He also sent the firm *Lord Arthur Savile's Crime* (which, although announced to be 'in press', never actually appeared under Heinemann's imprint).[34] Such activities may simply be evidence of Wilde's desire to maximize his income from existing publications; around November–December 1891, Wilde also wrote to David Nutt asking whether a new edition of *The Happy Prince*, one 'run as a Christmas book', might be produced to take advantage of seasonal demand.[35] Alternatively, these

---

[31] Mason, 369.   [32] *Heritage*, 113–14.

[33] See Carl J. Weber, *The Rise and Fall of James Ripley Osgood* (Waterville, Maine: Colby College Press, 1959).   [34] *Letters*, 294 and n.

[35] *More Letters*, 102. The Christmas market was extremely important for children's literature; in a letter to Macmillan, suggesting they miss the Christmas trade in order to improve the production values of *Through the Looking-Glass*, Dodgson admitted 'you will think me a lunatic for thus wishing to send away money from the doors; and will tell me perhaps

approaches may hint at a growing dissatisfaction with Osgood, McIlvaine, for during the autumn of 1891 Wilde was also negotiating with other publishers over new projects. For example, in October 1891, Wilde met Heinemann to discuss the possibility of writing the introduction for two plays of Maeterlinck in an English translation. This project came to nothing, although it was clearly taken seriously enough for there to have been a public announcement of it which later had to be denied. Thus in the January 1892 issue of *The Bookman* the following appeared:

Notwithstanding a recent announcement, it is not Mr Oscar Wilde who is writing the essay on Maurice Maeterlinck, introductory to the translation of *La Princesse Maleine* and *L'Intruse*, which Mr Heinemann is shortly to publish. This introductory paper has been undertaken by Mr Hall Caine.[36]

In the autumn of 1891 Wilde was also reported (somewhat surprisingly) to have been writing a serious religious story; the November issue of *The Bookman* confidently announced that:

Mr Oscar Wilde is writing a story which will be a study of Christianity from the standpoint of one who regards it as a great world-force, and independently of any doctrinal bias. One of the scenes will be laid in the Holy Land, but the story will deal with modern, not early, Christianity.[37]

This project also failed to materialize, and it is not known whether Wilde had a publisher for it. It is tempting to think that he may have been inspired by Renan's famous *Vie de Jésus* (1863) which he had apparently been looking at a year or so earlier, for there are allusions to it both in *Intentions* (in 'The Critic as Artist') and in 'The Soul of Man Under Socialism' (which appeared in the *Fortnightly* in February 1891). However, it is equally possible that the announcement was simple self-promotion, orchestrated by Wilde in order to represent himself as being both busier and more versatile in his

that I shall thus lose thousands of would-be purchasers, who will not wait so long, but will go and buy other Christmas-books' (quoted in Muir, *English Children's Books*, 141). The fact that Nutt resisted Wilde's suggestion is probably evidence that the second edition of *The Happy Prince* was indeed selling badly—perhaps not many more copies than the annual 150 which Wilde reported in 1894. However, other publications by Nutt were doing very well: for example, his *Celtic Fairy Tales* was listed in the November 1891 issue of *The Bookman* as one of the five best-sellers in London—a detail which in turn suggests that the disappointing sales of *The Happy Prince* had little to do with Nutt's lack of expertise. (See *The Bookman*, I, no. 2 (Nov. 1891), 67.)

[36] Ibid., no. 4 (Jan. 1892), 126; see also n. 1.   [37] Ibid., no. 2 (Nov. 1891), 49.

talents than was in fact the case. We have already noted in Chapter 2 Wilde's readiness (in the *Biograph and Review*) to advertise work not yet completed, nor even properly started; in Chapter 4, we will show that he had the same over-optimistic estimate of his productivity in the promises he made to theatre-managers. Significantly, in the December 1891 issue of *The Bookman*, there appeared yet another puff for Wilde's work:

Mr Oscar Wilde has just finished a play, which will be produced at the St James's Theatre. Mr Wilde wrote 'Dorian Gray,' as it appeared in magazine form, in three weeks, but the plot had of course been forming in his mind for a long time. The opium den scene (which occurs only in the revised volume form) is, for all its fidelity of detail, a purely imaginary description, as Mr Wilde recently said that he had never set foot in an opium den in his life.[38]

On this occasion the announcement seemed designed to serve two purposes; to alert the public to the forthcoming production of *Lady Windermere's Fan* (which, as we noted, had been accepted by George Alexander in late October for the St James's), and to try to stimulate sales for the book version of *Dorian Gray*. The sources of these notices, which appear in a section of *The Bookman* entitled simply 'News Notes', are never specified; but it seems likely that the information about Wilde originated with Wilde himself, and was an attempt to keep his name before the public—or, more precisely, to advertise himself to those in the publishing trade (who were, after all, the main purchasers of *The Bookman*). Such self-advertisement, in its turn, makes little sense unless Wilde was keen to attract houses more prestigious than that of Osgood, McIlvaine.

What, then, can we learn from Wilde's commerce with publishers in 1891? In particular, was it that 'annus mirabilis' which critics (and particularly Ellmann) have often taken it to be? First, all but one of Wilde's publications in 1891 were what we can describe as 'made' books, put together for what seem to be basically commercial reasons. As we have emphasized, all of the stories in *Lord Arthur Savile's Crime*, all of the essays in *Intentions*, two of the pieces in *A House of Pomegranates*, as well as *The Picture of Dorian Gray*, had appeared in periodical form. The only entirely new work in print in 1891 was *The Happy Prince and Other Tales*, although it was so only by default, because Wilde had tried but failed to place any of the

---

38 Ibid., no. 3 (Dec. 1891), 88.

stories in periodicals. Book publication was of course less ephemeral than publication in the periodical press, and it is wholly understandable that Wilde was keen to acquire the prestige that would accrue from being known as an author of books. But there was at least an equal interest in the commercial prospects that book publication offered: the touting of a second or third edition of a work to different publishers shows a man as concerned with money as much as kudos. Second, we would do well to register the sheer number of publishers with whom Wilde was negotiating: Nutt, Ward, Lock, Heinemann, and Osgood, McIlvaine. Of these four, one (Nutt) was a small specialist house, and a further two (Heinemann and Osgood, McIlvaine) had begun as part of what we have called the 'bubble-economy' in publishing in the 1890s. None of these houses had anything approaching the prestige or marketing skills of Macmillan, which rejected all of Wilde's proposals for books. It is worth pausing here to consider in more detail the significance of Wilde's repeated overtures to Macmillan and the reasons behind their repeated refusals.

II

Wilde first approached Macmillan as early as June 1878, when he wrote to George, who had accompanied him on an undergraduate tour of Greece in April 1877, to enquire whether his father's firm (which George had entered in 1874) might publish his Newdigate Prize poem *Ravenna*. George congratulated Wilde on his success, but pointed out that although he personally would 'have been glad to oblige', the house of Macmillan did not 'care much for publishing prize poems' and would not take on Wilde's.[39] This letter set a pattern for Wilde's dealings with Macmillan: he would always make an approach via his friendship with George, but was nearly always rejected. His next known contact with the house was made just under a year later. Correspondence with George in the spring of 1879 refers to the possibility of Wilde producing translations from Herodotus and Euripides. George had been made a full partner in

---

[39] *OWR*, 90. George Macmillan went on to advise Wilde to have the poem printed in Oxford; this may be a reference to the tradition of using Thomas Shrimpton to publish Newdigate Prize poems under the imprint of the University arms. At all events, the poem appeared under this imprint on 26 June. Shrimpton's ledger for Wilde's account shows that he was given 100 free copies, but he went on to purchase a further 75; see Mason, 245.

January 1879, and had taken responsibility for publications on music, the classics, and natural history. He was behind such important works as the *Journal of Hellenic Studies*, which was begun in 1880, and it was probably he who proposed the translations to Wilde.[40] In a letter dated 22 March Wilde indicated that he could have the translation work completed by 1 September. Macmillan's reply on 24 March welcomed the suggestion and offered half-profits and an advance of £25 or £30 for Herodotus and half-profits or £45 down for the plays. These were reasonable terms for an unknown author of academic works; but the plans came to nothing.[41] The negotiations probably had their origins in Wilde's ambitions for an academic career (as we described in the previous chapter, in 1880 Wilde had advertised himself as a writer on 'Greek art'.) But they were almost certainly given up after he failed to win his Magdalen fellowship.

Wilde's next known contact with Macmillan was in 1881 when he sent a sonnet 'for approval' to *Macmillan's Magazine*; no poem of Wilde's ever appeared in that publication, so we must presume that its editor, George Grove, refused it.[42] Some years later in the spring of 1886 Wilde again approached George Macmillan, this time with the offer of a translation of Turgenev's short story 'A Fire at Sea' (which had been written originally in French). George turned down

[40] See Seiler, *The Book Beautiful*, 33; the standard history of the firm is Charles Morgan's *The House of Macmillan* (London: Macmillan, 1943). In describing Wilde's transactions with Macmillan we have found useful some of the details compiled by Anya Clayworth in ' "Laurels Don't Come For The Asking": Oscar Wilde's Career as a Professional Journalist'. Unpublished Ph.D. thesis (University of Birmingham, 1996), 80–9.

[41] *Letters*, 59 and *More Letters*, 31 n. The terms Macmillan proposed to Wilde were fairly standard for serious literary or critical works. Walter Pater, for example, was offered (and accepted) a £50 advance on half-profits for *Marius*; moreover he was to keep the sum whether or not his share actually reached £50. Alexander Macmillan's explanation to Pater of the economics of such terms is interesting, for it suggests that the profit margins on serious literature were small and the financial risks borne by the publisher disproportionately high. Macmillan wrote: 'I suspect that authors do not realize that in the case of half profits arrangements the publisher only charges the actual cost of production and advertisements. House rent, clerks' salaries, our own time, thought, correspondence: whatever they are worth are supposed to be paid out of *our* share of profits. I am fully and keenly aware [of] how little the money result ever is to writers like yourself [who] by careful elaboration of thought and skill work out results that have intellectual value. But I think we do our best for the higher literature, as distinguished from the merely popular' (Seiler, *The Book Beautiful*, 92). George Macmillan had made a similar point in his offer of half-profits to Wilde, commenting that classical translations were not work 'for which we could afford to make large payments because the . . . outlay is considerable and the return rather slow' (ALS George Macmillan to Wilde, British Library, Macmillan MSS. Add. 55408, vol. 2). [42] *Letters*, 75.

the piece, explaining to Wilde (in a letter dated 7 April) that 'our experience of foreign fiction has been so uniformly discouraging that we have determined to make no further ventures in that field'.[43] Oddly, however, the translation was published just a month later in the May issue of *Macmillan's Magazine* (54: 319). Anya Clayworth has speculated that Wilde's original approach to George may have been for a prospective book (perhaps an anthology of Turgenev's short stories); and that on refusing it, George himself may have passed the piece for consideration to Mowbray Morris, the editor of *Macmillan's Magazine* from late 1885. Alternatively, it is possible that Wilde submitted the story to Morris independently.[44] Corroboration that the publication did come about through Wilde's initiative may be found in the fact that just a couple of months earlier, in March 1886, Wilde had been commissioned by Joseph Comyns Carr to write a piece for the *English Illustrated Magazine*, another title owned and published by Macmillan (although they exercised little control over its contents).[45] This essay, entitled 'London's Models', did not appear until the January 1889 issue; nevertheless, the commission itself may have given Wilde the confidence in late April 1886 to send the Turgenev translation to another Macmillan periodical.

In 1886 Wilde was certainly very interested in Macmillan publications and keen to make use of all his contacts with the house. For example, in the late autumn of that year he approached Comyns Carr with his short story 'The Happy Prince'. On this occasion, though, Comyns Carr appears not to have been impressed; Wilde later described how his piece 'languished in the manuscript chest of [the *English Illustrated*] for eighteen months' before he finally got it back.[46] However, on the return of his story, and in a manner which

43 ALS George Macmillan to Wilde, British Library, Macmillan MSS. Add. 55421, vol. 3. The significance of this part of the Macmillan archive was first noticed by Clayworth in ' "Laurels Don't Come For The Asking" '.

44 Clayworth, ibid. 90–1. John Morley assumed the editorship of the magazine in 1883. Illness forced his retirement around Sept./Oct. 1885. There is no clear agreement about when precisely Morris took over, although he was in total control by the end of 1885.

45 *More Letters*, 80–1.

46 Ibid. The letter in which Wilde reports Comyns Carr's conduct is dated Jan. 1889. However, the 'eighteen months' mentioned in this letter almost certainly date back from *Jan. 1888*, for it was around that time (as we describe below) that Wilde resubmitted his story for consideration by Macmillan. Of course it is possible that there was more than one text of the story—that Wilde might have simultaneously sent copies to Macmillan and Carr. Such a circumstance, however, seems highly unlikely; after all, if there were multiple copies, then

seems to reverse his touting of the Turgenev translation, Wilde decided to try Macmillan again but by a different route; this time he offered the story as part of a collection. Correspondence between Wilde and George dating from October 1887, in which Wilde asks whether Macmillan would send some of their books for him to review in the *Woman's World*, suggests that the two men were still on good terms, and the continuation of their friendship may have prompted Wilde's approach to the firm.[47] In this instance, though, there is no direct record of Wilde's proposal, nor of Macmillan's rejection of the project. However, a surviving reader's report (dated 16 February 1888) explains why the stories were returned to their author:

There is undoubtedly point and cleverness in the way in wh[ich] these stories are told. The writer has, no doubt, the literary knack—the point and finish. You feel at once the hand of the man who knows how to write. Two or three of the stories are very pretty, but I can hardly say as a whole that they have any striking imaginative brilliance—nor do I think that they would be likely to rush into marked popularity. They are pretty and bright, but they hardly strike into the reader's mind. They are good and respectable. Whether they are more than that, I doubt.[48]

Nutt must have taken up the volume fairly soon after this refusal, for *The Happy Prince and Other Tales* appeared under his imprint in May. It is worth remembering, though, and as we described earlier, that the sales of the book were limited: Macmillan's reader was proved right in his judgement that the volume would not be popular.

By the end of the 1880s, the balance of Wilde's refusals and acceptances at the hands of Macmillan seems to point firmly towards rejection—or, at the very least, to the firm's growing conviction that Wilde would not sell as an author of books. Nevertheless, it seems that there was still enough warmth in Wilde's relationship with George, and sufficient encouragement in his publications in Macmillan periodicals, for a further approach in 1890, this time

Wilde would hardly have been so anxious to get his manuscript back. As a token of friendship, Wilde later gave the manuscript to Leonard Smithers, a gesture which again makes little sense if there had been more than one copy of it (*Letters*, 221 n.).

47 See *Letters to Macmillan*, ed. and selected by Simon Nowell-Smith (London: Macmillan, 1976), 176.

48 The report is held in the Macmillan archive in the British Library; see Macmillan MSS Add. 5594; 16 Feb. 1888. The relevant parts of it are reprinted in Ian Small (ed.), *Oscar Wilde: Complete Short Fiction* (Harmondsworth: Penguin, 1994), p. vii.

with a proposed book-version of *Dorian Gray*. Wilde sent the manuscript (again to George) in mid-June 1890. This time, however, the reply came back from Alexander, who made it clear that George, who had been away, had not read the novel; more to the point, Alexander did not think it worthwhile to wait for George's opinion before returning the manuscript with what seems like indecent haste:

It is a weird tale & some of the conversation is most brilliant. I am afraid however that it would not do for us to publish. We have done very little in the way of such strong situations, and I confess there is something in the power which Dorian Gray gets over the young natural scientist, & one or two other things which is rather repelling. I dare say you do not mean it to be. I am sure it is not for us, & I do not like to keep it any longer.[49]

The abruptness of this response ('I do not like to keep it any longer'), together with Alexander's comment that he was 'returning it by hand' suggest a desire to be rid of the book as swiftly as possible. Given his long-standing friendship with George (who had recommended him for membership of the Savile Club in 1888), Wilde may have felt aggrieved at the speed with which the manuscript was returned and may have suspected a degree of personal animosity (although he might have attributed it to a father's, as much as a publisher's, prejudice). Nevertheless, just a few months later, in October 1890, Wilde approached the firm once more, this time with a collection of criticism entitled simply *Essays* (and almost certainly the pieces later published as *Intentions*). The volume was sent out for a reader's review, but was again rejected on the grounds that Wilde did not possess 'the sort of reputation—clever and accomplished writer as he is—that would help a volume of miscellanies from his pen'.[50]

In May 1892 Wilde made one final overture to Macmillan, proposing the publication of *Lady Windermere's Fan*. In that month's issue of *The Bookman* there is an intriguing announcement concerning the forthcoming publication of the play:

Mr Wilde's highly successful play, 'Lady Windermere's Fan,' is shortly to see the light in book form. The version will be much longer and more

---

[49] *OWR*, 79.

[50] See Warwick Gould, 'The Crucifixion of the Outcasts: Yeats and Wilde in the Nineties', in George Sandulescu (ed.), *Rediscovering Oscar Wilde* (Gerrards Cross, Bucks: Colin Smythe, 1994), 185.

elaborate than that now being produced at [the] St James's Theatre, as Mr
Wilde deliberately cut out some of the most brilliant dialogues in order
that the play might not occupy more than a certain time. Those who have
seen the book version of 'Lady Windermere's Fan' are of opinion that it
reads even better than it acts. It is not unlikely that the play will be the subject of an action in France, as a type-written copy which Mr Wilde had lent
to a friend in Paris was seen by some unscrupulous person, who made and
circulated a wretchedly imperfect and mutilated copy.[51]

As we noted earlier, it seems likely that Wilde was the source of this
information. However the claim that he had to cut 'brilliant dialogues' which he later restored is disingenuous. As we show in
Chapter 7, Wilde found completing the play difficult: lack of material, not its superabundance, was the problem. Moreover Wilde appears to have jumped the gun, for Macmillan declined the offer, and
it is therefore difficult to imagine how there could have been a 'book
version' for anyone to have seen in May 1892.[52] It is possible that
Wilde had another publisher in mind, although it is unclear who
this might have been. As we describe in Chapter 5, the earliest evidence of any publisher's firm commitment to the play is a draft contract between Wilde and the Bodley Head dated May 1893 (the firm
published *Lady Windermere's Fan* in September that year). An
unauthorized (and undated) text given the title *Lady Windermere's
Fan* was published in Britain by Samuel French; textually it is different from every other surviving acting or published version of the
play and seems to have been based upon an early acting draft.[53] It is
highly unlikely that the Samuel French text could be the 'longer and
more elaborate' version of *Lady Windermere's Fan* referred to in the
notice in *The Bookman*; however, it is just possible that French's
unauthorized edition could have been based on the 'wretchedly imperfect and mutilated copy' produced by 'some unscrupulous person'. If so, part of the notice might be true; but still unaccounted for
is Wilde's French friend (who might possibly have been Pierre
Louÿs, to whom Wilde was corresponding in the early summer of
1892). Of course, the most likely explanation of *The Bookman* notice
is the simplest: that Wilde was indulging in some 'puffing' and in
the process was being economical with the truth.

---

[51] *The Bookman*, II, no. 8 (May 1892), 37.   [52] *Letters*, 341 n.
[53] See Ian Small (ed.), *Oscar Wilde: Lady Windermere's Fan* (1980; London: A & C Black,
1999), p. xxxvi.

It is easy to interpret Wilde's constant appeal to Macmillan for approbation in terms of his courting of literary prestige; after all, Macmillan was probably the most important nineteenth-century British literary publisher, a house whose name, along with those of Smith, Elder and perhaps Routledge and Longman, could confer literary distinction as well as commercial security. Macmillan published, among other authors, Tennyson, Hardy, Pater, James, Arnold, Christina Rossetti, and Kipling; in addition, and as their correspondence reveals, Macmillan were scrupulous and often generous in their dealings with their authors. Moreover, following American copyright legislation in April 1891, Macmillan proved themselves adept in manipulating the large and expanding American market for British books. Throughout the 1890s, *The Bookman* carried numerous reports on the importance and professionalism of the American book trade: for example, a piece in the March 1892 issue entitled 'Some Impressions of a Bookman in America' noted that 'bookmaking and bookselling is a far more important branch of business in America than at home'; almost a year later, in the February 1893 issue, it was observed that 'in the United States . . . in one house alone they have machinery continually working, which is capable of printing, folding, stitching, covering, and cutting the edges of no less than 20,000 sets of a nine-volume edition of Dumas' works in one day'.[54] The New York branch of Macmillan had become an independent firm as early as 1890, trading under the name of Macmillan and Co.[55] To be a Macmillan author, then, was an understandable ambition for any writer, and particularly for Wilde, who (as we noted in Chapter 2) had been alert from his earliest days as a professional writer to the huge potential of the American market. Furthermore, Wilde may have thought that his friendship with George gave him a personal advantage with the firm.

On the other hand, Macmillan's interest in Wilde seems to have diminished as his celebrity (or notoriety) increased, and their correspondence over *Dorian Gray* suggests that it was Wilde the man, as much as his work, who was 'not for us'. Nevertheless there is a lot to be said for Macmillan's commercial judgements of Wilde's prospects. Nearly all the books they turned down—*The Happy*

54 *The Bookman*, II, no. 7 (April 1892), 19; and *The Bookman*, III, no. 17 (Feb. 1893), 144.
55 The London partners were directors of the new firm; see Seiler, *The Book Beautiful*, 34.

Prince, Dorian Gray, and *Intentions*—achieved only moderate sales.[56] Moreover, in the case of *Lady Windermere's Fan,* the market for reading editions of plays in 1892 was still young, highly specialized, and extremely risky. Even successful dramatists, such as Henry Arthur Jones, did not make much money for Macmillan; late in his life Jones was forced to admit to Frederick Macmillan that he had always been 'a "worst seller" '.[57] In fact, with the exception of Leonard Smithers's editions of *The Ballad of Reading Gaol,* no nineteenth-century publisher ever succeeded in turning Wilde into anything approaching a best-selling author. The literary works which topped the best-seller lists in the autumn of 1891 (when *The Bookman,* which recorded their sales, first appeared) were Rudyard Kipling's *Life's Handicap,* Walter Scott's Waverley novels, Richard Le Gallienne's *Book Bills of Narcissus,* and W. E. Henley's *Lyra Heroica*; in addition, Dickens, Thackeray, Eliot, Carlyle, and J. M. Barrie were listed as 'stock authors'—that is, writers for whom there was always a steady demand.[58] A slightly later issue of *The Bookman* (March 1892) described the British book-buying public falling into six classes: 'clergymen', 'doctors', 'lawyers', 'men of leisure', 'women of culture', and 'a very large class of readers whose purchasing powers never rise beyond a novel with which to while away an idle hour—a useful class because they clear away a great

[56] In a letter to Walter Pater, discussing the print-run of the second edition of *The Renaissance,* Alexander Macmillan defended his desire to print 1,250 copies (rather than Pater's proposal of 1,000) on the grounds that 'the last 250 make a considerable difference in the money result and they are sure to sell' (Seiler, *The Book Beautiful,* 77). It is worth remembering that only 1,000 copies of both *Dorian Gray* and of the first edition of *The Happy Prince* were printed. In fact, with the exception of *The Ballad of Reading Gaol,* all of Pater's books outsold those of Wilde, even though most of them were priced rather higher: *The Renaissance* went through four editions in Pater's lifetime. *Marius* went through two in its first year (the first comprised 1,000 two-volume sets at 21s.; the second doubled the print-run to 2,000). *Imaginary Portraits* was Pater's cheapest book at 6s., but it too ran to two editions of 1,000 and then 1,250 copies. *Appreciations* (as we described earlier) followed a similar pattern of two editions of 1,000 and 1,500 copies, priced at 8s. 6d. The last book published in Pater's lifetime, *Plato and Platonism* (1893), was printed in an edition of 2,000 priced at 8s. 6d. Finally it is worth remembering that none of these figures include sales in America which were similarly robust. (See Seiler, *The Book Beautiful,* 36–52.)

[57] Quoted in John Russell Stephens, *The Profession of the Playwright* (Cambridge: Cambridge University Press, 1992), 137.

[58] *The Bookman,* I, no. 1 (Oct. 1891), 31; no. 3 (Dec. 1891), 106; no. 4 (Jan. 1892), 140. Indeed the editorial of the Jan. 1892 number of *The Bookman* printed a list of the 'twelve English authors, arranged in the order of what I should consider their selling value: Rudyard Kipling, R. L. Stevenson, H. R. Haggard, A. C. Doyle, 'Q', W. Clark Russell, Miss Braddon, Ouida, William Black, Thomas Hardy, "Duchess" J. S. Winter' (131).

deal of stock on which there is a good margin of profit'.[59] Wilde had certainly failed to reach the last of these groups—those readers of what *The Bookman* termed 'light literature'; but neither to date had he been very successful with any of the smaller groups, made up, as they were, of the 'superior customer' who desired 'mental food' and 'the best class of books'. It is significant that the interest of the Bodley Head which, as we have said, was to publish most of the rest of Wilde's work, was in markets rather different from any of those identified by *The Bookman*: the Bodley Head looked to newly-emerging connoisseur markets of just a few hundred copies, reader-ships with which large houses like Macmillan were not concerned.

III

Leaving aside the details of Wilde's dealings with his various pub-lishers in 1891, there are some larger points about book and period-ical publication which are relevant to an understanding of his career in the early 1890s. The argument that book publication conferred prestige upon a writer (of a kind which was generally unavailable to the journalist or reviewer) is usually taken from the example of writ-ers such as Pater or Arnold who published 'serious' essays in distin-guished large-circulation periodicals (including *Macmillan's Magazine*, the *Cornhill*, and the *Fortnightly Review*), and who then collected those pieces in 'serious' books (such as *Culture and Anarchy* or *Studies in the History of the Renaissance*). With the work of Arnold and Pater there is an obvious sense of continuity between the intellectual ambitions of their periodical publications and those of their books. More importantly, there is also a consistency of mar-keting, in the sense that both book and periodical addressed broadly the same groups of readers.

Intentions (at 7s. 6d.) was the only example of Wilde's publica-tions which follows this pattern although, as we have noted, the low-ered price of the second edition suggests a less secure demand than that for Pater's work (the price of the second edition of *The Renaissance* was raised to 10s. 6d.).[60] Wilde's other books were

59 *The Bookman*, I, no. 6 (March 1892), 211.

60 The book publication of 'The Soul of Man Under Socialism' is often assumed to fol-low the pattern of *Intentions*. However, and as we argue in Ch. 6, it was issued under very dif-ferent circumstances: first, Wilde had almost no involvement in its publication; second, it

aimed at rather different audiences: at the mass or popular market, on the one hand, and the connoisseur or coterie reader, on the other. From a commercial point of view, *Intentions* was also the only work (up to 1891) that seemed to hit its intended market and was therefore (in publishing terms) a modest success; ironically, though, it was also the one kind of work that Wilde never repeated. The most obvious explanation (as we note in Chapter 7) is that in 1891 Wilde simply did not have to hand enough substantial critical work to make up a further volume of essays—it had been something of a struggle to find sufficient pieces for *Intentions*. He might also have been discouraged by its unsympathetic reception. More importantly, perhaps, Wilde must also have realized that whatever prestige accrued from the book publication of critical articles, for him there was not enough money in it, even if (and unlike *Intentions*) such a volume were to receive unqualified praise. As we noted in the previous chapter, both Pater and Arnold had income from other sources: and as letters from the Macmillan archive confirm, neither expected to earn a living from serious literature. Wilde, however, was not so happily placed. It is thus entirely unsurprising that, in the late autumn of 1891, he saw his future lying not in further volumes of essays, nor in further collections of popular fiction; success rather seemed to lie in writing for the commercial theatre and in coterie publishing.

One further complicating factor to Wilde's reputation in late 1891 and early 1892 concerns his personal life. Some of the mud first thrown by George Du Maurier and the satirists of a decade earlier had stuck: it was still possible for Wilde to be dismissed by the popular press as the parochial Irishman and dilettante. For example in mid-1892, after *Salomé* had been refused a licence by the Lord Chamberlain's Office, *Punch* published a cartoon of Wilde dressed as a French legionnaire above some lines adapted from W. S. Gilbert:

> In spite of great temptation,
> To French na–tu–ra–li–sa–tion,
> He'll remain an Irishman![61]

was priced very cheaply with a print-run of only 50 copies. Such a small number could hardly have been profitable; indeed there is some evidence that publication of the book was undertaken more for personal than commercial reasons.

[61] *Punch*, 103 (9 July 1892), 9. The reference is to an interview given by Wilde shortly before the Lord Chamberlain's decision, in which he was reported as saying: 'If the Censor

W. B. Yeats was one of the few writers at this time to make a virtue of Wilde's Irishness, but in terms which were hardly likely to endear him to the British reading public. In his review of *Lord Arthur Savile's Crime* for *United Ireland*, Yeats claimed that he saw in Wilde's 'life and works an extravagant Celtic crusade against Anglo-Saxon stupidity'.[62] For modern critics, this kind of oppositional identity is to be commended; it invites us to revalue contemporary reviewers' confusions about Wilde's intended readership as an admirable refusal on his part to be categorized. But as we have argued, for the prospective publisher of Wilde, Richard Le Gallienne's wry observation, that 'one hardly knows yet what to expect of him', takes on a different character. However admirable unpredictability or generic uncertainty appear to be in the eyes of the modern critic, for the contemporary publisher they presented acute marketing problems. If we look at matters from the perspective of Elkin Mathews, who bought up the unsold sheets of *Poems*, it is very difficult indeed to see how Wilde's reputation in late 1891—which was, if anything, a reputation simply for being controversial—could help sell the kind of poetry which the Bodley Head was about to specialize in.

The extent of the problem Mathews faced can be better appreciated by returning to the fate of *A House of Pomegranates*, the work that immediately preceded (by six months) the Bodley Head *Poems*. To the innocent eye, the marketing strategies of both publishers look similar. *A House of Pomegranates* was aimed (as the *Saturday Review* had noted) at a connoisseur market; and the book, at £1 1s. ($5 for the American edition), was priced accordingly. Osgood, McIlvaine had commissioned Charles Ricketts to design the book and Charles Shannon to provide four full-page illustrations, including an elaborate title-page. The volume had linen boards with a moss-green binding and gilt motifs. Ricketts had been used by Ward, Lock for the designs on the cover of the book version of *The Picture of Dorian Gray*; and Osgood, McIlvaine had also used designs by Ricketts for their issues of *Intentions* and *Lord Arthur Savile's Crime*, although on both occasions these designs were

---

refuses *Salomé*, I shall leave England and settle in France where I will take out letters of naturalization. I will not consent to call myself a citizen of a country that shows such narrowness in its artistic judgment. I am not English. I am Irish—which is quite another thing'. Mason 373; unfortunately Mason does not give his source.

[62] *Heritage*, 111.

modest in scale, in line with the prices of the volumes: 7s. 6d. and 2s. respectively. In other words, the extravagant appearance of *A House of Pomegranates* represented something of a new departure, for both Wilde and Osgood, McIlvaine. Wilde himself was clearly proud of Ricketts's work; following the publication of some adverse comments on the book's design in the *Speaker* on 28 November 1891, he responded in the 5 December issue:

The artistic beauty of the cover of my book resides in the delicate tracing, arabesques, and massing of many coral-red lines on a ground of white ivory, the colour-effect culminating in certain high gilt notes, and being made still more pleasurable by the overlapping band of moss-green cloth that holds the book together.[63]

The bindings and illustrations for *A House of Pomegranates* had in fact provoked two quite different sorts of complaint. Some critics had objected to them on stylistic grounds: that the draftsmanship was poor and that they were unsuitable as illustrations for fairy-tales.[64] Others objected to the quality of the printing, that the production values of the book, particularly the four plates, left much to be desired. As Mason observes, after the book had been printed, it was noticed that the plates were covered with a dusty deposit. To remove it involved rubbing away the surface of the ink, and this in turn resulted in a fading (to the point of invisibility) of Shannon's delicate designs.[65] The *Saturday Review* caustically observed that:

being printed in a very faint grisaille on very deeply cream-tinted plate paper, they [the illustrations] put on about as much invisibility as is possible to things visible, and as they are arranged, neither facing letterpress nor with the usual tissue guard, but with a blank sheet of paper of the same tint and substance opposite them, a hasty person might really open the leaves and wonder which side the illustration was.[66]

For a volume explicitly designed to appeal to the collector or connoisseur market, where the materiality of the book was as important as the text itself, this mishap over the production of the plates was unfortunate. They were printed in Paris by what Mason calls an 'improved' process which was apparently not overseen closely either by printer or publisher. The situation suggests a lack of professionalism on the part of Osgood, McIlvaine; more to the point, it contrasts markedly with the excellent production values of the

---

[63] Mason, 366–7; see also *Letters*, 301.   [64] *Heritage*, 113; Mason, 365.
[65] Ibid.   [66] *Heritage*, 114–15.

Bodley Head books (usually printed by the Chiswick Press or T. and A. Constable, both of which were known for the quality of their work). Mathews and Lane were to become market-leaders in the fashion for beautiful books; it was their practice to include in end-matter the praise of reviewers—not particularly for the author nor the work, but rather for the quality of the printing and for the publisher's style. The Bodley Head edition of *Lady Windermere's Fan*, for example, carried over a dozen pages of such advertisements:

To MESSRS. ELKIN MATHEWS AND JOHN LANE almost more than to any other, we take it, are the thanks of the grateful singer especially due; for it is they who have managed, by means of limited editions and charming workmanship, to impress book-buyers with the belief that a volume may have an aesthetic and commercial value. They have made it possible to speculate in the latest discovered poet, as in a new company—with the difference that an operation in the former can be done with three half-crowns. *St James's Gazette*.[67]

Significantly, Wilde (despite his public protestations to the contrary) was only too well aware of the deficiencies in the printing of *A House of Pomegranates*. In 1891, he wrote to Dodd, Mead & Co. (the American outlet of Osgood, McIlvaine) concerning their arrangements to publish the work in the United States. He suggested that their edition 'will have to be unillustrated' because 'the drawings and designs belong to Messrs Osgood & McIlvaine who do not wish to part with them'. Wilde failed to mention that the most likely reason that his British publisher wished to retain the plates was because of their poor quality. In an ironic (or perhaps hopeful) note Wilde concludes his letter by commenting that he anticipates that 'the book will be well printed and bound'.[68] An even more revealing letter (of June 1893) concerns Wilde's approach to Bertram Grosvenor Goodhue, a partner in Copeland and Day, another American publisher, asking whether the 'artistic and distinguished firm' whose work he had 'often admired' would bring out an edition of *A House of Pomegranates* (possibly using the unsold sheets from the Osgood, McIlvaine edition). Wilde again concedes that it 'would be better to omit the illustrations, lovely as they are'.[69] On this occasion Copeland and Day declined the offer, although a year later they did bring out American editions of *Salome* and *The Sphinx*.

[67] Oscar Wilde, *Lady Windermere's Fan* (London: Bodley Head, 1893), 2 of end-matter.
[68] *More Letters*, 106.   [69] Ibid. 121–2.

A second trend which *A House of Pomegranates* seemed designed to exploit was the increasing public appetite for fairy-stories which had taken place from about 1870 onwards, but which, by 1890, was beginning to decline. (It is worth reiterating the fact that Nutt did not take up Wilde's suggestion in the late autumn of 1891 for a new edition of *The Happy Prince*.) In 1891 the market for fairy-stories was certainly not a homogeneous one. There were a number of archival or archaeological anthologies of fairy-stories (analogous in status to the contemporary collecting of folklore and mythology). Exemplified by the collections of Andrew Lang and Joseph Jacobs in the late 1880s and 1890s, they were aimed at adults, and were to be distinguished from the market for children's fairy-stories, supplied by writers such as Jean Inglow, Christina Rossetti, or George MacDonald. Confusingly, in recent years modern critics have tended to revalue children's fairy-stories (particularly those by women writers) to suggest that they possess subversive subtexts aimed at an adult reader.[70]

Christina Rossetti's *Speaking Likenesses* (1874) is taken to be typical of this strategy. Some commentators have pointed to a tension between the naive language and simple illustrations, which indicate a very young intended audience, and the dour moralizing with its emphasis on the pragmatic and quotidian, which seems to satirize exactly the kind of magical logic which for the child is the fairy-story's most appealing feature. Modern critics typically go on to celebrate this kind of ambiguity on the grounds that it evidences a 'subversive' attitude towards what is held to be a highly ideological or patriarchal literary form. However winning this kind of interpretation may be, it is unfortunately at odds with some of the publishing details of Rossetti's book.

Significantly, she placed it with Macmillan, who had already published her poetry (both in *Macmillan's Magazine* and in a collection, *The Prince's Progress and Other Poems* (1866)). Moreover, Rossetti made it clear to Macmillan that her stories were intended 'for a child's Xmas volume'; she reported to her brother, Dante Gabriel, that she had written something 'with an eye to the market'.[71] Finally, Rossetti (or Macmillan) chose Arthur Hughes as an illustrator.

---

[70] See e.g. Nina Auerbach and U. C. Knoepflmacher (eds.), *Forbidden Journeys: Fairy Tales and Fantasies by Victorian Women Writers* (London: University of Chicago Press, 1992).

[71] Quoted in Kathleen Jones, *Learning not to be First: The Life of Christina Rossetti* (Windrush Press: Gloucestershire, 1991), 163–4.

Hughes is best remembered today for his association with the Pre-Raphaelites, but in the late nineteenth century he enjoyed a parallel reputation as an illustrator of children's literature. He was known in particular for his charming illustrations for George MacDonald's two volumes of fairy-stories, *Dealing with Fairies* (1867) and *At the Back of the North Wind* (1871); he had also illustrated Christina Rossetti's book of children's verse, *Sing-Song* (1872). *Speaking Likenesses* was poorly received by critics, and their disappointment did centre on the confusion of the moral of the stories: the *Academy*, for example, claimed that:

This will probably be one of the most popular children's books this winter. We wish we could understand it . . . but the present-day fairy tales fatigue us, because we feel we ought always to be watching for some hidden joke or deep meaning.[72]

Comprehensibility might be thought to be a paramount consideration for fairy-stories, and despite the *Academy*'s prediction, the book also sold poorly. As Percy Muir describes, the first edition was remaindered in a cheaper binding, and without the Arthur Hughes design in gilt on the front cover.[73] In other words, regardless of how we are tempted to interpret and value *Speaking Likenesses* today, it remains the case that in the late nineteenth century it was advertised, identified, and so (presumably) read as a children's book; and, on those grounds, it failed, both commercially and critically. Another way of putting this is to say that there does not seem to have been any obvious market at the time for that kind of subversive 'adult' fairy-tale which modern critics praise.

We should not be at all surprised by this situation, for (as we have hinted already) any form of generic ambiguity presented marketing difficulties for nineteenth-century publishers (and of course continues to do so for their twentieth-century successors). At a basic level, it was unlikely that a potential purchaser would be prepared to spend the same amount of money on a book designed for reading to (or for the use of) a child, as on a book designed for an adult. By the same token, it seems certain that the adult purchaser of fairy-tales—the specialist 'collector'—would be prepared (and might even expect) to pay a special price for the right sort of book. Such reasoning explains why Nutt produced only sixty-five copies of the

72 The Editor, 'Current Literature', *Academy*, 6 (5 Dec. 1874), 605–6.
73 Muir, *English Children's Books*, 153 n.

large-paper edition of *The Happy Prince*. It seems likely that Wilde's and Osgood, McIlvaine's strategy was designed to exploit what they saw as an overlap between the new connoisseur market for beautiful books and that represented by the adult collector of fairy-tales. More precisely, they might have thought that the market for adult fairy-tales could be expanded by appealing explicitly to the tastes exploited by the trade in beautiful books. Such a situation would explain why the marketing of *A House of Pomegranates* was so different from that of *Intentions* and *Lord Arthur Savile's Crime*. It would also explain the use of Shannon and Ricketts to provide the design and illustrations; unlike Walter Crane and Arthur Hughes, neither had reputations as illustrators of children's books. That said, the poor sales of *A House of Pomegranates* (even compared with Wilde's other volumes) suggests that the strategy was either poorly implemented or misplaced.

We have alluded already to shortcomings in the material quality of the book; but there was also a problem with the work's identity. The generic markers in the text did not coincide closely enough with what was expected from a book of such high price. Put simply: the stories in *A House of Pomegranates* were not different *enough* to signal unequivocally that they were intended for adults, and this confirms the suspicion that Wilde's and his publisher's identification of them as adult material was a marketing rather than creative decision. Influenced no doubt by the expectations set up by *The Happy Prince*, some reviewers of *A House of Pomegranates* continued to see Wilde as a writer of children's fairy-tales. Hence the perplexed tone of the reviewer in the *Pall Mall Gazette*, who was struck by inconsistencies in style—by the way 'pretty poetic and imaginative flights' would 'wander off too often into something between a "Sinburnian" ecstasy and the catalogue of a high art furniture dealer'—and by the strangeness of the illustrations which seemed 'unsuitable' for children.[74] In a letter written at the end of November 1891, Wilde attempted to defend his book from precisely this kind of misidentification. In a direct response to the *Pall Mall Gazette*, he argued that *A House of Pomegranates* was a book intended for adults, and not, as the paper's reviewer had intimated, one for children:

---

[74] *Heritage*, 113–14.

[The reviewer] starts by asking an extremely silly question, and that is, whether or not I have written the book for the purpose of giving pleasure to the British child. Having expressed grave doubts on this subject, a subject on which I cannot conceive any fairly-educated person having any doubts at all, he proceeds, apparently quite seriously, to make the extremely limited vocabulary at the disposal of the British child the standard by which the prose of an artist is to be judged! Now, in building this *House of Pomegranates*, I had about as much intention of pleasing the British child as I had of pleasing the British public.[75]

Wilde's tactic, when on the defensive, was invariably to impugn or ridicule the judgement of his accuser. But on this occasion, the allegation of misjudgement might more appropriately have been levelled at Osgood, McIlvaine and Wilde himself. Given the inherent ambiguity in the notion of an 'adult' fairy-tale, and the consequent difficulties in identifying a distinct market for such a genre, it does seem perverse to have assumed that a public who knew Wilde already as a writer of delicate children's tales would automatically accept him as a writer subverting this tradition. It is even harder to believe that this minority readership could have supported an initial print-run of 1,000 copies. As the reviewer in the *Athenaeum* noted, if 'Oscar Wilde [had] been good enough to explain' that *A House of Pomegranates* was 'intended neither for the "British Child" nor for the "British Public" ', then its only possible readership had to be 'the cultured few who can appreciate its subtle charms'.[76] Such an 'exiguous band', however, must have expected a book that was rare, expensive, and very beautiful. *A House of Pomegranates* succeeded fully on only one of these counts: at £1 1s., it certainly was expensive, but with a print-run of 1,000 copies it was not particularly rare, and neither, with its faded plates, did it wholly please the eye. It is worth noting that the print-run of comparably priced Bodley Head books were significantly smaller and advertised as exclusive when they were put on sale. It is also worth recalling that Ward, Lock printed only 250 copies of the large-paper edition of *Dorian Gray*, which they too priced at £1 1s., and Nutt, as we have said, printed a mere 65 copies of the £1 1s. large-paper edition of *The Happy Prince*. In the autumn of 1891 Osgood, McIlvaine were probably hoping to capitalize on Wilde's 'other' identity as the controversial author of the sensationalist *Dorian Gray*. But even here there was a difficulty, for the populist and explicitly melodramatic and satiric

[75] *Letters*, 301–2.   [76] *Heritage*, 117.

elements of that novel appealed to a readership that was still markedly different from the 'cultured few' willing to pay a guinea for a book of just over 150 pages.

IV

To come back to the point at which we began this chapter: the Bodley Head edition of Wilde's *Poems*. A glance at the binding and the title-page reveals Elkin Mathews's more acute sense of matching the market, the author, the product, and the print-run. In short, it shows that he (and later, John Lane) possessed a much better understanding of the diversification that was taking place in literary markets than Osgood, McIlvaine had. The Bodley Head Wilde was dramatically distinctive, intended to appeal to a completely different kind of reader and market than his earlier publications. Although the production values of *Poems* (1892) were in line with those intended by Osgood, McIlvaine for *A House of Pomegranates*, even down to using once again designs by Charles Ricketts (by this time Wilde and Ricketts had become closely associated in the public eye), the marketing of the book was quite different. Importantly the Bodley Head's treatment of Wilde was in no sense special for them, in that it did not trade solely on exploiting his personality in the way of Lippincott and Ward, Lock; rather Wilde was merely a notable example in a highly successful general remarketing strategy. *Poems* (1892), that is, was sold in part as a type of publication—as one of a series, rather than the unique book advertised by Osgood, McIlvaine. Mathews and Lane directed Wilde's work at an audience who had already developed a taste for expensive and beautifully produced books of poetry.

In the early 1890s the Bodley Head habitually bought up remaindered copies of books published during the previous decade, confident that they could repackage and resell them to a new market. As James G. Nelson, the historian of the firm, explains, a parallel to Wilde's case can be seen in the fate of a much less well-remembered volume of poetry by three Balliol College men (H. C. Beeching, J. W. MacKail, and J. B. B. Nichol). The collection, called *Love in Idleness*, was published originally by Kegan, Paul, and Trench in 1883. The Bodley Head bought the unsold sheets, re-bound them in imitation vellum, and pink paper-covered boards with a vignette on the title page designed by William Scott. The repackaged volume, which sold well, seems to have been designed to appeal explicitly to the connoisseur and book-collector as much as to the reader of poetry. As Nelson points out, this marketing ploy was repeated with other remaindered authors from the Kegan, Paul, and Trench list. Reissued works included William Watson's *The Prince's Quest* (originally published in 1880, and reissued in 1892, the second Bodley Head edition being brought out in 1893), Frances Wynne's *Whisper!* (originally published in 1890, and reissued in 1893), and Colonel Ian Hamilton's *The Ballad of Hádji* (originally published in 1887, and reissued in 1892).[77] It seems that Lane and Mathews were initially interested in Wilde insofar as he could be re-presented as part of the exclusive list of distinctive poetry which they were beginning to establish. Wilde's reputation as a sensationalist or as a children's author, or even as a critic, was largely irrelevant to this strategy—a factor which the visual attractiveness and opulence of the Bodley Head edition of *Poems* seems carefully designed to emphasize. As we shall argue in Chapter 5, it was only following the success of *Poems* that Lane and Mathews decided that it was worthwhile keeping Wilde as a Bodley Head author: they wanted Wilde only after they were certain that their tactic of repackaging and redefining him had been proved to work. On the other hand, and as we elaborate in the next chapter, it is also true that their confidence in Wilde was confirmed by his parallel success as a dramatic author.

In order to appreciate the distinctiveness of the Wilde that Mathews and later Lane created, it is worth returning to the details of the original publication of *Poems* in 1881 by David Bogue (not a house of particular note). Wilde's deal with Bogue stipulated that Wilde should meet all the production costs of the volume. Although some critics have seen in this detail evidence of a kind of 'vanity' publishing on Wilde's behalf, we should not read too much into this part of his financial arrangements. It was quite usual for even established late nineteenth-century authors to undertake to meet the printing costs of a book, or at least to assume some of the risk. (For example, on 24 May 1867, Matthew Arnold wrote to Macmillan, then in the process of publishing what would become *New Poems*, to remind them that 'with this book I revert to my original practice, which I think on the whole preferable, and publish at my own

---

[77] James G. Nelson, *The Early Nineties: A View from the Bodley Head* (Cambridge, Mass: Harvard University Press, 1971), 79.

risk'.)[78] Advances on royalties and the funding of the production
and distribution costs of books by the publisher was a practice more
typical of publishing in the 1890s than the 1880s; and we have suggested that the Bodley Head actually pioneered such tactics in order
to ensure author loyalty.

The details of the contract which Wilde signed with Bogue reveal
that he was not particularly disadvantaged. On the contrary, there is
evidence of some compromise between Wilde and Bogue, because
what appears to be a standard printed contract was altered in ways
intended to be generous to Wilde: what he was required to pay was
certainly less than Bogue routinely asked. Manuscript emendations
(shown below as italic type) and deletions (shown by strikethrough)
to the printed contract which Wilde signed indicate how much
the standard charges were changed. The relevant clauses are as
follows:

Memorandum of Agreement, made this *seventeenth* day of *May* 18 *81*
BETWEEN *Oscar Wilde, Esq*
of Keats House, Tite St, Chelsea, London on the One Part,
and DAVID BOGUE, of 3, St Martin's Place, Publisher, on the Other Part.
It is agreed:-
I.—That the said DAVID BOGUE shall be the sole Publisher of a Work entitled
   Poems by Oscar Wilde
of which the said *Oscar Wilde* is Proprietor.

II.—That all charges in relation to the Work be paid by the said Proprietor.

III.—That ~~half~~ *one third of* the estimated cost be paid when the MS is sent
to the Printer, and ~~the balance~~ *one third* when the work is ready for issue *and
the balance two months after the date of publication.*

IV.—That the said David Bogue shall account for all the copies he may dis-
pose of at ~~half the published price~~ *the trade sale price and thirteen as twelve
deducting a commission of ten per cent.*

V.—That the said David Bogue shall take upon himself the risk of bad
debts.[79]

---

[78] Cecil Y. Lang (ed.), *The Letters of Matthew Arnold*, iii (London: University Press of
Virginia, 1998), 142. Interestingly, Arnold entered into a quite different financial arrangement with George Smith, who published his prose. He wrote to Smith on 1 March 1867 asking for a loan of £200 on the following terms: 'I should like to borrow the money on my
promissory note, at 5 per cent., to be repaid £100 this time next year, and the other £100 the
same time the year after. . . . I can offer you, by undertaking to write in no periodical but the
"Cornhill" so long as the money is unpaid, a sort of security' (118).
[79] Clark Library. Wilde MSS. W6721Z M533 1881 May 17. Stuart Mason printed the

The remaining two clauses specify dates when accounts were to be rendered, and nominate procedures for the arbitration of disputes between author and publisher. We should notice that the alterations to the contract are in Wilde's favour, and it is tempting to interpret them as revealing a willingness on Bogue's part to take account of Wilde's lack of resources in 1881. Wilde was not being asked to put as much money 'up front' as was usually the case with Bogue's authors. It could be argued that Bogue's generosity indicates his sense of Wilde's promise as a poet.

It is worth remembering that by 1881 Wilde was widely published as a poet. Between 1877 and the appearance of *Poems* in 1881, he had published some forty poems in Irish, American, and English periodicals. His first published poem was as early as 1875 when he had just turned 21. In the following year, eight poems appeared in print, seven in Irish publications (in the *Dublin University Magazine* and in *Kottabos*) and one in the English *Month and Catholic Review*. His most successful year prior to the publication of *Poems* (1881) seems to have been 1877 when he published nine poems in Ireland and at least two (and perhaps three) in the United States.[80] The next year (1878) saw two more poems published in Ireland as well as his Newdigate Prize poem at Oxford, *Ravenna*. In 1879 Wilde published two further poems in Ireland and five in England. In 1880 and 1881, this success continued with eight more poems appearing in England. By any standards, this was an impressive body of work for a man only in his twenties. It is understandable that Wilde should have taken from this experience the sense that he was building a literary reputation, one that a volume of collected poems would help to consolidate. The pattern of his early publications suggests a growing confidence in which he moves from a local, university, Dublin, and Oxford audience towards the more cosmopolitan markets of London and Boston (in publications such as *Biograph and Review* and the Boston *Pilot*). When Wilde was considering publishing a volume of poems in England in the early 1880s the occasion must have seemed propitious to him (and possibly to

first clauses of the contract and noted the manuscript changes in it. He failed to note, however, the original terms of the standard contract.

[80] The uncertainty over Wilde's American publications derives from the fact that Mason suggests in a manuscript note to his own copy of *Bibliography of Oscar Wilde* (held in the Clark Library) that 'Italia' was published in the Boston *Pilot* in 1877, a detail which (because of the extreme rarity of that publication) it has not been possible to confirm.

Bogue). As a young poet, already widely published, and flushed
with success from Oxford, he had some reason to believe himself to
be the latest upholder of the tradition of earlier Newdigate winners
such as John Ruskin, Matthew Arnold, and John Addington
Symonds.

However, in the late nineteenth century to publish a collection of
poems was a significantly different undertaking from placing single
works in a variety of periodicals. First, the readership and market
for a volume of poetry were very different from the readership for a
periodical. The market for such books was much smaller, more critical, and not bound by loyalty to a title which periodicals aimed to
exploit. Second the economics of publishing a book of poetry was
wholly different from that of periodical publishing. With the exception of the Bodley Head in the 1890s, publishers tended to find
poetry, particularly the work of new poets, unprofitable. Katharine
Tynan, a contemporary of Wilde (and also a Bodley Head author)
commented that the late nineteenth century was 'an age as stony to
poetry as the ages of Chatterton and Richard Savage'.[81] Finally, individual poems, when collected, possessed a very different identity
and status from that conferred by their occasional publication. It is
perhaps relevant that the periodicals in which Wilde had published
his poems were in the middle-price range: most were between 6d.
and 1s. They were more expensive than truly mass circulation titles
(such as *Tit-Bits*), but still considerably cheaper than 'quality' or
elite journals. It is also worth noting that the periodicals in which
Wilde's poetry had appeared were of a general, rather than an exclusively literary, appeal. By contrast, *Poems* (1881) with a price of
10s. 6d. and an initial print-run of just 750 copies seems to have
been aimed at a more discriminating and wealthy market. In this
sense Wilde's periodical success with his poetry could not guarantee
equal success with a book publication.

To return to Bogue's contract with Wilde: the emendations to
Clause IV suggest that instead of taking 5s. 3d. per copy as his profit
(that is, half the published price of 10s. 6d.) Bogue's commission
was only 10 per cent of the trade price (which, in the late nineteenth

[81] Tynan's comments appeared in the *Irish Daily Independent*; they are quoted in Nelson,
The Early Nineties, 84. Wilde's reaction to the problematic market for poetry in the late 19th
cent. has been discussed by Josephine M. Guy, ' "Trafficking With Merchants for His
Soul": Dante Gabriel Rossetti Among the Aesthetes', *Proceedings of the British Academy*
(forthcoming).

century was typically just over 80 per cent of the published price), plus an additional twelfth of the published price per copy ('thirteen as twelve'). On these figures Bogue's take is about 1s. 9d. per book. On the total first print-run of 750 copies, he must have anticipated a profit of around £65; on the second printing (of 500 copies), a further £45. The first print-run was divided into three so-called 'editions' which, except for the title page, were identical. The book was then reset, with a number of revisions to the text and to the book's sections, reprinted and advertised as the fourth and then the fifth editions; only around half of these copies sold.

Bogue's attempt to stimulate sales by creating what a modern bibliographer would see as 'fake' new editions was not unusual. As Allan C. Dooley has argued, the meanings of terms such as 'edition' and 'impression', when used by nineteenth-century publishers, often do not correspond to their modern usage. For example, publishers would routinely advertise as new editions what in practice were simple impressions (that is reprintings made from the same plates) in order to boost sales; they would also divide first print-runs into separate editions if a book did not sell. Dooley quotes a letter from George Henry Lewes to the Edinburgh publisher Blackwood about George Eliot's *The Spanish Gypsy* (1868):

As from all appearance the poem is likely to go on selling don't you think it would be polite and fair to call every 1,000 a new edition? Absurd as the motive is people *are* influenced in their desires to possess a work by the knowledge that a great many other people possess it, and I often hear the number of editions referred to as proof of excellence.[82]

On some occasions, nineteenth-century publishers reversed this process; they attempted to make a new edition—that is, what modern bibliographers would identify as a revised and reset text—look like an impression, in order to disguise the fact that the author had corrected it. The example which Dooley gives is George Chapman's 1865 edition of Robert Browning's *Poetical Works*; although it was completely reset and incorporated many textual changes, Chapman contrived, through using the same typefaces, line spacing, pagination, and binding to make it appear identical to the 1863 *Poetical Works*. Dooley speculates that Chapman was either trying not to offend readers who had recently bought the 1863 edition; or (more

---

[82] Quoted in Allan C. Dooley, *Author and Printer in Victorian England* (London: University Press of Virginia, 1992), 88.

likely) he was trying to avoid paying Browning, for a new edition commanded a larger fee than a reprint. David Bogue's practice, then, was perfectly in keeping with late nineteenth-century publishing techniques, although it was a strong indication that the volume was failing.

Mathews and Lane bought the 230 copies left unsold from Bogue's fourth and fifth editions. The Bodley Head edition was only 220 copies, as the sheets of ten copies were spoiled during binding.[83] Mathews and Lane removed the two pages of Bogue's advertisements and bound the sheets in new covers from a design by Ricketts, together with a new title page, also designed by Ricketts. Some small details are indicative of the lengths to which the publishers went to match the volume to the needs of their intended consumers. A letter from Mathews to Wilde reveals the trouble that was taken to ensure that the design of the book was perfect: Mathews tried out at least two different cloths for the binding before he and Wilde settled on their final choice. In addition, each copy was numbered and signed by Wilde. In a manner reminiscent of Nutt's signing and numbering copies of the large-paper edition of *The Happy Prince*, each copy of *Poems* (1892) was given a material rarity, in addition to any literary distinction which inhered in the text. This emphasis on the materiality of the book is to be seen in a further production detail: the top of each volume was trimmed and gilded. The Bogue edition had also been gilded, and Mathews wished to retain this distinctive mark of lavish production. However, a letter dated 13 February 1892 from Leighton Hodge, the binder employed by the Bodley Head, reveals that this 'luxury' was more appearance than reality:

Dear Sir,

Oscar Wylde [sic] *Poems*

The extra price for gilding the tops of the above will be 4/- per 100 making our estimate for binding 66/- per 100.[84]

The total extra cost for gilding the entire edition was therefore slightly under 10s., or just over a third of one per cent of the net price of the entire run.

---

[83] See Mason, 322.
[84] ALS from Leighton Hodge to Elkin Mathews, dated 13 Feb. 1892. Clark Library. M429L W6721 [1892?].

As we have said, this limited luxury edition (priced at 15s., half as much again as the Bogue editions) sold out within days. The Bodley Head went on to publish six of Wilde's books in all: *Poems*, *Salomé*, in both English and French editions, *The Sphinx*, *Lady Windermere's Fan*, and *A Woman of No Importance*. In addition there were plans to publish an expanded version of his essay 'The Portrait of Mr W. H.', under the new title of *The incomparable history of Mr W. H.*, as well as *The Duchess of Padua*. Wilde was to become as important to the Bodley Head as the Bodley Head was to be to Wilde, and his subsequent transactions with the firm bear testimony to their perfecting a strategy to match market, author, and book. At the same time, that relationship was only made possible because Wilde had recently been freed from deriving his main income from publishing books by success in the commercial theatre, and that success in turn depended upon his active management at the hands of two other professionals, George Alexander and Herbert Beerbohm Tree.

4

The Dramatist

The shape of Wilde's career in the winter of 1891–2 has some parallels with his career a decade earlier: on both occasions he was anticipating the publication of a volume of poetry and had hopes that a play was to go into production in the West End. As we have described, on 24 January 1882 David Bogue printed a further 500 copies of Wilde's *Poems* (1881). It is unclear whether he planned at the outset to divide them into two further editions (the fourth and fifth) or whether, as before, the decision was made after slow sales. Importantly, though, what became the fourth and fifth editions were fairly heavily revised. There were changes at the level of individual lexical items, and two stanzas from one of the most controversial poems, 'Charmides', were deleted with the result that over half the volume had to be repaginated. Wilde may have also wished to give the volume more coherence, for he increased the number of its sections from eight to twelve by the addition (in the place of what were blank pages in the 1881 editions) of new half-titles. Wilde had already revised some poems from their periodical form to their first book publication; the small-scale lexical (as opposed to the structural or organizational) revisions for the 1882 editions could have been made at any time from June 1881 onwards (when *Poems* first appeared). However, it is inconceivable that Wilde should have organized these revisions in any systematic way and reshaped the volume by a date earlier than the end of September 1881, for there would have been no point in doing so until he was certain that Bogue was about to proceed with a second printing.[1] Furthermore, the revisions must have been completed by the time Wilde set off for his American lecture tour on 24 December.

---

[1] The revisions are discussed in Mason, 289–319. For a full account, see Fong and Beckson (eds.), *Oscar Wilde: Poems and Poems in Prose* (Oxford: Oxford University Press, 2000).

The revisions may have been prompted by the slow sales of the first three editions, but it is tempting to believe that Wilde had been galvanized into reshaping (and to a degree, reconceptualizing) the volume by the Oxford Union's rejection of the book at their meeting on 3 November 1881. Wilde was deeply offended by what he perceived to be the discourtesy and narrow-mindedness which that decision represented; in a letter to the Union secretary he regretted that 'there should still be at Oxford such a large number of young men who are ready to accept their own ignorance as an index, and their own conceit as a criterion of any imaginative and beautiful work'.[2] While this show of wounded pride is understandable, the fact remains that Wilde did take the opportunity to revise the volume: if he had been so certain of the poems' value as 'imaginative and beautiful work', he would hardly have bothered. In December 1881, then, Wilde may have been looking forward to a better reception for this new edition. At around the same time, he was also hoping that his first play, *Vera*, would go into production. The previous year, when he submitted *Vera* to E. F. S. Pigott, the Lord Chamberlain's Examiner of Plays, Wilde had confessed that he was 'working at dramatic art because it's *the democratic* art, and I want fame'.[3] So compelling was that desire for fame that Wilde had arranged and paid for a special performance of *Vera* scheduled for the morning of Saturday 17 December 1881 at the Adelphi Theatre, with Mrs Bernard Beere (who later was to take the role of Mrs Arbuthnot in the first production of *A Woman of No Importance*) in the title role.[4] This performance is best seen in terms of Wilde's attempt to advertise his work, for it was one aimed at the theatrical world and not the public. As John Russell Stephens has argued, by the 1880s the single matinée performance had become an established route by which a new dramatic author could be given a trial before being accepted for an evening run. Wilde clearly hoped that *Vera* would be taken up for a commercial production; indeed the actress and writer Elizabeth Robins reported that Wilde offered her

[2] *More Letters*, 36–7.   [3] Ibid. 32.

[4] Ellmann suggests that Wilde's friend Dion Boucicault was to direct (146). Boucicault's involvement, however, is unlikely for two reasons. In the first place, and as we mentioned in Ch. 2, Boucicault had sharply criticized the play; in the second place, and as George Rowell has argued, Boucicault had engagements in Dublin and New York in November and December 1881. See George Rowell, 'The Truth About *Vera*', *Nineteenth Century Theatre*, 21: 2 (Winter, 1993), 94–100; see also *Encyclopedia*, 35–6.

exactly this advice when she was trying to establish herself in Britain.[5]

If we move forward ten years to the late autumn of 1891, we find Wilde in a similar situation, for he had just signed the contract with Mathews to produce a new edition of *Poems*, and he was also anticipating a production in the new year of *Lady Windermere's Fan*.[6] Once more, Wilde was looking forward, and with more justification than in 1881, to the possibility of combining commercial success from the theatre with the prestige which would accrue from a limited edition book. The difference between these two moments is that Wilde's plans in 1881 did not bear fruit in the ways in which he had hoped. A notice (which, as we shall show, was somewhat disingenuous) appeared in the *World* on 30 November 1881 announcing the cancellation of the matinée performance of *Vera*: 'Considering the present state of political feeling in England, Mr Oscar Wilde has decided on postponing, for a time, the production of his drama *Vera*.'[7] As we have indicated, *Poems* (1882) was not a success either, and the new editions did not generate any positive reviews. Wilde might have been further disheartened by the reception of the American editions of *Poems* (published by Roberts Brothers in Boston); poor reviews appeared in early 1882 when he was a few weeks into his American tour. American critics were just as negative as their British counterparts had been. Moreover, although the first American printing is reported to have sold quickly, it was priced at only $1.25 and is unlikely to have earned Wilde much money.[8]

The parallels between Wilde's aspirations in the winters of 1881–2 and 1891–2 remind us how little his fundamental ambitions for his career had changed over that decade; at the same time, they should also alert us to the differences which the arrival of large sums of money from 1892 onwards were to make to his ability to realize those ambitions. The relative failure of *Vera* to generate the income

5 John Russell Stephens, *The Profession of the Playwright* (Cambridge: Cambridge University Press, 1992), 4; see also *Letters*, 222–3.

6 Ellmann claims that Wilde's agreement with Alexander (signed in the autumn of 1891) specified a February production of *Lady Windermere's Fan*. However, as we explain later, there is no evidence that such a definite promise had been made, although rumours of a performance were circulating in January.

7 See Mason, 254, and Frances Miriam Reed (ed.), *Oscar Wilde's Vera; or, the Nihilist* (Lampeter, Dyfed: Edwin Mellen Press, 1989), p. xxvii.

8 It is worth noting that Mason quotes a report that the American edition sold out 'within a few days of its appearance' (324). He does not, however, give a source.

for which Wilde had hoped forced him to focus most of his energies on commercial publications; by contrast, the immediate financial return from *Lady Windermere's Fan* enabled him to pursue the more rarefied market of limited editions and thus to acquire for his work the distinction which their coterie readerships (with their discriminating tastes) conferred. Before exploring this relationship between financial and artistic success, and the conditions which determined its form, it will be useful to compare Wilde's successful and unsuccessful attempts to establish himself in the popular theatre, in order to document more precisely the impact on his career of the financial disappointments of his first two plays.

We noted in Chapter 2 that Wilde attributed the failure of *Vera* in part to his own inexperience as a dramatist. Ten years later, Wilde still confessed to finding writing for the theatre difficult. *Lady Windermere's Fan* was commissioned by George Alexander in July 1890 when Alexander was negotiating (or about to negotiate) his initial lease for the St James's Theatre.[9] According to Richard Ellmann, Wilde's first thought was to offer Alexander *The Duchess of Padua*, which had yet to be produced in Britain; but Alexander asked Wilde to write on a more modern subject, and offered him an advance of £50 against the delivery of a new play by 1 January 1891.[10] The deadline passed, but no play was forthcoming; in some embarrassment Wilde wrote to Alexander on 2 February 1891, explaining that:

[9] Ellmann records that Alexander first approached Wilde for a play late in 1890 (Ellmann, 314). However, both Joel H. Kaplan ('A Puppet's Power: George Alexander, Clement Scott, and the Replotting of *Lady Windermere's Fan*', *Theatre Notebook*, 46: 2 (1992), 59–73) and Beckson (*Encyclopedia*, 178) give July 1890 as the date when the play was commissioned. The July dating is corroborated by a letter dated Jan 1892 from Alexander to Clement Scott; in it Alexander mentions commissioning the play '18 months ago when my larder was empty' (see Kaplan, 62). Alexander took over the tenancy of the St James's Theatre in late 1890; the first play he staged was R. C. Carton's *Sunlight and Shadow* which began its run on 31 Jan. 1891 (see Raymond Mander and Joe Mitchenson, *The Lost Theatres of London* (London: Rupert Hart-Davis, 1968), 475).

[10] Beckson claims that Alexander offered Wilde an advance of £100 (*Encyclopedia*, 178), a sum confirmed by Alexander many years later in a letter to Ross. See Margery Ross (ed.), *Robert Ross: Friend of Friends* (London: Jonathan Cape, 1952), 152; see also Ch. 3, n. 3. However, this figure is disputed by Ellmann on the basis of another letter from Wilde to Alexander (which we quote) and which mentions returning an advance of only £50. It seems unlikely that Wilde could have been mistaken about the sums involved. It is perhaps worth noting in passing that Ellmann's account does, however, contain a different error: he confuses the date at which Wilde offered to return the advance with the date when the initial agreement was drawn up. Hence he claims (illogically) that Wilde was given an advance in Feb. 1891 to write a play which was due for submission in Jan. 1891 (Ellmann, 314).

I am not satisfied with myself or my work. I can't get a grip of the play yet: I can't get my people real. The fact is I worked at it when I was not in the mood for work, and must first forget it, and then go back quite fresh to it. I am very sorry, but artistic work can't be done unless one is in the mood; certainly my work can't. Sometimes I spend months over a thing, and don't do any good; at other times I write a thing in a fortnight.[11]

Wilde offered to return the advance and end the agreement, a proposition which the patient Alexander obviously declined, although he had to wait another eight months for his play to materialize. This apparent defeatism on Wilde's part may perhaps have been because he recalled how difficult he had found the writing of his earlier plays. In 1880–1, when he was relatively unknown and hawking *Vera* to the theatrical profession, any anxiety had been disguised from all but his closest friends. In public Wilde had been very keen to project confidence, to the extent that he went ahead and printed a few copies of the play at his own expense, which he then sent to a number of leading actors and actresses. This form of self-publication was not at the time particularly unusual for dramatic authors. Until the last decade of the nineteenth century, contemporary drama, if published at all, tended to appear in flimsy sixpenny pamphlets which were aimed at amateur dramatic clubs. As John Russell Stephens has argued, quality editions of play-texts were relatively rare, and tended to be reserved for authors such as Tennyson or Bulwer Lytton who had established their reputations in other genres.[12] In these cases publishers relied on an author's general prestige, rather than a market for plays, to sell a play-text: it was Tennyson or Bulwer Lytton and not the genre who attracted the reader. In fact, the market for durable editions of play-texts—the whole concept of the 'reading text'—did not develop until the 1890s when the passing of the American copyright Act (in 1891) made it economically viable by restricting the opportunities for piracy. But even then the market was slow and unpredictable, and few dramatists or publishers could make money out of it.

Part of the problem was educating the book-buying public into accepting the idea of the play-text as *literature*—as a work of written art which would endure beyond the occasion of its performance. Indeed, the status of the play-text as literature was contested even in the 1890s. For example, Edmund Gosse, a critic who had seen his

---

[11] *Letters*, 282.   [12] See Stephens, *The Profession of the Playwright*, 135–7.

mission to defend literary (although not necessarily scholarly) standards, assumed that true literary merit was conferred by book publication rather than performance. On receiving Wilde's gift of the Bodley Head edition of *Lady Windermere's Fan* in December 1893, he commented on its 'brilliant merit . . . which is only enhanced by the absence of stage disturbance'. Gosse went on 'I have just read it through, & I think more highly of it than ever. We might still have a drama, if they would only close the play-houses.'[13]

Gosse's assumption that literariness was a quality inherent in writing and style (rather than performance) echoed Henry Arthur Jones's comment in the preface to the first book publication of his play *Saints and Sinners* (1891), in which he claimed that if 'a play-wright does not publish within a reasonable time after the theatrical production of his piece, it will be an open confession that his work was a thing of the theatre merely, needing its garish artificial light and surroundings, and not daring to face the calm air and cold daylight of print.'[14] Importantly the commercial publication of play-texts, when it did occur, did not pre-empt or replace the habit of private publication. So dramatists as popular as Pinero or Jones, whose work was published by Heinemann and Macmillan respectively, continued to produce private pre-performance editions of their works in small numbers. These private copies could be lavish and in some cases were indistinguishable from commercial publications. However, their use was restricted to rehearsal and prompt copies, although they were also given to friends as gifts and invariably one would serve as the licensing copy submitted to the Lord Chamberlain's Examiner of Plays. Private publication could pre-date commercial publication by several years: houses such as Macmillan only became involved once a play was a proven success on the stage. In 1881, then, Wilde, by paying for the publication of *Vera* and assiduously working his contacts in the theatrical world, was following the only route available for the aspiring drama-tist. The business of the dramatist—Wilde's business—was self-advertisement, an activity which demanded self-assurance and financial resources in equal measure.

[13] *OWR*, 84–5. In 1886 Gosse had been subjected to a devastating and very public con-demnation of his standards of scholarship by John Churton Collins, a former friend and later professor of English at the University of Birmingham.

[14] Quoted in Stephens, *The Profession of the Playwright*, 134–5.

Ellmann speculates that the postponement of the performance of *Vera* can be attributed to 'official pressure' following the assassination of Czar Alexander II in March 1881, pressure which came perhaps from the Prince of Wales himself who had married the sister of the new Czarina. There is, however, no evidence for any such intervention, and it seems hard to believe that the possibility of giving offence was not considered until only days before the scheduled performance (and eight months after the assassination itself). George Rowell offers a much more plausible if more mundane explanation, that it was simple lack of money which caused the play's withdrawal.[15] We do know that Marie Prescott (who staged the American production) thought the play an expensive one: she later quoted Wilde a minimum of $5,000 for what she termed a 'bare production'.[16] *Punch* for its part was not taken in by the explanation that had been given in the *World*, and on 10 December 1881, under the heading 'Impressions du Théâtre' (a pointed allusion to a section of *Poems* (1881)), took the opportunity for some punning at Wilde's expense:

The production of Mr Oscar Wilde's play *Vera* is deferred. Naturally no one would expect a Veerer to be at all certain: it must be, like a pretendedly infallible forecast, so very weather-cocky. *Vera* is about nihilism: this looks as if there were nothing in it.[17]

Undeterred Wilde took his play with him on his American tour and with the help of Richard D'Oyly Carte, and his business manager, Colonel W. F. Morse, set about trying to interest the American theatrical profession. The most promising response came from Steele Mackaye (James Morrison Steele, an actor-manager and dramatist) who began negotiations with Mary Anderson, an actress whom Wilde greatly admired. When these fell through, he suggested that Wilde should approach another American actress, Marie Prescott. Prescott was enthusiastic, but an agreement was reached only after many weeks. Wilde initially began discussing terms with William Perzel, Prescott's manager and second husband. However,

[15] See Rowell, 'The Truth about *Vera*', 99; see also Reed, *Oscar Wilde's Vera*, p. xxvii, and Ellmann, 146, both of whom elaborate on the issue.   [16] Mason, 260.
[17] *Punch*, 81 (10 Dec. 1881), 274; the paragraph continued with a joke at the expense of Wilde's social celebrity: 'But why did Mr O'Wilde select the Adelphi for his first appearance as a Dramatic Author, in which career we wish him cordially all the success he may deserve? Why did he not select the Savoy? Surely where there's a Donkey Cart—we should say D'Oly Carte—there ought to be an opportunity for an "Os-car"?'

they could not agree, and Prescott wrote to Wilde directly with new terms.[18] She offered $1,000 for the sole rights to perform the play (although it was to remain Wilde's property) and a further $50 fee (which Prescott confusingly calls a royalty) for every performance. It is not clear how much of an improvement this offer represented over Perzel's original overtures, but Prescott was keen to emphasize the advantages of the arrangement. She insisted that Wilde would be virtually guaranteed 'seven performances a week' and thus the prospect of a regular weekly fee of $350. This amount compares very favourably with the royalties (based on a percentage of gross takings) which Wilde negotiated some years later for the American touring production of *Lady Windermere's Fan*. On that occasion (as we describe below) Wilde received between $200 and $350 dollars a week as his take from gross receipts of between $4,000 and $6,000. It also compares well with the performance fees commanded by other dramatists in Britain: for example in the 1860s Tom Robertson was given the 'top rate' fee of £5 a night by the Bancrofts at the Prince of Wales and managed to negotiate £10 a night from Edward Sothern at the Haymarket for the 1869 run of *Home*; James Albery, a dramatist of proven box-office appeal, was offered six guineas (£6 6s.) by the normally parsimonious Henry Irving for the 1881–2 revival of his *Two Roses* at the Lyceum.[19] Prescott went on to remind Wilde that a dramatist as experienced as his friend Dion Boucicault 'engages his plays this way only', and that 'twenty-five dollars [was] the highest royalty [i.e., set fee] he ever got and now he's glad to get ten dollars a performance'.

As a final justification Prescott set out an estimate of profits based on weekly costs to the company (which included items such as salaries, Wilde's fee, travelling expenses, and so on) of $2,000. She went on to explain that:

if we play on shares with a manager—say 50 per cent of gross receipts—we might draw 5,000 or $6,000 gross, giving us $2,500 or 3,000. Now that would be very nice for us if it kept up and give us a chance to get our money back. But suppose we only draw *down stairs* audiences and get but 3,500 to 4,000 gross—then we are out! So on the average I am sure my outline of contract is just to us both.[20]

---

[18] Prescott's long letter is printed in full in Mason, 259–65; Mason dates it 9 Jan. 1883; Hart-Davis, who mentions the same letter, prefers a date of March/April (*Letters*, 142), although he does not give any reason for that preference.

[19] Stephens, *The Profession of the Playwright*, 62–4.   [20] Mason, 260.

Her figures show that Prescott was planning on making a weekly profit of between $500 and $1,000; she had, though, the additional burden of having to recoup the anticipated initial outlay (which she had calculated as $9,000) necessary to set up the production. Furthermore, if houses were not good—if they drew only a 'down stairs' audience—then the play could easily run at a loss. Prescott was at pains to point out that Wilde's set fee protected him from poor houses (which a percentage royalty would not). She alludes to what seems to have been an objection from Wilde, that he stood to gain nothing from very good houses—from what Prescott calls 'playing to 8,000 a week'. Wilde did accept her terms, although it is clear that for future productions of his plays (at least all those for which records survive) he would opt for a percentage of gross takings; these decisions turned out to be wise, for the Society Comedies had profitable runs, both in Britain and (for the most part) in the United States. The terms he agreed with Prescott promised (if *Vera* had been a success) to bring him an income of around £70 a week while the play was in production; moreover Prescott had planned an extensive tour of 'large cities' for the 1883 season and 'small places' for the season the year after.[21] The closure of the first American production of *Vera* at the Union Square Theatre, New York in August 1883 after only one week (of a projected four-week run) must have been a bitter disappointment, not only for Wilde, but also for Prescott who had invested considerable sums of her own money (she claimed to have spent $700 simply on advertising and $1,650 on renting the Union Square Theatre).[22] Prescott did subsequently take the play on tour, opening for a week in the Detroit Opera House in late December 1883. It is clear, though, that the play never made either Prescott or Wilde the sums which she had anticipated.

While Wilde had been negotiating about *Vera* with Marie Prescott, he appears to have remained in contact with Mary Anderson, for in the winter of 1882–3 he also finalized terms to produce for her a new 'tragedy' (the play which would become *The Duchess of Padua*). Mason prints a draft of an agreement drawn up between Wilde and Anderson's representative, probably her manager, Hamilton Griffin, in which Wilde was offered the sum of $5,000: $1,000 on signing the contract and a further $4,000 on Anderson's 'acceptance & approval'. Once again, these were good

---

[21] Letter from Marie Prescott to Wilde dated 11 Feb. 1883; quoted in ibid. 266.
[22] Ibid. 267 and 272.

terms for an unproven dramatist: $4,000 would have been roughly equivalent to 11–12 weeks of the performance fee offered by Prescott, but without any risk on Wilde's part. The deal is also very similar to the one which George Alexander is reported to have first offered Wilde for *Lady Windermere's Fan*: that is, £1,000 as a fee to buy the rights of the play.[23] Ellmann claims that the contract with Anderson was agreed in early December 1882.[24] The play itself was finished in Paris on 15 March 1883 (despite the contract specifying delivery on or before 1 March).[25] Wilde wrote to Anderson a long letter dated 23 March in which he painstakingly explained various details of the play's plotting and characterization. He took every opportunity to remind Anderson of how seriously he had taken his commission, commenting: 'I remember what you talked to me about it: I think I have produced exactly what you desire.' He ended his letter with a flourish: 'believe me that writing this play for you has been a task of pleasure, and a labour of love.'[26] All in all, the letter is an anxious attempt to 'sell' the play and discloses a deep lack of confidence on Wilde's behalf. That anxiety turned out to be well placed, for Anderson was unimpressed. After some enquiries from Wilde, she telegrammed her refusal in late April.

It is tempting to see Wilde's early dramatic career only negatively: to stress the lack of interest among British theatre-managers for his work, and the largely unsuccessful attempts to sell his plays in America. It is not at all clear, however, that Wilde himself saw his first two plays in these terms; rather his repeated attempts (up to 1892) to find a producer for *The Duchess of Padua* point to a real commitment to high tragic drama. Moreover there was at least one lesson which Wilde must have learned from *Vera* and *The Duchess of Padua*, and that was just how much money a successful dramatist could earn in the popular theatre. If Anderson had accepted *The Duchess of Padua* in March, and if Prescott's run with *Vera* had gone its full four weeks, then by the autumn of 1883 Wilde would have

---

[23] For details of the agreement over *The Duchess of Padua*, see Mason, 357. (Ellmann (199) confusingly substitutes pounds for dollars when describing it.) The figure of a fee of £1,000 for *Lady Windermere's Fan* is mentioned by Hesketh Pearson (in *The Last Actor-Managers* (London: Methuen, 1950), 28) in a report of a conversation between Wilde and Alexander, but no source is given. The figure is repeated in Ellmann (315) and, as we noted in Ch. 3, in a letter from Alexander to Ross in 1908. This anecdotal evidence apart, there seems to be no firm confirmation of the sum involved. It has, however, been so often quoted that it has become concretized into an accepted 'fact' about Wilde. See e.g. the otherwise reliable Stephens, *The Profession of the Playwright*, 78.

[24] Ellmann, 199.   [25] *Letters*, 136 n.   [26] Ibid. 137 and 142.

earned around $7,400, in addition to the fees earned from any tour-
ing productions of *Vera*. That he found himself at the end of the
year with 'only' around $2,700 was obviously disappointing, but it
was still a useful sum of money. The theatre held out the prospects
of substantial earnings, but they were uncertain and irregular—too
irregular to be the sole means of support for a man engaged (on 26
November 1883) to be married.

I

The first (but tentative) evidence that Wilde turned his attention
back to the commercial theatre concerns a fragmentary manuscript
draft of an early play entitled *A Wife's Tragedy*. It has been dated
(mainly on stylistic grounds) by Rodney Shewan as having been
written some time in the late 1880s—that is, after *Vera* and the
Duchess of Padua but before *Lady Windermere's Fan*. Shewan argues
that the draft is best understood as a 'trial run for *Lady Windermere's
Fan*'; nevertheless it is clear that the play was abandoned at a very
early stage in its composition.[27] Interestingly, *A Wife's Tragedy* is
not the only unfinished play in the Wilde canon. Critical accounts of
the drama dwell almost exclusively on the completed and performed plays; as a consequence Wilde is typically presented as a
writer whose dramatic career begins, as we have indicated, with two
relatively unsuccessful works (which can be bracketed off as juvenilia), includes an attempt at avant-garde or experimental drama
(*Salomé*), and concludes with a sequence of highly successful society comedies in which he is seen to have found his style and voice.
This narrative suggests Wilde acquired most of his theatrical skills
during the short three-year period between 1892 and 1895, a view
most familiar from the pioneering criticism of Ian Gregor in 1966,
but which underlies many more recent accounts.[28] The difficulty
with such a story is that it erases the time which Wilde spent inves-
tigating other sorts of drama: *A Wife's Tragedy*, *A Florentine*

[27] See Rodney Shewan (ed.), '*A Wife's Tragedy*: An Unpublished Sketch for a Play by
Oscar Wilde', *Theatre Research International*, 7: 2 (1982), 75–131.

[28] See Gregor, 'Comedy and Oscar Wilde', *Sewanee Review*, 74: 2 (1966), 501–21; but, as
we explain in Ch. 7, this narrative informs accounts by later critics, such as Kerry Powell, Sos
Eltis, and Peter Raby. See Powell, *Oscar Wilde and the Theatre of the 1890s* (Cambridge:
Cambridge University Press, 1990); Eltis, *Revising Wilde: Society and Subversion in the Plays
of Oscar Wilde* (Oxford: Clarendon Press, 1996); Raby, *The Importance of Being Earnest: A
Reader's Companion* (New York: Twayne, 1995).

Tragedy, *La Sainte Courtisane*, and *The Cardinal of Avignon*. These were unfinished, but it is important for us to acknowledge that cumulatively they are evidence of a breadth in Wilde's dramatic interests.[29] To put this another way: alongside the society comedy (a sub-genre which Wilde did perfect) he retained a lifelong interest in another sort of drama altogether, one more self-consciously 'literary'. Wilde was much less successful with these plays, but this is not necessarily an indication that he valued the genre less. Rather his repeated attempts to write more serious drama suggest a higher ambition than straightforward commercial work. On the other hand, the growing tension between these ambitions and the financial need to write for commission meant he had less and less time to devote to more serious drama. In this respect, Wilde's career as a playwright exhibits in miniature, as it were, the tensions of the whole of his career, the way in which the need to make money led him to modify his literary ambitions.

That Wilde started but failed to finish at least five plays (this figure includes the scenario for *Mr and Mrs Daventry* in 1900) should also remind us that dramatic writing did not come particularly easily to him. In the summer of 1890, when Alexander commissioned *Lady Windermere's Fan* with an advance of £50, he seemed much more sanguine about his prospects than he had been in 1880 when he was finishing *Vera*. It is worth remembering that he had been given four times Alexander's advance in 1883 to write for Mary Anderson. Interestingly in September 1890 Wilde turned down a request for a play from his friend the actor Norman Forbes-Robertson because Forbes-Robertson would not pay enough. 'If you want a play from me,' Wilde wrote, 'I would require £100 down on the scenario being drawn out and approved of, and £100 on the completion of the manuscript. Then royalties of course to follow.' Anything less, Wilde suggested, would be 'speculative' work, and as someone who 'was always in need of money', he had 'to work for certainties'. He concluded, rather pompously, by pointing out that Forbes-Robertson would 'find it good economic policy to pay a good price for good plays'.[30] Wilde's apparent inability to get to grips with the writing of *Lady Windermere's Fan* might have been

---

[29] The Clark Library possesses a photostat of an autograph page of what might be another unfinished play, 'Beatrice and Astone Manfredi'. See Clark Library. Wilde W6721M2. However the fact that Wilde habitually changed characters' names from draft to draft may indicate that it more properly belongs to another work.   [30] *Letters*, 275–6.

due to his sense that Alexander's meagre £50 advance undervalued him, but it is equally plausible that the delay was because Wilde had several other irons in the fire. In the first place, he had been trying to revive interest in *The Duchess of Padua*. Lawrence Barrett, an American actor-manager, staged a short production of it on Broadway from 26 January to 14 February 1891. Wilde's negotiations with Barrett date back as far as 1882, when Wilde reported in a letter to Mary Anderson that Barrett had already made 'a very large offer for the play' (which Wilde, at that time, rejected).[31] In the summer of 1889 Barrett contacted Wilde again to ask whether he was still willing to let him have the play, although Barrett clearly wanted 'alterations' to be made to the text, and these Wilde declared himself 'very glad' to undertake. In the same letter Wilde also mentions that he had been approached by another American, the actress Eleanor Calhoun, although she had not yet made an offer.[32] It seems the contract with Barrett was not finalized until late in 1890, when Wilde wrote formally accepting his offer.

We do not know the exact terms which Barrett and Wilde agreed, although Wilde requested £100 (his usual figure) as an advance or as a 'forfeit in case of the play not being brought out'. In the same letter Wilde also acceded to Barrett's request that the title be changed to *Guido Ferranti* in order, in Wilde's words, 'to preserve the secret of authorship'.[33] Once again, we can only speculate why Barrett did not want Wilde's name associated with the production; it might have been to do with memories of the failure of *Vera* in New York, or it might have related to the adverse publicity over *Dorian Gray*. Either way, it is interesting that Wilde's celebrity was not perceived in positive terms. There were plans to take *Guido Ferranti* on tour, but Barrett's death on 20 March 1891 stalled them, and the production was taken over by a new company formed by the actress Minna Gale, who had taken the lead role in the Broadway staging. Gale began her tour half a year later on 31 August in Philadelphia, but Wilde's play was only one in a repertoire of six, and it was therefore not performed very often. As a result Wilde earned little money from the tour, a fact which gave him considerable annoyance, as he had 'assigned my American rights' to Gale on the understanding that she would 'emphasise' the play and 'assert it in each town'.[34]

---

[31] Ibid. 127.   [32] *More Letters*, 85.   [33] Ibid. 91–2.
[34] For the relevant correspondence, see *Letters*, 307, and *More Letters*, 104–6.

Although it is impossible to reconstruct Wilde's motives in the last months of 1890 with any precision, it seems likely that Barrett's acceptance of *The Duchess of Padua* provided a welcome diversion from the writing of *Lady Windermere's Fan*. Certainly it prompted Wilde to put his energies into trying again for a British production. In the last chapter we suggested that in early 1891 Wilde seemed more concerned to 'make' books from already published material than to write new works. It could be argued that his attitude towards *The Duchess of Padua* was part and parcel of that same ambition to make a little material go a long way; alternatively, and as we have already suggested, it might be indicative of a desire on Wilde's part to see this kind of tragic drama succeed. At the beginning of February 1891, he wrote to Charles Cartwright and Henry Irving, inviting both actor-managers to produce the play. The offer to Cartwright was made only half-seriously, for Wilde began by mentioning the 'great success' of Barrett's American staging, and then went on to suggest that his play required: 'One quite beautiful heroine / One passionate *jeune premier* / One evil old man'; moreover, 'it would cost a lot of money'. It seems that Wilde's approach to Cartwright was somewhat opportunist, prompted perhaps by Cartwright's decision to go into theatrical management—in Wilde's terms 'to take a theatre'.[35] By contrast, the letter to Henry Irving is altogether more serious and ingratiating. In it Wilde again mentions Barrett's production, insisting that it was 'an immense success'; he claims 'at Barrett's request' to have 'acknowledged authorship by cabling my thanks to the public for their reception of my play'. This self-promotion was clearly designed to kindle Irving's interest in *The Duchess of Padua*. So was Wilde's all-too obvious flattery, his suggestion that Irving was 'the one artist in England who can produce poetic blank-verse drama', and that his theatre was 'the one link between our stage and our literature'. This was high praise indeed, given the contemporary tendency (which we have mentioned already) to dissociate theatrical and literary achievements. As Wilde reminded Irving, he had already lavishly praised him in his recently published 'The Soul of Man under Socialism' in the *Fortnightly Review* in February 1891, and the coincidence of the dates suggests that log-rolling was in the forefront of Wilde's mind. At the same time he clearly had some anxiety about the play's prospects, for his

---

[35] *Letters*, 285.

suggestion to Irving was modest—that he 'have it produced for one performance, to be put regularly in the bills if you and the public take pleasure in it'.[36] Like Alexander, Irving was unpersuaded, and in his reply of 18 February he politely thanked Wilde for the opportunity to read the play, but nevertheless declined it.[37]

This activity on Wilde's part hints that in the winter and spring of 1891 he was reluctant to knuckle down to the work of writing *Lady Windermere's Fan*. He also may have been waiting to find out the fortune of those 'made' books—whether there was the possibility of establishing himself as a critic (with *Intentions*) or, and this is more likely, whether there was a future as a writer of popular fiction (with the book version of *The Picture of Dorian Gray* and *Lord Arthur Savile's Crime*) before he committed himself once again to the theatre. In other words, Wilde's failure to make progress with *Lady Windermere's Fan* may be because there was the possibility of success in other fields. It is worth remembering that by the reckoning in Wilde's letter to Forbes-Robertson, the £50 advance on *Lady Windermere's Fan* would have made the writing of that commercial play tantamount to 'speculative' work (and, as we argue below, Alexander seemed to have shared this view, because he too turned out to be less than fully committed to it). It was probably only when the very modest nature of his achievements both as a critic and as a writer of fiction became apparent to him, and when the prospect of a British production of *The Duchess of Padua* had all but disappeared, that he seriously applied himself to writing his new play. There is evidence from Wilde's correspondence that most of *Lady Windermere's Fan* was composed in the summer of 1891 (that is a year after it had been commissioned) during a trip to the Lake District; by October it was finished and Wilde was ready to read it to Alexander.[38]

The opening night of *Lady Windermere's Fan*, and of Wilde's self-congratulatory speech to the audience at its conclusion, have become a clichéd episode in the story of his success. Contemporary reviewers (and most modern critics) see in it an attitude of extreme arrogance. It is plausible, however, to suggest that an equally strong emotion on Wilde's behalf was simple relief. At last he had achieved what had been his ambition for over a decade—that 'fame' which he had described to E. F. S. Pigott in 1880. Significantly, and as Joel H.

---

[36] *Letters*, 286. [37] *OWR*, 80. [38] See Ellmann, 314, and *Encyclopedia*, 178.

Kaplan has pointed out, the relationship between Wilde and Alexander was not straightforward, and the success of the play by no means a foregone conclusion. Correspondence between Alexander and the theatre critic Clement Scott shows that the initial reason for commissioning a play from Wilde (in the summer of 1890) was to use Wilde's name to 'bring to the St James's the smart society circles in which Wilde himself already moved'. In other words, Alexander's commission was explicitly a marketing gambit, to 'make the St James's . . . a glittering fixture in London's Social Season'.[39] Ellmann reports that Alexander's first reaction to the play in October 1891 had been unambiguously positive: *Lady Windermere's Fan* was 'simply wonderful'.[40] However, a letter from Alexander to Scott dated 13 January 1892 shows that in reality he had been far from happy with Wilde's work and was reluctant to put the piece into rehearsal. There had been rumours that winter of an imminent production, but they had almost certainly been started by Wilde. Significantly, Alexander states that although he had given Wilde 'a considerable amount down in fees' (presumably the £50 advance Wilde mentions in his letter of February 1891 and perhaps a further amount on the delivery of the finished play), nevertheless they did not 'bind [him] to any time for production'. Kaplan convincingly demonstrates that Alexander was precipitated into staging *Lady Windermere's Fan* in early 1892 only by the failure of *Forgiveness*, a comedy by Joseph Comyns Carr (ironically one of Wilde's periodical editors) which had opened on 30 December 1891. Alexander had planned to follow *Forgiveness* with R. C. Carton's *Liberty Hall*; however Carton fell ill, and his play was unfinished, leaving Alexander no option but to fall back on *Lady Windermere's Fan*.[41] (A fuller account of Alexander's reservations about the play, and the revisions he insisted be made, are given in Chapter 7). *Lady Windermere's Fan* opened at the St James's Theatre on 20 February 1892 and ran for an initial 156 performances; it was

[39] Kaplan, 'A Puppet's Power', 62.

[40] Ellmann, 315; Ellmann's source is Alexander himself, who was quoted in newspaper articles some twenty years after the event. It is possible that Alexander's memory was unreliable, or that in retrospect he was trying to disguise the fact that initially he had little confidence in Wilde's abilities.

[41] Kaplan, 'A Puppet's Power'. It is worth noting that Alexander did stage *Liberty Hall* in 1892; Carton commented that 'no dramatic author was ever more fortunate in his company—and *his manager*'. Carton also wrote to Alexander to tell him of his pleasure at the size of his first royalty cheques. See Stephens, *The Profession of the Playwright*, 75 and 168–9.

then taken on a short provincial tour before it returned to the St
James's on 31 October where it ran until the end of November
1892.[42] In addition, the play was produced in the United States in
1893 and in Australia in May–June 1894.[43]

The contract Wilde signed with Alexander (which was probably
drawn up on his formal acceptance of the play in October 1891) has
unfortunately not survived, with the consequence that literary and
theatre historians have been forced to speculate about the terms
which Wilde agreed. These speculations are in turn based on the
figures quoted first by Hesketh Pearson and subsequently repeated
by Richard Ellmann and John Russell Stephens, that Wilde earned
£7,000 in total from *Lady Windermere's Fan*. However, it is not at all
clear how Pearson computed this figure, nor the productions to
which it refers.[44] In fact, and unknown to Pearson, Ellmann, and
Stephens, some of the account sheets for productions of Wilde's
Society Comedies, including *Lady Windermere's Fan*, have survived, and give us a much more accurate indication of the terms
Wilde negotiated and the kind of sums which he earned. The
records are by no means complete, and they do not give a full picture; moreover those which have survived reveal that the takings
from the plays could vary quite significantly from day to day as well
as month to month, a circumstance which Marie Prescott had been
keen to impress upon Wilde ten years earlier. Nevertheless, we can
reconstruct from these surviving account sheets an outline of the
main features of the business aspects of Wilde's work for George
Alexander and later for Herbert Beerbohm Tree, the manager of the
Theatre Royal, Haymarket.

The statement of returns for *Lady Windermere's Fan* from the St
James's Theatre account sheets show that for the week ending 11

[42] The dates for the second London run are taken from *Encyclopedia*, 178.

[43] The Australian production was arranged by Dionysus George (Dot) Boucicault, Dion
Boucicault's son who ran the Bijou Theatre in Melbourne from 1886 to 1896 as well as the
Lyceum Theatre in Sydney. On 22 April 1894 he wrote to Wilde promising him 'all the
papers, and photographs of the scenes & principal characters.' See *OWR*, 92. Correspondence
dated Oct. 1891 from Wilde to Princess Alice of Monaco, brought to our attention by Merlin
Holland, and to be included in his new edition of Wilde's letters, mentions a forthcoming
production of a play in London, and the possibility of arranging a prior production in Paris.
This may refer to *Lady Windermere's Fan*, but there is no record of a French production of
that play.

[44] Pearson, *The Last Actor-Managers*, 28; Pearson asserts that 'the original run [of *Lady
Windermere's Fan*] brought him £7,000'. He goes on to claim that the information derived
from a reported conversation (which he does not source). See also Ellmann, 315; and
Stephens, *The Profession of the Playwright*, 78.

March 1892 (about a month into the play's run) the total gross was £646 2s. 6d. Wilde had agreed with Alexander that Wilde's royalty per week on the first £600 should be 5 per cent and 7½ per cent on all gross takings thereafter. The principle of a profit-sharing deal, as opposed to a single payment for purchase of all performance rights or flat-rate performance fees, had been pioneered in the 1860s by Dion Boucicault who had advised Wilde on the business aspects of his American tour in 1882. Boucicault's preferred arrangement in Britain was a share (sometimes up to 50 per cent) in all takings (less house expenses) above a certain agreed nightly minimum. The idea of sliding percentage royalties, which became common in the 1890s, did not strictly speaking involve profit-sharing. However, the system did allow authors to benefit proportionately from improved business at the box office (exactly the issue that Wilde had contested with Marie Prescott). One of the earliest known examples of such a contract is that drawn up between George Sims and Wilson Barrett in June 1881 for Sims's drama *The Lights O'London*: Sims was offered a set fee of £2 2s. for each performance when box office receipts did not exceed £600; this changed to a sliding scale of a 5 per cent royalty of gross receipts over £600 and up to £700, 7½ per cent of gross receipts over £700 and up to £800, and 10 per cent of gross receipts over £800. Such conditions were a marked improvement on Sims's first play, *Crutch and Toothpick*, which he had sold outright for a fee of only £150—the same amount as he earned for the first week's performances of *The Lights O'London*.[45] The terms which Wilde was offered for *Lady Windermere's Fan* were thus fairly typical of the time. His contract for *A Woman of No Importance* in the Herbert Beerbohm Tree Archive in the University of Bristol Theatre Collection has a similar (although, for Wilde, more generous) system of graded percentages.

In the week in question, then, Wilde received in total for *Lady Windermere's Fan* some £43 15s. 1d. for six performances. Other weeks tell a similar story. For the week ending 25 March 1892, the total gross on eight performances (which included two matinées) was £663 18s. 6d., from which Wilde received £46 12s. 5d. A little later in the run, in the week ending 13 April, the total box office gross for six performances was £526 9s. 6d., from which Wilde would have taken almost £37. The same is true of weeks nearer to the end of the play's run: for the week ending 8 July, Wilde received slightly over £48. These figures suggest that in addition to a royalty, Wilde was receiving some sort of extra weekly payment. It does not seem to have been a bonus for matinée performances (of the kind he later negotiated with Tree), and in the absence of a contract, we cannot be sure about the reasons for the extra sums involved. What is certain, though, is that Wilde earned what was for him a great deal of money from *Lady Windermere's Fan*, a play which, we should remember, was his first West End production. On the first London run of 156 performances alone Wilde would have received around £1,000, an average of about £7 per performance.[46]

Unfortunately no accounts for the British provincial tour of *Lady Windermere's Fan* have (to our knowledge) survived; it was undertaken in autumn 1892 by J. Pitt Hardacre, a theatrical manager whom Hart-Davis claims specialized in touring productions.[47] It is extremely unlikely that the takings of the touring production of the play would have been more than in the West End, as provincial audiences were less wealthy and less numerous than their metropolitan counterparts. Moreover, where figures have survived for provincial tours of Wilde's plays (as, for example, with *A Woman of No Importance*, the figures for which are given below), they indicate that earnings fluctuated considerably from theatre to theatre and region to region; Wilde's weekly earnings rarely (if ever) reached a half of those from the West End. After its short provincial tour, *Lady Windermere's Fan* returned to the St James's for a second London run from 31 October until 30 November, and, in all, for a further forty-one performances. Once again no account sheets for this period have survived, but it is likely that returns were similar to those for the first run. If so, Wilde would have received around a further £280. A reasonable estimate for the play's total London earnings for Wilde for 1892, then, is a sum of around £1,300. The provincial tour could only have lasted for a maximum of three months, or about ninety performances. Even if earnings per performance were half of those received in London, Wilde's total earnings for the year would have not been significantly higher than £1,600.

In contrast to the British tour of *Lady Windermere's Fan*, there do exist some returns for the successful 1893 North American run of

---

[46] Clark Library. Wilde W6721Z L157 1892, Mar. 11 to July 8. It is worth noting that our figure of £7 per night gives weekly earnings totally at odds with Stephens's calculation of £200.   [47] *Letters*, 325 n.

the play. In New York Wilde was in account with the American producer Charles Frohman, and correspondence from Elisabeth Marbury, Wilde's New York agent, shows that he was contracted to receive 5 per cent of the first $4,000 taken, and 10 per cent of everything taken thereafter (Marbury herself took a commission of 8 per cent of Wilde's royalty). Wilde's decision to employ Marbury was probably prompted by his experience of the staging (in the United States in 1891) of *The Duchess of Padua*. As we have indicated, Wilde was paid very poorly for Gale's tour, receiving royalties for only eight performances. He wrote to her in December 1891 complaining that he had let her have the play 'on absurdly low terms', and had suffered what he called 'a severe monetary loss', and a 'grave injustice'.[48] When *Lady Windermere's Fan* was performed in Palmer's Theatre in New York City (in February and March, 1893), it was grossing between $4,000 and $6,000 a week, with Wilde receiving between $200 and $350 a week. (This latter amount was similar to the fee which Marie Prescott had offered for a week's performances of *Vera*). It is worth stressing that these figures were significantly larger than Wilde's earnings from the London run of his play, and are another indication of the potential of the North American market for British cultural products. The figures from Chicago tell a similar story. For the week ending 21 October 1893, the play grossed $4,569.75, and Wilde received $300, less $36 for copyright typing (his royalty in Chicago was 7 per cent rising to 10 per cent). Later in the Chicago run takings fell away, and for the week ending 4 November 1893 Wilde received only $142.48 on a gross take of $2,212. In the extended tour of Kentucky and then Indiana and Montreal, the gross takings fell to $1,681 for a week, giving Wilde a royalty of only $108.30. In St Louis, however, Wilde's earnings returned to their early Chicago levels.[49]

Although we do not have anything that resembles a complete picture of the North American tour, the returns we do possess suggest that Wilde's earnings averaged about £55 per week in New York (and thus about £550–£600 in total there) and around £30 per week for the rest of the country and Canada. If we assume continuous performances from May until November (although such an uninterrupted tour is unlikely), then the maximum that Wilde could have received is a further £900. The most generous calculations,

48 *More Letters*, 104–5.
49 Clark Library. Wilde W6721Z 1893, Feb. 13 to 1894, Jan. 27.

then, suggest he would have earned no more than £1,600 from Britain and £1,400 (after deducting Marbury's commission) from the United States for *Lady Windermere's Fan*; in fact, his combined income probably amounted to less than £3,000. No returns from the Australian production could bring this figure to even half of that mythical £7,000 which has passed into scholarly folklore. It is worth reiterating John Russell Stephens's observation that £100 per night or £600 per week was the generally agreed 'base-line' from which sliding-scale percentages usually began.[50] Put another way, these sorts of receipts were regarded by theatre-managers as break-even figures, and were the gross which the average play was expected to yield if a run were to continue. The figures we have quoted show that receipts for the first British production of *Lady Windermere's Fan* never rose significantly above this crucial £600 threshold, and on occasions fell a little below it. Wilde's earnings, then, were nowhere near those of the 'top league' of dramatic authors, who consistently reached sliding-scale royalties of 10 per cent or even 15 per cent. Pinero, for example, was reputed to have earned £30,000 from *The Second Mrs Tanqueray*; the *Era* reported that Sims earned the same amount for *The Lights O'London*. Jones earned £150,000 over his writing career.[51] Furthermore, the first run of *Lady Windermere's Fan*, although it was long compared to those earlier in the century, was merely average for the 1890s: very successful dramas ran for up to a year, and first runs of 200–300 nights were not uncommon. For Wilde, *Lady Windermere's Fan* was a success, but in terms of the commercial theatre in the 1890s, it was only a modest one. Moreover, whether or not it made Wilde the most sought-after *man* in London (as Ellmann claimed), it did not appear to make him the most sought-after *dramatist*: after all, his next per-formed play, *A Woman of No Importance*, was staged by Herbert Beerbohm Tree, who was an old friend.

These caveats aside, the sums *Lady Windermere's Fan* earned Wilde were substantial, and represented a huge improvement over his earnings from books. They were certainly closer to those com-manded by successful writers of popular fiction (who could receive between £1,000 and £3,000 for the serialization rights of a novel). A comparison in the opposite direction, one provided by Wilde's own family, further emphasizes how impressive these sums were: they

[50] Stephens, *The Profession of the Playwright*, 78.   [51] Ibid. 76–7.

were earned by Wilde at a time when his wife Constance was writing to Arthur Lee Humphreys (who was to publish Wilde's *The
Soul of Man* in 1895) lamenting the fact that craftsmen, such as the
carpenter whom the Wildes had employed for ten years, were
'utterly unable to get work, and either helped to swell the ranks of
the unemployed, or when starvation stared them in the face became
labourers with a labourer's wages of 6d. an hour'.[52]

II

There is considerable speculation about the origins and genesis of
Wilde's next play, *Salomé*. Karl Beckson follows Hart-Davis in
quoting a diary entry for 27 October 1891 from the poet William
Scawen Blunt in which he recalls Wilde reporting that 'he was writing a play in French to be acted in the Français [*sic*]'.[53] If this
memory is correct, it would suggest that Wilde began thinking
about *Salomé* almost as soon as he had finished *Lady Windermere's
Fan*. Given the delays over the latter play, it seems unlikely that
Salomé was begun any earlier than the autumn of 1891. There is
some (although mostly unreliable) evidence that Wilde worked on
Salomé during a stay in Paris in November and December of that
year. Ross, however, recalled in 1910 that *Salomé* was largely written
on Wilde's return and during a brief visit to Torquay from late
December 1891 to January 1892.[54] Ross also claimed that *Salomé*
was 'not written with any idea of stage representation'. Certainly
the play is very different in character from *Lady Windermere's Fan*,
was not written to commission, and therefore represented (to use
Wilde's terms) 'speculative' work. It may have been that the financial security promised by Alexander's acceptance of *Lady
Windermere's Fan* liberated Wilde into experimentation; likewise
that play's successful run may have emboldened Wilde to test his
experiment on the public. By June 1892 rehearsals for *Salomé* had
begun (in French) at the Palace Theatre with Sarah Bernhardt in
the title role. However, the performance plans were suddenly can-
celled when the play was refused a licence by Pigott. Wilde responded by announcing in the press his determination to take
up French citizenship and to organize a performance in France

---

[52] Clark Library. ALS Constance Wilde to Arthur Lee Humphreys. Wilde W6711L
H924 1894, Oct. 22.

[53] See *Encyclopedia*, 324; and *Letters*, 305 n.   [54] See Ellmann, 342–3.

(although such a production did not take place until February 1896, when Wilde was in prison).

Despite the self-dramatization in Wilde's response to Pigott's judgement, it is difficult to know how much of a surprise it really was. Even by Wilde's own account, the planned staging at the Palace Theatre had been a decision made on the spur of the moment, prompted in part by Sarah Bernhardt's interest in the work. Importantly, there is no evidence that Wilde had any pre-performance copies of the play printed (as he had done for *Vera*) either in England or France. Also significant is the fact that he appears never to have considered offering the play to the North American market; Wilde may have had reservations about its appeal to a non-European audience. In an interview which Mason quotes but does not source, Wilde declared his intention to publish even before the Lord Chamberlain's decision was made fully public. Moreover, the play was turned into a reading-text remarkably quickly. Although the book did not appear until early 1893 (under the joint imprint of the Bodley Head and the Librairie de l'Art Indépendant), there is a corrected proof copy of *Salomé* (marked up partly in Wilde's hand) dated as early as 12 July 1892—that is, very close to the refusal of a licence.[55] As we shall describe in Chapter 7, Wilde revised his other published plays, the Society Comedies, continuously and heavily, and often on the advice of his actor-managers, who contributed significantly to their performed versions; in addition, there are fundamental (and often structural) differences between the texts of prompt-copies and those of the book editions. By contrast, evidence from the extant drafts of *Salomé* suggests that this play, although worked on by Wilde over a period of several months, did not undergo the same pattern of revision: crucially the changes made to prepare the text for publication seem to have involved what were largely grammatical errors, identified for Wilde by his francophone friends. *Salomé*, that is, did not need much work to transform it into a reading-text. Taken together, this information points inescapably to the conclusion that *Salomé* is a genuine exception in Wilde's dramatic *oeuvre*, and that its success ought to be explained in terms of Wilde's dealings with Mathews and Lane rather than with theatrical institutions. (It is perhaps worth remembering that the 1894 English version of the play, with its eleven elaborate illustrations by

<hr />

55 See Mason, 371, and *OWR*, 154.

Aubrey Beardsley, reinforced the work's identity as a literary, not a dramatic text).

Wilde began writing his next play, *A Woman of No Importance*, in the summer of 1892 after a short trip to Bad Homburg with Douglas. Whatever sort of experiment *Salomé* represented, its failure as a piece of theatre was unequivocal, and it seems that Wilde was keen to return almost immediately to the more profitable formula of the society comedy. A letter to Herbert Beerbohm Tree which Hart-Davis tentatively dates 1 September 1892 indicates that Wilde had almost finished the first three acts of *A Woman of No Importance*, and hoped to have it 'all ready in ten days or a fortnight at most'. He concluded by assuring Tree: 'If you will send me your dates I would read it to you somewhere about the end of this month.'[56] Wilde kept to this timetable, for a contract with Tree was signed by mid-October. It is interesting that this play came much more easily than *Lady Windermere's Fan* had done, and the later plays were to do. Hart-Davis's dating of certain letters indicates that Wilde was still in Germany up to the third week of July 1892. *A Woman of No Importance* was thus probably complete (in a form suitable to be read to Tree) in a little over two months. It is not clear whether the play was formally commissioned, or whether Wilde had been offered an advance, but it does seem that the work had in some sense been promised to Tree, for he was given first refusal of it.

Tree had known Wilde for some years, at least since 1888 when Wilde's first reference to him appears in his surviving correspondence. There is evidence that as early as December 1891 Wilde approached Tree with a play, almost certainly *The Duchess of Padua*, which Alexander, Cartwright, and Irving had already turned down: Wilde was nothing if not persistent in his promotion of this early work. A letter bearing that month's date from Tree to Wilde indicates that Tree was the fourth manager in Britain to decline the play; although he thought the piece 'dramatic and stirring', it needed 'a deal in the way of rewriting' (it had already been rewritten for Barrett, although Wilde might not have sent him the Barrett version). Moreover, at that time Tree was already committed to 'two elaborate productions'. Interestingly, the letter also reveals that Tree had been following Wilde's career closely, for he reveals that he and his wife had heard 'talk of a new play by you', presumably a

---

[56] *Letters*, 320.

reference to the rumours circulating in the late autumn of 1891 of a spring production of *Lady Windermere's Fan*.[57] Given the friendship between the two men, it is perhaps not surprising that Wilde offered Tree his next new play—*A Woman of No Importance*. The deal they agreed is set out in a letter dated 13 October 1892; it indicates the following royalties:

when the gross receipts for six performances are under £600 you shall pay me nothing, when the gross weekly receipts are over £600 and under £800 you shall pay me 6%, when the gross weekly receipts are over £800 and under £1,000 you shall pay me 7½%, and when the gross weekly receipts are over £1,000 you shall pay me 10% of such gross receipts, it being understood that the sums stated are in each case for six performances and that £100 shall be added to such sums for seven or eight or more performances. In the provinces of Great Britain and Ireland, the said play shall be our joint property, but if you elect to play it yourself in the provinces, you shall pay me 5% of the gross receipts.[58]

It has been assumed by critics that this letter represents Wilde, now secure in his abilities as a dramatist, dictating terms to Tree (as he had tried unsuccessfully to do with Norman Forbes-Robertson two years earlier). In fact the opposite turns out to be the case. As Joel H. Kaplan has observed, the discovery of a letter by Tree which pre-dates that of Wilde, proves that it was Tree who set the terms which Wilde was merely reiterating. The only real element for negotiation was the position which the play would occupy in Tree's season.[59] Nevertheless, the contract was an improvement over the terms Wilde accepted for *Lady Windermere's Fan*. To be more precise, Tree wanted to reward success: if *A Woman of No Importance* did well Wilde stood to earn considerably more than he would have done for similar houses for *Lady Windermere's Fan*; by the same token, if the play fared less well than his first, his earnings would have been negligible.

A Woman of No Importance received its first performance on 19 April 1893, running until 16 August, with a break of three nights: the run, that is, was similar in length to the first West End run of *Lady Windermere's Fan*. While reviews (as with all of Wilde's work) were mixed, the play was better received than its predecessor. Moreover its gross takings exceeded that of the earlier play. The

[57] *OWR*, 83.   [58] *More Letters*, 118.

[59] Joel H. Kaplan, 'Oscar Wilde's contract for *A Woman of No Importance*', *Theatre Notebook*, 48: 1 (1994), 47.

statement of receipts at the Haymarket for *A Woman of No Importance* for the period from April to August 1893 are more detailed than the figures from the St James's for *Lady Windermere's Fan*: there are many records that show daily rather than weekly takings, and some give details of exactly how those takings were made up. They show that while the cash taken at the door did not fluctuate, house (or pre-performance) bookings slowly declined over the play's run. This detail is explained by the practice in the 1890s of theatres accepting advance bookings only for their more expensive seats, those in the dress-circle and boxes. Unreserved seats were much cheaper. There are no records for the first weeks of the run, but during May it was consistently grossing figures of around £200 per night. For example, the twenty-first performance on 9 May took over £230; by the end of that month (on its forty-second performance), it still took £211. At the height of its success, then, Wilde would have been earning well in excess of £120 per week; in weeks with matinées, which would have triggered the extra payment of £100 to which his letter of 13 October refers, this figure would rise to over £200. These earnings coincide fairly accurately with Wilde's later recollections in 1900 that he 'used to draw £170 to nearly £200 a week'.[60] By the middle of July, the gross takings had declined to around £150 per night, and by its hundredth performance on 2 August, they had declined further to about £120 a night.[61]

Generally speaking, then, the returns for *A Woman Of No Importance* were about a half as much again as those for *Lady Windermere's Fan*. There are several ways of accounting for the difference between the figures. Seats might have been more expensive, or the proportion of expensive to cheaper seats might not have been identical. (The Haymarket was, if anything, slightly smaller than the recently refurbished St James's.) We cannot therefore make any simple correlation between gross earnings and popularity, although it seems plausible that Wilde's growing success as a dramatic author was confirmed by growing box-office receipts.

A Woman Of No Importance, like *Lady Windermere's Fan*, was taken on an extended provincial tour of England; unlike *Lady Windermere's Fan*, some records for that provincial tour in the autumn of 1893 have survived. Three companies were touring simultaneously with the production, and the financial arrangements

60 *Letters*, 841; Hart-Davis's dating is tentative.
61 Clark Library. Wilde W6721Z W872 1893, Mar. 9 to Aug. 2.

between Beerbohm Tree and Wilde—as Wilde had indicated in his letter of 13 October 1892—were conducted not on a royalty basis, but rather via the kind of profit-sharing agreement pioneered by Boucicault. After a deduction was made for expenses, a profit was declared for each touring company for each performance. The profits were then divided between the touring company, which took 50 per cent, and Wilde and Tree, who took 25 per cent each. So company 2, playing at the Theatre Royal, Preston on 6 October 1893 showed a loss; by contrast, company 3, performing on the same night at the Lyceum Theatre, Ipswich earned a small profit, while company 1, playing at the City Theatre, Sheffield, again on 6 October, earned a substantial profit of £41 15s. 3d. Total expenses incurred by all three touring companies would typically average between £60 and £100 a night depending upon the venue and travel arrangements; receipts varied between £62 and £275 (in Sheffield) per night. The total profits also varied considerably from week to week; for example, on the week ending 13 October 1893, they were £60 5s. 4d. The tour included the Theatre Royal, Middlesborough, performances in Islington for two (not continuous) weeks, a week in the Opera House, Leicester, and a week in the Grand Theatre, Derby. The accumulated sums which Wilde was earning from these provincial tours were not insignificant, even though individual performances would not realize as much money as those in the West End. For example, the records of Tree's three touring companies show total profits for the fortnight between 20 November and 2 December 1893 at around £163. Wilde's share of these profits was £40 16s. 10d. In addition, a few details of the New York production of *A Woman Of No Importance* also survive. They show Wilde receiving exactly the same royalties for *A Woman of No Importance* as he had for *Lady Windermere's Fan*—5 per cent on the first $4,000, and 10 per cent of gross takings thereafter. So for a total of nine performances Wilde received a royalty of $289.72.[62] Clearly we cannot be sure of how representative this record of nine performances is of the whole run; however, the figure is roughly comparable to a week's takings from the New York run of *Lady Windermere's Fan* and therefore it does not seem unreasonable to estimate that Wilde's total income for the American production of *A Woman Of No Importance* was probably no more than £200.

[62] Clark Library. Wilde W6721Z W8721 1893, Oct. 6 to Dec. 2; Wilde W6721Z 1893, Feb. 13 to 1894, Jan. 27.

The history of the composition and production of *An Ideal Husband* is more difficult to piece together than that of the earlier two Society Comedies. Part of the problem lies in the complication that from the spring of 1893 until the spring of 1894 Wilde was working simultaneously on several different projects and was negotiating with several different theatrical managers. There is also a problem of evidence: it is unfortunate that much of our information about this period in Wilde's creative life relies on his own account of it in *De Profundis*, a document for which accuracy was not a principal aim, and which was written long after the events in question. According to *De Profundis*, Wilde began work on *An Ideal Husband* some time in the early summer of 1893 when he rented a cottage at Goring-on-Thames in Berkshire.[63] Once more it seems that the impetus to begin a new work was the success of a previous one: *A Woman of No Importance* had begun its run in the middle of April. In contrast to that play, however, the writing of *An Ideal Husband* did not go well, and Wilde describes taking a set of rooms in St James's Place in the autumn (the apartment was rented from October 1893 to March 1894) in order to be better able to concentrate on his work—to be free, that is, from interference (principally from Alfred Douglas). In *De Profundis* Wilde explained the reason for the urgency as follows: 'I had broken my contract with John Hare [manager of the Garrick] for whom I had promised to write a play, and who was pressing me on the subject.'[64] In a letter which Hart-Davis tentatively dates as December 1893, Wilde wrote to Bosie with 'horrid news': Hare was about to return 'to town' and Wilde explained that he was 'going to make an effort to induce him to see that my new play is a masterpiece'. But Wilde had 'grave doubts'—presumably because the 'masterpiece' was yet to be finished.[65]

In fact Wilde was still working on *An Ideal Husband* in January 1894, although a letter dated that month to Lewis Waller, an actor who had appeared in Tree's No. 1 (northern) touring production of *A Woman of No Importance* in the autumn of 1893, shows that the play was finally nearing completion: Wilde claimed that he had finished 'three acts' of a play that he was writing for Hare, and was hoping to complete the fourth act 'in the next fortnight'.[66] Indeed Wilde was optimistic enough to put to Waller a new proposition for what he called a 'Triple Bill'. It is not clear at this stage exactly

[63] See *Letters*, 426 ff.   [64] *Letters*, 426.   [65] Ibid. 347–8.   [66] Ibid. 349.

which three plays Wilde had in mind; but he was certainly contemplating producing some new material for Waller, for he explained that he would 'begin to write' at 'the end of the month', and that the 'plays' would be 'ready by the middle of March'. It seems very unlikely that *An Ideal Husband* could have been a part of the proposed triple bill, because it was already promised to Hare. It is probable that one of the new plays was *A Florentine Tragedy* and another may possibly have been *La Sainte Courtisane*, for in *De Profundis* Wilde claims to have been working on both these pieces at the same time that he was finishing the 'last three acts' of *An Ideal Husband*.[67] Neither play, though, was ever completed (although *A Florentine Tragedy* was later offered, in its unfinished state, to George Alexander in February 1895).[68] Interestingly, the terms which Wilde set out to Waller for this triple bill did not, on this occasion, involve royalty payments: 'royalties on a triple bill which would be played at most two nights a week', Wilde argued, 'would not be anything important'. Instead Wilde reverted to the kind of agreement which he had signed with Mary Anderson: he asked Waller for 'a certain sum of money down, and a certain sum on completion'.

In January 1894 Wilde also wrote to George Alexander; he was anxious to explain to his former actor-manager exactly why it was Hare (and presumably not Alexander) who had been given the first refusal on what would become *An Ideal Husband*. Unfortunately only a fragment of this letter survives, but its conciliatory tone suggests that Wilde was attempting to forestall any possible offence which Alexander might take. He praised the 'artistic manner' and 'artistic care' with which Alexander had produced *Lady Windermere's Fan*; in addition he paid tribute to Alexander's 'charming theatre', commenting that 'it would be a great delight' if Alexander were to put on some 'other play' by Wilde. On this occasion, Wilde explained, he was 'anxious to have some work of mine produced by Hare' because of what Wilde calls Hare's 'wonderful stagecraft'.[69] We do not know exactly when Wilde had approached Hare with proposals for a new play (nor indeed whether it was Hare who first made overtures to Wilde); neither do we know exactly when the contract which Wilde claimed to have broken had been signed. However, we can be reasonably certain that negotiations could not have begun much before April 1893, for Wilde was preoccupied until the middle of that month with preparations for the

[67] Ibid. 427.   [68] Ibid. 383.   [69] Ibid. 349–50.

production of *A Woman of No Importance*. In a similar manner we can speculate that terms were probably finalized by May, for there is evidence that Wilde had made plans to rent the cottage at Goring where he claimed to have started composing *An Ideal Husband* as early as the very beginning of April.[70] (By this time Wilde had established his habit of going away from London in order to write—to Cromer in Norfolk for *A Woman of No Importance*, and later to Worthing in Sussex for *The Importance of Being Earnest*.) Significantly, May is also the month in which Alexander's enormously successful production of Arthur Wing Pinero's *The Second Mrs Tanqueray* began: it was to fill his theatre for virtually a year. The first run of *The Second Mrs Tanqueray* was from 27 May to 28 July 1893; it was then taken on a provincial tour and returned to the St James's on 11 November for a second run until 21 April 1894. Wilde's decision in the spring of 1893 not to offer his next play to Alexander may have been because of the busy season at the St James's. At that time Wilde already had one successful West End production to his name, and was anticipating another; we can speculate that he may have thought that he was in a position to negotiate better terms with other managers (details of the contract with Hare have not survived). It is also possible that Wilde may have wanted to protect his newly-won reputation from direct comparison with the work of Pinero. A production at a different (and rival) theatre may have offered Wilde a better chance to consolidate his reputation. Moreover, Hare's initial interest in the play must have suggested to Wilde that he was, by 1893, an author whose work was in demand.

Worried that he might have offended Alexander, it is possible that Wilde, as he suggests in his letter of January 1894, did follow up his offer of another play. In a letter dated 20 April 1894, Wilde wrote to Alfred Douglas that he thought 'of writing *The Cardinal of Avignon* at once. If I had peace, I would do it'.[71] Like *A Florentine Tragedy*, *The Cardinal of Avignon* was never finished; all that has survived of it is a scenario (in the hand of Wilde's friend More Adey, dated 1896, when Wilde was in prison) and a notebook draft of what appears to be the second act. Ellmann reports that Wilde sent

---

[70] A letter of 22 April from Dot Boucicault to Wilde mentions the cottage at Goring-on-Thames. Boucicault implies that he had already received a letter from Wilde describing the cottage in some detail, for Boucicault asks for 'a room looking on to the river'. See *OWR*, 92.

[71] *Letters*, 355.

Alexander the scenario of *The Cardinal of Avignon* in August 1894, although he gives no source for his information, and we cannot even be sure that the Adey manuscript is an accurate copy of Wilde's.[72] However, if Ellmann is correct, and Wilde had offered *The Cardinal of Avignon* to Alexander, then his decision to start work on this new play must have been made after he had completed the troublesome *An Ideal Husband* for Hare (and while he had two unfinished plays still on his hands, *A Florentine Tragedy* and *La Sainte Courtisane*, works which he had also started in the early spring of 1894).

Gaps in Wilde's correspondence inevitably mean that parts of the narrative which we have outlined are speculative. Wilde certainly *talks* of working (from the summer of 1893 until the summer of 1894) on four plays: of finishing *An Ideal Husband* (for Hare), writing *A Florentine Tragedy* and *La Sainte Courtisane* (perhaps for Waller), and of thinking of writing *The Cardinal of Avignon* (perhaps for Alexander). Ellmann understandably interprets these comments as evidence of a period of intense productivity which he sees lasting until early 1895. However, it is worth remembering that of the four plays in question, only one was finished, two more (*A Florentine Tragedy* and *La Sainte Courtisane*) were short, and only partly written; and the fourth was little more than a sketch. It is equally possible, then, to see the same period as one of a series of false starts disguised by anxious self-publicity. Wilde was, after all, negotiating with one manager (Waller) and perhaps also Alexander, at the same time as he was struggling to fulfil contractual obligations to another (Hare). This pattern of activity is reminiscent of his anxious advertising of the *Duchess of Padua* to Irving and Cartwright in the winter of 1890–1 while he was under contract to Alexander to write *Lady Windermere's Fan*. The difference of course is that in the winter and spring of 1893–4 Wilde was promising much more than he could reasonably expect to deliver.

This suspicion that Wilde was overestimating (or, to be less generous, deliberately misrepresenting) his creative energies can be seen in the way his negotiations with Lewis Waller over the proposed triple bill developed. At the end of January 1894, Wilde wrote again to Waller, making it clear that one of the three plays for the triple bill had to be *Lady Windermere's Fan*; and that Waller must agree to the terms required by Alexander, who still owned the rights

[72] Ellmann, 389.

to the play.[73] For the second piece, Wilde suggested Waller take (from Tree) *A Woman of No Importance*; this arrangement would leave Wilde with just one new play to write for Waller (presumably the unfinished *A Florentine Tragedy* or perhaps *La Sainte Courtisane*). The letter also indicates that Wilde's initial idea for running a triple bill for 'two nights' a week had been over-ambitious, for he now claimed that 'one night a week would be the most one could play it'. On the other hand, Wilde was adamant that Waller (and his partner, Harry Morell, Tree's business manager) must not include on the bill a play by any other author. Indeed the programme seems to have been designed on Wilde's part not so much as an opportunity to show new work, but rather as a means to maximize income from existing material. As Wilde pointed out, *Lady Windermere's Fan* had 'not been played in the big towns since 1892'. We might note in passing that Wilde's attitude to his unfinished short plays seems not to have been so different from his attitude to his Society Comedies, for although he was prepared to start them without any commission (and along the lines of what he had called earlier a 'speculation'), he was consistent in refusing to finish them until he had received a firm commitment for performance.

To return, though, to our account of *An Ideal Husband*: Wilde finished the play more or less as he reported in his first January letter to Waller, because Hare had received a copy of it by the early spring of 1894. However, in a barely legible letter (tentatively dated 11 April 1894), Hare voiced a number of reservations about the work: fundamentally, he pointed out that it was very late (as we have said, evidence from *De Profundis* suggests that *An Ideal Husband* had been due no later than the autumn of 1893, and perhaps as early as the summer of that year). Had Wilde complied with the original timetable, Hare claimed, the play could have been produced to follow *Diplomacy*, Clement Scott's and B. C. Stephenson's translation of Victorien Sardou's *Dora*, which Hare staged with great success at the Garrick and which ran for 174 performances from 18 February to 14 July 1893.[74] Wilde's play would presumably have followed in the autumn after the summer break. In the spring of 1894, Hare claimed that for his new season he already had 'a comedy that suits

73 *Letters*, 350.
74 In an interview with Gilbert Burgess entitled 'A Talk with Mr Oscar Wilde', published in *The Sketch* a few days after the opening night of *An Ideal Husband*, Wilde referred to *Diplomacy* as 'a rather ordinary travesty of . . . *Dora*', and defended his own work from

me as well'.[75] This is almost certainly a reference to his revival of Edward Bulwer Lytton's satire *Money*, which he staged from 19 May to 20 July 1894 and then revived from 27 October to 22 December 1894. *Money* was already a proven success and it is understandable that Hare was unwilling to replace it with the untried *An Ideal Husband*. Hare ended his letter, however, on a positive note, promising to return the manuscript only if he and Wilde could not agree upon a new date for production. Hart-Davis and Beckson both report that Hare turned down *An Ideal Husband* because 'he considered the last act unsatisfactory'.[76] Neither provides any evidence to support this claim, and Hare's letter points explicitly to the fact that scheduling was the difficulty. It concludes by inviting Wilde to 'definitely settle its production at the Garrick'. In a part of the letter that is unfortunately very difficult to read, Hare alludes to Wilde's relationships with 'other managers' and their 'temporary difficulties'; he also hints at the possibility that Wilde's play would—in his words—'immediately . . . follow Pinero'. The reference is not clear, but it is tempting to link these two pieces of information and suggest that the allusion is to the possibility of Alexander staging a Wilde play (perhaps *An Ideal Husband* or possibly the putative *Cardinal of Avignon*) after the second run of *The Second Mrs Tanqueray* (which was due to finish on 21 April 1894). We can speculate that Wilde was ironically in the same position as he had been a year earlier: that there was no space in Hare's (or perhaps) Alexander's seasons with which he was happy. Here it is perhaps worth repeating Joel H. Kaplan's claim about Wilde's negotiations with Tree, that Wilde was 'an author more in a position to debate production dates than fees'.

Unable to agree terms or—more likely—a production date with Hare, Wilde sent the play to Waller and Morell for production at the Haymarket. This decision is understandable given that Wilde had been in negotiation with them since January over his proposal for a triple bill. In the event, that project came to nothing: the failure might have been because the third (and new) piece for the programme had not been finished; or because Waller was unwilling to accept Alexander's conditions for *Lady Windermere's Fan*.

allegations that he had plagiarized Sardou (Mason, 441). Wilde's claim is substantiated by the fact that the Lord Chamberlain's copy does not contain any reference to Mrs Cheveley's bracelet/necklace, which in the published edition is central to the plot.

[75] *OWR*, 85.   [76] See *Letters*, 348 n., and *Encyclopedia*, 147.

Alternatively the unexpected offer of *An Ideal Husband* may simply have represented a better business prospect. A letter to Charles Sugden dated July/August 1894, and written in response to a request for a part in *An Ideal Husband*, indicates that by the summer casting for the play was already well under way (Wilde notes that Waller had agreed to play one of 'the two big parts', that of Sir Robert Chiltern). The timing of the casting of the play is confirmed by a more precisely dated letter of 18 August from Waller to Wilde which refers to Tree's consent to release Mrs Patrick Campbell should she like the work.[77] We can therefore be very certain that agreement with Waller and Morell had been reached fairly soon after Hare's rejection in April. The play finally opened at the Haymarket on 3 January 1895 and it ran for 111 performances until 6 April, when Tree (who had returned from a tour of America) required the auditorium for a revival of Charles Haddon Chambers's *John-a-Dreams*; the success of the first run of *John-a-Dreams* in the autumn of 1894 was almost certainly the reason for the delay between the casting of *An Ideal Husband* and its first production. Waller and Morell transferred *An Ideal Husband* to the Criterion (usually let to Charles Wyndham) where it ran from 13 to 27 April. On 5 April, the day of Wilde's arrest, Waller had Wilde's name removed from the playbill but it was restored on Wyndham's insistence when the play transferred to the Criterion. *An Ideal Husband* opened for its first American run in New York at the Lyceum Theatre on 12 March 1895; it was reported some weeks later that the management of the theatre had followed Waller in removing Wilde's name from the playbills and programmes.[78]

The statement of returns from the Haymarket for *An Ideal Husband* are not as full as those for Wilde's first two Society Comedies. They are not broken down in a way that permits us to reconstruct the details of Wilde's contract; none the less they indicate that the play consistently earned the same sorts of sums as the first two comedies. The early performances of *An Ideal Husband* each grossed figures well in excess of £100. By its fiftieth performance on 16 February 1895, it was still taking £135. Takings fell somewhat through March and April, but the 106th (matinée) and 107th

---

[77] See *OWR*, 87.

[78] Mason, 438. Wilde's bankruptcy records (see n. 79) indicate that the play was performed in July 1895 (after Wilde's imprisonment) in Margate and in the Grand Theatre, Islington.

(evening) performances on 3 April together still took over £190. Details about payments to Wilde by Waller and Morell in the Public Record Office give further information, suggesting a sliding scale of royalties from six per cent to ten per cent and what may be additional cash payments made at intervals during the play's run. They show that in the first nine weeks of its run the play grossed between £900 and £1,300 a week, and for its entire run Wilde received something over £1,600.[79] Unfortunately, we have no details about the length of the American run, nor about Wilde's earnings from it. However the play is unlikely to have survived later than the end of April, when *Earnest* closed, and therefore we can be fairly safe in assuming earnings (based on earlier American productions of his Society Comedies) of around a maximum of £300.

III

Richard Ellmann claims that 'none of Wilde's plays cost him less effort than the best of them. *The Importance of Being Earnest* flowed from his pen'.[80] There is certainly a pleasing symmetry in the idea that Wilde's most light-hearted and good humoured play was largely free from the anxiety which attended the composition of most of the rest of his dramatic works. Unfortunately, however, the evidence does not support such a comfortable assumption. *The Importance of Being Earnest* was substantially drafted during a relaxed family holiday (with Constance and the children) in Worthing in August and September 1894. The idea for a new play seems to have been first conceived in July (presumably after terms had been agreed with Waller for *An Ideal Husband*), and it is clear that Wilde's explicit motive for writing was a financial one. During that summer Wilde frequently complained of being in desperate need of money; it is worth remembering that the delay in completing *An Ideal Husband*, and the subsequent difficulty in scheduling its production, had meant that an important source of income was closed off until the winter at the earliest (*A Woman of No Importance* had ended its run a year earlier). Anxious for money, Wilde wrote to Alexander offering him first refusal of the scenario for the play

[79] Clark Library. Wilde W6721Z I19 1895, Feb. 4 to Apr. 5. The payments by Waller and Morell are from Wilde's bankruptcy records (Public Record Office B9/429). There is a degree of inconsistency between these two sources. Moreover the percentage royalties in the bankruptcy records are themselves inconsistent.   [80] Ellmann, 398.

which became *Earnest*: he described it as having 'lots of fun and wit', and with an emphasis on 'dialogue' rather than plot, which Wilde described as 'slight'.[81] The letter is not dated and exists in full only in typescript; we can be fairly sure, however, that the date was earlier than August because Wilde talked of wanting 'to go away and write it'. Similarly, it is unlikely to be much earlier than July, because Wilde was still in negotiations in the early summer over *An Ideal Husband*. Wilde requested from Alexander an advance of £150 which he offered to return if, 'when the play is finished', Alexander thought it 'too slight—not serious enough'. Wilde was candid about his urgent need for money, and appealed to Alexander's friendship as much as to his own reputation as a dramatist: 'my dear Aleck, I am so pressed for money that I don't know what to do. Of course I am extravagant . . . you have always been a good wise friend to me— so think what you can do.' Wilde promised to finish the work by October, claiming that he had 'nothing else to do'. (Later he wrote frankly to Charles Spurrier Mason that he was anticipating his new play would once again 'bring me in a lot of red gold'.)[82] It is worth recalling Wilde's earlier letter to Alexander, dated January 1894, in which he had attempted to make amends for any bad feelings which might have been caused by his decision to work with John Hare, offering Alexander some 'other play' in the future. Seven months later, the financial pressures produced (in part) by the difficulties which had ensued over the staging of *An Ideal Husband* had placed Wilde in a rather different position: the dramatist who in January had felt himself in such demand that he was proposing triple bills was now turning to an old colleague for help. Cumulatively these details give the lie to the assumption embedded in Ellmann's account that writing became progressively easier for Wilde, and that he, in turn, became progressively more in demand.

Alexander's response to the scenario which Wilde proposed has unfortunately not survived; however, it can be partly reconstructed from Wilde's own allusions to it in a further letter to Alexander also written in the summer of 1894. Wilde began this letter by mentioning that correspondence (presumably Alexander's first reply to the original offer of the new play) seemed to have gone

[81] A portion of the letter appears in A. E. W. Mason, *Sir George Alexander and the St James's Theatre* (London: Macmillan, 1935); it was reprinted in *Letters*, 359. The full text was first printed by Peter Raby in 'The Making of *The Importance of Being Earnest*', *TLS* no. 4629 (Dec. 1991), 13. See also *OWR*, 65–8.   [82] *Letters*, 364.

astray. Wilde wondered 'what could have become of your letter', explaining that he had interpreted Alexander's apparent 'silence' as rejection—he had assumed Alexander thought the play 'too farcical' and had been offended by his request for 'some money' (presumably for that £150 advance). The letter continues, however, by alluding to a difference of opinion over the question of 'American rights'; Alexander apparently wanted to acquire the play for performance both for London and for a planned American tour. This part of the letter reveals once again the fact that money was uppermost in Wilde's mind:

As regards the American rights: when you go to the States, it won't be to produce a farcical comedy. You will go as a romantic actor of modern and costume pieces. My play, though the dialogue is sheer comedy, and the best I have ever written, is of course in idea farcical: it could not be made part of a repertoire of serious or classical pieces, except for fun . . .

I would be charmed to write a modern comedy-drama for you, and to give you rights on both sides of the disappointing Atlantic Ocean, but you, of all our young actors, should not go to America to play farcical comedy . . . Besides, I hope to make at least £3000 in the States with this play, so what sum could I ask you for, with reference to double rights? Something that you, as a sensible manager, would not dream of paying. No: I want to come back to you. I would like to have my play done by you . . . but it would be neither for your artistic reputation as a star in the States, nor for my pecuniary advantage, for you to produce it for a couple of nights in each big American town. It would be throwing the thing away.[83]

Wilde's letter appears to be evidence of a disagreement between him and Alexander over what *Earnest* was worth, particularly in the United States. Wilde already had experience (from *Lady Windermere's Fan* and *A Woman of No Importance*) of the substantial earnings which the North American market could produce, even though his estimate of £3,000 is larger than the returns from the American productions of those two earlier plays. It seems from Wilde's letter that Alexander's offer had been to tour *Earnest* as 'part of a repertoire of serious or classical pieces'. Of course it was exactly this kind of arrangement that had so disadvantaged Wilde during Minna Gale's tour with *The Duchess of Padua*, and Wilde almost certainly felt that Alexander was underestimating the appeal of *Earnest* for an American audience. (However, Alexander's judgement proved to be correct, for the play flopped in New York.)

[83] Ibid. 368–9.

At the same time, Wilde seems to have been anxious not to offend Alexander, for in a further letter (also written that summer) he 'scribbled off' the scenario for yet another play, one which Alexander could 'have for America' and one in which Wilde planned for 'the sheer passion of love to dominate everything'. It was, in Wilde's view, a work more suited to Alexander's acting talents. (This scenario was later sold to Frank Harris and is now known as *Mr and Mrs Daventry*.)[84]

Other correspondence during August and September 1894 shows that Wilde continued to work on *Earnest* during those months: he wrote to Douglas claiming that it was 'really very funny' and that he was 'quite delighted with it' even though it was 'not shaped yet'.[85] In fact the work was not brought to a state which Wilde considered finished until the end of October when he had returned to London. Mrs Marshall's Typewriting Agency completed a four-act typescript dated 31 October which Wilde sent off to Charles Frohman offering him the American rights. Wilde had of course worked with Frohman some eighteen months before with the American production of *Lady Windermere's Fan*, and Frohman's brother Daniel would produce *An Ideal Husband* in New York in March 1895. Charles took up the offer, and staged a short but (as we have noted) unsuccessful run of *Earnest* at his Empire Theatre in New York in late April 1895.[86] In late October 1894 Wilde was also contacted by Alexander who asked if he might read the finished play. The tone of Wilde's reply (which Hart-Davis dates around 25 October, but which the date-stamps from Mrs Marshall's Typewriting Office on the four-act typescripts suggest may be later) indicates that Alexander was not asking to see a work which he had formally commissioned. If this is true, then it is unlikely that Wilde ever received the £150 advance he had requested in July. This detail is significant, for critics have habitually viewed *Earnest* as Alexander's play. Karl Beckson, for example, states

---

[84] *Letters*, 360–2. Confusingly, Hart-Davis dates this piece of correspondence as having been written *before* the letter quoted previously in which Wilde comments on the suitability of *Earnest* for an American production. It is also worth pointing out that Alexander's American tour never materialized. See Joseph Donohue (with Ruth Berggren) (ed.), *Oscar Wilde's The Importance of Being Earnest: The First Production* (Gerrards Cross, Bucks: Colin Smythe, 1995), 38. [85] *Letters*, 362.

[86] Donohue (with Berggren), *Earnest: The First Production*, 38; *Letters*, 841 n. Karl Beckson notes that the run 'lasted little more than a week' and that American audiences were 'meagre' (*Encyclopedia*, 154).

explicitly that 'Alexander ... had commissioned Wilde to write [it]'.[87] Wilde's response to Alexander's request does not support this view. Although he agreed to send Alexander the 'first copy' of the new play (that is, one of the four-act typescripts of *Earnest*), he did so only grudgingly.[88]

In terms very reminiscent of correspondence during the summer of 1894, Wilde did everything to put Alexander off the play, reminding him of its profound unsuitability for Alexander's acting style—he was 'a romantic actor' and 'the people it wants are actors like Wyndham and Hawtrey'; it was also, in Wilde's eyes, unsuitable for the St James's Theatre. Wilde suggested that a 'farcical comedy' would alter 'the definitive artistic line of progress you have always followed'. Wilde's repeated emphases on the farcical character of the play strongly indicate that when he was putting flesh on the scenario in Worthing in the summer and autumn of 1894, Alexander was no longer at the forefront of his mind. He was, after all, fully aware that Alexander's strength was not farce, and if he had hoped better to persuade Alexander with the finished play, his writing up of the farcical elements makes no sense. Wilde ended his letter by noting that he already had 'very good offers from America for it', a pointed reference to the earlier disagreement over Alexander's wish to purchase the American rights at what Wilde thought was a discount.[89] It was certainly not an encouraging letter, and Wilde may have felt piqued that Alexander had been unwilling to support the play at an earlier stage in its composition—when, that is, Wilde desperately needed money. Alternatively, it is equally likely that he had already begun tentative negotiations with other actor-managers, for when Alexander decided to reject *Earnest*, the play was quickly taken up by Charles Wyndham for the Criterion.[90] Raymond Mander and Joe Mitchenson observe that the Criterion under Wyndham's management had achieved 'a brilliant reputation as a home of light comedy'. In the 1890s some more serious works, including Henry Arthur Jones's *The Case of Rebellious Susan*, had been staged there; but comedy was still the theatre's forte. 1895 also

---

[87] *Encyclopedia*, 154.

[88] Donohue (with Berggren), *Earnest: The First Production*, 39. Peter Raby's account of the genesis of the play also suggests a lack of transparency in Wilde's dealings with Alexander. See Raby, 'The Origins of *The Importance* of *Being Earnest*,' *Modern Drama*, 37 (1994), 139–47.   [89] *Letters*, 376.

[90] Donohue suggests the typescript stamped 1 Nov. 1895 could have been prepared for Charles Wyndham. See Donohue (with Berggren), *Earnest: The First Production*, 39.

saw the production of a musical farce entitled *All Abroad*.[91] Wyndham, of course, was the very actor whom Wilde had claimed to prefer to Alexander for one of the male leads, and it is possible that Wilde had written up *Earnest* as a farce with Wyndham and the Criterion in mind.

Our knowledge of Wyndham's involvement in *Earnest* comes principally from a letter (of 18 February 1895) which he wrote to Henry Arthur Jones in which he reported that *Earnest* had originally been his play, and that it had been scheduled for production later that year. However, Wyndham had agreed to transfer the play to Alexander following the unexpected failure of Alexander's January production of Henry James's *Guy Domville*, the terms for which Alexander had negotiated as far back as the summer of 1893.[92] The disastrous first night of *Guy Domville* left Alexander in what Wyndham ineloquently called a 'hole': James's play struggled through only thirty-two performances before it closed. Interestingly Wyndham claims that it was Wilde, and not Alexander, who asked for *Earnest* to be transferred to the St James's. Moreover, Wilde's motives seem to have been almost entirely selfish, for the arrangement promised Wilde a much earlier run (and therefore an immediate source of income) than that permitted by Wyndham's schedule. Further correspondence from Wyndham suggests that he did not ask Alexander for the usual 'premium' to compensate for the loss of his artistic property, nor did he request the return of any advance which had been offered to the author on the signing of their agreement.[93] We do not know the exact nature of the terms Wilde negotiated with Wyndham, but the evidence suggests that Wilde may have retained the advance by promising Wyndham the first refusal of his next play after *Earnest*. In a letter to More Adey, dated February 1897, Wilde talks of owing Wyndham £300: as Hart-Davis points out, this may be the amount Wilde was paid (and retained) on first signing over *Earnest* to Wyndham.[94]

91 Raymond Mander and Joe Mitchenson, *The Theatres of London* (London: New English Library, 1975), 59–61.   92 Stephens, *The Profession of the Playwright*, 75–6.

93 The correspondence is quoted in *Letters*, 419 n. Donohue notes that as part of his negotiations with Wyndham, Alexander 'stipulated that "my scenario" was to be exempt from the agreement'. See Donohue (with Berggren), *Earnest: The First Production*, 40 n. Donohue also suggests that this may be a reference to the play outline which Wilde had sent to Alexander in August and which (as we have noted) later formed the basis of *Mr and Mrs Daventry*. Whether or not Alexander did acquire the rights to this scenario in the summer (and there is no positive evidence that he did), he was to show no further interest in it.

94 *Letters*, 418–19 n.

It might be thought that Alexander's predicament over *Guy Domville*, and his pressing need for a new play, would have altered the balance of power in his relationship with Wilde. However, Alexander proved as uncompromising in his demands for changes to *Earnest* as he had been over *Lady Windermere's Fan*, further evidence that Wilde's actions were almost entirely motivated by the needs of his personal life, and not by feelings of generosity towards Alexander. Alexander's attitude also reminds us that Wilde's works were never to be his first choice: at the time of their writing, he was rarely more than lukewarm about them. Wilde refused to make changes (just as he had with demands to restructure *Lady Windermere's Fan*). Alexander then took matters into his own hands, by cutting a whole scene (the 'Gribsby' episode, which is discussed in Chapter 7).[95] Following further tensions during rehearsals, Wilde finally acceded to Alexander's request that he leave matters in Alexander's hands alone. On 17 January Wilde set off with Douglas for a holiday in Algiers and Blidah. He returned in time for the dress rehearsals. As with the disagreements over *Lady Windermere's Fan*, at this point in the play's genesis it is difficult to sort fact from fiction. Wilde's reactions to Alexander's changes to his play have survived in a number of versions.[96] Whether or not these anecdotes are true, it is significant, as we describe in Chapter 7, that when Wilde came to put together the book version of the play, he kept faith with Alexander's structural changes. It is also worth emphasizing that Alexander's treatment of Wilde was no different from his treatment of the other dramatists with whom he worked (a fact which in itself is revealing of Alexander's sense of Wilde's status, and of the power-relationship between manager and author). Alexander had a reputation for cutting and rewriting the works he produced. In 1914 in a letter to Robert Ross concerning a revival of *An Ideal Husband*, he commented that '[w]e shall have to go through it carefully, and cut some of the more melodramatic phrases and you will have to *re-write* it in places . . . When you have any leisure just have a go at it and I will, too, and then we can compare notes'.[97]

[95] See Donohue (with Berggren), *Earnest: The First Production*, 41.

[96] According to Ellmann (406), Wilde commented to Alexander: 'Yes, it is quite a good play. I remember I wrote one very like it myself, but it was even more brilliant than this.'

[97] Quoted in Margery Ross, *Robert Ross. Friend of Friends* (London: Jonathan Cape, 1952), 259.

Wilde's contract with Alexander has not survived. George Bernard Shaw reported that Wilde had negotiated 'substantial advances' together with a sliding-scale royalty of 'up to 15% for full houses'. As his source for this information Shaw cited Wilde's bankruptcy proceedings, but he seems to have exaggerated or misremembered, for surviving account sheets from the St James's Theatre tell a different story.[98] Nevertheless Wilde's contract with Alexander was a marked improvement over the terms he accepted for *Lady Windermere's Fan*: his royalty had increased sharply to 10 per cent of all gross takings (rather than, as with *Lady Windermere's Fan*, 5 per cent on the first £600 and 7½ per cent thereafter). This arrangement was more generous for it effectively doubled the royalty which Wilde received. These better terms can be explained in a number of ways: it may be that Alexander valued Wilde more highly in 1895 than he had in 1892; alternatively, it may be that the failure of *Guy Domville* had strengthened Wilde's negotiating position. However, Alexander's reservations about Wilde's play, together with the fact that Wilde came to him, make both of these explanations unlikely. Much more plausible is that Alexander felt obliged to match the terms offered by Charles Wyndham.

The statement of receipts for *The Importance of Being Earnest* show that on 14 February 1895 (the first night) the play grossed £156 7s. 6d., and that on the five days between 16 February and 22 February the box-office take ranged from £118 16s. to £183 17s., giving a total for the first full week of performance of £903 14s., of which Wilde's share would have been over £90.[99] Through March the play carried on averaging between £80 and £110 on weekdays, rising to £160 on Saturdays; so, for example, the statement of returns at the St James's show the play grossing £1,088 2s. from eight performances for the week ending 8 March, with Wilde's royalty being some £108.[100] These figures give a total of around £1,200 for Wilde for the play's run—that is, they were well over twice the weekly earnings for *Lady Windermere's Fan*, although its run was of course only half the length of the first play. The evidence from the return sheets for the St James's indicates that Alexander does not

98 Stephens, *The Profession of the Playwright*, 79 and 209. Records of Wilde's bankruptcy proceedings are held in the Public Record Office. In them Alexander and Wyndham give evidence of their payments to Wilde, but this may not be completely reliable.

99 Clark Library. Wilde W6721Z 134 1895, Feb. 14 to Apr. 4 1895.

100 Clark Library. Wilde S143Z S797 1895, Mar. 8.

seem to have included the matinée bonus which Tree had offered and which occasionally pushed Wilde's weekly earnings from the Haymarket for *A Woman of No Importance* to nearer £200. At the same time, we should remember that from 14 February 1895 *An Ideal Husband* and *Earnest* were running concurrently, and from that day until the plays were taken off, Wilde's combined weekly earnings were at a minimum around £150 per week, but on many weeks probably rose to at least £250. The American production of *Earnest* lasted for only a week, and Wilde's earnings from it would therefore have been negligible.

In light of the sums Wilde received for his Society Comedies, his often expressed need for money in the early summer of 1894 may strike the modern reader as puzzling. It is doubly difficult to account for that need if we persist in the traditional view of his career as one following (from 1891, and in Russell Jackson's words) 'an irresistible upward curve'.[101] Wilde's references in his letters to his own extravagances obviously tell part of the story. For example, in *De Profundis* he records spending between £80 and £130 a week on entertaining Alfred Douglas, and claimed to have spent £5,000 in total on Douglas from the autumn of 1892 up to his imprisonment.[102] The other part of the explanation for Wilde's self-declared poverty is that the success which is taken to characterize his career between 1891 and his trial in 1895 was by no means consistent. The contracts and receipts which we have detailed in this chapter, although not exhaustive, indicate that from February 1892 until his trial in the spring of 1895 Wilde earned in total somewhere around £10,000. This sum is only an estimate, and based on partial evidence. However, the order of magnitude seems correct: that is, the margin of error is in hundreds, not thousands, of pounds. Furthermore, these figures also show that Wilde enjoyed only two periods of sustained financial success. The first lasted from the spring of 1893 until the end of that year: this was the period of the London runs of *A Woman of No Importance* (the play from which he received his highest weekly earnings), of the American tour of *Lady Windermere's Fan*, and of his most financially successful publications with the Bodley Head (which included *Salome*, the most profitable book published by that firm, and the book edition of *Lady*

[101] Russell Jackson (ed.), *The Importance of Being Earnest* (1980; London: A & C Black, 1990), p. xv.   [102] *Letters*, 428.

Windermere's Fan). The second period of financial success occurred from February 1895 until the first trial, and was brought about by the simultaneous West End runs of the last plays. Ironically, though, this was also the period when Wilde's resources were being put under their greatest pressure. Interestingly, in a letter to Frank Harris written in 1900 (which we have already quoted), Wilde remembered 1893 as his most financially productive year, and that recollection is borne out by his abundant self-confidence in the first months of 1894, when he had plans for any number of new dramatic ventures.

Equally, though, we need to recall the difficult periods of the late career. There is Ellmann's so-called 'annus mirabilis' of 1891, a year which, however, did not involve any financial miracles, for Wilde's books in that year earned very little money; in addition there was the fallow winter of 1891–2, when Wilde was waiting for projects to materialize; and there is nearly all of 1894. Alongside these periods, it is also worth remembering the number of Wilde's incomplete or aborted projects: in the theatre, *A Wife's Tragedy*, *A Florentine Tragedy*, *La Sainte Courtisane*, *The Cardinal of Avignon*, the projected triple bill for Lewis Waller, and the *Mr and Mrs Daventry* scenario. Equally, there were projects for books which came to nothing: the expanded version for book publication of 'The Portrait of Mr W. H.', the Bodley Head edition of *The Duchess of Padua*, and the approaches to other publishers which proved fruitless.

These caveats aside, it is undeniably the case that Wilde was earning from the theatre sums of a completely different order of magnitude from his earnings either as a journalist, critic, or writer of popular fiction. These sums in turn allowed him the luxury of becoming an author whose prime appeal was to a coterie readership. At the same time, those 'beautiful' books produced by the Bodley Head were just as implicated in the realities of the market-place as the more obviously commercial work for the West End theatre. As a result the distinction to which Wilde frequently referred, that between commercial and speculative (or literary) work, never really held in practice. As we shall argue in the next chapter, his dealings with the Bodley Head were also driven by financial imperatives, and his book publications were no less free from the pressure of market forces than his plays were.

5
The Bodley Head

From the late 1880s onwards a persistent note of antagonism towards the values of the popular press, and (in Conrad's terms) its
'beastly bourgeois' readers, appears in much of Wilde's writing. In
his 1891 essay, 'The Soul of Man Under Socialism', Wilde re-
proached 'the public' for 'continually asking Art to be popular'. It
should, he claimed, never try to be so, and went on:

The popular standard is of such a character that no artist can get to it. . . .
It is all too easy, because the requirements of the public as far as plot, style,
psychology, treatment of life, and treatment of literature are concerned,
are within the reach of the very meanest capacity and the most unculti-
vated mind. It is too difficult, because to meet such requirements the artist
would have to do violence to his temperament, and would have to write not
for the artistic joy of writing, but for the amusement of half-educated
people, and so would have to suppress his individualism, forget his culture,
annihilate his style, and surrender everything that is valuable in him.[1]

This was an odd stance for an author who had already tried to make
a name by appealing to readers of popular fiction and children's
fairy-stories. With hindsight it is tempting to conclude that Wilde
was protesting too much. However, the contradiction was characteristic, for in his reviewing for the *Pall Mall Gazette* (in the 1880s)
Wilde had also adopted the perverse tactic of using the pages of the
popular press in order to condemn its values. There he is often to be

[1] Ross, *Intentions and The Soul of Man*, 301 and 303. Wilde's words once again echo those
of Gissing's Jasper Milvain in *New Grub Street*: 'If only I had the skill, I would produce
novels out-trashing the trashiest that ever sold fifty thousand copies. But it needs skill, mind
you; and to deny it is a gross error of the literary pedants. To please the vulgar you must, one
way or another, incarnate the genius of vulgarity. For my own part, I shan't be able to address the bulkiest multitude; my talent doesn't lend itself to that form. I shall write for the
upper middle-class of intellect, the people who like to feel that what they are reading has
some special cleverness, but who can't distinguish between stones and paste' (*New Grub
Street* (1891; Harmondsworth: Penguin, 1987), 43–4).

found praising work precisely because of its inaccessibility to a popular readership—to readers, that is, of papers like the *Pall Mall Gazette* itself. For example, in a notice of Joseph Knight's *Life of Dante Gabriel Rossetti* written for that paper Wilde set out to rescue Rossetti's reputation from what he termed the 'vulgarisation' of the 'mob of magazine-hacks', arguing that Rossetti 'never trafficked with the merchants for his soul, nor brought his wares into the market-place for the idle to gape at'.[2]

Along with this frequent disparagement of public taste there was often an equally bitter denunciation of a press—those 'magazine-hacks'—who pandered to it. The problem with journalism, for Wilde, was 'its tradesman-like habits'; journalists were too much at the service of the public, inviting members of it 'to give their views . . . to carry them into action, to dictate to the man upon all other points'. For Wilde, the public and the press worked in concert to 'limit' the freedom of the artist. In 'The Critic as Artist', he went so far as to describe the tenacity of 'modern journalism' in terms of the 'great Darwinian principle of the survival of the vulgarest'.[3] And later, in a letter published in the *Pall Mall Gazette* in 1894, Wilde defended himself from an allegation of plagiarism, claiming that 'it would be too much to expect any true literary instinct to be found among the members of the staff of an ordinary newspaper'.[4] Journalism was also the target of many of Wilde's aphorisms. The best-known published example is from 'A Few Maxims For the Instruction of the Over-Educated' in the *Saturday Review* in 1894 where he protests that 'the only thing that the artist cannot see is the obvious. The only thing that the public can see is the obvious. The result is the criticism of the journalist'. Better examples are to be found in Wilde's manuscript notebooks, which contain a larger selection of aphorisms, although many remained unpublished. There we find the following rebukes:

[2] 'A Cheap Edition of a Great Man', *Pall Mall Gazette* (18 April 1887); Ross, *Reviews*, 148 and 151.

[3] Ross, *Intentions and The Soul of Man*, 312–14 and 114. Wilde's disparaging use of the term 'tradesman' is common to many discussions about literary taste in the late 19th cent. For example George Moore also condemned the 'censorship of a tradesman' in his pamphlet, *Literature at Nurse, Or Circulating Morals* (London: Vizetelly & Co, 1885), 3.

[4] *Letters*, 372. The charge was from T. P. O'Connor in his paper the *Sunday Sun*. O'Connor had wrongly attributed to Wilde some doggerel verse which he then claimed had been plagiarized. Wilde's two letters of complaint were printed under the heading 'The Ethics of Journalism'. Ironically, after his release from prison, Wilde thought about trying to sell *The Ballad of Reading Gaol* to O'Connor for the *Sunday Sun*.

The journalist is always reminding the public of the existence of the artist. That is immoral of him. The journalist is always reminding the artist of the existence of the public. That is indecent of him.

In the presence of a work of art the public should applaud and the journalist be silent. In the well-thumbed lexicon of the journalist there is no such word as success.[5]

Wilde's attitude to the press was not, however, a wholly negative one. In 'The Soul of Man Under Socialism' he excluded from his scorn a small but special category of journalists in whose ranks he would undoubtedly have placed himself. These were:

men of education and cultivation, who really dislike publishing these things [i.e. scandals], who know that it is wrong to do so, and only do it because the unhealthy conditions under which their occupation is carried on oblige them to supply the public with what the public wants, and to compete with other journalists in making that supply as full and satisfying to the gross popular appetite as possible. It is a very degrading position for any body of educated men to be placed in, and I have no doubt that most of them feel it acutely.[6]

The distinction which Wilde wants to draw is between the journalist who is an unwilling victim of the market and the journalist who knowingly caters to it. While it is easy to see the reasons why at a personal level Wilde would have found this argument attractive, it is much more difficult to see how such a distinction would have worked in the real world of periodical publishing—that is, to see how magazine readers would be able to distinguish between the two sorts of author whom Wilde has in mind. Moreover Wilde actually lived the paradox he was deprecating because his wish to make money from his writing did not prevent him from resisting the idea that sales—and therefore public opinion—were in any way a measure of its value.

Behind Wilde's scorn for the 'vulgarity' of public opinion and of journalism there is an assumption of a community of 'right' or 'good' taste, a community whose values coincide with the writer's own; satisfying these tastes does not therefore entail any loss of integrity on the author's behalf. At first glance Wilde seems to be revisiting an argument familiar from the 1860s and 1870s in which the artist with integrity works (or advertises himself as working)

5 Clark Library. Wilde MSS W6721M3. E64. [189-?]; see *OWR*, 130–1. Clark Library. Wilde MSS W6721M3. P572. [188-?]; *OWR*, 142.

6 Ross, *Intentions and The Soul of Man*, 314.

without regard for public opinion. In this polemic, the general public (to whom we referred in Chapter 3 as the common reader) is assumed to be an unfit judge in matters of artistic taste. Rather, judgement is alleged to reside in a hypothetical or ideal readership. This readership is in turn defined negatively, and in opposition to the values predicated of the common reader. Characterizations of such a readership are frequently to be found in the polemic of that group of writers with whom Wilde is traditionally associated— Dante Gabriel Rossetti, Algernon Swinburne, and Walter Pater were all involved in vigorous defences of their work in the face of what they, like Wilde, claimed were vulgar misreadings by a public insufficiently sensitive to comprehend the subtlety of real literary value. In Swinburne's terms, the ideal reader, in contrast to the actual reading public, was one prepared to 'read in a fit frame of mind';[7] in Pater's frequent formulations, literary art is to be understood in terms of 'the scholar writing for the scholarly'.[8] In this conception of the relationship between the writer and an audience, the reader discovers the writer by a (supposed) process of natural recognition or appreciation. Lionel Johnson's concept of a 'little clan' of like-minded souls (which he formulated in an essay celebrating Pater in 1900) captures this sense of exclusiveness established through a kinship of refined taste.[9] Similarly Rossetti's much earlier definition of the 'fit reader', as one who is prepared to look past 'an author's difficulties to the spirit which shines through them', is suggestive of a special compact or trust between reader and writer, where the reader is required to take responsibility for understanding a sensibility greater than his or her own.[10]

The obvious shortcoming of this conception of the relationship between reader and writer is the refusal to recognize the fact that books are commodities, that they are bought and sold. Readerships of printed works have therefore always been defined in part by commercial considerations and by the economics of publishing. The Aesthetes as a group were not unaware of the commercial realities of the literary culture of their age, but they attempted to distance

---

[7] The phrase is from a digression on Browning in Swinburne's *George Chapman* (1875), repr. in Clyde K. Hyder (ed.), *Swinburne as Critic* (London: Routledge and Kegan Paul, 1972), 157.

[8] Walter Pater, 'Style' in *Appreciations* (1889; London: Macmillan, 1912), 17.

[9] See Johnson, 'For a Little Clan', *Academy*, 59 (13 Oct. 1900), 314–15.

[10] Dante Gabriel Rossetti, '*Madeline* with other Poems and Parables. By Thomas Gordon Hake, M. D.', *Academy*, 2 (1 Feb. 1871), 105–7.

themselves from it by making a strong distinction between the ownership of an object and its value as a source of aesthetic pleasure or experience. Characteristically it was Pater who articulated this distinction most carefully when, in his essay 'Style', he emphasized that a particular aesthetic experience is unique to the individual, and that the potential for aesthetic experience (understood as a special class of experience) is available only to 'a select few', to ' "men of a finer thread" '; put more forcefully, it was available only to 'the sensitive . . . [to those] "who have intelligence" '.[11] In other words, Pater suggested that the numbers of books which are sold or circulated (and therefore the absolute numbers of their readers) had no necessary relationship with the aesthetic value of those books, simply because only a small number of readers would experience the books that they possess as works of art.[12]

This distinction between buyers and readers, or between the commercial and literary values of a book, is perfectly valid, but it is not one that publishers, who are principally concerned with readers *as buyers*, would necessarily be concerned with, now or in the late nineteenth century. Moreover, in the hands of Rossetti, Swinburne, and Pater the distinction was a somewhat disingenuous one, in the sense that all three were partly insulated from the commercial aspects of publication, for they enjoyed the luxury both of other forms of income and an already established and loyal readership. It is certainly the case that Swinburne, Rossetti, Pater, and Lionel Johnson had little trouble finding commercial houses to publish their work, and the modern critic might be struck by the irony that their rarefied or precious conceptions of a readership went hand in hand with relatively robust sales for their books. Rossetti's first volume, *Poems* (1870), went through six editions in the space of a year; his second volume, *Ballads and Sonnets* (1881), ran to four editions in less than two years. Swinburne's *Poems and Ballads* (1866), despite a mixed critical reception, was said to have exhausted six editions by 1873, and 39 by 1916. The first edition of Pater's two-volume *Marius the Epicurean*, with a print-run of 1,500, sold out within months of its first publication in 1885. Even Lionel Johnson's critical essay, *The Art of Thomas Hardy* (1894), had a print-run of

[11] Pater, *Appreciations*, 18 and 36.
[12] For an elaboration of this argument, see Josephine M. Guy, 'Aesthetics, Economics and Commodity Culture: Theorizing Value in Late Nineteenth-Century Britain', *English Literature in Transition*, 42: 2 (1999), 143–71.

1,500.[13] Of course these sales did not represent mass markets, but they do suggest that the works in question were commercially viable.

By contrast, Wilde was for several reasons differently placed when he appropriated the polemic of his fellow-Aesthetes. First, and most obviously, because he was a professional author he simply could not afford to ignore buyers. Second, the market for his work was not nearly as healthy as it was for that of Swinburne, Rossetti, or Pater. Although some of his books had sold, each had been bought by, and seemed designed to attract, readerships very different from each other, and different again from the constituency to whom Swinburne, Rossetti, and Pater could appeal. In other words, Wilde as an author in the 1880s had not attracted a loyal 'little clan'; he does not seem to have established a rapport with a homogeneous group of readers prepared to take his talent on trust. Third, and most importantly, Wilde's public involvement with the press and his readiness to use it to advertise himself made it virtually impossible for him to arrogate to himself the artistic 'high ground' of his predecessors. There was a certain consistency in the public statements of Rossetti, Swinburne, and Pater and the artistic lives which they professed (and often endeavoured) to lead; by 1880 all three, albeit in slightly different ways, had or were about to remove themselves from the public gaze, and could therefore claim with some legitimacy that they were unconcerned with public opinion.[14] Wilde's position in 1880 could not have been more different, in the sense that his career from the very outset demanded maintaining a high and often exaggeratedly flamboyant public profile, both in the British and American press. His attempts to appeal to that 'little clan' of discriminating readers were therefore bound to ring hollow.

[13] Figures for Pater's sales are given in Robert Seiler, *The Book Beautiful* (London: Athlone Press, 1999), 180–4; the sales for Swinburne are taken from T. J. Wise, *A Bibliography of the Writings in Prose and Verse of Algernon Charles Swinburne* (London: privately printed, 1919); even allowing for Wise's characteristic inaccuracy, the figures are still impressive. The print-run for Johnson's book is given by James G. Nelson, *The Early Nineties: The View from the Bodley Head* (Cambridge, Mass.: Harvard University Press, 1971), 90.

[14] At this time Rossetti lived as a virtual recluse in his Cheyne Walk home (although there is evidence that he did attempt to manipulate reviews of his work). Swinburne, although outrageous and combative in the 1860s, had, by the 1880s, been restored to a quieter life by Theodore Watts-Dunton. According to contemporaries such as George Moore and Wilde himself, Pater's name had also become a byword for privacy and an almost pathological shyness.

Like Wilde's contemporaries, modern literary historians have tended to be suspicious of Wilde's rhetoric in the 1880s about the autonomy of art and the artist. None the less they have been willing to see his post-1891 publications—his set of limited-edition books published by the Bodley Head—as a change of direction, as evidence of a self-conscious repudiation of the values of the mass market, a move in turn made possible by the fact that, by 1892, he was earning enough money from the theatre to allow him not to compromise his literary art. In other words, Wilde's Bodley Head books have been seen primarily as aesthetic objects (both textually and materially), designed not to make money but rather to appeal to the taste of those readers in possession of Pater's 'special kind of temperament': they have been taken as an indication that Wilde had finally found that elusive readership with tastes as non-commercial as he pretended his own were. Exactly these sorts of sentiment have recently led Peter D. McDonald to define Wilde as a 'master-purist'. For McDonald, Wilde was a writer for whom 'the literary field exists in and for itself', and who consequently valued only 'non-fungible goods (that is art for art's sake or peer recognition)'. McDonald distinguishes Wilde from 'the profiteers', a group who valued 'the most fungible good of all, namely, money' and who measured their work in terms of its 'accessibility to the greatest number'.[15]

Wilde might have appreciated being labelled a purist, for it ironically takes his boasts about the nature of his literary art at face value; or, more precisely, it assumes, as the Aesthetes took pains to argue, that a lack of concern with absolute numbers of book-buyers—or with writing with an eye to pleasing the public—automatically equated with a disdain for the commercial elements of publication. Wilde's presentation of himself certainly centred on propagandizing exactly this separation between 'taste' and 'trade' (a distinction which he also emphasized in the Society Comedies). However, his decision (made in late 1891) to appeal, as he put it in the preface to *The Picture of Dorian Gray*, to 'the elect', turns out in practice to have been based not on 'purism' at all, but on its exact opposite, pragmatism and a sound commercial sense.

When in August 1893 Wilde made a decision to sign over to Mathews and Lane the rights to a string of new works, he was for the

---

[15] Peter D. McDonald, *Literary Culture and Publishing Practice, 1880–1914* (Cambridge: Cambridge University Press, 1997), 14.

first time committing *all* his publications to that 'elect'. He was also for the first time committing himself to—and being accepted by—a single house. Why did this change came about? Part of the answer lies with the Bodley Head, which as far as we know was the first firm (since the uneven efforts of Osgood, McIlvaine) to indicate a willingness to take Wilde on as an author (with an *oeuvre* and a style) rather than as the writer of single books. This confidence in turn confirms the arguments of historians such as James G. Nelson that Mathews and Lane were publishers significantly more adventurous than their competitors. Such an observation, however, begs another large question—what was the advantage *for Wilde* in this arrangement? As we have suggested, Wilde was undoubtedly attracted by the image of himself which Mathews established with *Poems* (1892); one of taste, refinement, and exclusiveness, it matched very precisely (and perhaps for the first time) Wilde's public rhetoric about the role of the artist. More importantly, by 1893 Wilde may have been persuaded that there was now a viable market for expensive limited editions. Significantly, in January 1893, a report in *The Bookman* noted that:

one of the features of the past season [i.e. autumn 1892] has been the growing demand for large paper copies and first editions of important works. Collectors of these editions have of recent years been largely on the increase, and the demand has assumed proportions quite out of keeping with the numbers printed. This demand has caused several books to be out of print before publication. . . . A first edition of 1,000 copies of Hawthorne's 'Wonder Book,' illustrated by Walter Crane, was all disposed of by the day of publication. . . . These demands testify to the growing interest in first editions by authors and artists of repute.[16]

The tradition of producing large- or fine-paper editions was not a new one, although it had become much less common by the second half of the nineteenth century. Nevertheless, at a time when the general pattern of Victorian publishing was to produce books increasingly economically, the conspicuous extravagance of large margins on hand-made paper found an enthusiastic if small market—one

---

[16] *The Bookman*, III, no. 16 (Jan. 1893), 112. This demand for expensive limited editions lasted throughout the 1890s but was more or less exhausted by the turn of the century. John Sloan observes that 'in 1900 the publisher Grant Richards referred regretfully to "those happy days . . . when Lane could work off editions on unsuspecting booksellers and infatuated undergraduates" ' (John Sloan, 'In a Music Hall', *Review of English Studies*, 46 (1995), 435.)

willing to pay a substantial premium for quality materials and higher craftsmanship. The decision in the summer of 1891 to produce *A House of Pomegranates* in a limited and expensive edition, together with Wilde's defence in the press of its exclusiveness, suggest that such a change of strategy was already in his mind when Mathews approached him with the proposal to reissue *Poems*—that Wilde, too, had noticed the developments in the market which were later described in *The Bookman*. Moreover, the success of *Poems* (1892), when *A House of Pomegranates* had failed, may have confirmed the rightness of the strategy, and have indicated to Wilde that the Bodley Head (rather than Osgood, McIlvaine) was the publisher in the best position to carry it out.

Understanding Wilde's dealings with Mathews and Lane in terms of marketing decisions allows us to glimpse in his attitudes to his eight (projected or actual) Bodley Head books a cynicism and worldliness far removed from the disinterestedness of the Aesthetic or 'purist' ideal. It turns out that unlike Pater, Wilde and his publishers were concerned with readers insofar as they were buyers, to the extent that they defined ideal readers mainly in terms of their purchasing power. Put crudely, in his actual publishing practices Wilde seemed content to collude with Lane in conflating aesthetic with monetary value: a social exclusiveness, which the Aesthetes had represented as a refinement of the spirit or temperament, was translated in Wilde's Bodley Head books into a simple financial elitism. We will show that Wilde was fully aware that rarity could be created by manipulating the market: that is, material rarity—the newly-revived publishing phenomenon of the limited edition— could confer on his work (or be a substitute for) an aesthetic distinction which his peers had consistently refused to recognize in his writing alone.

Despite his protestations to the contrary, Wilde's practice was effectively reversing the terms of Pater's careful argument. Pater had insisted that the small numbers of readers who would experience a book as a work of art had no necessary relationship with the number of buyers of that book (or its price). An aesthetic experience, that is, has no direct relation with a market because (by definition, and as Pater had implied) it is non-material, although, of course, it is often produced by an experience of a material object. Wilde and the Bodley Head, by contrast, worked on the opposite assumption: that artificial restrictions (which were often restrictions determined by price) on the number of books (and therefore on the number of purchasers) became the absolute guarantee of a work's value as art. Nothing exemplifies this mode of operation better than the practice of signing and numbering copies, as Wilde did with *Poems* (1892). The signatures and numbers guaranteed the value of the book as a specific object, as a limited commodity. By such an action rarity was not the intangible consequence of an individual and intensely private interpretative transaction; rather it was crudely physical, the outcome of a limited print-run and clever marketing. The notice of Wilde's volume in the May 1892 issue of *The Bookman*, together with the advertisement which the Bodley Head placed in the June issue, explicitly drew attention to these material signifiers of the book's value:

A very rich and striking cover in white and gold has been designed by Mr Charles Ricketts for the new edition of Mr Oscar Wilde's 'Poems,' which Messrs. Elkin Mathews and John Lane are about to issue.

Poems, by Oscar Wilde. 200 copies only with Decorated Title-page and End Papers. The binding, 'The Seven Trees,' is in gold on iris (cloth), designed by C. S. Ricketts. Each copy signed by the Author. Post 8vo, 15s. net. Very few remain.[17]

James G. Nelson has observed that the Bodley Head's practice of issuing only limited editions, and hence its attempt to present aesthetic value in terms of material rarity, did not go unnoticed and that there were 'many charges in the press that a considerable amount of calculation and, to a certain extent, manipulation of the book market was being indulged in' by the firm.[18] Wilde's decision to publish with the Bodley Head inevitably identified him in the public eye with these sorts of criticisms—in the words of W. Roberts in an article entitled 'The First Edition Mania' in the *Fortnightly Review* in 1894, they linked him to a situation where 'every little volume of drivelling verse becomes an object of more or less hazardous speculation, and the book market itself a Stock Exchange in miniature'. They linked him also to a business where 'the only two motives which have operated in the making of these [limited edition] books are the getting of the smallest amount of text into the widest size of page, and the skill which can spread over the greatest amount of space the smallest quantity of original

[17] *The Bookman*, II, no. 8 (May 1892), 37; and II, no. 9 (June 1892), 65.
[18] Nelson, *The Early Nineties*, 81.

thought'.[19] The outcome, for Roberts, was that limited edition books were produced as commodities for booksellers to speculate in. Indeed *The Bookman* drew attention to a study by one M. G. de Sainte Heraye on this speculative element in bookselling, on 'the art of advertisement'—or, as *The Bookman* helpfully labelled it, '*puffisme*'; it nominated Wilde as worthy of inclusion in such a work, along with H. M. Stanley (who had made both his name and fortune by his discovery of David Livingstone).[20] It is hard to believe that Wilde was unaware of this controversy. All the evidence suggests that Wilde was deeply complicit in what Roberts termed the 'artful machinations of a few in the trade'. This is borne out most dramatically in a letter of November 1894 to a different publisher, Wilde's friend Arthur Humphreys. Humphreys was in the process of bringing out a selection of Wilde's aphorisms (chosen by Constance) entitled *Oscariana*. Wilde was clearly unhappy with Humphreys's plans to market the book, and urged him to adopt practices similar to those which had been employed by the Bodley Head. More precisely, Wilde made clear to Humphreys that the reputation of the book was to be assured as much by its pricing and format, as any textual qualities:

I think the book [i.e. *Oscariana*] should be dearer than 2/6—all my books are dear—and it would look like underselling the other publishers, who have given their consent for extracts. I think also it should be bound in cloth, and look dainty and nice. I don't want a 'railway bookstall' book. In England a paper-covered book gets so dirty and untidy: I should like a book as dainty as John Gray's poems by Ricketts. I think also there should be fifty large paper at a guinea: the book could be five shillings.

After the *Green Carnation* publication, this book of 'real Oscar Wilde' should be refined and distinguished: else, it will look like a bit of journalism.[21]

Wilde's allusion was to the Bodley Head's 1893 edition of Gray's *Silverpoints*, a volume that was set in italics throughout and was published in an unusual format (eleven centimetres wide and twenty-two high) with binding, title-page, and initials all designed by Ricketts. Wilde's memory of the quality of *Silverpoints* (the publication of which he offered to part-subsidize) was accurate, but his

[19] William Roberts, 'The First Edition Mania', *Fortnightly Review*, 55 NS (Jan.–June 1894), 347.
[20] *The Bookman* II, no. 11 (July 1892), 106.   [21] *Letters*, 378.

recollection of his own books was rather more selective.[22] As we pointed out in Chapter 3, not all of Wilde's books had in fact been 'dear': *Lord Arthur Savile's Crime* had been only 2s.; there had also been cheap (that is, 3s. 6d.) editions of *The Happy Prince* and *Intentions*. In 1895, and contrary to Wilde's wishes, Humphreys did bring out both *Oscariana* and (later that year) the book version of 'The Soul of Man Under Socialism' in cheap 'paper covers'. In 1898, when his disgrace had virtually excluded him from the ranks of established houses, Leonard Smithers published *The Ballad of Reading Gaol*, also in a cheap format—2s. 6d. The half-dozen books which Wilde published with the Bodley Head were therefore hardly typical of his *oeuvre*. Their appearance was quite different from his other books: they were priced to reach a different buyer, and they sold in fewer numbers. At the same time, Wilde clearly saw them exemplifying exactly the kind of authorial persona with which he wished, in 1894, to be identified. 'Refined and distinguished', that persona appears (and has been taken) to be the very opposite of the journalist or 'magazine-hack'. Yet both conceptions of the author shared one very important common ground: the assumption that aesthetic discrimination correlated with and could be represented by price. In its crudest formulation, cheapness implied tastelessness, and expensiveness suggested connoisseurship.

We suggested in Chapter 3 that a further factor in Wilde's decision in August 1893 to give to the Bodley Head the sole rights over his *oeuvre* was the stage success of *Lady Windermere's Fan* and *A Woman of No Importance*; these had, for the moment, made earnings from his books a less pressing consideration. In fact this last issue is a complex one: as we will show, Wilde often disagreed with Mathews and Lane about the pricing of his books, and those disagreements were because he thought they were being undersold. But this wish not to be sold cheap was motivated by a number of rather different considerations.

First, Wilde's desire for his books to be priced as highly as possible (much higher, incidentally, than most other books on the

---

[22] In a letter of 17 June 1892 to Wilde, Mathews and Lane agreed to publish *Silverpoints* on the understanding that Wilde undertook 'the cost of the designs—block for same—paper, printing and binding of an edition not exceeding 250 copies.' The Bodley Head was to take a commission of '40% on the published price' of each copy sold. See *More Letters*, 117. However, a later agreement, drawn up on 4 Jan. 1893 and superseding the first, reveals that the Bodley Head underwrote the costs of the volume themselves. See Nelson, *The Early Nineties*, 95.

Bodley Head list) seems, as we have said, to have been determined mainly by his sense of the value which such pricing signified to the reader. For example, when Wilde signed the contract for *The Sphinx* in 1892 (and at a time when he was assured of income from the production of *Lady Windermere's Fan*), he virtually prohibited the Bodley Head from producing cheap, popular editions of the work on the grounds that they would spoil its reputation for exoticism and exclusivity.[23] On other occasions, though, when he was more pressed for money, Wilde's haggling about pricing was driven by a more straightforward anxiety about a book's profitability. It does not seem to be the case that from 1892 onwards Wilde's theatrical earnings made him wholly (or consistently) indifferent to the sums which he could earn from books. We have described in the previous chapter the way in which his income from his plays fluctuated between early 1892 and mid-1895, and how in particular Wilde seems to have been very pressed for money during most of 1894. It is worth recalling that John Hare's refusal of *An Ideal Husband* had taken place in April, and that the consequent delay in the production of the play had deprived Wilde of royalty income from plays for the remainder of that year. His correspondence in the summer of 1894 reveals that the relatively modest amounts to be earned from his Bodley Head books had become unexpectedly important, given the fact that he was in a situation where—in his words—he had 'not a penny'.[24] But ironically, it was at precisely this time that Wilde's income from the Bodley Head threatened to dry up, for the partnership itself was on the point of dissolution. These circumstances explain why (as we describe later) Wilde's negotiations with Mathews and Lane in the summer of 1894 become marked by an increasingly impatient tone; and why, more particularly, he was so angry at the firm's slowness in bringing out an enlarged book version of his essay 'The Portrait of Mr W. H.'. While he had been prepared to wait for two years for *The Sphinx* to appear, in the summer of 1894 Wilde complained bitterly that 'Mr W. H.' had been in the firm's hands '*for more than a year*'.[25]

I

Money, then, and the pricing of his books, were always important in Wilde's dealings with Mathews and Lane, even if his concern was

---

[23] *Letters*, 319.   [24] Ibid. 359.   [25] Ibid. 367.

often more for its symbolic than economic value. Certainly when Wilde reached an agreement in 1891 with Elkin Mathews to reissue *Poems*, the actual earnings promised by this expensive, limited edition volume cannot have been his only consideration. Success defined in terms of royalties seems to have been reinforced by another kind of success which was to become equally important: what we have called the Bodley Head 'image' of Wilde. It may seem odd to describe an edition of just 220 copies (of which only 200 were for sale) as any kind of success.[26] After all, the number was considerably smaller than all of Wilde's other books up to that date. It was also many times smaller than Rudyard Kipling's critically acclaimed six-shilling *Barrack-Room Ballads* which, according to *The Bookman* in June 1892, was among the top five best-selling books in London, Liverpool, Edinburgh, Glasgow, Bradford, and Aberdeen.[27] The notion of success, however, has to be defined in relation to the specific cultural as well as financial circumstances of the edition. In contrast to Kipling's *Barrack-Room Ballads*, with its celebration of the heroism of ordinary lives, the cultivated exoticism of Wilde's volume, reinforced by the 'very rich and striking cover', was designed to be attractive to a more restricted, wealthier, and largely metropolitan clientele.

James G. Nelson notes that the expensive look of the typical Bodley Head book was often just that—an appearance. Unlike the economics of modern publishing, where small print-runs and fine editions are prohibitively expensive, in the 1890s limited editions were economically viable because of the historically low costs of book production: Nelson calculates that the Bodley Head could make a profit on print-runs of 350 while charging 'on the average no more than five shillings net per copy'.[28] A large proportion of the cost of any volume went on the setting of type, and this made publishing poetry (and, later, plays), with their small proportion of print to the page, an attractive prospect. The practice of the Bodley Head was to set poetry in large type, and this produced further savings because it involved less labour on the part of the compositor. When—as with Wilde's volume of poems—the printed sheets were bought from bankrupt or remaindered stock, costs were even lower.

---

[26] The new front-matter made the distinction by stating: 'This edition consists of 220 copies, 200 of which are for sale.'

[27] *The Bookman*, II, no. 10 (June 1892), 85.

[28] Nelson, *The Early Nineties*, 84.

We do not know exactly how much Mathews paid for the unbound sheets of Bogue's unsold fourth and fifth editions of Wilde's *Poems*; however, we do know that he spent £9 12s. 6d. on binding and on engraved blocks for the new title-page and covers.[29] Further details of expenses can be seen in the contract which Mathews signed with Wilde:

To Oscar Wilde, Esq
Poems

Dear Sir,

I undertake to issue your volume of Poems on the following terms viz:-

To instruct printer to supply Title-page with my imprint for 230 copies

On receipt of artists Designs for cover at cost of £5–5–0. Block to be prepared from same the cost of which as well as that of Title-page, Binding and Advertising to be first charges on the amount received for copies sold. The cost of advertising not to exceed £5–5–0.

For my Commission I agree to take 20% on the net published price, it being agreed that the book shall be brought out as a net one the price to be fixed when bound.

After the above charges have been met the balance to be remitted quarterly the first balance to be struck six months after publication

> I am yours faithfully,
>   Elkin Mathews[30]

So we know for certain that £20 11s. 6d. was spent on producing the book. This figure does not take account of the costs of printing the new end- and front-matter, nor printing the new cover with its design by Ricketts; nor, as we have said, the cost of buying the sheets. An analogous case of a volume made from bought remaindered sheets (this time from Kegan Paul) is Francis Wynne's *Whisper!*. The records of the Bodley Head show that the sheets for 308 copies were purchased, and the trade cost of the finished volume was only 2s., giving a total return to the Bodley Head of £30, a figure which suggests that the additional printing and production costs must have been very low indeed. Wilde's volume, by contrast, was priced at 15s., and (if we calculate from the example of other Bodley Head books) its trade price was probably 12s. 6d. The total amount realized from trade sales would, then, have been around £125. Mathews's commission (20 per cent of the net price) would have come to £30. Thus it does not seem unreasonable to assume that

---

[29] Ibid. 91.   [30] Clark Library. Wilde M429L W6721 [1892?].

Wilde himself would have received somewhere between £45 and £60 for the volume.

It is worth remembering that *Poems* (1892) required very little work from Wilde.[31] In a sense, the reissue of the volume represented money for nothing. None the less, in the context of his theatrical earnings, the sum he earned from it was not particularly impressive. More exactly, it was probably around the same amount as he earned weekly from the London or New York productions of his plays. Indeed what Wilde earned in absolute terms from all his Bodley Head books was slight compared with any of his theatrical earnings (even though *Salome* was the firm's most profitable book). Because we have no details of Wilde's contracts with David Nutt or Osgood, McIlvaine, it is impossible to know how the profits from *Poems* (1892) stood in relation to earnings from earlier books, nor whether the work earned Wilde more than those copies of Bogue's first four editions. To concede that *Poems* (1892) did not earn Wilde a large amount of money, however, is not to say that he was in any sense a 'purist' in his attitudes towards it, nor that financial considerations were not a significant factor in his later decision (in August 1893) to commit himself solely to the Bodley Head. As we have argued, Wilde's positive attitude towards the Bodley Head seems to have been conditioned largely by the way they made and (more importantly) *sold* books—a possibility which is entirely obscured by McDonald's distinction between 'purist' and 'profiteer'. In contrast to Lord Darlington's aphorism in *Lady Windermere's Fan*, being uttered six or seven times a week on the West End stage at the precise moment when *Poems* (1892) appeared—that only a cynic 'knows the price of everything and the value of nothing'— Wilde understood that for a writer with his uncertain reputation, price could be the most reliable indicator of value. And it is exactly this kind of reasoning which seems to have informed Wilde's decisions about the plans for the publication of his next work, *The Sphinx*. Produced more expensively and in more limited numbers than any of his other books, it represents the perfect illustration of what the Bodley Head's marketing strategies could do for him.

---

[31] We should note that there is a letter in the Clark Library to an unknown correspondent which is tentatively dated 1892, where Wilde asks to see proofs of his poems. If the date is correct it could refer to the Bodley Head edition. There is no indication whether Wilde's request refers simply to the volume's new matter, however. See *OWR*, 47–8.

Wilde's decision to offer the firm a second (and this time, new) work was almost certainly prompted by the fact that *Poems* (1892) had sold out within days. In a dismissive letter to Grant Richards, written in June 1892, Wilde refused to supply a copy for the *Review of Reviews* with a joke about the rarity of his volume:

The new edition of my poems is limited to 200 copies, and these are meant not for reviewers, but merely for lovers of poetry, a small and quite un-important sect of perfect people ... Its raiment, gold smeared on tired purple, might attract attention in the Strand, and that would annoy it, books being delicate and most sensitive things, and, if they are books worth reading, having a strong dislike of the public.[32]

We do not know whether it was Wilde or the Bodley Head who first mooted the idea of publishing *The Sphinx*. The first mention of the book in Wilde's correspondence is in a letter, written from Bad Homburg to Elkin Mathews in early July 1892, in which Wilde presses him to send the 'agreement for *Sphinx*'.[33] The timing is interesting, for Wilde had escaped to Germany in order to recover from the disappointment over Pigott's recent refusal (in mid-June) of a licence for *Salomé*. Constance described Wilde to her brother as being 'under a regime, getting up at 7.30, going to bed at 10.30, smoking hardly any cigarettes and being massaged'.[34] Another source of disappointment may have been the slow sales of the book version of *Dorian Gray* (as we suggested in Chapter 3, by this time it had probably sold only a few hundred copies).

The exotic qualities of *The Sphinx* have often been taken as evi-dence of Wilde's commitment to a decadent aesthetic: it seems to be the logical end of a progression which begins with the purple pas-sages added to *Dorian Gray*, and proceeds via the self-conscious stylization of *Salome* with its illustrations by Beardsley for the English language edition. However, the plans for publishing *The Sphinx* were being put in place at exactly the time when decadence (or at least Wilde's particular version of it) was apparently failing to sell—and this might explain Wilde's sense of urgency in his letter to Mathews. Certainly, it makes explicable his confidence in the firm (they had been successful in selling *Poems* in an exotic packaging), and it may also explain why Mathews, Lane, and Wilde settled upon producing *The Sphinx* in such a small and expensive edition, one

[32] *Letters*, 314.   [33] *More Letters*, 117.   [34] *Letters*, 316 n.

designed explicitly to appeal to that 'sect of perfect people' who, although 'quite unimportant', were none the less quite rich.

The contract was actually signed a little later in July. More elaborate than that for *Poems*, it had been drawn up by the law firm Markby, Wilde, and Johnson of Lincoln's Inn—a detail which suggests Wilde's growing sense of professionalism. Wilde's first contract with Mathews had stipulated a commission for the publisher. By contrast Lane, who was effectively the Bodley Head's business manager, agreed to meet all the costs of production of *The Sphinx* and to pay his author a royalty:

(1) The publishers shall pay the poet a royalty of 10% on the gross sum received on the sales rendering accounts every six months.
(2) The publishers shall determine all details respecting the publication, the price at which copies are to be sold and the number of copies for publication in this country, America and elsewhere.
(3) The artist will before the 1st day of October 1892 submit to the publishers for their approval ten designs for decorating colouring and fully illustrating the Poem also specimens of paper or other material and binding.
(4) The artist will execute and see to the reproduction of the designs when approved and prepare for and superintend through the press the said work and will make arrangements for the supply of all materials and labour for printing issuing and binding the first and other editions thereof according to his own judgment but at the expense of the publishers with the stipulation that their total expenditure exclusive of advertisements sales and fees paid to the author and artist shall not exceed £150 for an edition of 300 copies or less and £50 per 100 for any larger number which they may decide to produce.
(5) The publishers shall pay to the artist the sum of £45 which shall be paid as follows £10 [£30 marked out by John Lane and £10 inserted] on the 18th of July 1892 and £10 on the eighteenth of each month until the total amount shall have been paid.
(6) The copyright of the work and of the illustrations and designs and of all future editions thereof shall belong absolutely to the publishers [Wilde has written in here: 'personally.' In the margin by (6) Wilde has written: 'the publishers are not to have the right to sell the copyright of the poem, without the poet's sanction.']35

It is clear from this contract that Mathews and Lane were prepared to commit significant resources to the production of *The Sphinx*. The sum set aside for artwork alone was nine times what had been spent on artwork for *Poems* (1892). More importantly, the

35 Quoted in Nelson, *The Early Nineties*, 96–7.

contract indicates the firm's intention to make Wilde their most expensive author to date. *The Sphinx*, like *Poems* (1892), was designed
to sell in small numbers but at very high prices: two guineas (42s.)
for the small-paper edition and five guineas (105s.) for the large-
paper. It is worth remembering that the majority of the Bodley
Head's books (those with larger print-runs) were priced more modestly: the average was 5s., but on occasions they cost as little as 2s.

Visually, *The Sphinx* was a sumptuous book. The text of both editions was printed in small capitals and in three different ink colours
throughout: the running title and the illustrations are in red, the
thirteen fancy capital letters beginning each section and the guide
words at the foot of the page are in bright green, and the text of the
poem itself is printed in black. Some pages have only two, four, or
five lines of text, although the reason for this seems to have been as
much economic as aesthetic. In a letter to Ricketts Wilde expressed
his concern that 'the pages are terribly few in number', and suggested that Ricketts 'put fewer verses on each page [so] we could
easily have four or five pages more'.[36] Both editions contained ten
illustrations or designs by Ricketts, eight of which were full-page.
The paper was hand-made, with uncut edges. Both editions were
bound in vellum boards with gilt designs, also by Ricketts. (The designs on the covers for the large edition are slightly bigger, and are
enclosed by a decorative gilt margin.)

Despite the opulent and ornate appearance of the book, and the
resources lavished on its production, *The Sphinx* was priced to be
very profitable. Details from the Bodley Head's final inventory
sheets and from their contract with Wilde allow us to calculate the
potential earnings for both the author and his publisher. It was
planned to sell the book in both Britain and North America. We
know from the Bodley Head records that initially 303 small-paper
and twenty-five large-paper copies were printed. Of these, only 200
copies of the small-paper edition were advertised for the British
market and fifty for the North American. It is unclear whether the
extra fifty copies printed were a safeguard against an unusually high
number of anticipated spoils in the production process, or whether
(and this seems more likely) a further 'edition' was planned—in the
contract the Bodley Head had reserved the right to determine 'any
larger number which they may decide to produce'. Details about

[36] *More Letters*, 123.

other books from the Bodley Head's inventory suggests that they may on occasions have engaged in sharp business practice in that they sometimes printed more copies (and perhaps planned more 'editions') than they actually advertised were for sale.

We know that both editions of *The Sphinx* were to be sold in America at a slightly higher price than in Britain, but as we do not have information about the projected destinations of the twenty-five large-paper copies, calculations about the economics of the book cannot be precise. None the less, if we make the conservative assumption that all returns were at the British price, then those economics are as follows. Had the volume been successful (a point to which we shall return), the large-paper edition would have grossed (at trade prices) £112 5s. The small-paper edition (also at trade prices) would have grossed £437 10s., giving a total gross to the firm of almost £550. Wilde's royalty on this trade price would have represented £55. The Bodley Head were contracted to pay Charles Ricketts £45 for designing the book, and had reserved a maximum of £150 for printing and production costs. No records survive for the costs of advertising, but working with figures based on the amounts spent on other Bodley Head books, it is unlikely to have been more than £10. If *The Sphinx* had sold out, then the Bodley Head stood to earn a handsome profit of slightly under £300, or over £1 a copy, averaged over both editions.

However, the volume did not sell well and, as Stephen Calloway has noted, many unsold copies were later destroyed at a fire at the warehouse of the printers, the Ballantyne Press.[37] Significantly, though, the relative failure of the book did not become apparent until late 1894, long after Wilde had made his major contractual commitment to the Bodley Head. The important point to bear in mind is that in July 1892, when the contract for *The Sphinx* was signed, the Bodley Head saw in Wilde's work the prospect of exceptional profits. The advantage for Wilde lay in the opportunity of combining generous royalties (without having to risk any of his own capital) with an exclusivity and distinction which he had long desired. More precisely, the Bodley Head seemed uniquely able to manufacture (and to sell) exactly the kind of decadent exoticism— books of 'gold smeared on tired purple'—with which Wilde

37 See Stephen Calloway, 'Wilde and the Dandyism of the Senses', in Peter Raby (ed.), *The Cambridge Companion to Oscar Wilde* (Cambridge: Cambridge University Press, 1997), 53.

identified but which other publishers (particularly Osgood, McIlvaine) had failed to market. In another letter of July 1892 to John Lane, in which he enclosed the agreement for *The Sphinx*, we find Wilde crowing about his new-found status as a 'poet' (rather than simply 'author', as the contract had originally identified him), in a manner reminiscent of his rebuff to Grant Richards in June of that year. Wilde described the projected *Sphinx* as 'very rare and curious'; he went on to explain that:

A book of this kind . . . must not be thrown into the gutter of English journalism. No book of mine, for instance, ever goes to the *National Observer*. I wrote to [W. E.] Henley to tell him so, two years ago. He is too coarse, too offensive, too personal, to be sent any work of mine . . . Where in a magazine of art, either French or English, we know that an important appreciation will be written, we can send a copy, but ordinary English newspapers are not merely valueless, but would do harm. . . . I hope *The Sphinx* will be a great success.[38]

The self-satisfaction of the letter testifies both to Wilde's pride in his book, and the use he made of it (together with *Poems* (1892)) to distance himself from the journalist and author of popular fiction he had been only a year earlier. In the summer of 1892, then, the Bodley Head was already playing a key role in defining and embodying an alternative image of Wilde as an 'artist', when that term was understood to mean a writer who addressed himself to a coterie, to that 'sect of perfect people'. We need to see the agency of the Bodley Head working in two ways: it made a certain image of creativity possible for Wilde in the sense that it demonstrated that a certain kind of exclusive market did exist for him; on the other hand, that process of marketing—decisions about prices, bindings, print-runs, and so on—was itself instrumental in shaping this new image of Wilde in the first instance. It seems that by the summer of 1892 Wilde was beginning to see himself in terms explicitly associated with Bodley Head books: that is, he was making himself *into* a Bodley Head author as much as allowing the Bodley Head to discover and make *him*. The 1893 contract with Mathews and Lane consolidated both this strategy and the image it promoted, but not before Wilde's relationship with the firm had been severely tested.

[38] *Letters*, 318–19.

II

Reaching agreement over *The Sphinx* in early July 1892 freed Wilde
to concentrate on finding a publisher for *Salomé*. As we argued in
Chapter 4, there is evidence that Wilde began preparations to publish the play almost as soon as a licence had been refused. It was
eventually brought out in Paris in February 1893 under the joint imprint of the Librairie de l'Art Indépendant and Elkin Mathews and
John Lane. The Bodley Head's involvement in this first French-
language publication of the play was, however, both limited and
fraught with misunderstandings. Given that Wilde was already negotiating with Mathews and Lane over the publication of *The
Sphinx*, it might be thought that he would have given them the first
refusal of *Salomé*, and that they would have been keen to accept the
play. He was, after all, clearly anxious to find a publisher as quickly
as possible, and knew that the Bodley Head was interested in his
work. The evidence, though, suggests that the firm did not become
formally involved until rather later, for a written agreement was not
forthcoming until well after negotiations had been finalized with the
Librairie.

As we suggested in Chapter 4, the publication of play-texts for
private reading was a specialized part of the publishing trade of the
1890s, and the reputation of the Bodley Head by contrast centred
(at least in 1892) on their specialist publications of poetry. The firm
had only one dramatic work on its list by 1892, John Todhunter's *A
Sicilian Idyll*, which had been published by Elkin Mathews in
November 1890 in editions of 250 small-paper and 50 large-paper
copies, priced at 5s. and 10s. 6d. respectively. It is possible, then,
that Wilde had initially approached Mathews and Lane, but they
had been unwilling to underwrite the costs of *Salomé*. *A Sicilian
Idyll* had been warmly received on its private staging in May 1890
and the volume sold reasonably well (some advertising of May 1894
records that 'very few' copies remained, but of course this evidence
might not be reliable). However, *A Sicilian Idyll* cannot be seen as a
precedent, because *Salomé* was a much more controversial work: it
had been given no staging and had received only negative publicity.[39] It is equally likely that Wilde himself may have felt that a
French publisher, or a house more experienced in producing dramatic works, was more appropriate for a play-text in French.

39 See Nelson, *The Early Nineties*, 228 and 284.

Correspondence (dated December 1892) with E. Bailly, the manager of the Librairie de l'Art Indépendant, indicates that Wilde had negotiated to print 600 'exemplaires ordinaires' and fifty 'exemplaires sur Hollande'; matters had probably been finalized during a short trip Wilde had made to Paris in early November 1892.[40] The precise terms of Wilde's agreement with his French publishers are unknown, but evidence (detailed below) indicates that the production costs were funded by Wilde, with the Librairie presumably taking a percentage of the profits, in a manner that had been usual for British publishers up to the early 1890s. Proofs for the volume were in hand by late December 1892 and the book was planned to appear in late January the following year.[41]

The first evidence of the Bodley Head's interest in the book derives from a letter dated early February 1893 in which Wilde reports to Lane that *Salomé* was to be ready 'in a fortnight' and offers to sell him 25 of the 50 large-paper copies at what he terms a 'proper reduction' from the projected 'sale price' of '10s.'. This letter shows that there was (as yet) no contract with the Bodley Head for copublication, for Wilde urgently requests from Lane 'a formal note about the whole thing, so as to have no misunderstanding about the agreement. Pray do this at once'. In the remainder of the letter Wilde lists other grievances, and this in turn suggests that he was not wholly satisfied with the Bodley Head's business arrangements with its authors. He claims that 'a large number of my poems are still unpaid for' (a legitimate complaint, given that almost a year had passed since *Poems* (1892) sold out). He also questions Lane about the firm's apparent delay in paying Ricketts for his artwork on Gray's *Silverpoints*. Finally, he asks (in a tone which suggests it was a repeated request), 'how *The Sphinx* is progressing, and what date it is likely to come out on'.[42]

Stung by Wilde's obvious impatience, Lane telegrammed a reply which Wilde accepted (later that month) as 'a formal record of our agreement'. It is obvious, though, that he was still not happy and complained to Lane once again in terms which make clear the sequence of events leading up to the Bodley Head's involvement in the French edition of *Salomé*. The letter is worth quoting at length:

[40] For the dates of Wilde's trip, see Ellmann, 322; for the exchange with Bailly about print-runs, see *Letters*, 324–5. See also Mason (374–5) for another letter referring to the agreement made during the Paris trip.

[41] See *Letters*, 324–5.   [42] Ibid. 326.

You see now, I feel sure, how right I was in continually pressing you for a written agreement, and I cannot understand why you would not do so. I spoke to you on the subject at your own place; you promised to forward the agreement the next day; this was in November last; I spoke to you twice about it at the Hogarth Club, you made the same promise. I wrote to you endless letters—a task most wearisome to me—on this plain business matter. I received promises, excuses, apologies, but no agreement. This has been going on for three months, and the fact of your name being on the title-page was an act of pure courtesy and compliment on my part: you ask me to allow it as a favour to you; just as my increasing numbers printed from 250 to 600 was done to oblige you. I make no profit from the transaction, nor do I derive any benefit. As you are interested in literature and curious works of art I was ready to oblige you . . . [W]hen I did not hear from you in Paris last week I very nearly struck your name off the title-page of the book, and diminished the edition. As you advertised it, however, I felt this would have been somewhat harsh and unkind to you.[43]

Wilde's acrimonious tone, reminiscent of the hectoring moments in *De Profundis*, betrays a curious mixture of aloofness from, and indebtedness to, the Bodley Head: he represents himself both as doing a personal favour to Lane while acknowledging that without the Bodley Head's imprint (and presumably their marketing expertise) the volume would be 'diminished'. Lane's side of this correspondence is not known, and it is therefore impossible to be certain of the reasons behind his reticence. If Wilde's report about the increased print-run is correct, then it suggests Lane had confidence in the volume, for he was anticipating British sales of up to 350 small-paper copies. Lane's later procrastination might have had something to do with the forthcoming revival that autumn of *Lady Windermere's Fan*; it was scheduled to begin on 31 October, at around the very time when (if Wilde's memory is correct) he was first discussing the possibility of publishing *Salomé* with Lane as well as finalizing negotiations with the Librairie. At this time Lane was probably keen to retain Wilde as a Bodley Head author; but, pragmatist that he was, he might also have been waiting for Wilde's reputation as a dramatist (rather than a poet) to be confirmed by the second London run of *Lady Windermere's Fan*. Wilde ends his letter on a conciliatory note, accepting Lane's 'regrets' and hoping that 'we may publish some other book of mine, but it must be clearly

---

[43] *Letters*, 327.

understood that the business matters are to be attended to by your firm properly and promptly'.

Two further letters from Wilde to Lane, also dated February 1893, confirm Lane's commitment to the volume, and his continued keenness to do business with Wilde. It is difficult to ascertain exactly how many copies of *Salomé* Lane bought for the Bodley Head to sell in Britain. In the February letter quoted above, Wilde offers him half of the fifty large-paper copies; in his next letter, he informs Lane that he has decided to put only twenty-five 'on the market' and thus reduces what he is prepared to offer to ten copies. Lane, however, asked for more, and in a further letter Wilde promised to 'get them', noting that Bailly's failure to number the edition offered the possibility of 'printing more'. A final letter in the sequence suggests that Lane ended up with at least fifteen large-paper copies (for which he paid 5s. each, at a total cost of £3 15s.). He had already agreed to pay Wilde £35 for what were (presumably) 350 small-paper copies; however, he requested an additional 150.[44] When the edition was published (on 22 February) with the joint imprint of the Librairie de l'Art Indépendant and the Bodley Head on the title page, it was advertised, according to a brief note made by Mason, as consisting of 600 copies with 500 for sale.[45] If Lane had received those extra 150 copies, and if his original purchase from Wilde had been 350 (as the February letter certainly suggests), then the total number of books on sale in Britain would have been exactly 500. However, this would have left no copies for sale in France (by the Librairie) unless Wilde released for sale all or part of the 'extra' 100 copies which remained from the print-run. Matters are further complicated by another letter from Bailly to Wilde, dated 23 December 1892, which indicates that in November, when drawing up the original agreement, Wilde had planned to print only 500 small-paper copies, and that at some later date he had increased this number to 600.[46] These figures do not square with Wilde's February letter to Lane in which he complained of having to increase the print-run beyond the original plan of 250. (Wilde may

44 Ibid. 329. In his research for a new edition of Wilde's correspondence, Merlin Holland has discovered a letter from Wilde to Lane in which Wilde refuses to supply the further 150 copies until he receives payment for the first 350.

45 Mason, 370. Mason's figures are confirmed by an advertisement in *The Bookman* which states that the 'first edition [is] limited to 600 copies (500 of which are for sale) for Paris and London'. *The Bookman*, III, no. 18 (March 1893), 169.   46 Mason, 374–5.

have exaggerated his inconvenience in order to embarrass Lane; alternatively it is possible that an initial distrust of Lane led Wilde to hold back on the projected print-run of 600 in case Lane did not buy the full 350 copies. No written agreement with Lane had been reached by December.)

At all events, the Bodley Head stood to make a decent profit on its dealings over *Salomé*. With purple paper covers (chosen according to Wilde to 'suit' the 'gilt-haired' Douglas),[47] muted silver lettering, and a title-page designed by the Belgian artist, Félicien Rops, depicting a Satanic woman with angel's wings and the tail of a fish, the volume was distinctive; but it was not nearly as elaborate as the Bodley Head's own books, and was priced (in Britain) quite modestly—at 5s. for the small-paper copy and 10s. 6d. for the large-paper copy.[48] The Bodley Head placed an advertisement for *Salomé* in the March 1893 issue of *The Bookman*; unlike *Poems* (1892), no attention was drawn to the bindings or cover design, but there was a quotation from the *Daily Chronicle* which warmly defended the work from the criticism of the Lord Chamberlain:

Mr Oscar Wilde has produced a remarkable little tragedy, powerfully conceived, and conveying a striking picture of one of the most conspicuous fragments of history. It is written with perfect reverence throughout . . . and there is no reason whatever why 'Salomé' should not be acted, and witnessed by everybody. The fact that the Lord Chamberlain refused it a licence is likely to confer upon this play a reputation for impropriety of thought or language which it in no way deserves. If Madame Bernhardt had acted it, 'Salomé' would have been one of the most thrilling and solemn dramatic spectacles that had been seen for many a day.[49]

Mathews and Lane may have been nervous about sales of this controversial work, but they need not have worried. There is no record of remaindered or unsold copies for the French language edition of *Salomé* in the final inventory sheets of the Bodley Head, so we can safely assume that the volume did sell out. If we refer to the pattern of their pricing of other books, we can estimate that the trade prices would have been 4s. 2d. and 8s. 9d. If Lane's £35 was for 350

47 *Letters*, 333.
48 Karl Beckson comments that Rops had also illustrated the works of Baudelaire, Péladan, and Barbey d'Aurevilly, and was best known for his 'explicit sexual depictions'. It is not clear who commissioned Rops's art-work, nor how much he was paid; Wilde, according to Beckson, did not know the artist personally. See *Encyclopedia*, 325.
49 *The Bookman*, III, no. 18 (March 1893), 169; the ellipses are in the advertisement.

small-paper copies, then he was paying Wilde 2s. per book. This would have given the Bodley Head a profit of 2s. 2d. per small-paper copy, and 3s. 9d. on the larger format. If Lane had sold only 350 books, then his total profit (minus an estimated £5 for advertising) would have been a little over £35. If, though, he had bought and sold the 500 copies of the small-paper edition which he requested, then his total profits would have been around £52.

Wilde's earnings are more difficult to calculate. The December letter from Bailly to Wilde which we mentioned earlier indicates that Wilde was originally charged 400 francs for printing both 500 small-paper and fifty large-paper copies, with an additional 50 francs for the extra 100 small-paper copies ('pour le 100 en sus que vous demandez').[50] Bailly's letter continues with a request for a further 200 francs to cover unexpected costs for paper and for delays which Wilde had caused. (This last detail is presumably a reference to the time taken to incorporate the corrections suggested by Marcel Schwob, which in turn necessitated more proofs and the need to keep type standing.) Wilde, then, paid at least 650 francs for the production of the volume, a sum which suggests costs of approximately 1 franc for each small-paper copy. The small-paper copies to be sold in France were priced at 10 francs each (we have no record of the price of the large-paper copy). Without knowing the trade price, the costs of advertising and of Rops's art-work, the percentage of profits taken by the Librairie de l'Art Indépendant, or indeed the precise numbers of copies for sale in France and whether they did in fact all sell, it is obviously impossible to calculate Wilde's profits with any precision. In his letter to Lane, Wilde claims that the copies for the Bodley Head would give him no extra 'benefit'. If Wilde is being truthful, then it may be that the 2s. per book Lane was paying him was equivalent to Wilde's profit after subtracting the production costs plus the percentage taken by the Librairie. If we make informed guesses for trade prices and advertising, then we can estimate that Wilde may have made a profit of some 4 francs on each small-paper copy. If 100 copies had sold in France, this would have given a total profit of 400 francs, a sum additional to the £35–£50 which he probably received from Lane.

These figures are only estimates based on limited and occasionally contradictory information. None the less, as with some of our

50 Mason, 375.

calculations of Wilde's theatrical earnings, their order of magnitude is likely to be accurate. More importantly, if they are correct, they go some way towards explaining why, in the spring of 1893, Lane would have been keen to secure Wilde's *oeuvre* for the Bodley Head and to publish him as a dramatist as well as a poet. As we show below, the 1893 contract was principally for dramatic works, and thus represented a new departure for the Bodley Head. The profits from the French edition of *Salomé*, although not enormous, may have settled any lingering uncertainties in Lane's mind about Wilde's marketability as a dramatic author. Likewise, it must have been equally clear to Wilde that however much he distrusted Lane personally—and his letters of February 1893 are marked by a constant sense of irritation at what Wilde perceived as Lane's bad faith—the Bodley Head was conspicuously successful in selling his work to the elite, connoisseur market which he could now afford to appeal to. The considerably higher sales of the French edition of *Salomé* in Britain (in contrast to those sold in France) was a clinching proof, were one necessary, of the Bodley Head's success in packaging Wilde.

III

The agreement Wilde signed with Mathews and Lane at the beginning of August 1893 is by far the most detailed of any of his known contracts. Set out as a letter on the firm's headed notepaper, and dated 3 August, it is reproduced below in full. The two details worth noting are the contract's comprehensiveness and the fact that its terms differ from work to work:

To Oscar Wilde Esq
Dear Sir
Lady Windermere's Fan: a play
A Woman of No Importance: a play
The Duchess of Padua: a play

We agree to publish the above plays undertaking the whole cost of printing advertising and publishing in an edition of 500 small paper and 50 large paper copies at the respective prices of 7/6 net and 15/- net. The books to have a binding designed for each of them by Mr Charles Shannon. *The Duchess of Padua* to have an introduction by Mr Edgar Fawcett which you will arrange for. We agree to pay you a royalty of 10% on the published price of all copies sold.

The incomparable history of Mr W. H.
We agree to publish this book on the same conditions as the foregoing with regard to expenses undertaken by ourselves and to pay you a royalty of 20% on the published price of all copies sold. The edition to consist of 500 small paper copies at 10/- net and 50 large paper copies at 21/- net and to have a binding and initial letters designed by Mr Charles Ricketts.

Salomé, done into English
We agree to publish this play on the same conditions as the foregoing with regards to expenses undertaken by ourselves. The edition to consist of 500 small paper copies at 15/- net and 100 large paper copies at 30/- net. Ten full page illustrations by Aubrey Beardsley will be produced at our expense: of these we agree to furnish you with clichés to be used only for an edition to be issued in Paris and in addition to these clichés we further agree to pay you for translating and royalty the sum of 1/- per copy on the small paper edition and 3/- per copy on the large paper edition.

We also agree to supply you with three large paper and seven small paper copies of each of the books gratuitously.

We stipulate that the royalties agreed upon in the foregoing shall only become payable as the books are sold and within one month after each quarter-day provided that the book on which the royalty is payable shall have been published at least one clear month previous to such quarter-day.
Yours faithfully
I agree to the above
[signed over a 6d. stamp]
Oscar Wilde[51]

Negotiations for publishing the works listed in this contract had begun several months earlier; a draft version of the whole contract had been drawn up as early as May.[52] Furthermore, two of the books, the English-language *Salome* and *Lady Windermere's Fan*, were already in production by early June. In a letter to Wilde, dated 8 June, Lane enclosed 'a specimen page of "Lady Windermere's Fan" ' for Wilde's 'approval'.[53] A few days later Wilde wrote to Ricketts (the partner of Shannon, who was providing the designs for the play) commenting that he was 'quite charmed with the setting ... it looks delightful and is exquisitely placed'. However, Wilde judged it to be 'too late in the season to publish now'.[54] In Lane's letter of 8 June to Wilde, we also find evidence that plans for the English-language *Salome* were well advanced, for Lane reported

[51] Clark Library. Wilde MSS; uncatalogued.
[52] See Nelson, *The Early Nineties*, 244.
[53] *OWR*, 84.   [54] *Letters*, 341.

that he had just succeeded in commissioning Aubrey Beardsley to do the artwork. The sequence of events by which Lane's procrastination in the autumn of 1892 over the French-language *Salomé* was translated by the spring of 1893 into a commitment to publish what was effectively an *oeuvre* is not wholly clear. As we suggested earlier, the success of the French-language *Salomé* played a role; but another spur was probably the staging of *A Woman of No Importance*. It began its run at the Haymarket on 19 April, and its success would have been conspicuous at around the time when the draft contract was drawn up. The addition of *The Duchess of Padua* and 'The Portrait of Mr W. H.' to the list of proposed publications may have been at Wilde's insistence. Unlike the other works in the contract, both of these were relatively untested: *The Duchess of Padua* had yet to receive a British staging and no one at the firm had seen a manuscript for the extended version of 'The Portrait of Mr W. H.'

The contract specifies that the works were to be brought out in virtually uniform numbers: all were to be issued in 500 small-paper copies and all but one in fifty large-paper copies. These figures represent over double the number of copies for *Poems* (1892) as well as double the number of copies planned for *The Sphinx*. They suggest a growing confidence on the part of Mathews and Lane and confirm the evidence described above about the Bodley Head's likely purchase (and successful sales) of 500 copies of the French-language edition of *Salomé*. On the other hand, the pricing varied considerably from volume to volume. It appears that for marketing purposes Mathews and Lane were dividing Wilde's works into discrete categories. The dramatic texts (with the exception of *Salome*) were by the far the cheapest, at 7s. 6d. and 15s. for the small and large formats respectively. A letter from Shannon to Lane, written some time before the draft agreement was drawn up, reports that Wilde had agreed 'very wisely' to the price of '7/6 net' for the ordinary edition of *Lady Windermere's Fan*, but he had preferred a higher price of '1 guinea [21s.]', rather than 'the uniform price of 10/6', for the 'limited Edition de luxe'.[55] Wilde, it seems, wished to retain the exclusivity conferred by the high pricing of *The Sphinx* and *Poems*. The final price of 15s. may have been a compromise. Interestingly the figures specified in the August contract are in line with the Bodley Head's pricing of other dramatic works, including their

55 Nelson, *The Early Nineties*, 244.

plans for a new edition of John Davidson's *Plays*. Although Davidson's volume appeared in 1894, the terms had been negotiated in November 1893—that is, just a few months after agreement had been reached with Wilde. Davidson's contract also specified 'an edition not to exceed 500 copies at 7/6 net'.[56] The only other play-texts published by the Bodley Head at this time were two volumes by Michael Field: *Stephania* had been issued in an edition of 250 in 1892, priced 6s., and *A Question of Memory* appeared in November 1893 in a smaller edition of just 120 copies.[57] It seems that the Bodley Head's involvement in the market for play-texts was limited and cautious. Nevertheless, there is evidence that, in early 1893, they were beginning to develop a list with some coherence to it. As Nelson notes, three out of the four authors on it—Wilde, Michael Field, and Todhunter—had some form of association with Jacob Grein's Independent Theatre and with what Yeats termed the 'higher drama'. Davidson's plays had not been performed, but they were experimental in the sense that Davidson saw himself as attempting to evolve a new dramatic form for the future. Moreover, Davidson was already a Bodley Head author; in early 1893 the firm had issued his *Fleet Street Eclogues* with some success. Finally, in June 1894 the Bodley Head published Allan Monkhouse's *Books and Plays*, a volume which defended the influence of Ibsen on contemporary English dramatists.

The uniform pricing and print-runs planned for Davidson's and Wilde's plays strongly suggest that Mathews and Lane had in mind a common marketing strategy for them. Further evidence that these books were being thought of as a group is to be seen in Beardsley's frontispiece for Davidson's volume which included a caricature of Wilde. Wilde's plays in their turn were also designed to form a collectable set and were advertised as numbered volumes. There is evidence, though, that Wilde had initially been against this idea:

[56] Ibid. 231. As Nelson points out, Davidson's collection of three plays was originally published privately in 1889; a second edition was issued by T. Fisher Unwin in 1890. This sold poorly, and the remaining sheets were acquired by the Bodley Head and first brought out with their imprint (and with a new title) in 1893. The same year the firm also re-issued remainders of two other plays by Davidson. The Bodley Head's 1894 *Plays* (referred to here) contained all five works and was a new edition, with a frontispiece by Aubrey Beardsley.

[57] We have found no record of the price of this volume, but it is likely to have been in the five to six shilling range, in line with other volumes of Michael Field's work published by Elkin Mathews and by the Bodley Head. Michael Field was, of course, the pseudonym of Katharine Bradley and Edith Cooper, her niece.

Shannon's letter to Lane, quoted earlier, reported that 'Oscar is averse to the idea of their [i.e. *Lady Windermere's Fan*, *A Woman of No Importance*, and *The Duchess of Padua*] being all bound in the same cover'.[58] Nevertheless the small-paper copies of *Lady Windermere's Fan* (Volume I) and *A Woman of No Importance* (Volume II) were produced with identical red-brown linen boards, gilt-lettering and generically similar embossed gold floret motifs designed by Shannon. The same was true of the large-paper copies, the only difference being that they were more expensively bound in yellow buckram. Interestingly, the design and materials were reproduced exactly by Leonard Smithers in his later editions of *An Ideal Husband* and *The Importance of Being Earnest* (Smithers did, though, have larger print-runs and charged higher prices for the large-paper editions).

The Duchess of Padua was never published in Wilde's lifetime. As we have indicated in Chapter 4, after writing the play in 1883, Wilde had made persistent and strenuous attempts to promote it with theatrical managers in both Britain and the United States; his efforts had been rewarded when the play was eventually staged (albeit briefly) in New York in 1891. It is therefore not surprising that the work was included in the 1893 contract. Significantly there appears to have been no interest in reprinting *Vera*, which had not been restaged (apart from some touring performances) since Marie Prescott's failed New York production a decade earlier. *The Duchess of Padua* was announced as Volume III in the set of Wilde's playtexts, and was advertised as appearing 'shortly' in both the Bodley Head's May 1894 book list, and later in October 1894 (when Lane had taken sole ownership of the Bodley Head name).

However, there is no evidence that these plans for publication were ever put into practice. Shannon's letter to Lane, written in the spring of 1893 (and quoted above), reported the 'order of plays' as:

1 Lady Windermere's Fan
2 The Duchess of Padua
3 The [*sic*] Woman of No Importance

He then added a note, instructing Lane that 'he had better write to [Wilde] concerning the proper order'—presumably a reference to rescheduling *The Duchess of Padua* as Volume III in the set.[59] When

---

58 Nelson, *The Early Nineties*, 244.   59 Ibid.

originally discussing terms with Mathews and Lane, Wilde may have been under the impression that the Bodley Head possessed a stronger commitment to *The Duchess of Padua* than was actually the case. It seems likely that the firm's interest in Wilde as a dramatic author rested mainly on those two plays which had been West End successes. When the firm was on the point of dissolution in the summer of 1894, Wilde reminded Mathews and Lane of their 'obligation to me to publish my five-act tragedy, *The Duchess of Padua*'. He also noted that they had 'never seen, nor expressed any desire to see a manuscript'—an observation which once again suggests that Mathews and Lane had been less than assiduous in their efforts to publish the work, and may have always harboured some doubts over its commercial prospects.[60] Wilde's reference to a manuscript is interesting, because twenty copies of the play had been privately printed in 1883 for theatrical purposes, although, as we noted in Chapter 4, Wilde had heavily revised it for Lawrence Barrett's New York production. It is not clear, then, what the published text of *The Duchess of Padua* would have been, nor whether it had ever been in any fit state for publication. Following what he calls the 'ransacking' of Tite Street after Wilde's bankruptcy proceedings, Wilfred Hugh Chesson describes buying Wilde's own copy of *The Duchess of Padua* in a bookshop in Chelsea and delivering it to Wilde in Paris on 5 July 1898.[61] Later that month Wilde sent a postcard to Ross confirming Ross's view that '*The Duchess* is unfit for publication'; Wilde went on to explain that it was 'the only one of my works that comes under that category. But there are some good lines in it'. Ross himself reported that a few months before his death Wilde acceded to this judgement, suggesting the play was 'unworthy of me'.[62] All of this indicates that Wilde may have had doubts about *The Duchess of Padua*, although it does not seem that he was prepared to admit them openly to Mathews and Lane.

The details in the contract relating to a new, English-language edition of *Salome* suggest that this volume, in contrast to the other play-texts, was conceived (and priced) to stand alongside Wilde's 'decadent' books: *Poems* (1892) and *The Sphinx*. The 10 per cent

---

[60] *Letters*, 367.

[61] Chesson's 'reminiscence' appeared originally in the Dec. 1911 issue of the New York *Bookman*; it is reprinted in *More Letters*, 197–8.

[62] See *Letters*, 757 and note. Ross must have disagreed, for he published the play in his 1908 edn.

royalty which Wilde was offered on his other plays was standard for the Bodley Head, and it promised to earn him (if the editions sold out) £22 10s. for each work. The terms for *Salome* were more generous, reflecting Wilde's anticipated work on the translation: they promised earnings of £40. However, Wilde's actual income from this book turned out to be larger, for the Bodley Head printed (and sold) more copies of *Salome* than specified in the contract, and more than they had advertised (their book lists indicate an edition of 500 small-paper copies). The firm's inventory sheets reveal that 755 small-paper copies were printed (200 of which were intended for sale in America), together with 125 large-paper copies; of these 605 of the small-paper and 115 of the large-paper copies had already been sold at the time of the dissolution of the partnership in the summer of 1894. These sales raised Wilde's earnings from the English-language edition of *Salome* to £47 10s.; the Bodley Head's profit-margin was a handsome £432 13s.—as we noted earlier, the English-language *Salome* turned out to be the firm's most profitable book.[63]

Profits aside, the actual production of *Salome* was complex and fraught, and was the cause of yet more ill-feeling between Wilde and Lane. One set of difficulties concerned the translation. The contract clearly nominates Wilde as the anticipated translator of his own text. However, at some point Wilde decided to let Douglas do the work—an unwise choice, because Wilde was less than satisfied with the result. In *De Profundis*, Wilde referred to Douglas's 'schoolboy faults' and declared the translation 'unworthy' of him 'as an ordinary Oxonian'. (This was a reference intended to contrast with Wilde's Oxford scholarship—a 'classical demyship'; Douglas was, however, less than ordinary in that he never took a degree.)[64] Douglas had his own version of events, and in his *Autobiography* vigorously defended his text, pointing to the time and care he had taken over it. He also claimed that Aubrey Beardsley (who had been commissioned to provide illustrations) then offered Wilde his own services as translator, but that Beardsley's efforts were also dismissed as 'utterly hopeless'. Wilde, according to Douglas, then reverted to his (that is Douglas's) text, to which he made but 'a few alterations'. As Karl Beckson notes, there is unfortunately no evidence to corroborate any elements of Douglas's account, and the

[63] For details, see Nelson, *The Early Nineties*, 109.   [64] *Letters*, 432.

textual provenance of the English-language *Salome* therefore remains open to question.[65] It is worth noting, however, that although the book was dedicated to Douglas, his name (as translator) was removed from the title-page; moreover, it is significant that (as we have noted) the August contract clearly specifies Wilde as the translator—according to the Bodley Head inventory sheets, he was paid the full sum for the royalty and translation. Both these facts suggest that Wilde had considerable control over the published work.

A second and equally serious set of difficulties emerged over Beardsley's artwork. Wilde's illustrators of choice had previously been Ricketts and Shannon: the latter was to provide designs for the Bodley Head editions of the Society Comedies, the former had worked on *Intentions*, *Lord Arthur Savile's Crime and Other Stories*, *Dorian Gray*, *A House of Pomegranates*, the Bodley Head *Poems*, and was contracted to work on *The Sphinx*. It is not clear whether it was Lane who first suggested Beardsley; but either he, or Wilde, may have been prompted by Beardsley's striking drawing 'J'ai baisé ta bouche', which appeared in the first issue of *The Studio* in April 1893 (and which in a slightly different version became 'The Climax' in the Bodley Head *Salome*). The Bodley Head agreed to pay Beardsley fifty guineas (£52 10s.) for the illustrations. This sum was significantly larger than the royalties Wilde would have received if the planned editions of 500 small-paper and 100 large-paper copies had sold out, and over seven pounds more than Ricketts was paid for designing and illustrating *The Sphinx*. A letter from Lane to Wilde, dated 8 June 1893 (and already quoted), suggests that securing Beardsley's agreement was viewed, by Lane at least, as something of a coup: 'I have this day seen Beardsley and arranged for 10 plates and a cover for 50 guineas!' he boasted. When Beardsley delivered his artwork the following November, both Lane and Wilde were unhappy, and a number of the drawings had to be changed. In a letter to Ross written later in 1893, Beardsley (referring to what he termed the '*Salome* Row' over his original cover design), described himself as having had 'a warm time of it between Lane and Oscar and Co'. He added that 'for one week the numbers of telegraph and messenger boys who came to the door was simply scandalous', and

[65] Alfred Douglas, *Autobiography* (1929; London: Martin Secker, 1931), 160. See also *Encyclopedia*, 325.

confirmed that 'Bozie's [*sic*] name is not to turn up on the Title'.[66] Wilde himself, in a telegram to More Adey, talked of the 'wicked Lane' having been 'routed with slaughter'—a comment which suggests that there was as much friction between Wilde and his publisher, as between either of them and Beardsley.[67]

The text for *Salome* was set up by 13 November and by December, Lane had chosen the binding for the small-paper edition.[68] Once again, Wilde's reaction was less than enthusiastic, and in a caustic letter he berated Lane for his lack of taste:

The cover of *Salome* is quite dreadful. Don't spoil a lovely book. Have simply a folded vellum wrapper with the design in scarlet—much cheaper, and much better. The texture of the present cover is coarse and common: it is quite impossible and spoils the real beauty of the interior. Use up this horrid Irish stuff for stories, etc: don't inflict it on a work of art like *Salome*. It really will do you a great deal of harm. Everyone will say that it is coarse and inappropriate. I loathe it. So does Beardsley.[69]

If we remember the care which Mathews had taken over the cover designs for *Poems*, Wilde's sense of grievance at Lane's high-handedness does seem understandable. Certainly, it does not appear that Lane had bothered to consult him on the matter. Interesting, too, is Wilde's reference to the appropriateness of 'coarse and common' covers for mere 'stories': Ward, Lock's 6s. edition of *Dorian Gray* had been bound in rough grey boards. As we suggested earlier, Wilde's experience of luxury materials and good design seems to have played an intimate role in his attempt, from 1892 onwards, to distance himself from his earlier life as a writer of popular fiction. Lane's tastelessness may have threatened that careful process of redefinition. Nevertheless Wilde's letter seems not to have had any effect, for when the book was published on 9 February 1894, it was bound in coarse-grained blue canvas boards with lettering on the spine and Beardsley's cover design in gilt. The large-paper edition, though, was more luxurious with green silk boards. As we noted earlier, the book sold well, although it received few significant notices in the English press, apart from a review in the *Studio*. That journal, while it liked the binding and printed a full-size reproduction of Beardsley's 'The Peacock Girl' (from *Salome*), none the less

---

[66] The letter is printed in Margery Ross (ed.), *Robert Ross, Friend of Friends* (London: Jonathan Cape, 1952), 28–9; 28. This version is slightly different from that given in *Letters*, 344.

[67] *Letters*, 347.

[68] See Nelson, *The Early Nineties*, 242.

[69] *Letters*, 348.

found nothing to say about the text and little to admire in the art-work, concluding archly that 'all collectors of rare and esoteric literature will rank this book as one of the most remarkable produc-tions of the modern press'.[70]

The last work included in Wilde's contract with the Bodley Head was the extended version of 'The Portrait of Mr W. H.', given the slightly revised title of *The incomparable history of Mr W. H.* The complex history of this work's composition has been painstakingly put together by Horst Schroeder.[71] The first version of 'The Portrait of Mr W. H.' was as a short story, probably written in early 1889, and published in *Blackwood's Edinburgh Magazine* in July that year (it may have been refused earlier by Frank Harris for the *Fortnightly Review*). As Schroeder points out, apart from a couple of hostile reviews, opinion was generally favourable. Wilde wrote to William Blackwood almost immediately (on 7 July) declining the suggestion that it be reprinted in *Tales from Blackwood*, and instead urged bringing it out in a 'special volume of essays'. When Blackwood hesitated, Wilde then suggested enlarging it for publica-tion by itself as 'a dainty little volume'.[72] Blackwood's response has unfortunately not survived, but it is likely to have offered Wilde some encouragement. According to Ricketts (who had provided a portrait to be used as a possible frontispiece) Wilde had an ex-panded version of the story ready for publication by the early au-tumn of 1889. Schroeder, however, argues that some details of the expanded version must have been added at a later date, and that Wilde must have continued working on it until at least the summer of 1891, and probably beyond that. It is not clear whether Wilde ever offered the expanded story to Blackwood; nor whether he tried other publishers. The 1893 contract with the Bodley Head is the first (and only) evidence of any publisher's commitment to it as a book.

The draft agreement with the Bodley Head, drawn up in May, is virtually identical to the August contract, and suggests that *The in-comparable history of Mr W. H.* was always conceived as an expensive book. (The only difference is that the draft specifies a price of 10s. 6d. against the contract's figure of 10s.; the advertised price of the

[70] 'New Publications', *The Studio*, 2 (1894), 185.

[71] See Horst Schroeder, *Oscar Wilde, 'The Portrait of Mr W. H.'—Its Composition, Publication and Reception* (Braunschweig: Technische Universität Carolo-Wilhelmina zu Braunschweig, 1984).

[72] See *Letters*, 246–7, and Schroeder, *Oscar Wilde, 'The Portrait of Mr W. H.'*, 22.

small-paper edition reverted to the original suggestion of 10s. 6d.)[73] Modern critics tend to see the additions to 'The Portrait of Mr W. H.' as an attempt to change its identity from a work of fiction— a short story—into literary criticism, a view consonant with Wilde's initial decision to republish it in a volume of essays. It is not certain, however, that this is how Mathews and Lane viewed the work. At first glance it seems to fit generically and stylistically with the other critical works on their list, several of which had a degree of eccentricity to them. It is possible to see these publications as companions to Wilde's, but they were noticeably cheaper than the price planned for his volume: Kenneth Grahame's *Pagan Papers* and John Davidson's *A Random Itinerary* were only 5s; at 8s. 6d. John Addington Symonds's *In the Key of Blue* was more expensive, but still less than *The incomparable history of Mr W. H.* would have been. By the same token, it is hard to see the work fitting in with the firm's plans for their fiction list. The Bodley Head list for 1893–4 contains very little fiction, but the titles which had been printed (including the first numbers in what was later to be Lane's Key Notes series) were, at 3s. 6d, once again relatively cheap. The high price for Wilde's 'story'—if story it is—thus sets it apart from both the Bodley Head's fiction and criticism. Perhaps the book was to have been a one-off, its price justified by Ricketts's artwork as much as Wilde's prose. That price does suggest that the market for Wilde's works was seen to be rather different from those of other authors. It is tempting to see Mathews and Lane making a distinction between the plays (which were more conventional) and the more rarefied, decadent works—*Poems*, *The Sphinx*, *Salome*, and perhaps the planned *The incomparable history of Mr W. H.*—for which they could charge higher prices. From Wilde's point of view, *The incomparable history of Mr W. H.* had the potential to be the most profitable of the group, for the generous royalty of 20 per cent would have earned him £60 10s.

The incomparable history of Mr W. H. was first advertised in the Bodley Head's 1893 autumn list of new books, where it was described as being 'in rapid preparation'.[74] However, later correspondence

---

73 The large-paper edition of *Lady Windermere's Fan* (1893) carries in its end-matter an announcement for: '*The Portrait of Mr W. H.: The incomparable and ingenious History of Mr W. H.*; initial letters and cover design by Charles Ricketts. 500 copies. 10/6d.'.

74 See Schroeder, *Oscar Wilde, 'The Portrait of Mr W. H.'*, 29. The list printed as part of the end-matter of John Davidson's *Fleet Street Eclogues* (1893), for example, suggests that

between Wilde, Mathews, and Lane flatly contradicts this claim, for at the time of the dissolution of the partnership, in August 1894, the book was nowhere near ready. Mathews and Lane had allowed their authors to choose how their works were to be distributed between the two partners when they broke up. Wilde wrote to the Bodley Head in August declaring that he wanted his plays to remain with Lane, and '*Mr W. H.*' to go to Mathews, on the grounds that such an arrangement 'would give an opportunity of making some alterations in the usual issue and price' for the planned enlarged version. Wilde continued: '300 or 250, and 50 large-paper would be better. Also the book should be a guinea. These, at least, are Mr Ricketts's views. This book should be out by the end of October.'[75] Wilde seems to be proposing that the print-run (as specified in the original contract) of 500 small-paper and 100 large-paper copies be halved. It is not clear to which issue his proposed price of 'a guinea' refers, but the context suggests that he may have wanted to double the price of the small-paper edition, from 10s. to 21s., in order to compensate for the reduced print-run. What is obvious, though, is that Wilde must have sensed Lane's and Mathews's misgivings about the volume—the poor sales of *The Sphinx* would by now have been apparent—and he may have been offering a compromise which would minimize their financial risks without fundamentally affecting the book's profitability. It is worth remembering that at this time Wilde was desperately short of money, and could not afford for the book simply to be dropped. This sequence of events would also explain Wilde's decision to give *Mr W. H.* to Mathews: his experience with *Poems* (1892)—200 copies priced at 15s.—might have indicated to him that Mathews was the partner more committed to marketing luxury editions.

A further letter of 3 September from Wilde to Mathews suggests that Mathews had responded to Wilde's proposition by asking whether he in fact might take the plays, and Lane *Mr W. H.* 'I have no objection at all to your having the plays', Wilde wrote, 'and hope they will be a success in your hands.'[76] On 7 September Wilde

Mr W. H. was in as advanced a state of preparation as *Lady Windermere's Fan* (end-matter, 13).

[75] *More Letters*, 124.

[76] *Letters*, 365. Hart-Davis comments that Wilde made a slip in this letter, by addressing it to Mathews instead of Lane. In fact correspondence from Lane to Wilde (printed in *More Letters*, 124–5) reveals that Wilde did make a slip, but not the one which Hart-Davis assumes. The letter is indeed addressed to Mathews; Wilde's slip occurs when he comments 'let

received another letter, this time from Lane, which contained bad news. Lane, it seems, had not been happy with Mathews's endeavours to reverse the terms of Wilde's original arrangements. In what seems to be an attempt to retain the plays for himself, Lane reported that he had agreed to give them up to Mathews, but only on the condition that Mathews also take *Mr W. H.*, a proposition which he presumably knew Mathews would reject. Lane explained the sequence of events to Wilde in a manner unflattering to his former partner:

it now appears that Mr Mathews has again communicated with you on the subject and he declines to have *Mr W. H.* at 'any price', but he wants the plays. Since I have pointed out that if he takes the plays he must also take *Mr W. H.* he declines both.

For my part I am perfectly willing to publish your plays and *Mr W. H.* provided I see and approve the latter before it is printed, but I am sure that you as a man of the world would not expect me or any other publisher to issue a book he had never seen.[77]

These exchanges indicate that while both partners wanted Wilde's plays, neither was keen on *Mr W. H.*, certainly on its own. Wilde was understandably annoyed, and wrote a bitter letter to both partners in which he reminded them of the precise details of the 1893 contract in which they had undertaken to publish *Mr W. H.*, pointing out that '[f]or the firm to break their agreement with me would be dishonourable, dishonest, and illegal'. However, after this angry outburst, Wilde suddenly offered a 'compromise': for '£25' Mathews and Lane could be 'let off' their 'agreement'.[78] This change of tactic seems odd, until we remember (as Wilde surely must have done) that just a few weeks earlier (in August) he himself had been in the process of renegotiating the terms of publication for *Mr W. H.*—evidence, as we have said, that he too shared some of Mathews's and Lane's doubts about the commercial viability of the work. Twenty-five pounds was considerably less than Wilde might have expected to receive in royalties had the original plans gone ahead, and the editions sold out. On the other hand, if the number of copies to be printed had been revised downwards (as the August letter indicates), but if their prices had been unchanged from the

Mr Mathews have "Mr W. H" '; this should be 'Mr Lane'. It is only this sequence of events which makes sense of Wilde's comments that he hopes the 'plays will be a success' in Mathews's hands; his earlier dealings with the plays had, of course, been with Lane.

77 *More Letters*, 125.   78 *Letters*, 366.

original contract, then Wilde could have counted on earnings of only £35–£40, a sum which makes the request for an immediate and assured £25 a reasonable bargain for both sides.

A curt letter followed from the Bodley Head which clarified matters: Lane would assume sole responsibility for honouring all the terms of the 1893 contract. Wilde's complaints were also dismissed on the grounds that he had never submitted to the firm the manuscript of *Mr W. H.*[79] Once again Wilde responded angrily. He pointed out that the manuscript had been in the hands of Ricketts for 'more than a year', and that Mathews and Lane had not been as exacting about his other works, accepting both *Salomé* and *The Duchess of Padua* without seeing a manuscript in advance. This claim was only partly true: the Bodley Head had already co-published the French-language version of *Salomé*, and could therefore be reasonably confident about the prospect of an English translation. *Lady Windermere's Fan* and *A Woman of No Importance* had appeared on the stage, and texts of them therefore existed. *The Duchess of Padua* and *Mr W. H.* were the only two works which Lane bought on trust; but they were also the only two never published. Several more letters were exchanged between Wilde, Mathews, and Lane: in all of them Wilde continued to insist that the 'arrangement to publish "Mr W. H." . . . be honourably and strictly kept'.[80] By the end of September, when it seemed that matters had finally been resolved, one further and unexpected complication arose: a letter from Wilde to Lane indicates that Ricketts was no longer available to design what Wilde referred to as his 'dainty book'. Lane was instructed to find 'someone else', before 'we proceed to our other schemes'.[81]

Whether Lane found—or even tried to find—another designer is unknown, but he did 'proceed to other schemes', for he continued with the publication of *A Woman of No Importance* in October 1894. Wilde's trials in the spring of 1895 halted any further publication of his works by either partner. However, it is difficult to avoid the conclusion that, had he set his mind to it, and had finished texts of both works existed, Lane could have published *Mr W. H.* and indeed *The Duchess of Padua* before the middle of 1895—the gap of time between late September and May was ample for both projects. It is hard not to agree with Wilde's own conclusion that the firm was 'not really interested' in either work.

[79] *More Letters*, 125.   [80] *Letters*, 368.   [81] *More Letters*, 127.

The trials, then, perhaps relieved both partners of unpleasant decisions. Wilde's imprisonment marked the end of his association with the Bodley Head (the tradename had now become the property of John Lane alone). Although he had no plans to publish any further books by Wilde, Mathews was even quicker than Lane to dissociate himself from Wilde. On 8 April 1895, Mathews wrote to *The Times* about Wilde's relationship with Edward Shelley, a former employee of the Bodley Head who was to be a witness against Wilde. Mathews claimed to 'know nothing of Mr Oscar Wilde except in a business capacity by publishing his *Lady Windermere's Fan* etc.', and declared that 'for several months I have ceased to be the publisher of any of Mr Oscar Wilde's books'.[82] The decision of both Mathews and Lane, acting as separate and independent publishers, to 'drop' Wilde may strike the modern reader as a form of bad faith; but from a commercial point of view, it was entirely understandable. It has been argued by many critics that Wilde's trials changed the literary and cultural map of Britain in the sense that it redrew the boundaries of acceptable taste: *The Yellow Book* folded, and the decadent sensibility associated with it became unmarketable. The merits of the work aside, it is quite possible to see *Mr W. H.* as simply a casualty of these changed conditions.[83]

The relationship between Mathews, Lane, and Wilde ended abruptly and on a sour note, but how exactly had Wilde benefited from that collaboration of just thirty-six months? First, the Bodley Head offered Wilde better terms than any of his other publishers, even though he was less than happy with some of their business practices. Wilde never earned large sums of money from his Bodley Head books, but in the summer of 1893 when he signed over his *oeuvre* to the firm, earnings from the theatre had almost certainly changed his attitude towards the profitability of books. At that moment, the value of the Bodley Head to Wilde lay principally in their success in creating an image and a style that allowed him to identify himself as a literary artist writing for a coterie—for his 'sect of perfect people'. Importantly, however, that identity and image was the

---

[82] Quoted in *Letters*, 312.

[83] We have suggested that the fatal delay in publishing *Mr W. H.* was probably due to Mathews's and Lane's doubts about its viability. However, it is possible that Wilde himself may have been partly to blame, in that he may not ever have brought the work to a state in which it was ready for publication. As we discuss in Ch. 7, the provenance of the one manuscript of the enlarged version of the story which has survived is doubtful.

outcome of decisions made about the materiality of his books—that is, their production values and their prices. The Bodley Head as a firm traded explicitly on these qualities, and their own advertising often quoted reviews which drew attention to them. For example, the large-paper edition of *Lady Windermere's Fan* (1893) glows with self-congratulation, and its end-matter reprints a tribute from the *St James's Gazette*:

To MESSRS. ELKIN MATHEWS AND JOHN LANE almost more than to any other, we take it, are the thanks of the grateful singer especially due; for it is they who have managed, by means of limited editions and charming workmanship, to impress book-buyers with the belief that a volume may have an aesthetic and commercial value. They have made it possible to speculate in the latest discovered poet, as in a new company—with the difference that an operation in the former can be done with three half-crowns.[84]

The paradox of the Bodley Head is laid bare in this advertising: initially it is claimed that a book's aesthetic value determines its commercial value, a position that in public Wilde was only too happy to corroborate. The concession, however, that the Bodley Head 'made it possible to speculate in the latest discovered poet' suggests that the relationship was in practice exactly the reverse, that material rarity stood for aesthetic value. In private, and particularly in his letters to Lane, Wilde disclosed that he was thoroughly implicated in this commodification of aesthetic value. His insistence that his books were to be produced as lavishly and priced as expensively as possible reveals that he was deeply alert to the fact that—in his own words—'his wares' were in a highly competitive 'market-place', and that what he called 'the public' and 'the idle' would have to be content merely 'to gape' at them.[85]

---

[84] *Lady Windermere's Fan* (1893), end-matter, 2.
[85] The quotations are, of course, taken from Wilde's review of Rossetti; see n. 2 above.

6

Post-Prison and Posthumous Works

It is tempting to understand Wilde's three trials as marking the final watershed of his life, and in so doing to endorse the judgement of Mathews and Lane that after them neither Wilde the personality nor Wilde the author were marketable. This perception of events is only partly correct. Wilde's arrest did compromise his reputation, and he was never again in his lifetime to be the dramatist whose satire was performed on the West End stage. Although *An Ideal Husband* and *The Importance of Being Earnest* did not close immediately after the case against Queensberry collapsed, neither production survived Wilde's prosecution. Moreover, none of the Society Comedies were revived until several years after his death. In a similar manner, mainstream publishers followed Mathews and Lane in shunning Wilde's name in a kind of literary black-balling which persisted until 1905 when Methuen published Ross's abridged edition of *De Profundis*. However, Wilde the writer did not disappear altogether. Paradoxically, his most successful book—if success is to be understood in terms of the number of copies sold—was a post-prison work, *The Ballad of Reading Gaol* (1898), which ran to six editions in only five months. It seems that Wilde was still a marketable author after his disgrace, but different strategies (and different publishers) were required to sell his work.

There had been what amounted to a rehearsal for these strategies in the two books by Wilde published by Arthur Humphreys, a bookseller and a friend of both Wilde and Constance: these works, both of which appeared in the first half of 1895, were *Oscariana*—a small anthology of Wilde's aphorisms—and the book version of 'The Soul Of Man Under Socialism'. Little is known of the circumstances surrounding the commissioning of either of them. Ellmann suggests that the arrangement for Humphreys to publish both books was made as early as the summer of 1894, a claim that is partly

borne out by a letter which Wilde wrote to Humphreys from
Worthing where he was holidaying during August and September
that year. In his letter Wilde enclosed what he called 'permissions'
(presumably to reprint excerpts from works already published) and
confirmed that he had not 'parted with the copyright of my books'.
Wilde also reminded Humphreys that he had not yet received his
'£50'.[1] The sum was probably a fee or an advance royalty, although
it is not clear whether it was for one or both books. Whatever the
case, it was still a generous commission, for both editions were initially printed in runs of only 50 copies, and unlike the limited editions of Wilde's Bodley Head books, both were priced cheaply.
There has been speculation by biographers of Constance that
Humphreys was motivated by personal rather than commercial
considerations. As we have said, he was a friend of both Wildes, and
there is evidence that he and Constance, if not actually conducting
an affair, were certainly extremely close to each other.[2] At all events
Humphreys could not have been unaware of the financial difficulties
of the Wilde household. It is worth recalling that in the summer of
1894, when he was trying to interest George Alexander in the scenario of *Earnest*, Wilde had asked (in July) for a '£150' advance, complaining 'I am so pressed for money that I don't know what to do'.
In August, in a letter to Charles Spurrier Mason, he was even more
desperate: 'I have no money at all, and indeed am at my wits' end
trying to raise some for household expenses and such tedious
things.'[3] The offer of a '£50' advance from Humphreys did therefore come at a very opportune moment.

Oscariana seems initially to have been Constance's idea; Ann
Clark Amor goes so far as to call it 'truly her personal project'.[4]
Wilde did, however, retain a degree of involvement with the book.
When the proofs arrived from Humphreys (in late November 1894,
according to Hart-Davis) he complained bitterly that:

[1] *Letters*, 364–5.
[2] See *Encyclopedia*, 410–11. Letters from Constance to Humphreys which suggest a degree of intimacy between the two were printed in part in the Sotheby sale catalogue for 22–23
July 1985. There is in the Clark Library, however, an unpublished letter from Constance to
Humphreys of 22 Oct. 1894 where she enquires after *Oscariana*, but admonishes Humphreys
that: 'I shall have to come up to town to-morrow morning to get a book from the London
Library, & I will come in & see you for a few minutes. But we must not talk of subjects that
we do not agree upon.' Clark Library. Wilde W6711L H924 1894, Oct. 22.
[3] *Letters*, 359 and 364.
[4] Anne Clark Amor, *Mrs Oscar Wilde: A Woman of Some Importance* (London: Sidgwick
and Jackson, 1983), 152.

the book is, as it stands, so bad, so disappointing, that I am writing a new set of aphorisms, and will have to alter much of the printed matter. The plays are particularly badly done. Long passages are quoted, where a single aphorism should have been extracted.[5]

It is not known whether Wilde undertook these revisions: he confessed later in the letter that 'to do it well requires time, and I am busy, with heaps of things, but I work a little at it every morning.' Manuscript notebook pages held at the Clark Library which contain a number of heavily corrected aphorisms might be evidence of this 'work', but none of the material appeared in *Oscariana*.[6] It is also significant that the name of the book's compiler was given simply as 'Mrs Oscar Wilde'. Interestingly, and as we have hinted in Chapter 5, for Wilde the appearance of the book seems to have been just as important as its contents. By November 1894 the Bodley Head partnership had been dissolved and Lane seemed to be dragging his feet over the publication of both *The Duchess of Padua* and *Mr W. H.* Yet Wilde was concerned that the firm's strategy of producing his books as if for a 'sect of perfect people' should be maintained. He thought it appropriate that *Oscariana* should be produced in the manner of his Bodley Head books, and set out to Humphreys his thoughts about the format, appearance, and price of the volume.

In Wilde's view, it ought to have sold at five shillings (with a more expensive version at twenty-one shillings) rather than at the price originally proposed by Humphreys, that of 2s. 6d. As Wilde (inaccurately) reminded Humphreys, 'all my books are dear'. Wilde also stipulated that Humphreys should bind the book in 'cloth' so that it looked 'dainty and nice'. 'Dainty' was a term he had used in his correspondence with Mathews and Lane, describing the projected *Mr W. H.* as 'a dainty little volume'. In Wilde's vision, *Oscariana* was to be 'refined and distinguished', a 'work of art' as opposed to 'a bit of journalism'. Humphreys's suggestion of using 'paper-covers' compromised this image, making the book indistinguishable from what Wilde termed a ' "railway-bookstall" book' and thus identifying it with the tastes of the common reader rather than with that 'sect of perfect people' which he had grown accustomed to addressing. Wilde was also concerned that paper covers could become 'dirty and untidy'.[7] Wilde's dislike of cheap binding dates back to the mid-1880s; reviewing a collection of ballads called *Low Down* in

5 *Letters*, 378.   6 These are printed in *OWR*, 127–31.
7 Wilde had had similar concerns over *Poems* (1892); see Mason, 322.

1886, he had referred disparagingly to the 'cover . . . of brown paper like the covers of Mr Whistler's brochures'.[8]

In the event, Wilde's instructions seem to have been ignored, for the fifty copies of the first issue of *Oscariana* (which appeared in January 1895) were bound in buff-coloured paper: the covers had red and black lettering and were decorated with a small floret motif. There is no record of the price, but the quality of the book's printing and binding strongly suggests that Humphreys kept with his original proposal of 2s. 6d. A further 200 copies, identically bound, were printed in May in the middle of the trials: unlike Lane, Humphreys, perhaps for personal reasons, kept faith with Wilde.[9] In contrast to the Bodley Head books, *Oscariana* is ordinary in appearance: the volume does not draw attention to its materiality, and it did not advertise itself as a collector's item. There was no design-signature, and although it was printed on Van Gelder paper, it was an exceptionally plain book. Moreover Wilde's suggestion for an expensive large-paper version priced at one guinea was never taken up during his lifetime. Mason notes that around 1903 a prospectus advertising twenty-five copies of such an edition was issued, and some copies were printed. It is, however, unclear whether this edition was an authorized one sold by Humphreys himself: Mason observes that the prospectus was 'fictitious' and was almost certainly issued by a different bookseller or publisher.

In May 1895 Humphreys also issued fifty copies of *The Soul of Man* in a format similar to *Oscariana*: bound in light brown paper wrappers with the title-page printed in red, it is also an unprepossessing book and was again probably sold for 2s. 6d. Unlike *Oscariana*, however, it seems that Wilde had little interest in this second project. The *Fortnightly* version of 'The Soul of Man' had been published as far back as February 1891; at that time, and in a letter about proofs to an unidentified correspondent, Wilde had complained about 'an error of setting' in which a paragraph 'is out of place'.[10] The transposition makes the essay at that point quite incoherent, and it is understandable that Wilde asked for it to be corrected 'at once'.[11] Nevertheless the correction was not made,

---

[8] 'The Poet's Corner', *Pall Mall Gazette* (27 Sept. 1886); repr. in Ross, *Reviews*, 90.
[9] Mason gives no indication of the price of the second impression.   [10] *OWR*, 46.
[11] The transposed passages occur between 306 and 308 in the *Fortnightly Review*, 55 (1891); see also Horst Schroeder, 'A Printing Error in "The Soul of Man Under Socialism" ', *Notes and Queries*, 43 NS: 1 (March 1996), 49–51.

either because the letter arrived too late, or perhaps because the re-vision was too difficult or expensive. Significantly this paragraph remained misplaced in the 1895 book edition—a detail which sug-gests that on this occasion Wilde did not see proofs; or, equally significantly, that if he did, he no longer cared about the essay in the way that he had cared in November 1894 about *Oscariana*.

In contrast to the essays reprinted in *Intentions* there are almost no differences between the periodical and book versions of *The Soul Of Man*. The book omits just one word used in the periodical; it also omits the frequent italicization used to highlight particular phrases and aphorisms found in the periodical version. This decision may have been a matter of the house-style of the Chiswick Press, or it may possibly have been designed to make the work appear more ser-ious. One reviewer of the *Fortnightly* version had associated the use of frequent italics with a playful intention to be provocative—to 'startle and excite talk'.[12] There is, however, no evidence that Wilde was responsible for these changes to accidentals, and considering the speed with which his personal life was moving towards crisis in the spring of 1895, this apparent lack of interest is hardly surpris-ing: he was probably too preoccupied with his impending libel suit against Queensberry. Wilde's (and perhaps Humphreys's) percep-tion of the book's prospects were doubtless affected by the revela-tions emanating from the witness box at the Old Bailey. It is possible to see the timing of the republication of what was effectively a de-fence of freedom as an attempt on Humphreys's (or Constance's) behalf to justify some of Wilde's behaviour; it may seem analogous to Ross's attempt in 1905 to rehabilitate Wilde's reputation with his carefully edited version of *De Profundis*, which presents Wilde as a repentant sinner rather than a recriminating lover. However, the tiny print-run of *The Soul Of Man* (fifty copies, compared with 10,000 for the first edition of *De Profundis*) does not support this view; it seems likely that Humphreys went ahead with the edition as a token of friendship and support. It is also significant that *The Soul Of Man* was not reprinted by Humphreys until well after Wilde's death. Humphreys's tactics suggest extreme caution: the 'Wilde' he presented in May 1895 was quite distinct from the decadent author of extravagant books such as *The Sphinx* and the English edition of *Salome*; moreover the returns for Humphreys from *Oscariana* and

---

[12] *Spectator* (7 Feb. 1891); quoted in Mason, 73.

The Soul Of Man must have been negligible, and this in turn re-inforces the suspicion of some biographers that the venture was not commercially motivated. Humphreys did eventually make money from Wilde, but not until well into the twentieth century. In 1904 he combined elements of the two books into a new work by 'Sebastian Melmoth' which was republished several times (Sebastian Melmoth was the pseudonym that Wilde adopted in France and Italy after his release from prison). Humphreys also republished *The Soul Of Man* and *Oscariana* separately several times between 1907 and 1912.[13]

I

By contrast, Leonard Smithers, who was the sole publisher of Wilde's post-prison works, certainly was commercially motivated, and as a consequence was forced to confront head-on the problem of the dramatic change in Wilde's reputation. In the first half of the twentieth century Smithers acquired notoriety as a dealer who was reported by Vincent O'Sullivan to have said that he would 'publish anything that the others are afraid of'.[14] Rupert Hart-Davis makes the point that this description is something of an unfair caricature, and that Smithers's risk-taking had at least two sides to it. If at times his publishing policy could appear little more than a rationalization for printing pornography, on other occasions it could be justified in terms of upholding an aesthetic ideal, that of avant-garde experi-mentation. It is worth bearing in mind that Smithers launched the *Savoy*, the only British avant-garde periodical to be published in the years between Wilde's arrest and the turn of the century. Smithers, then, should also be remembered as the one London publisher, after the withdrawal of the *Yellow Book* by John Lane, who was consist-ently prepared to take the risk of publishing controversial material and authors. Wilde would frequently joke about this ambivalent reputation. 'Very intoxicated but amusing' is how he described his first impression of Smithers to Ross in July 1897.[15] To Reginald Turner he was more forthcoming, although his judgement had not changed. Smithers was:

a priest who serves at the altar whose God is Literature . . . wasted and pale—not with poetry, but with poets, who, he says, have wrecked his life

---

[13] For details of these editions, see Mason, 406–7 and 558.
[14] See *Letters*, 627 n., and *Encyclopedia*, 345.   [15] *Letters*, 627.

by insisting on publishing with him. He loves first editions, especially of women: little girls are his passion. He is the most learned erotomaniac in Europe. He is also a delightful companion, and a dear fellow, very kind to me.[16]

Smithers had first corresponded with Wilde as early as 1888, when he had praised *The Happy Prince*; a decade later he encouraged a friendship with Wilde by sending him a parcel of books on his release from prison.[17] The gesture was appreciated, prompting Wilde to comment in his letter of thanks (dated 4 August 1897): 'I hope very much that some day I shall have something that you will like well enough to publish.'[18] Further correspondence in August shows that Wilde's confidence in Smithers, both as a friend and as a publisher, grew quickly. In a letter dated 18 August he advised Ernest Dowson that Smithers would be an ideal publisher for his proposed translation of Pierre Louÿs's *Aphrodite*. Dowson, according to Wilde, might expect to earn 'a lot of money by royalties'—a comment which suggests that Wilde had already received the impression that Smithers would be a publisher prepared to offer generous terms. Indeed by this time he had almost certainly reached an agreement with Smithers to publish *The Ballad of Reading Gaol*. (A later letter from Wilde to Smithers suggests that he had originally offered Wilde 'the entire profits' for the poem, although they ultimately agreed that Wilde should take only 'half profits', an arrangement Wilde considered to be more 'business-like'.[19]) In the same letter to Dowson, Wilde referred to progress with his poem. Believing that it would be 'very good', Wilde had begun it as early as June 1897 at Berneval-sur-Mer.[20] Although by mid-August the poem was still unfinished, Wilde had ambitious plans for it. He informed Dowson that he was 'going to try and get a lot of money for it from the *New York World*', a goal that was to be realized through the good offices of Robert Sherard, and which shows that Wilde was keen from the very beginning to maximize his income by selling the work separately in Britain and the United States (as he had learned to do earlier with his Society Comedies). A few days later, on 24 August, Wilde wrote to Smithers to ask him to arrange for the unfinished manuscript of *Reading Gaol* to be typed 'on good paper' (presumably in order to be able to correct it legibly) and 'bound in a

[16] *Letters*, 630–1.
[17] Wilde gave Smithers the manuscript of 'The Happy Prince'; see ibid. 221.
[18] Ibid. 629.   [19] Ibid. 651.   [20] Ibid. 586.

brown paper cover'—Wilde, it seems, was 'sick of [his] manuscript', and in need of some encouragement to complete the work.[21]

Smithers's reply, dated 2 September, makes it clear that despite the work's unfinished state, plans for its publication were already well advanced. Smithers's confidence seems to have been high, for he had approached Aubrey Beardsley to design a frontispiece. Wilde wrote back on 4 September, to acknowledge receipt of the type-script, and to offer some ideas of his own for the book's design. He suggested the Belgian painter, Fernand Khnoppf, as a possible illus-trator, if Beardsley continued 'hedging', and commented that the design should be 'something curious . . . Death and Sin walking hand in hand, very severe, and mediaeval'. In addition, divisions be-tween the parts of each canto were to be marked by 'a little design of three flowers, or some decorative motive, simple and severe'.[22]

Wilde's reasons for placing with a publisher of Smithers's mixed reputation a poem as serious and populist in its appeal as *Reading Gaol* are not obvious. However, we should remember that despite his optimistic plans for earnings from the American market, Wilde had few other options: if Smithers had not approached him, it is un-likely that any other British publisher would have brought out a post-prison work. By contrast, Smithers's interest in Wilde is more easy to explain: the businessman who traded on controversy must have seen in Wilde a potential which he moved quickly to secure. In the early summer of 1897, he seems to have assiduously (if not ex-actly cynically) cultivated Wilde's friendship, recognizing perhaps the congruence of the needs of the outsider–writer and the out-sider–publisher.

Wilde's decision to give his work to Smithers may also have been dictated by an intimation that his powers as a writer had been un-dermined by his prison experience. Smithers may have been the only publisher to approach Wilde after his release, but he was not the only man of business to do so. In August 1897 Wilde had re-ceived another and what appears on the surface to have been a rather better proposal. The American dramatist and manager Augustin Daly had offered Wilde an advance to write a play for Ada Rehan; the amount is unknown, but Wilde described the offer as 'generous'. Rehan was an actress who had won great popularity under Daly's tutelage; in the autumn of 1891, Wilde had sent Daly a copy of *Lady*

<hr />

[21] Ibid. 632, and 635; see also Mason, 410.   [22] *Letters*, 637.

Windermere's Fan in the hope that Rehan might take the part of Mrs Erlynne.[23] Daly's approach to Wilde eight years later suggests that his theatrical reputation had not been wholly destroyed by his disgrace, and that there were some managers (albeit in the United States and so safely removed from the reverberations of Wilde's conviction and imprisonment) who were prepared to invest in his talent. It might be thought that Wilde would have jumped at this opportunity, as it offered him a route back to the lucrative earnings of American (and perhaps eventually of West End) theatres. Wilde, however, declined the offer. Part of the problem was that he already felt under an obligation to George Alexander and Charles Wyndham. More truthfully perhaps, he confessed that he was 'not yet in train for work', having still not recovered the 'concentration of will-power that conditions and governs art'—he was finding the completion of *Reading Gaol* difficult enough. Wilde nevertheless did not reject the offer out of hand: he hoped 'later on . . . to think out something' that Daly would 'like'.[24]

In a further letter to Smithers dated 14 September, Wilde spoke optimistically of his intention to finish 'my poem', and also to 'begin my play' (the reference may be to a work for Daly or perhaps to the plays he 'owed' Wyndham and Alexander). The same letter, though, also hints at difficulties. Wilde explained that he was now trying to place *Reading Gaol* with the *New York Journal* (instead of his earlier idea of trying the New York *World* which by this time had presumably turned him down). The *Journal* had been brought out in 1895 by the flamboyant and immensely wealthy William Randolph Hearst; it had a reputation both for sensationalism and (as Wilde later crudely put it) for possessing 'millions'.[25] On the advice of Clyde Fitch, Wilde hoped to be offered '£200', but expected to receive at least '£100'.[26] Interestingly, Wilde had employed the literary agent, James Brand Pinker, to negotiate for him.

Pinker's first occupation, like that of Wilde himself, had been a jobbing journalist from which he had progressed (again like Wilde) to magazine editorships. However, in 1896 he had given up this

<hr/>

[23] *Letters*, 296.

[24] Ibid. 634. Evidence that Wilde recognized the financial potential in new work for the theatre can be seen in an earlier letter to Ross, dated 2 June 1897, in which he declared himself 'determined to finish the *Florentine Tragedy*, and to get £500 for it—from somewhere. America perhaps' (*Letters*, 591). Wilde's failure to get on with this work—the play, as we have said, was never completed—may have informed his response to Daly.

[25] *More Letters*, 158.   [26] *Letters*, 640.

work in order to concentrate his energy on setting up as a professional literary agent. He had offices in Arundel Street in the Strand and in a very short time had made something of a name for himself. An interview with Pinker, printed in the April 1898 issue of *The Bookman*, described him as 'young, shrewd, business-like' and in possession of 'genuine literary instinct'. Pinker made a particular point of reading for himself all the manuscripts which were submitted to him, and making his own judgement as to which publisher or journal they were best suited; he took pride in being able to single out and promote work with distinction. Pinker had also won recognition for promoting the careers of young or unknown writers. Among his clients in 1898 were H. G. Wells, Ernest Rhys, and George Egerton (Mary Chavelita Dunne); later he acted for Joseph Conrad and D. H. Lawrence. In the interview he justified the agent's role on the grounds that 'reputations are made and destroyed so rapidly to-day that a man wants all the "tips" he can get'.[27] An astute businessman who nevertheless had a reputation for good taste and for successfully promoting new and difficult writers—in these ways Pinker must have been a sound choice for Wilde in late 1897, knowing, as he did, that he would have to publish anonymously. Likewise, Wilde may have provided an interesting challenge for Pinker. Wilde's decision to engage Pinker suggests that he was following closely the most recent developments in literary culture in Britain and America. On the other hand, it is worth noting that according to Wilde the *New York Journal*'s first offer, made via Pinker, had been '£1,000' for 'an interview'. It was Wilde's notoriety, more than his literary talent, that was in demand. Meanwhile, Wilde himself was still desperately short of money—he asked Smithers to 'advance' him '£20' on the still incomplete *Reading Gaol*.

The Wilde who came to an accommodation with Smithers in the summer of 1897 is, then, a curious mixture of confidence and

[27] *The Bookman*, XIV, no. 79 (April 1898), 9–10. A piece in a later issue indicates that there was some ambivalence in the trade about the growing power of literary agents. There is discussion of an article by one W. H. Rideing in which it is claimed that agents were responsible for a gross inflation in the advances paid to authors and (more perniciously) for destroying talent by 'booming' young writers. The inexperienced writer was pressed to produce work too quickly and to a formula, with the result that he or she turned into a 'diffuse and tedious hack, undesired by anybody, undesired even by the literary agent himself' (*The Bookman*, XIV, no. 82 (July 1898), 89). It is worth noting that *The Bookman* did not entirely agree with Rideing's argument; the portrait painted of Pinker suggests that he was more discriminating and honourable than the average agent.

anxiety. There is strong evidence of the persistence of many aspects of the 'old', pre-trial, entrepreneurial writer. First, there is the familiar obsession with money and particularly with clinching a good deal. More precisely, Wilde's efforts to negotiate separate American rights for *Reading Gaol* suggest that he had lost none of his acute sense of the potential of the North American market. Second, there is his difficulty in completing a promised work. It is worth reiterating the fact that Wilde, despite representing himself as a naturally gifted artist of great facility, often found the reality of writing sustained or long pieces of work difficult. *The Sphinx* took years to complete; *Lady Windermere's Fan* and *An Ideal Husband* were both delivered very late.

The genesis of *Reading Gaol* illustrates two other elements in Wilde's writing practices, both of which he had habitually disguised in public, and which are discussed in more detail in Chapter 7. He delivered the poem to Smithers in bits and pieces—a poem by instalments, as it were. Extra lines or extra stanzas would arrive by post to be added to the typescript, in a manner reminiscent of the piecemeal way in which some parts of the Society Comedies were composed. Then there is the scarcely acknowledged involvement of other hands. Smithers had been instructed by Wilde to send a typescript copy of the unfinished poem to Ross so that Wilde might benefit from Ross's 'suggestions and criticisms'.[28] Ross took this responsibility seriously and proposed numerous emendations to the poem's style, structure, and vocabulary, some of which Wilde took to heart. Later Ross corrected proofs for Wilde, a task that Wilde was content to delegate.[29] At one point Wilde ordered Smithers to stop sending him proofs on the grounds that he (Wilde) possessed a '*maladie de perfection*' and did not want to 'polish for ever'.[30] The decision to enlist Ross's help points to an anxiety behind Wilde's frequent pronouncements that the poem was 'very good'; as we argue below, some months earlier (in May 1897) Wilde had already entrusted Ross with responsibility for producing a typescript from the prison manuscript now known as *De Profundis*. As Wilde's 'textual confidant', Ross now took over aspects of the roles previously undertaken collectively by James Stoddart, Dion Boucicault, Herbert Beerbohm Tree, George Alexander, Marcel Schwob, and Pierre Louÿs. On the other hand, there were strict limits to Ross's

[28] *Letters*, 649.   [29] See ibid. 654–5 and 683.   [30] Ibid. 696.

involvement: Wilde later quarrelled with him over his attempt to intervene over the pricing and format of *Reading Gaol*; Ross had approached Smithers directly and without consulting Wilde. In his correspondence to Smithers Wilde emphasized that Ross was only a '*literary* friend', and was not to be involved in any of their business arrangements.[31] Finally, Wilde's letters to Smithers exhibit a continuing concern with his works as products—with the materiality and embodiment of the text (and particularly with its pricing). In *De Profundis* Wilde claimed to have undergone a moral re-education in prison, but there is no evidence that such a change in values affected how he operated as a writer. Rather, there are abundant indications that he still understood his literary works as much as commodities as anything else, even if those commodities were now harder to sell.

Wilde also retained from his pre-prison days a tendency to plan more projects than he could possibly hope to complete. *Reading Gaol* was not the only piece he had in mind in the summer of 1897. In late September he wrote to Ross from Naples about an Italian translation and production of *Salomé*; another letter, dated 1 October, talks of resuming work on 'the *Florentine Tragedy*' and beginning a new play, '*Pharaoh*'. Growing confidence in *Reading Gaol* had also prompted Wilde to request from the *New York Journal* '£300 at least—more, if possible'; constantly hopeful of receiving American money and particularly of being a beneficiary of the Hearst millions, he boasted in a letter to Reginald Turner that he was 'going to ask huge sums from America'.[32] However Wilde's letters are also marked by numerous complaints about poverty. Grievances of this sort were not new, but the poverty to which Wilde refers in 1897 was of a different order from his financial difficulties in the summer of 1894. The double-bind was that Wilde's penury made multiple projects necessary but at the same time they ensured an over-commitment which would be impossible to meet. We should not forget that in attempting to restart his career in 1897 Wilde began from a position of severe disadvantage, and this inevitably conditioned the power structure of his relationship with publishing institutions in general, and with Smithers in particular.

Disappointment with Smithers and with the prospects for *Reading Gaol* quickly surfaced. By the beginning of October

---

[31] Ibid. 689.   [32] Ibid. 649–50; see also n. 24.

Smithers, although in possession only of an unfinished typescript, was nevertheless negotiating with Wilde over its production. One of Wilde's anxieties concerned the length of his work. Again we find echoes of early worries and correspondence, particularly of his concerns over the length of *The Sphinx* which he had set out in letters to Lane and Ricketts. Wilde suggested to Smithers, as he had to Ricketts, how the layout of the book might be adjusted to make the most of the relatively small body of text. 'By spacing the intervals of the poem well I think it will be almost a book. Wherever a space occurs one should have a fresh page—begin a fresh page.'[33] The problem of length was finally solved not by the provision of additional material, but by Smithers's decision 'to print on one side only' of the paper.[34]

A further worry was financial: Wilde continued to press Smithers for a £20 advance on profits, which he insisted was his 'right' on 'business grounds', as opposed to a 'personal and private loan'. To strengthen his case, he reported that the poem was no longer to be first published 'in some paper'. It seems that Wilde was pointing out to Smithers what he had learned from *Dorian Gray*—that prior publication in a cheap magazine would 'have damaged' Smithers's sale. 'People', Wilde pointed out, 'will not pay half a crown for what they can buy for a penny.'[35] In practice, though, Wilde's generosity may have been an attempt to disguise failure, for few magazines had made offers for the poem, nor had Pinker managed to sell the American rights.[36] Throughout the first half of October, Wilde persisted in his attempts to exploit the American market, enlisting the help first of Ross and then of More Adey in order, in his words, to 'stir Pinker'. Ross may not have been his best advocate, however, for in a letter to Smithers which Hart-Davis tentatively dates 6 October 1897 he had reported: 'He [i.e. Wilde] asks me to see Pinker, though in what capacity he does not say . . . I do not think his work has any market value, but I may be quite wrong.'[37] At one stage Wilde seems to have had hopes of receiving at least '£500' for his poem.[38] Ironically, the more discouraging the news from America, the higher the price Wilde seemed to place on his work.

---

[33] *Letters*, 650.   [34] Ibid. 688.   [35] Ibid. 651.

[36] Ibid. 652. Wilde mentions an offer from Robin Grey, the editor of the *Musician*; however, we cannot be certain that Wilde was telling the truth.

[37] Ibid. 653 n.   [38] Ibid. 653.

Towards the end of October, however, he was facing failure; Wilde commented to Smithers that Ross thought Pinker was 'not to be trusted', and told Smithers: 'treat the whole affair as if you were the owner of the American copyright.'[39] A little later he sent Smithers a formal document enabling him to assert his rights in the poem.[40] Wilde acknowledged to Ross that he feared he had 'built air-castles of false gold on my dreams of America'.[41] But Wilde was not quite ready to give up and suggested that Smithers get in touch with Elisabeth Marbury, the agent who had earlier handled the copyrights and royalties for the American productions of the Society Comedies. Wilde thought she might succeed where Pinker, now considered by Wilde to be 'an absurdity', had failed. Wilde's dismissal of Pinker is almost certainly unfair; as we suggested earlier, Pinker had a reputation for succeeding with difficult writers, and his failure to place Wilde's work should perhaps be read less a testimony to his—that is, Pinker's—inadequacies than to the enormous difficulties posed by Wilde's reputation. The new plan, suggested to Wilde by Reginald Turner, was to use Marbury to 'syndicate' the poem—that is, to arrange simultaneous publication in a number of different periodicals and different countries. Wilde, ever ambitious, had in mind the Paris edition of the *New York Herald*, the *New York Journal*, and the London *Sunday Sun* (edited by an old foe, T. P. O'Connor).[42] Wilde's earlier anxieties about damaging the book sale in Britain seem to have been conveniently forgotten. The plan, though, came to nothing and by early November, Wilde was forced to acknowledge that America (or more properly, the American press) was as hostile to him as Britain and the British. He wrote plaintively to Ross: 'I see that the difficulties about America are terrible. It is a sort of dreadful shock to me to find that there is such a barrier between me and the public.'[43] A week later, he declared to Smithers that he now had 'no hopes' of America, although he took the precaution of urging Smithers to secure copyright as there was still 'a *chance*—just a chance—of a big sale'.[44] By 19 November, however, Wilde finally admitted to Smithers that 'America is a foolish dream as far as buying my poem goes'.[45]

[39] Ibid. 666.   [40] Ibid. 669.   [41] Ibid. 668.
[42] Ibid. 666; see also Ch. 5, n. 4.   [43] Ibid. 671.   [44] Ibid. 675.
[45] Ibid. 676. Ironically, the decision to syndicate the work probably tied Wilde's hands, for the need to negotiate terms collectively made deals on an individual level unattractive. It

It is tempting to attribute to Wilde a certain naivety in his approach to publishing *Reading Gaol*: that he was unwilling to recognize that no amount of entrepreneurial dealing could overcome the difficulties posed by his reputation. The failure fully to acknowledge the weakness of his position also influenced his dealings with Smithers. Their principal disagreement occurred over the pricing of the volume. Wilde was anxious that the book should earn him money and was dismayed to find that Smithers had in mind a limited print-run of only 600 copies (500 for sale and 100 for the press and the author), and a rather cheap price of 2s. 6d. Wilde's view, set out in a letter to Ross, was that the price of 2s. 6d. demanded a printing of at least '1500 copies', while a limited print-run was justified only by a higher price of '5s.'.[46] In a further letter to Ross Wilde continued to complain, pointing out that an edition of '500 at 2/- (100 for reviews, author, etc.) would only fetch £40, which would only just cover expenses of paper, printing, etc., with £10 for advertisements, and leave nothing at all for me'.[47] To Smithers himself, Wilde argued that the economics of such an edition would 'leave me £20 in your debt'.[48] It seems that it was Smithers's excessive caution which had prompted Wilde's renewed attempt to publish the poem first in the British periodical press—(as we noted earlier) in the *Sunday Sun*, and also in *Reynolds News*, a popular but sensationalist Sunday newspaper. Ross strongly disapproved of Wilde's actions, and Smithers too may also have given Wilde some kind of ultimatum, for in a later letter (dated 27 October) Wilde withdrew his threat to publish in a British newspaper, confessing 'if I have to choose between *Reynolds* and Smithers, I choose Smithers'.[49] Wilde may also have been mollified by Smithers's decision to leave the type of the first edition standing in order to allow for the possibility of quickly printing a second impression in another run of 500 copies. (Smithers anticipated printing 1200 copies in all— presumably 100 from each impression would have been reserved for the author and for reviewers.) Smithers had also changed his mind

is interesting that Wilde did not at this time try the former editor of the *Fortnightly Review*, Frank Harris; Wilde judged him to have been too 'offensive'; see *Letters*, 663.

[46] *Letters*, 654 and 663.   [47] Ibid. 661.

[48] Ibid. 663; Smithers had already advanced Wilde £20 on the edition against sales.

[49] Ibid. 667. In later correspondence, however, Wilde claimed to Ross that Smithers 'did not care twopence' whether he published the poem first in a paper. Such a view seems unlikely, and may have been reported by Wilde in order to justify his resentment at Ross's intervention with his publisher, noted earlier; see *Letters*, 691.

about the price and now suggested 3s. 6d., terms which Wilde found more attractive.[50]

No sooner had Wilde and Smithers reached an agreement about the price and the print-run, than another bone of contention appeared. Wilde received first proofs on 19 November, and found fault with almost everything: the paper was 'awful', the spacing wrong, the title-page 'not good', the dedication '*revolting*'; even the full-stops were 'characterless', and there were objections to the changes Smithers had made to Wilde's spelling. Most important of all, however, in Wilde's view the volume looked 'too meagre for a 3/6 book'. He explained:

When one remembers what thick cloth-bound volumes the public buys nowadays for 3/6 or 2/6, it seems to me that they will think twice before they pay 3/6 for what looks like a thin sixpenny pamphlet, lacking in all suggestion of permanence of form. The public is largely influenced by the *look* of a book. So are we all. It is the only artistic thing about the public.[51]

Wilde was not exaggerating when he claimed that a well-bound book could be bought for as little as 2s. 6d. Although 3s. 6d. was the average price for cloth-binding without gilt, *The Bookman* had on occasions carried advertisements for such volumes priced as low as 1s. 6d.[52]

Ten days later, Wilde was still finding faults (although strangely he attributed them to the printers, the Chiswick Press, who had produced his Bodley Head books, rather than to Smithers) and he was still making changes to his text. The title-page proved to be a particular nub of disagreement: Wilde continued to object to the spacing and the size of type, especially that used for the 'C.3.3. signature'. (The first six editions did not carry Wilde's name as author, only his prison number at Reading Gaol.) There was also continuing bickering over the price. Given his initial objections to Smithers's plans for a cheap edition, ironically Wilde now held out for cheapness, believing that the 'ultimate shape' of the volume—that it was a 'meagre pamphlet'—made a price of 3s. 6d. simply 'impossible': 'no one', he explained to Smithers, 'except a damned and chosen few, would buy it; they would be content with reviews and pirated quotation'.[53] However, in early December when Wilde received the second proofs printed on Van Gelder paper, he declared himself 'delighted with the *size* of the book' and now thought that his earlier suggestion of '2/6' was a 'fortunate' price, and proposed that Smithers might after all raise it to 3s. (The first edition was eventually sold at the lower price of 2s. 6d; Smithers initially printed only 400 copies, but when these sold he quickly printed a further impression of 400, making a first edition of 800 in total.) In addition, Wilde had some suggestions about marketing the book, which again were in flat contradiction to his earlier worries that it was not cheap enough. Wilde now advocated an exclusivity (and perhaps some astute business practices) reminiscent of his Bodley Head days:

Do you think you might, to give the book a *cachet*, prefix a note that 25 large paper copies are printed, of which 22 are for sale, say at 10/6, and also that the edition is limited to 500 copies? When there is a demand, we can put second edition on the next 500 . . . I think that *some* large paper copies could be sold. I am sure of it. But of course the cover should be slightly different.[54]

On 7 February 1898 Wilde finally received the finished book. He was still unhappy with the 'signature' of authorship, asking Smithers to 'cut' the final 'C.3.3.' from a second edition. In all other respects, though, he seemed pleased, commenting that the 'cover is very nice [it was bound in white linen with cinnamon covers], and the paper excellent', and that 'the title-page is a masterpiece—one of the best I have ever seen'.[55]

The only outstanding issue was the continuing problem of publication in America, and the failure of Marbury (like Pinker) to secure a deal for serialization there. Wilde had hoped to circumvent the problem of his American reputation by publishing anonymously. As he put it to Smithers: 'I see it is my *name* that terrifies.'[56] However, Marbury wrote to Smithers from New York in January 1898 with the disappointing news that '[n]obody here seems to feel any interest in the poem, and this morning I received from the *Journal* their final offer, which, alas, is only $100'. This was a poor response indeed from the periodical financed by the Hearst 'millions', and it was rejected.[57] The first American book edition of *Reading Gaol* did not appear until 1899.

53 *Letters*, 689.   54 Ibid. 693–5.   55 Ibid. 699.   56 Ibid. 698.
57 Ibid. 699 n; see also Mason, 415–16.

Reading Gaol sold well and a second (corrected) edition of 1000 copies was in hand by mid-February. Wilde was encouraged, and urged Smithers to advertise in the hope that there might be 'a great popular sale'. To Ross also, he spoke of his anticipation of a 'popular "rush" '.[58] Smithers had fallen in with Wilde's earlier suggestion of a limited large-paper edition, printing (according to Mason) 30 copies on Japanese vellum priced at a guinea. Wilde then suggested a further 'Author's Edition' of signed copies with 'a cover by Ricketts—a new colour and a *remarque* in gold': this too appeared in March 1898 in a run of 99 copies priced 10s. 6d (although Wilde had thought 15s. more appropriate, pointing out to Smithers that 'my signature should be worth more than Japanese paper').[59] Bound in linen in Wilde's favourite colours, purple and white, with a leaf design by Ricketts, it was closer in appearance to his Bodley Head books than any other edition of *Reading Gaol*. Three further cheap editions, all priced at 2s. 6d. were printed between March and May 1898: the fourth with a print-run of 1,200 copies, and the fifth and six in runs of 1,000 copies. Wilde's name did not appear until the seventh edition (of 2,000 copies) of 1899, the last to be authorized by him. Finally, Wilde also arranged for a French translation by Henry Davaray, which appeared first in the May 1898 issue of the *Mercure de France* and then in book form (selling at two francs) in the autumn. The only reward he anticipated from the French edition was the 'profitable pleasure of looking at the daffodil paper cover'.[60]

The publication history of *Reading Gaol* allows us to see very sharply concerns and values which had always characterized Wilde's attitudes towards his books. They centred on the recognition that—to use Wilde's words once more—'the public is largely influenced by the *look* of a book. So are we all'. This focus on the book as product could at times be reduced to an anxiety about finding a price which corresponded to its material rather than textual value. In Chapter 5 we suggested that Wilde's experience with the Bodley Head taught him that an expensive limited edition could, for him, be more advantageous than a cheap run of 1–2,000 copies—the numbers in which his pre-Bodley Head books sold—because it combined a modest financial return with significant cultural prestige. *Reading Gaol*, however, presented a problem for this

---

[58] *Letters*, 703 and 705.   [59] Ibid. 708 and 711.   [60] Ibid. 742.

strategy. First, in 1897–8 Wilde needed money in a way that he had not when he agreed to the Bodley Head's marketing tactics. Second, the exotic Wilde persona which had been substantially responsible for selling the expensive Bodley Head books was now ironically the chief obstacle to sales. Wilde's negotiations with Smithers, and more particularly with Pinker and Marbury, suggest that he was trying to come to terms with these changes in his reputation—that he was enlisting their help to sell his works in a different way to a different sort of audience. Similarly Wilde's concerns over the pricing of *Reading Gaol* indicate a sensitivity to markets beyond those of the collector or connoisseur buyer to which his Bodley Head books had been directed. On the other hand, once it became clear that the poem was selling well, and that there was potential for a 'popular rush', Wilde immediately pressed Smithers for an expensive limited edition. The 'sect of perfect people' might have become 'a damned and chosen few', but Wilde still hankered after the approval which their tastes conferred on a book. It is perhaps ironic that the anonymous *Reading Gaol* was the one work where Wilde came closest to achieving his dual ambition of exclusivity and popularity. In his lifetime he sold 7,000 cheap copies of the work, and two expensive limited editions.

On the other hand, the term 'popularity' needs some contextualization: print-runs of 1,000 copies were still modest for a book selling for as little as 2s. 6d. The numbers were similar to the sales achieved by poets such as Richard Le Gallienne (who was employed full-time as a reader for the Bodley Head), but considerably less than canonical poets such as Tennyson. Moreover, poetry itself was rarely on the best-seller lists of 1898 (an interesting exception was W. E. Henley's *Poems*); rather it was the 6s. novel which, according to *The Bookman*, was the leading line. In the late spring of 1898 *Reading Gaol* was competing with such popular novels as H. G. Wells's *The War of the Worlds*, Hall Caine's *The Christian*, a new edition of Thackeray's *Vanity Fair*, and Mary Elizabeth Braddon's *Rough Justice*.[61] Nevertheless *Reading Gaol* was easily Wilde's

[61] These works, including Henley's *Poems*, appeared on the best-seller lists published in the spring and early summer issues of *The Bookman*; see *The Bookman*, XIII, no. 78 (March 1898), 172; XIV, no. 80 (May 1898), 32; XV, no. 81 (June 1989), 62. Unsurprisingly, there are many works on their lists which today are forgotten: Anthony Hope's *Simon Dale* or Mrs C. Praed's oddly-titled, *The Scourge-Stick*. An indication of the order of sales (and profits) to be gained from a best-seller can be glimpsed in a discussion in the July 1898 issue of *The Bookman* of Hall-Caine's *The Christian*. The piece by W. H. Rideing, which we cited earlier

best-selling book while he was alive, and it is therefore interesting to document its economics.

The printer was Charles Whittingham at the Chiswick Press, a firm habitually used by the Bodley Head, and the records of the Press show that Smithers's bill for the first six editions came to £42 1s. 9d.[62] The total printing costs for all the copies manufactured in Wilde's lifetime (including the 2,000 of the seventh edition) were unlikely to have been greater than £60. Typically binding costs would have been somewhere between £2 and £3 per 100 copies. Added together, the costs of all the editions would have been approximately £60 for printing and paper, £150 for binding, and perhaps a further £30 for advertising, giving a total of somewhere around £240. The returns on net sales were probably around £730 for the cheap editions, plus a further £65 for the two large-paper editions, giving a total of just under £800 and profits of around £560, of which Wilde's share, if he had retained half-profits on all the editions, would have been £280. Wilde himself claimed to Otho Lloyd that he only received 3d. a copy for the cheap editions of the poem, giving him a return of only £87 10s., and a figure of less than £120 in total for all editions. The discrepancy between this figure and that suggested by the economics of the book's production can be explained in a number of ways. First, we cannot be sure that the agreement for Wilde to receive half-profits was retained through all the editions; neither can we be sure that he was completely truthful in his report to Lloyd. In any case, as Wilde was still an undischarged bankrupt, it is likely that the Official Receiver took a large part of all of Wilde's earnings. All this notwithstanding, it is ironic that Wilde's most popular and most profitable book earned him so little money.

Wilde followed the fortunes of *Reading Gaol* keenly: he troubled Smithers constantly for news of sales, and bombarded him with ideas for advertising. In late March, for example—and in a complete

---

(see n. 27), used *The Christian* as an example of the inflated earnings of popular authors. Rideing claimed that following its successful serialization in British and American magazines, the novel went on to sell around 150,000 copies in book form in the two countries, earning its author '81,000 dols.' in total. *The Bookman* contested Rideing's figures, claiming, for example, that he had overestimated the amount Hall-Caine had been paid for serialization rights (it suggested a total of £3,000, rather than Rideing's $36,000). Significantly, however, *The Bookman* did not contest the numbers of books sold. See *The Bookman*, XIV, no. 82 (July 1898), 89.

[62] *Letters*, 715.

contrast to his disdain in 1894 for ' "railway bookstall" books'—he ordered Smithers to 'supply' W. H. Smith's bookstalls with 'a placard'; he later admitted that a popular sale 'largely depends' on Smith. Smithers was also asked by Wilde to place 'a leaflet, with criticisms, . . . into the leaves of a good magazine . . . like Pear's soap, and other more useful things'. Wilde ended his letter with the perceptive comment that he felt 'like Lipton's tea'; by now he had completely embraced the idea that books and the personality of their authors were commodities.[63] In May he had an idea for a further, cheaper edition, asking Smithers's views on the cost of '1000 copies at 1/'. The selling point was to be a preface by some notable public figure with an interest in penal reform; Wilde suggested the Irish MP, Michael Davitt, who had been frequently imprisoned because of his political activities. Smithers's response was to propose an even cheaper, sixpenny version with a print-run of 10,000. Wilde, though, disagreed, and his objections were pragmatic rather than principled: he pointed out that 'sixpence [is] too little . . . The profit is far too small'.[64] Discussions about a cheap popular edition continued throughout May, but the project failed to come to anything.

II

Reading Gaol was only the first work by Wilde which Smithers published. As early as the autumn of 1897 (that is, well before the success of *Reading Gaol* was apparent) he approached Wilde with a view to publishing *The Importance of Being Earnest* and *An Ideal Husband*. According to Wilde, Smithers offered him '£50' to purchase both plays, a sum which Wilde considered disappointing. He reminded Smithers that both plays had 'been great *successes*, [had] been admired, etc., and belong to a series of published plays that were sold out almost at once'.[65] This last reference was of course to the successful Bodley Head editions of *Lady Windermere's Fan* and *A Woman of No Importance*. It is difficult to know exactly how much money Wilde received for his last two Society Comedies, because the evidence is confusing. In the archives of the Bodley Head there is a document dated 27 April 1899, and signed by Wilde, in which

[63] *More Letters*, 170, and *Letters*, 736.
[64] *Letters*, 733 and 740. It should be noted that Hart-Davis takes the text of the second letter from the 1939 Spoor sale catalogue, and its authenticity is not therefore certain.
[65] *More Letters*, 159–60.

Oscar Wilde agrees to sell to Leonard Smithers all his right and interest in the publication in book form of *An Ideal Husband* and *The Importance of Being Earnest* for thirty pounds and acknowledges the receipt of that sum.[66]

There is also a letter from Wilde to Smithers dated August 1899 in which Wilde asks for 'the £20 for the two plays'; this may be a request to Smithers to make up the amount to his original offer of £50.[67] Earlier correspondence from Wilde to Ross in the spring of 1898 suggests that Wilde may have had some hesitation about assigning both works to Smithers. It was not until May that year that he wrote to Ross informing him that he had finally decided to let Smithers '*buy The Importance of Being Earnest*'.[68] On the other hand, plans for the publication of *An Ideal Husband* seem to have been under way as early as late October 1897, for Wilde had written to Smithers (in a letter tentatively dated by Hart-Davis as 29 October) with instructions to ask Shannon to design the cover, in order that the volume form a 'series' with the Bodley Head editions of his plays.[69] These same instructions were later repeated (and with more detail) in May 1898 in relation to *The Importance of Being Earnest*: again Wilde demanded that the 'type, paper, setting, margin, etc.' should be 'identical' to the Bodley Head books, and that Shannon should 'do a similar cover, same cloth, same colour, and similar design'.[70]

In nearly all respects Smithers fell in with Wilde's wishes, although there were some differences between his editions of Wilde's plays and those of the Bodley Head. The first concerned the pricing and size of the print-runs. Smithers doubled the numbers of copies of each play, printing editions of 1,000 small-paper copies at 7s. 6d. and 100 large-paper copies at 21s.—that is, higher than the Bodley Head price of 15s., but the figure which Wilde had preferred in his original negotiations with Lane. (Smithers also printed twelve 'presentation' copies of each play on Japanese vellum; but they were not for sale.) The second difference was a decision to publish both plays semi-anonymously, by replacing Wilde's name on the title-page with the phrase 'by the author of *Lady Windermere's Fan*'. It is not clear who made this decision, nor why; nor, indeed, why there was no acknowledgement of *A Woman Of No Importance*. In a letter to

---

[66] Ibid. 160 n.; *Letters*, 765. [67] *Letters*, 808.
[68] Ibid. 739. [69] Ibid. 669. [70] Ibid. 736.

Smithers, dated 23 November 1898, Wilde seems to have acceded only reluctantly to this description of his authorship.[71] However, given his frequently voiced anxieties about the 'terror' inspired by his name, it is possible that his preference might have been for total anonymity, rather than (and as Karl Beckson hints) for an explicit reference to his name.[72] On the other hand, it is worth remembering that the plays themselves could hardly have been mistaken for the work of any other dramatist. Moreover, and as Wilde himself had earlier pointed out to Smithers, the sales of play-texts were wholly dependent upon their previous success in performance. There would have been no point in attempting to disguise their origins, but either publisher or author seems to have been apprehensive of the consequences of drawing too much attention to Wilde's name.

At some stage a decision was made to bring out *Earnest* first. Wilde had hoped for publication of the play by early June 1898, once more for simple financial reasons—'so as to have at least six weeks' run for its money'.[73] The summer months were the quietest period of the theatrical calendar, and thus a poor time for publishing play-texts. Earlier Wilde had delayed the publication of *Lady Windermere's Fan* when he realized that it could not be brought out much before July. In the event June was too optimistic a date, and neither play appeared until the following year. Some of the delay was inevitably caused by the fact that Wilde no longer had a manuscript of either work. In May 1898 he asked Ross to have a typed duplicate made of Alexander's prompt-copy of *The Importance of Being Earnest*. (The significance of these circumstances for the revisions Wilde made are discussed in Chapter 7.) Exactly the same arrangements had been made in October 1897 to provide Wilde with a text for *An Ideal Husband*; Wilde himself reported having written to Waller to ask him to send Smithers his copy of that play. The problem, as Wilde put it, was that his own manuscript, 'as all my things[,] . . . disappeared at the seizure of my house'.[74]

Earnest was published in February 1899. Wilde had revised it extensively, taking great care in preparing it for press. However, and in contrast with his attitude a year earlier towards *Reading Gaol*, he had little optimism about its prospects. He wrote pessimistically to Frank Harris:

71 *More Letters*, 173.   72 *Encyclopedia*, 154.
73 *Letters*, 736.   74 Ibid. 669.

I do not fancy the play will have anything like the success of *The Ballad*. It is so trivial, so irresponsible a comedy: and while the public liked to hear of my pain—curiosity and the autobiographical form being elements of interest—I am not sure that they will welcome me again in airy mood and spirit, mocking at morals, and defiance of social rules. There is, or at least in their eyes there should be, such a gap between the two Oscars.[75]

To Ross, he repeated his anxieties, wishing the play 'was a more wonderful work of art—of higher seriousness of intent'.[76] Wilde's acknowledgement that his reputation and that of the play would be inevitably linked in the eyes of the public makes the decision to remove his name from the title-page even more difficult to understand. As matters turned out, some of Wilde's fears were realized, for the press barely noticed the volume, a circumstance which may have muted his enthusiasm for *An Ideal Husband*. Wilde wrote to Smithers in March 1899 complaining that he was finding the task of correcting this play 'a great trouble—worse than a new play. I am quite exhausted'.[77] A little later he asked Ross: 'when it is in proof, will you look over it and tell me your views,' just as he had done with *Reading Gaol*.[78] Later Wilde informed Smithers that he believed it 'reads the best of my plays'.[79] *An Ideal Husband* appeared in July 1899.

It is not known whether Wilde received any payment from the sales of the two plays in addition to the original purchase fee. In his correspondence with Smithers there is no mention of a royalty payment. The dating (April 1899) of the agreement in the Bodley Head archive may indicate that it took some time for Wilde and Smithers to agree terms; moreover the slow sales of *Earnest* might explain why Wilde eventually relinquished his publishing rights to both works for such a modest sum. Further indications that Wilde probably received little from the sales of the works are to be found in the state of Smithers's own finances. Wilde received news early in the summer of 1900 that Smithers's business had collapsed (he was formally declared bankrupt on 18 September of that year).[80] There is something of an irony in that fact that Smithers, attempting to make capital out of the career of one bankrupt, should end up a bankrupt himself.

As a publisher and unofficial banker, Smithers was now of little use to Wilde, and any opportunity that he had once offered Wilde of

[75] Ibid. 780.   [76] Ibid. 783.   [77] *More Letters*, 180.
[78] *Letters*, 789.   [79] *More Letters*, 181.   [80] *Letters*, 829 n.

a route back to a professional writing career was closed. However bleak Wilde's prospects looked, he did not give up. For his last project he turned his attention once more to the theatre and to his old sponsor, Frank Harris, who now effectively superseded Smithers as Wilde's financial and artistic 'manager'. Around the end of September 1900, Wilde agreed to sell Harris 'the plot and scenario' for a play provisionally entitled *Her Second Chance*. Harris had first approached Wilde for a 'comedy' in February 1898 (he may have been prompted by the strong sales of *Reading Gaol*). Wilde had then refused on the grounds that he had lost '*la joie de vivre*'.[81] The scenario offered to Harris a year and a half later was not new. It had been sketched out as far back as August 1894 in a letter to George Alexander, following his refusal (in July) of the scenario for *The Importance of Being Earnest*. In the summer of 1900 Harris had originally proposed that he and Wilde collaborate in order to ensure the work's completion. However, it appears that Wilde's contribution was minimal, and by the end of September Harris, according to Wilde, had already fleshed out the scenario into a 'finished' play. Wilde complained that he had 'not seen a line of it'; nevertheless, his financial difficulties, coupled with his own creative inertia, determined him to accept Harris's work as a *fait accompli*, and he set out the following terms:

£200 down
£500 shares in the Reserve
¼ of profits of play.[82]

Harris agreed, and proposed to send Wilde a sum of £175 as an advance on profits. Wilde wrote to Harris on 26 September, acknowledging receipt of the money (although he had not actually received it) and formally assigning to him 'the entire rights in the plot and scenario'.[83] The play was staged with a new title, *Mr and Mrs Daventry*, at the Royalty Theatre on 25 October 1900 with Mrs

---

[81] *Letters*, 708.   [82] Ibid. 836.

[83] Ibid. 836. Harris did not send Wilde the full £175, because (as we discuss below) he discovered that other managers had rights to the scenario. Harris therefore withheld £125 of the money due to Wilde in order to compensate these individuals. In a letter to Harris, dated 12 Oct., Wilde complained about this treatment, pointing out that he had acknowledged receipt of the £175 in anticipation of Harris sending it, and that Harris had now broken 'the agreement'; characteristically Wilde refused to see that he had been in any way at fault (see *Letters*, 837).

Patrick Campbell and Fred Kerr in the title roles; it ran for 116 performances, closing on 23 February 1901.[84]

For an author who had once been so confident of his genius, and
who had identified his personality so closely with his writing,
Wilde's willingness to cede creative responsibility to Harris seems
like an acknowledgement of defeat: it is a striking example of how
important money, rather than artistic integrity, had now become for
him. However, and as Harris quickly found out, there were other
reasons why Wilde had agreed terms so promptly: apparently he
had already sold the scenario several times over. In a letter to More
Adey, written shortly after Wilde's death, Ross claimed that Harris
had to buy off, at the cost of £100 each, no fewer than five separate
claimants to Wilde's work. The complex history of Wilde's efforts
to sell the *Mr and Mrs Daventry* scenario is usually seen as evidence
for the final failure of his creative energy for which he compensated
by underhand financial deals with his theatrical connections. Wilde
was under stress in his post-prison years, and this may have led him
to promise more than he could possibly deliver. Nevertheless there
are many similarities between his attitude towards marketing this
work and the tactics he used earlier in his career.

The first of those on Ross's list of claimants was the English theatrical manager, Horace Sedger. Wilde had sold him the rights to
the scenario together with those for his 'next modern play' as far
back as October 1898.[85] The second individual to advance Wilde
£100 was Leonard Smithers: according to Wilde, he and Smithers
reached an agreement in the spring of 1899, and only after Sedger
had already 'resigned all claim' in the scenario. Wilde was under the
impression that Smithers was acting on behalf of another party, and
that he was merely the '*l'homme de paille*'.[86] Correspondence in
1899 reveals that Wilde also entered into negotiations with the
English actor, Kyrle Bellew. Wilde's acquaintance with Bellew went

[84] See *Encyclopedia*, 224. The play closed for two weeks in the middle of its run to observe
mourning following the death of Queen Victoria.   [85] *Letters*, 762.

[86] It seems that Smithers had been underhand in dealings with Wilde, for he had been
working secretly with two agents, referred to in Wilde's correspondence simply as 'Roberts'
and 'Sequale'. Hart-Davis speculates that the shady nature of the negotiations points to the
presence of Sir Randal Roberts. Roberts was an English theatre-manager of dubious reputation whom Wilde knew. Wilde's main complaint against Smithers was that he had used the
subterfuge of Roberts and Sequale in order to 'get round him'—that is, to persuade him to
'agree to much lower terms' for his play, a mere '£100' (or '£25' for each act) rather than the
£400 which had apparently been offered to him at some stage in the negotiations. See *Letters*,
796–8.

back to the early 1880s, when he had proposed him for the part of the Czarevitch in the planned American production of *Vera*. Bellew himself was a close associate of the American actress, Cora Brown-Potter, another of Wilde's 'clients'. In fact Bellew and Brown-Potter were negotiating together, although it appears that they initially approached Wilde separately and with different proposals. Wilde claimed to Frank Harris that he reached terms with Brown-Potter (which again included a £100 advance) only after an earlier agreement with Bellew had 'lapsed' because of Bellew's failure to honour his financial commitments (which unusually seemed to involve, according to Wilde, a number of weekly payments of '£5').[87] It is not known when exactly the agreement with Brown-Potter was formally signed. However in March 1899, Wilde ordered Smithers to send to her a copy of the recently published *The Importance of Being Earnest*; in July, Bellew was sent a copy of *An Ideal Husband*.[88] These gifts suggest that Wilde may have been trying to encourage their interest (earlier in his career he had attempted to promote *Vera* in the same way, by giving copies of the privately printed work to various actors, actresses, and theatrical managers). A year later, on 22 March 1900, Brown-Potter wrote to Wilde enquiring after her commission: 'When will you give me over my play? Don't you think I have been very patient with you about it? Let me hear from you by return post.'[89] Wilde claimed to Harris that it was 'impossible' to 'break' with her, in part because he had already accepted (and presumably spent) her £100 advance.[90] Wilde's belated sense of honour towards Brown-Potter is interesting, for it contrasts markedly with his attitude to another of the claimants to the rights over the scenario: the Australian theatrical manager, Louis Nethersole, the brother of the actress, Olga, whose performances Wilde had admired in the late 1880s.

According to Ross, Nethersole, like Smithers and Brown-Potter, had also been sold the rights for '£100' and had also later been repaid by Harris.[91] Wilde vehemently denied that Nethersole had any rights to the play, and claimed that he had purchased the scenario on

---

[87] *Letters*, 834. The circumstances of this deal have echoes with Wilde's earlier negotiations with Marie Prescott over *Vera*: on that occasion too Prescott had to intervene with an improved offer when Wilde had failed to reach terms with Perzel, her husband and manager. Perhaps Wilde found business with women easier.

[88] *Letters*, 792 and 805 n.

[89] Ibid. 830 n.

[90] Ibid. 834.

[91] Ibid. 847.

false pretences from 'a scoundrel called Eliot . . . [who] had no right to sell it, or deal with it, or adapt it, or do anything with it at all. His selling it to Nethersole was a fraud'. There is evidence that Nethersole may never have received the scenario he paid for.[92] Wilde also denied that Smithers retained any rights. He argued that Smithers (like Sedger before him) had agreed to 'surrender' his rights if Wilde refunded Smithers his original sum.[93] If Wilde was correct on these points, then he would have entered into his agreement with Brown-Potter in good faith.

The last claimant to the scenario on Ross's list was Ada Rehan. Wilde's negotiations with her began indirectly in August 1897 when Augustin Daly had approached him for a play for her. As we noted earlier, at the time Wilde had refused. A few months later, however, in late November 1897, Wilde instructed Smithers to write to Daly that he was now ready to 'begin a comedy for him for £100 down, and £100 for each completed act, the royalties to be such as I received for my last American play. Miss Marbury will let him know the contract'. These advance payments were larger than anything that Wilde had commanded at the height of his success, and he anticipated that they 'would . . . see me through the winter'.[94] It is not known whether Daly received this communication, but if he did, he seems not to have acted upon it. After a chance encounter with Daly and Rehan in Paris a year and a half later Wilde reported to Ross that 'they . . . want me to write something for them'.[95] Slightly later Wilde wrote to Smithers that 'Daly, who has just died, had made us a large offer for the American rights of our play'.[96]

This reference to 'us' and 'our' is interesting, for Wilde can only have had in mind the *Mr and Mrs Daventry* scenario, which he had sold to Smithers earlier that spring. But June 1899 was also the time when Wilde was probably in discussions with Brown-Potter and Bellew to sell the rights of the same scenario. Negotiations with

[92] Ibid. 838. In an unpublished letter of 2 Dec. 1899 Nethersole asks Wilde: 'When are we to see the scenario of the play? I am waiting anxiously for it. Kindly hurry.' (See Clark Library. Uncatalogued MSS. ALS Nethersole to Oscar Wilde.)

[93] This sum was to be taken from the profits of the production Wilde was negotiating with Bellew and Brown-Potter. There is no reason to disbelieve Wilde: as we argued earlier, there is evidence that Smithers was acquainted with Wilde's dealings with Bellew and Brown-Potter (he had sent them copies of Wilde's plays). Moreover, the later payment of £100 by Harris to Smithers may have been in lieu of the performance fees—the payment to Smithers is not necessarily an indication that Smithers still had a legal right to the scenario. (See ibid. 839.)   [94] Ibid. 689.   [95] Ibid. 800.   [96] Ibid. 801.

Daly came to a dramatic end with his sudden death on 7 June, and it may have been this event that decided Wilde finally to give the play to Brown-Potter and Bellew in a deal which refunded Smithers the sums that he had paid for the rights. Alternatively, it is possible that Wilde had already agreed terms with Brown-Potter, but only for the British rights. Such an account would explain why Wilde was apparently simultaneously negotiating with two parties in the summer of 1899—he was only acting in a way broadly similar to the manner in which he had sold his earlier plays.

Rehan later described Wilde's kindness after Daly's death, which for her was both a personal and a professional tragedy: 'Oscar Wilde came to me and was more good and helpful than I can tell you—just a very kind brother.'[97] Some months later, in February 1900, Wilde agreed terms with Rehan for 'a new and original comedy, in three or four acts', which he was to complete by 1 June. The contract specified a £100 advance on royalties, with a further £200 on Rehan's acceptance of the manuscript. The royalty earnings themselves were as follows: for production 'in London at a first-class West-end theatre' they were to be set on a sliding-scale of '5% on gross weekly takings up to £600', increasing by increments to '10% on the gross over £1,000'; royalties for British productions outside London were set at a flat 6%, while for the USA and Canada they were '5% on the weekly gross up to $3,000 dollars, 10% on the next $3,000 and 15% on all receipts above this sum'.[98] These details suggest that Rehan may have known about, and indeed followed, the instructions Wilde had earlier directed Smithers to send to Daly—that he should contact Elisabeth Marbury to find out about Wilde's usual contractual arrangements. Of course this agreement with Rehan does conflict directly with the terms Wilde said he had reached with Brown-Potter the previous year. It does seem to indicate a degree of double-dealing on Wilde's behalf. Up to this point, he had received £500 (not counting the £50 from Harris) for the various sales of the scenario. Ross himself reported Wilde's comment that the play was 'my only source of income' in the sense that it was a work 'on which I could always have raised £100'—a report which reinforces the sense of Wilde deliberately exploiting the gullibility of his theatrical acquaintances.[99]

[97] *Letters*, 800 n.; Hart-Davis's source is Graham Robertson's *Time Was*.

[98] Quoted in Russell Jackson, 'Oscar Wilde's Contract for a New Play', *Theatre Notebook*, 50 (1996), 113–14.   [99] *Letters*, 847.

Ross's interpretation, however, is not the only possible explanation of events. It is perhaps significant that Wilde himself viewed the Brown-Potter and Rehan claims as equally legitimate. By contrast Wilde did not recognize Nethersole's claim, and believed that Smithers and Sedger had both agreed to relinquish their rights to the scenario. There is evidence to suggest a dispute between Sedger and Wilde over the nature of the agreement they had signed. At the beginning of March 1899 Wilde wrote to Ross to contradict an advertisement which Sedger had placed announcing Wilde's authorship of a new play: 'there is no truth at all in Sedger's advertisement, and I am very angry about it. It is quite monstrous. My only chance is a play produced anonymously.'[100] This last detail about anonymity is important for it also figures in the contract which Wilde later drew up with Rehan:

The name of the author of the play is not to be printed or announced on any theatre programme, bill or advertisement, unless it is so agreed mutually by the party of the first part [Wilde] and the party of the second part [Rehan], and the party of the second part is to have the right to produce the play anonymously.[101]

In his account of Rehan's dealings with Wilde, Russell Jackson finds this clause 'striking' and links it to the absence of Wilde's name on the title pages of *An Ideal Husband* and *The Importance of Being Earnest*. In fact the issue of anonymity seems much more pertinent to Wilde's views of the staging rather than publication of his plays. It is possible that in publicly announcing Wilde's name, Sedger, in Wilde's view, had reneged on some aspect (perhaps an informal one) of their agreement. When Wilde found he was unable to finish the play promised to Rehan by 1 June (as his contract had stipulated), he wrote to her fairly promptly offering (as he had once with Alexander) to return the advance, although he would need what he termed 'a little time' to repay it.[102] Rehan was disappointed but agreed. Wilde failed to return the money before his death, but there is no sense that, at the time, he thought he was deceiving or misleading her.

Another factor in Wilde's behaviour concerns his understanding of the relationship between a scenario and a finished play. Wilde

---

[100] Ibid. 783–4.   [101] Jackson, 'Oscar Wilde's Contract for a New Play', 114.
[102] *Letters*, 814 n. The phrase 'a little time' derives from a letter from John Farrington, Rehan's theatrical agent, to Wilde concerning the fee owed her. Farrington is apparently quoting Wilde's own words.

reminded Harris that Harris himself had 'taken legal opinion' and discovered that 'there was no copyright in a plot'.[103] It is plausible that Wilde, familiar with the pattern qualities of society drama, had never viewed a scenario as a precise blueprint for a finished play. Indeed, as we describe in the next chapter, drafts of the Society Comedies reveal that plots of the finished plays are often quite different from the scenarios offered to theatre-managers; moreover Wilde could move characters and large blocks of dialogue from one work to another. So it is possible that Wilde believed that the same scenario could be worked up to produce quite different plays. In his own mind, Wilde may have felt that the agreements that he signed with Rehan and Brown-Potter would have resulted in substantially different *works*, even if the scenarios were similar.[104]

As one might expect, Wilde's explanation to Harris of how he sold the scenario of *Mr and Mrs Daventry* is characterized by angry self-justification: he represents his dealings as complex but fundamentally honest, casting himself as the injured party—a tactic familiar from correspondence throughout his career, and best seen in *De Profundis*. Wilde may have overstated his vulnerability, and he only gradually told Harris the whole truth. Nevertheless Wilde's dealings with the scenario should not be nearly as damaging to his reputation as Ross (and some literary historians after him) have implied. On the contrary, it is possible to see in Wilde's negotiations evidence of the financial acumen which had helped him to become the successful dramatist of the early 1890s. It is also perhaps worth noting Wilde's lack of faith in Ross's business sense: however good Ross was as a 'literary friend', Wilde constantly complained about his meddling in money matters.

A more important lesson to be taken from the dealings over *Mr and Mrs Daventry* is the way they testify to the enduring quality of

103 *Letters*, 838.

104 Ellmann maintains that there was a further claimant on the scenario, the American impresario Charles Frohman; he reports that Wilde signed an agreement with Frohman on 4 Oct. 1899. (See Ellmann, 544.) Ellmann unfortunately gives no source for this information, and he is almost certainly mistaken. It is significant that Frohman's name is not mentioned in Ross's list of claimants. Moreover, where he does appear in Wilde's correspondence, it is in a letter written in Nov. 1900 to Harris, when Wilde asks him to 'try and get Frohman to take the piece' (i.e. *Mr and Mrs Daventry*). This request makes no sense if Wilde had, as Ellmann claims, already reached agreement with Frohman in the previous year. Frohman would of course have been a natural choice for an American production of *Mr and Mrs Daventry*; as we noted in Ch. 4, he had at one time negotiated with Wilde about an American tour of *Lady Windermere's Fan* and had staged the New York production of *The Importance of Being Earnest* (see *Letters*, 841).

Wilde's reputation among theatre-managers. Wilde seems to have been in as much demand after his disgrace as immediately before it. Besides Sedger, Smithers, Nethersole, Brown-Potter, and Rehan, Wilde had also had discussions about new works with George Alexander and Charles Wyndham (both of whom were contractually 'owed' plays by him). Wilde spoke to Reginald Turner of his intention to begin a play for Alexander as early as October 1897, although he was then honest enough to acknowledge that another 'comedy' would be unlikely as his 'sense of humour is now concentrated on the grotesqueness of tragedy'.[105] Wilde wrote to Wyndham in the spring of 1900 with several suggestions about possible subjects for a new drama, none of which had anything to do with the *Mr and Mrs Daventry* scenario. Rather Wilde had in mind for Wyndham a historical theme.[106] In addition, and as we noted earlier, during his self-imposed exile Wilde also referred to work on a play entitled *Pharaoh* as well as *A Florentine Tragedy*: nothing has survived of the first piece; the second (begun as early as 1894) was never completed. As we have said, Wilde always found the writing of plays difficult, and had nearly always delivered them late. In the light of his attempts to restart his career as a dramatist, and the number of managers still interested in his work, we should perhaps be cautious about writing off the post-1897 years as straightforward failure.

Apart from plans for West End dramas, there is evidence that Wilde had other literary projects in mind. He corresponded with Dalhousie Young in September 1897 about a libretto for *Daphnis and Chloe* (apparently making use of some lyrics by Douglas). Wilde asked for the familiar '£100 down, and £50 *on production*', and for profits on the publication of the libretto to be shared between himself and Bosie.[107] Wilde failed to produce the work and in July 1898 explained himself to Ross on the grounds that the money advanced

[105] *Letters*, 659. Alexander had been estranged from Wilde for some time after his disgrace; but when the two men finally met in the early summer of 1900, they resumed their friendship. Alexander later bequeathed the acting rights of *Lady Windermere's Fan* and *The Importance of Bring Earnest* to Wilde's sons. Time also mellowed Alexander's view of Wilde's theatrical abilities. He wrote to Ross in 1906: 'I've been studying [*The Duchess of Padua*] very carefully, and I have come to the conclusion that I ought to have played [it] fifteen or twenty years ago'. Later in 1909 he wrote again to report that his revival of *The Importance of Being Earnest* had 'really caught on', that he 'turned money away from the "*pit and gallery*"—how this would have pleased [Wilde]!' Margery Ross (ed.), *Robert Ross, Friend of Friends* (London: Jonathan Cape, 1952), 132 and 173.
[106] *Letters*, 818.   [107] Ibid. 639 and 646.

by Young had been meant 'half as a gift, half as an encouragement';
no timetable had ever been mentioned, and so Wilde believed
that he had not broken any trust.[108] Other projects which were
unfinished (or perhaps never even begun) include a short story
which Wilde mentioned to Ross in May 1898, and proposals made
to Smithers in the same month for a novel and for a volume of
French short stories in translation—Wilde volunteered to 'help in
the selection'.[109] In Wilde's post-prison correspondence there are
also references to various pieces of journalism which never materialized, including a promise in May 1899 from William B. Fitts (an
editor on the staff of the *North American Review*) for £75 for an
article.[110]

III

A simple contrast between the number of projects Wilde promised
from 1897 onwards and the number he actually completed (apparently only one work) would support the view that by 1898 Wilde
was spent as a writer. Ellmann succinctly captures this sense of inevitable decline and defeat in his characterization of the period from
1897 to 1900 as 'the left-over years'.[111] Of course there is some
truth in this judgement, in that the number of original works produced in the five years between Wilde's arrest and his death were
fewer than those produced between 1890 and 1895. There is, however, less of a discrepancy in the number of works *published*: the
book versions of *The Soul of Man*, *An Ideal Husband*, and *The
Importance Of Being Earnest*, as well as *Reading Gaol*, all appeared
after Wilde's arrest. Moreover it is worth stressing that our sense of
Wilde's enormous productivity in the first half of the 1890s derives
largely from the success of the Society Comedies; but critics such as
Kerry Powell have argued that these plays have a large number of
formulaic elements to them, as well as some degree of repetition.[112]
We also need to bear in mind the immense change in Wilde's personal situation. Restarting his career was hindered by a number of
factors, each of which separately presented a major handicap.

---

[108] *Letters*, 755.   [109] Ibid. 732 and n., 746, and 744.
[110] Ibid. 796 and n.   [111] Ellmann, 515.
[112] See Kerry Powell, *Oscar Wilde and the Theatre of the 1890s* (Cambridge: Cambridge
University Press, 1990).

The first problem, to which we have already alluded, was Wilde's name. For an author who had so persistently and self-consciously traded on personality, and who had been complicit in the ways in which publishers promoted his work via his name, to be forced to write anonymously amounted to a personal affront. More importantly, it required Wilde to rethink the whole basis of his creativity. Second, we should not overlook the enormous material obstacles confronting Wilde after his release from prison. Practically he was short of the basic tools of the writer, particularly books. In *De Profundis*, he described his attachment to his home and his 'charming things'—particularly 'my Library with its collection of presentation volumes from almost every poet of my time, from Hugo to Whitman, from Swinburne to Mallarmé, from Morris to Verlaine; with its beautifully bound editions of my father's and mother's works; its wonderful array of college and school prizes, its *éditions de luxe*, and the like'.[113] It is also worth bearing in mind that Wilde's theory of literary creativity had been based not on original thought, but on the original use of the ideas of others. The books which contained these ideas were no longer available in the series of hotel rooms that were Wilde's home for most of the final three years of his life. The peripatetic nature of that life also made communication with London difficult. Combined with a (for him) debilitating lack of money, it is not surprising that Wilde found these conditions uncongenial to writing. Moreover, in the 1880s and 1890s Wilde had always linked his creative powers to his capacity to earn money, and had been honest enough to acknowledge that the life of the *poète maudit* was hardly an ideal.

Some of the most compelling evidence for acceding to Ellmann's portrayal of Wilde, as a man in decline in those 'left-over years', seems to be provided by Wilde himself. In the spring of 1898 he acknowledged to Carlos Blacker that *Reading Gaol* was his '*chant de cygne*', and that 'I don't think I shall ever write again: *la joie de vivre* has gone, and that, with will-power, is the basis of art'.[114] In some ways this prophecy turned out to be true, and it is tempting to use Wilde's intimation of it to explain why he worked so hard to market the poem. However, such an argument has an important and unfortunate consequence: it inevitably leads one to view all Wilde's negotiations from 1898 onwards in terms of duplicity and deceit, an

---

[113] *Letters*, 451.   [114] Ibid. 715.

interpretation which surviving evidence does not support. Moreover a shabby and grasping Wilde is ironically quite at odds with the
figure of the tragic and broken man whose decline is to be pitied.

Happily there is a strong counter-argument to this view, one reminiscent of the case H. C. Robbins Landon has made about Mozart
in his final years, and one quite compatible with our sense of Wilde
the would-be literary entrepreneur: neither Wilde (nor Mozart)
knew that death was imminent; neither planned to die.[115] It is quite
plausible that Wilde made promises, and accepted money on account of them, with the intention of delivery at some point in the
future. It is worth reiterating that, even at the height of his success,
Wilde had a history of over-commitment, of advertising more work
than he could ever finish; likewise he had made a habit of delivering
completed work late—particularly his plays, which could be delayed by more than a year. In the past—and as with Rehan—he had
offered to return advances when he thought that it was unlikely he
would be able honour an agreement. On these occasions, Wilde's
dealings have never been seen as being motivated by duplicity or deceit, either by contemporary or subsequent commentators. Rather
his actions can be more easily understood as the pragmatic persistence of the professional. The Wilde of the early 1890s, who worked
harder at selling an existing work (such as *The Duchess of Padua*)
than writing a new one (such as *Lady Windermere's Fan*), and who
would enter into simultaneous negotiations with several theatre-
managers, promising more work than he could write—all of this is
very comparable with his dealings in 1899 and 1900. It is only *our*
knowledge of Wilde's impending death, and *our* knowledge that
those agreements could never be fulfilled, that allows him to be cast
as deceitful.

A final piece of evidence that strengthens the case for a continuity between the pre- and post-prison Wilde is to be found in the textual history of *De Profundis*, a work nearly always overlooked in the
narrative of Wilde's decline and failure. It is a document of well over
50,000 words, and is thus similar in length to the Lippincott *Dorian
Gray*. It was written under conditions more extreme than any of
Wilde's other works, a circumstance that has led critics to treat it as
an exception. Since the manuscript was published by Rupert Hart-
Davis in 1962, and its provenance and authority thus established, it

---

[115] See H. C. Robbins Landon, *1791: Mozart's Last Year* (London: Thames and Hudson,
1988).

has been usual to identify *De Profundis* as a private letter to Lord Alfred Douglas. A further reason for the traditional exclusion of it from the *oeuvre* of Wilde the professional writer is that a published version did not appear until five years after his death; moreover it was one heavily edited by Ross. However, there is strong evidence to suggest that Wilde himself conceived his manuscript letter as a work of literature (or the basis of a work) intended for publication—that for him it was not only (nor perhaps even primarily) a private letter to his lover. If we recognize *De Profundis* as an unfinished literary work, written with extraordinary speed and facility in the first twelve weeks of 1897, and comprising Wilde's second longest piece of prose, then the balance of creative work in the years preceding and following his arrest is dramatically altered.[116]

IV

In order to substantiate our claim that Wilde's manuscript was written with a view to publication, it is necessary to re-examine the history of its composition. Wilde wrote it in the early months of 1897 in prison at Reading.[117] The text was certainly finished by 1 April 1897, because on that day Wilde wrote to Robert Ross telling him to expect the manuscript in the post.[118] Actually the manuscript was retained by the prison authorities until Wilde's release on 18 May and was not given to Ross until 20 May when Wilde met him in Dieppe. The letter of 1 April also appointed Ross as Wilde's literary executor and as a consequence contains a detailed account of Wilde's last known intentions towards his manuscript. In brief, Wilde told Ross to read it and then have it 'carefully' copied for him (that is, Wilde), using Mrs Marshall's Typewriting Office in the Strand, an agency which Wilde and his managers had used for the Society Comedies.[119] Wilde stipulated that the transcription should be typed on 'good paper such as is used for plays'. He also stipulated that 'a wide rubricated margin should be left for corrections'.[120] Wilde habitually made marginal glosses and corrections to his own typescripts, often in coloured ink or pencil. The detailed instruction about the margin points to an intention to revise the

---

[116] There is a difficulty of terminology here. The title *De Profundis* was given by Ross to his 1905 abridged edition. To avoid confusion, henceforth we refer to the manuscript document housed in the British Library simply as 'the manuscript'.

[117] Hart-Davis dates the manuscript 'January–March'; see *Letters*, 423.

[118] Ibid. 512 ff.   [119] Ibid. 512–13.   [120] Ibid. 513.

typescript at a later date. It is worth repeating that Wilde asked Smithers to have the unfinished manuscript of *Reading Gaol* typed so that he could continue to work on it more easily. The use of typescript copies were integral to the way Wilde wrote: they were rarely final or fair copies, merely another form of a working draft. In other words, Wilde's comments suggest that the manuscript was intended as a letter (and as such finished) and simultaneously as the draft for some possible future work. It seems, then, that Wilde's instructions indicate that the letter was never just a letter. Wilde told Ross to send the manuscript to Alfred Douglas via More Adey, who was also to read it. Importantly, Wilde instructed that Douglas should not be told that a copy had been taken unless he complained 'of injustice in the letter or misrepresentation'—which of course he later did.[121] In the event, Ross decided to send not the original, but the typed copy to Douglas (who later claimed that he destroyed it).[122]

We should notice here how difficult it is to reconcile these instructions with the traditional (post-Hart-Davis) view of the work as a private letter. How often are letters circulated to other readers before their delivery to their recipients? Genuine love-letters are rarely copied in advance of their delivery; nor, if copied, are they retained in a form which allows for later correction or revision; nor indeed are they given titles—Wilde referred to his manuscript as 'his Encyclical Letter' and half-humorously offered the title of *Epistola: in Carcere et Vinculis* for it. (In addition, it was not Wilde's custom to keep copies of his own correspondence as he instructed Ross to do with the manuscript.) If the manuscript were simply a love-letter, who were the later putative corrections to be made for? Paradoxically, the Wilde who asks selected individuals to read his manuscript sounds very like the Wilde who sent drafts of his plays to Boucicault and Tree, and who would later send proofs of *Reading Gaol* and *An Ideal Husband* to Ross.

In the letter of 1 April 1897, Wilde made further stipulations which reinforce this sense that his manuscript was conceived as the basis for a publishable literary work. He suggested that Ross should have a second typewritten copy made for Ross himself, because as Wilde's literary executor he needed to 'have complete control over

---

[121] *Letters*, 514.

[122] This was clearly not Wilde's instruction in April or May of 1897, although we cannot discount the possibility that he changed his mind, and informed Ross privately of that change.

my plays, books and papers'. We might legitimately wonder why Ross would ever need control over a private love-letter, especially one sent to a rival for Wilde's affection.[123] In addition, Wilde also asked Ross to arrange for two typed copies of an abridgement of the manuscript to be made. These would include material from what Wilde referred to as folio 9 to folio 14 of the manuscript letter. These extracts were to be—in Wilde's words—'welded' by Ross with anything else 'you may extract that is good and nice in intention, such as the first page of sheet 15'. These typed copies were then to be sent to a woman whom Wilde identifies as the 'Lady of Wimbledon'— that is, to Adela Schuster—and to Frances Forbes-Robertson; she could in turn permit her brother Eric to read it.[124] At this point in his letter, Wilde seems to have in mind a substantially different work from his manuscript. The abridgement is not commensurate with the love-letter itself, but nor does it seem to be equivalent to the future emended—'corrected' is Wilde's word—work derived from the typed transcript with the 'wide rubricated margin'.

We do not know whether these abridgements were ever made, nor whether Schuster or the Forbes-Robertsons would have been told that they had received a truncated version of a private letter intended for Douglas. What is important is that there is clear evidence that Wilde had in mind several different uses for the material in his manuscript; only one of these involved a private letter to his lover (and even then it was not to be that private, having been read in advance by Ross and Adey). Second, it is equally important to register Wilde's desire to enlist the help of others—Ross and Adey—to realize his intentions; more particularly, the role Wilde assigned to Ross seems similar to that given to him in shaping *Reading Gaol*, a work conceived unambiguously for publication.

Wilde's instructions to Ross in his letter of 1 April were detailed. Nevertheless, they were not carried out precisely. We know that Ross made one typescript copy which he sent to Douglas. We also know that he kept the manuscript for a period of several years and eventually lodged it in 1909 in the Library of the British Museum in order to protect himself from possible litigation (and Wilde's work

---

[123] This second typed copy was presumably to have been made from the first, because the manuscript by this time should have been dispatched to Douglas. As we explain later, Vyvyan Holland claims that this second typescript was in fact a carbon copy of the first, a claim which is plausible if Ross always intended to retain possession of the manuscript himself.   [124] *Letters*, 513.

from possible destruction) at the hands of Douglas. There is no direct evidence that the second typescript was ever made, nor that it was delivered to Wilde for correction. However Wilde's correspondence with Ross in the summer and autumn of 1897 indicates that he was very eager to receive such a typescript and therefore that presumably he still had plans to produce a publishable literary work from it.[125] There is abundant circumstantial evidence that a second copy of the manuscript was made. The first kind of evidence comes from Vyvyan Holland, Wilde's son and a friend of Robert Ross. In 1949 Holland published what he claimed was the 'complete' 'carbon copy' of the typescript dictated by Ross from Wilde's manuscript to a typist. (The top typescript was the one sent to Douglas.) Holland is adamant that the carbon copy made in 1897 was 'still in the possession of Robert Ross' when he died in 1918 and that it then passed to him. Holland waited until after the death of Douglas in 1945 before publishing it. Like Ross he was alert to Douglas's predilection for the libel court.[126]

There is no reason to doubt Holland's account, for it is difficult to see what other source he could have used for his text. However, since the publication of the British Library manuscript by Hart-Davis, critics have been reluctant to accept the authority of Holland's text. In fact Hart-Davis himself (understandably) began this process by suggesting that Holland's text was incomplete and inaccurate; he identified four sorts of discrepancy between it and the manuscript: misreadings of Wilde's handwriting, '[a]ural misprints, probably caused by Ross's dictating to an ill-educated typist', changes in Wilde's 'grammar and syntax', and the shifting of passages.[127] Hart-Davis's account is underwritten by a traditional (and now dated) theory of editing, in which the manuscript is always judged to be the authentic and primary witness to the text, because it is the one nearest to the author's intentions. Other versions are by definition corrupt, forms of 'foul papers'. Hart-Davis seems to have made this assumption in ignorance of Wilde's writing practices. As we have said, Wilde habitually revised from typescript, and there is plenty of evidence, especially from the plays and *Reading Gaol*, to show that the process of typing somehow made a work more concrete and real to him—that it was part and parcel of the creative

---

[125] See *Letters*, 609 and 624.
[126] Vyvyan Holland (ed.), *De Profundis: The Complete Text* (London: Methuen, 1949), 9.
[127] *Letters*, 424.

process. If we treated all of Wilde's works in accordance with the principles behind Hart-Davis's editorial practice, then Wilde's *oeuvre* would look very different indeed. It is also worth pointing out that Hart-Davis's editorial practice has a tautologous relationship with his identification of the manuscript as a letter: it excludes seeing it as any other kind of document.

Because Hart-Davis (and nearly every critic after him) seems unaware that Wilde might have had multiple intentions towards his manuscript, he refuses to entertain the possibility that the carbon copy might have had Wilde's authority: that the discrepancies which Hart-Davis notices between the manuscript and Holland's 1949 edition might have been made in consultation with Wilde, or—and this is more likely—might have had his authority through the delegation of editorial responsibility to Ross. We are now in the realm of hypothesis because the fate of the carbon copy is not known. Nevertheless there is a further factor which supports the claim to authority of the Holland text, and therefore that Wilde intended that his manuscript be turned into a literary work. Whether or not Wilde ever received a copy of the text, he certainly had ample opportunity to discuss the manuscript with Ross. Ross spent ten days with Wilde in Dieppe in June 1897 before returning with the manuscript to London, and it seems highly unlikely that he and Wilde did not discuss the work which had so absorbed Wilde for the previous months. It is possible that Ross could have taken away a list of Wilde's corrections, additions, and emendations. This is to say the transposition and deletion of material mentioned by Hart-Davis, together with the changes in grammar, may have a completely different explanation—that they were approved by Wilde. Strong evidence for this is to be found in the striking similarities between Ross's 1905 abridged version and the corresponding sections of the Holland text: both contain exactly the same substantive 'deviations' from the manuscript.[128]

At first glance, it seems that there might be a banal explanation for this similarity: that Ross was working from the carbon-copy which Holland later published. But in 1905 Ross still had the manuscript in his possession: even if he did use the carbon-copy as printer's copy, he did not correct proofs against the manuscript. Why not? Why would he change Wilde's text in the unauthorized

---

[128] See [Robert Ross, ed.] *Oscar Wilde: De Profundis* (London: Methuen, 1905).

manner which Hart-Davis suggests, particularly when the manuscript itself was so readily accessible—perhaps even on his desk?
Why would he reproduce a typist's 'aural misprints'? A close study
of the variants shows them to be carefully thought-out, often
involving fine nuances of meaning, anything but 'misprints'.
Furthermore, where Ross's 1908 collected edition of Wilde repro-
duces previously unpublished material (such as *A Florentine
Tragedy*) Ross reveals himself to be a careful and exacting trans-
criber of Wilde's handwriting. Finally, even if Ross did introduce
some variants into the typescript and carbon-copy on his own initiative, this on its own is no reason to discount their authority. As we
shall elaborate in Chapter 7, we know that there was a strong collaborative element to most of Wilde's *oeuvre*.

As we have hinted, it is not known what happened to Holland's
carbon copy, and therefore the evidence finally to settle these issues
is not available.[129] What evidence we do possess, however, settles
the lesser issue of the identity of the manuscript and Wilde's intentions towards it. The very instruction to produce a typescript for
'correction', taken with Wilde's relationship with Ross (as literary
executor and what he called a 'literary friend'), and the ample opportunities the two men had to discuss the text, entitle us to consider that the manuscript was intended to become the basis for a
literary work as much as it was a letter. That literary work was
unfinished, in the sense that (as far as we know) Wilde never did correct or work on a typescript for publication, but it was one much
nearer completion than any of the play scenarios which he con-
cocted after his release from prison. More importantly it was a work
more likely to appeal to that 'public [which] liked to hear of my
pain—curiosity and the autobiographical form being elements of
interest'. The reason for Wilde's failure to return to the work is almost certainly his reconciliation with Douglas. This is not to say,
however, that Wilde necessarily forgot the work completely, nor that
he would not have returned to it had he lived longer.

V

We have suggested that there are many continuities in Wilde's attitudes towards writing before and after his disgrace. There is the

---

[129] Vyvyan Holland's son, Merlin Holland, reported in conversation that he has no memory of the carbon copy in his father's house; he suggested that it might have been sold.

time and energy which he devoted to selling his work; his obsession with obtaining a series of £100 advances for the *Mr and Mrs Daventry* scenario is similar to his earlier pre-trial determination not to involve himself with what he called 'speculative' writing. There are also his consistent difficulties in finishing long pieces of work and delivering copy to a deadline. There is the pragmatic desire to make a given piece of text (and often single ideas and jokes) serve a variety of purposes, and a willingness (and often a need) to work collaboratively and to delegate creative responsibility to others. Finally there is the persistence of the journalist's (or journeyman's) understanding of creativity as a means of earning money—a position that often led Wilde to over-commitment or to misrepresent his creative energies. In all these traits, and therefore throughout Wilde's career, we can witness the emergence of a writer determined to tune himself to the demands of the modern age, one willing to acknowledge that writing had become as much product as art.

Wilde's post-prison career is not then the tragedy identified by biographers such as Ellmann, that he was simply a broken man. His writing life in France and Italy was anything but purposeless and without application. The irony of Wilde's life, if there is an irony, was that he was excluded by those very writing conditions which he had so successfully exploited in the first half of the 1890s. More specifically Wilde had sold an image of himself as much as his work, and this fact was as true of his signed journalism as it was of his plays and his Bodley Head books. The forms of professional writing with which Wilde was most familiar and which offered the greatest financial prospects in 1897 were drama and writing for the popular press; but ironically it was exactly these forms which he could not exploit without a name. By 1900 journalism had become inextricably linked with the cult of the 'personality', but as a tradeable item Wilde's public personality was now of little or no value. In a similar way, the cult of playwriting as a kind of public performance, which once again Wilde had perfected, virtually ensured his ostracism from the London stage. Wilde seemed to realize as much despite the many offers he received. Interestingly the two sustained works which he did produce after his conviction and disgrace, *Reading Gaol* and *De Profundis*, continued to trade strongly on his life, but both represented the limits of how a suffering, contrite personality could be exploited creatively.

7

The Writer at Work

To document the mundane details of the writing career of an author so publicly disdainful of the quotidian aspects of his craft as Wilde might come as a surprise. Nearly every attempt in recent years to revalue Wilde's worth as a writer has ignored details like the nature of his contracts, the amount of money he earned, the material qualities of his books, and concentrated on the textual rather than the material aspects of his writing. In the 1970s and 1980s the aim of these sorts of accounts was to replace the myth of Wilde the dilettante who, according to Gide, had put his talent into his works and his genius into his life, with another myth, this time one of Flaubertian seriousness, where writing is a search for 'le mot juste', and where creativity is perspiration rather than inspiration.[1] The problem with these recent refigurings of Wilde, however, is that they seem incompatible with those other aspects of his career which we have been at pains to establish in the previous chapters—basically that sense of Wilde as a writer who could not ignore the fact that literature was in part a commodity, and who was as much concerned with what he called 'the *look* of a book' as with the integrity of the work itself. This discrepancy between the way Wilde actually sold his works and the ways in which recent critics have theorized his creativity is disturbing: it suggests that examining textual evidence in isolation from the material elements involved in authorship may have led to misrepresentation. To put the issue bluntly, can the 're-vising Wilde' (to use the title of Eltis's 1996 study) be accommodated to a Wilde preoccupied with the market-place? And how does knowledge of Wilde's concern with literature as product require us to reconsider our understanding of his habit of rewriting?

[1] This change of emphasis was largely due to the work of text-editors, whose interest in Wilde's composition revealed the considerable care taken in some revisions.

If we were looking for one word to sum up what the last chapters have revealed about Wilde's attitude towards his career, then 'opportunism' would be as good a candidate as any. The most striking element in this opportunism is his pragmatism and willingness to compromise. Wilde nearly always wrote for money; paradoxically, as he became more successful and his earnings increased, money became more rather than less important to him. The element of versatility that characterized his early career virtually disappeared once he found a market—the fashionable West End theatre—which combined social and artistic prestige with income. It is worth recalling that of the books published during the period of his success as a dramatist, not a single one represented new work: financial security did not propel Wilde into any form of creative risk-taking; rather the opposite.[2] By his own admission, once Wilde knew his market value, he was unwilling to undertake what he termed 'speculative work'.

A second and related feature of Wilde's opportunism is his willingness to work with others. Despite advertising the uniqueness of his genius, Wilde was often prepared to delegate creative responsibility, inviting other minds to exercise some control over the kind of writer he was to be. That control took a variety of forms: in the early stages of his career figures such as Dion Boucicault and Hermann Vezin were invited to criticize work in progress; later, despite being more successful and therefore perhaps more sure of his talents, Wilde still let others (particularly Ross) take some responsibility for the final shape of a work. Suggestions made by editors (such as Stoddart) were often acceded to, in much the same way as Wilde complied with the demands of his theatre-managers, particularly Alexander and Barrett. Finally, Wilde was also more than happy to allow his image as a writer to be determined by publishers, book-designers, and those with a more sophisticated understanding of the book trade. What is striking is not simply the consistency of these kinds of collaborations, but the fact that they appear, if anything, to have increased as Wilde's fame grew. Once again there seems to be an inverse relationship between success and creative autonomy— and this in turn suggests that for Wilde collaboration was the result of a willing pragmatism rather than, as some critics have suggested, a form of coercion and censorship.

[2] *The Sphinx*, published in 1894, may appear an exception to this argument; however it had been begun much earlier, perhaps as early as the late 1870s.

A third feature of Wilde's opportunism was his lifelong readiness to maximize the use of his material. He was reluctant to discard 'failed' work and quick to adapt successful material for new purposes. We have seen this already in what we have termed the phenomenon of the 'made' book and in the energy which Wilde put into placing works such as *The Duchess of Padua*. Wilde found writing difficult; more precisely, he found long stretches of sustained original thought daunting. Despite his display of intellectual virtuosity, he was a writer with a relatively small repertoire of ideas which he reused constantly. We see this economy of creativity not only in his published works, but also in his correspondence, and it testifies to an awareness of the limitations of his imaginative resources. In turn this self-awareness may explain why financial success did not liberate Wilde's creativity, but led instead to a form of conservatism where he was content to work with well-established formulas. Ironically the break with pattern writing, which we see in works such as *Reading Gaol* and *De Profundis*, was not a free choice by Wilde; rather it was dictated by the catastrophic changes in his material and personal circumstances following his imprisonment.

In public (that is, in his criticism, in interviews, and in letters to the press) Wilde certainly propagandized a Romantic notion of the autonomy and integrity of the artist—what Peter D. McDonald has called a 'purist' position. However in his dealings with the culture industry of Britain in the 1880s and 1890s he was much more in sympathy with the consumerism then beginning to emerge. The very vehemence of Wilde's public celebrations of the autonomy of the world of art may betray his fear that the opposite was the case— it may betray an anxiety about the depth of his immersion in market values. Alternatively it is equally likely that Wilde's celebrations of the artist are simply a cynical extension of those market-values, insofar as he realized that Romantic mythologies were attractive precisely because they pretended to eschew market forces. In terms of literature, these mythologies traded on exactly the demand for exclusivity and rarity which ironically, as Thorstein Veblen was to argue in his *Theory of the Leisure Class* (1899), a mass market was instrumental in bringing about.

All of this is not to deny that Wilde worked hard at his writing, and took his career very seriously. *De Profundis*, his spiritual autobiography, abounds in reproaches to both Douglas and himself for wasting time which would have been better spent writing.

Moreover, Wilde's worries about money and sales did not preclude an equally strong concern for his artistic reputation. The highlighting of exactly these ambitions explains why some critics have attached so much significance to Wilde's habit of revision. They have tended to make an automatic correlation between the effort spent on rewriting and what Peter Raby has termed Wilde's 'artistic seriousness'. It is 'an attitude', Raby claims, 'to which the numerous drafts and rewritings of all his comedies . . . testify'.[3] However, revision and rewriting, taken in themselves, reveal very little about what value ought to be attached to particular works, either by the author or by later critics: a bad writer may have to revise more often than a good one, and revision itself is not necessarily an index of improvement. More importantly most critics have ignored the fact that Wilde was an inconsistent reviser, and that some works, particularly the short fiction, underwent very little change on republication.

Understanding the process of revision always takes place in relation to ideas about the identity and integrity of a work. Certain editors will invariably see that integrity existing in the earliest complete draft of a work, and subsequent revisions to that draft (made to facilitate publication or performance) will be seen as forms of corruption. Exactly this position has led some critics to argue for the integrity of the four-act version of *The Importance of Being Earnest*, rather than the performed and published three-act version.[4] Other editors have a more teleological conception of composition in which the last version of a work overseen by the author is held to embody his most valid intentions towards it; in this view the last versions of Wilde's works published during his lifetime are held to possess the greatest integrity and authority.[5] Arguments like these, because they are incompatible with each other, have divided critics about the relative merits of, say, the periodical and book versions of *Dorian Gray*. And these disagreements in turn have obscured the fact that both positions—the first-text and last-text theses—have an important common ground: they both postulate the existence of a single authentic version of a work, even if they cannot agree on which

[3] Peter Raby, 'Wilde's Comedies of Society', in Peter Raby (ed.), *The Cambridge Companion to Oscar Wilde* (Cambridge: Cambridge University Press, 1997), 143.

[4] See e.g. Terence Brown's case for the text printed in Merlin Holland (ed.), *The Complete Works of Oscar Wilde* (Glasgow: HarperCollins, 1994), 351–6.

[5] This presupposition underlies Sos Eltis's study of Wilde's Society Comedies. See Eltis, *Revising Wilde: Society and Subversion in the Plays of Oscar Wilde* (Oxford: Clarendon Press, 1996).

version embodies that authenticity. Significantly both understand the process of revision and redrafting in relation to that authentic version.

There are, however, a number of other ways of conceptualizing the relationship between versions and works, and these have a dramatic impact on our understanding of revision.[6] Some authors, most notably perhaps D. H. Lawrence, revised so systematically and continuously that the opposition between authentic and inauthentic versions of their works makes little sense. As Lawrence's editors have argued, such revisions seem to have been made in particular circumstances to suit particular occasions, so much so that it is possible to think of individual versions possessing the status of separate works.[7] In these cases it can seem pointless to construct a stemma, for the arrangement of versions and works into a hierarchy will do little but exhibit the prejudices of the modern editor. We need, then, to be alert to the fact that we cannot take for granted a narrative of development which orders versions into a sequenced history. Holding to such an assumption may distort the way in which we identify versions. To put this into the terminology of editorial theory, we ought to be cautious about the narrative paradigms which we bring to our interpretation of textual stemmata. For the purposes of understanding Wilde's writing, the choice need not necessarily be between a progression towards, or away from, the perfect text. It is equally possible that Wilde's revisions were made locally to produce different texts to suit different circumstances. *Dorian Gray* provides a good test of this hypothesis: it is not clear whether from Wilde's (or any other) point of view the longer and later book version was necessarily better, or worse, than the earlier and shorter Lippincott version. The additions and emendations to the second version (as we describe later) were made for a variety of reasons, and it is more honest (if less tidy) for an editor to acknowledge that, like Wordsworth's *Prelude*s and Shakespeare's *King Lear*s, the two versions constitute works conceived for different purposes. The logic

---

[6] For the theorization of the relationships between versions and works, see George Bornstein and Ralph G. Williams (eds.), *Palimpsest: Editorial Theory in the Humanities* (Ann Arbor: University of Michigan Press, 1993).

[7] See e.g. John Worthen, 'D. H. Lawrence: Problems with Multiple Texts', in Ian Small and Marcus Walsh (eds.), *The Theory and Practice of Text-Editing* (Cambridge: Cambridge University Press, 1991), 14–34; and Michael Black, 'Editing a Constantly-Revising Author: the Cambridge Edition of Lawrence in Historical Context,' in Mara Kalnins (ed.), *D. H. Lawrence: Centenary Essays* (Bristol: Bristol Classical Press, 1986), 191–210.

of this proposition is that judgements about the value of particular versions should be made in relation to a knowledge of their various functions. This way of understanding revision, which ties rewriting to local circumstances, is one perfectly compatible with the picture we have drawn of Wilde the opportunist, of a writer driven by the need to respond to cultural and economic changes in the literary market-place.

It is interesting that studies of Wilde's writing practices have been restricted either to individual works or to individual genres.[8] This piecemeal approach has tended to prevent critics from appreciating the diversity of Wilde's motives for revision and from realizing that there is no consistent pattern to his rewriting throughout the *oeuvre*. We have noted already that some works were revised far less systematically than others. The obvious (if banal) explanation for this is that Wilde found some sorts of writing more difficult than others, and some revision more worth his time and trouble. Equally obvious (and equally banal) is the fact that Wilde spent most time and most effort on the works which had the potential to earn him the greatest money and fame and which simultaneously required the greatest financial commitment from others: these works were of course the plays. However, the picture is more complicated than such reductive explanations suggest, because if we look at the whole of Wilde's output, we see that his pattern of revision differed not only between but also within works. As we will show, a single text could be revised in quite disparate ways, ranging from fastidious changes to individual lexical items, to what appears to be a more casual importation of whole blocks of material, designed principally to pad out a piece. To make sense of such apparently contradictory practices we need to be aware that Wilde revised in response to a number of imperatives, only some of which concerned the aesthetic value of the work.

In assessing the careers of writers, the same kind of narrative which orders versions in relation to works is also typically used to organize works in relation to each other within an *oeuvre*, with the result that originality and a sense of growing maturity tend to be

---

[8] In addition to Eltis's work, see also Lawrence Danson, *Wilde's Intentions: The Artist in his Criticism* (Oxford: Clarendon Press, 1997); Donald Lawler (ed.), *Oscar Wilde, The Picture of Dorian Gray* (London: W. W. Norton, 1988); Bobby Fong, 'The Poetry of Oscar Wilde: A Critical Edition'. Unpublished Ph.D. thesis (University of California, Los Angeles, 1978); and Bobby Fong and Karl Beckson (eds.), *Oscar Wilde: Poems and Poems in Prose* (Oxford: Oxford University Press, 2000).

valued over repetition and familiarity. The unthinking assimilation of just such a concept of creativity may explain why critics have found it so difficult to account satisfactorily for other elements in Wilde's writing practices—namely, his lifelong habit of plagiarism and self-plagiarism and the use of schematic and often repetitive plot devices and themes.[9] Of course many forms of writing (and many writers who seek commercial success) do trade quite deliberately on the formulaic: the pleasure of recognition is a response intrinsic to most popular genres, and certainly to those new forms of literary entertainment which emerged in the second half of the nineteenth century, including collections of fairy-tales, sensation fiction, and most theatrical entertainments—that is, precisely the forms with which Wilde first experimented in his attempts to establish himself. However, the sense of repetition that we experience in Wilde's *oeuvre* is not confined to these generic borrowings. For many readers of Wilde, one work seems uncannily to recapitulate the concerns of others, even when the genre is quite different. So at times it is possible to see Wilde's actual and individual works as embodiments of some ideal but unwritten text, a Platonic Wilde text, as it were. It is exactly this sort of familiarity which is typically viewed pejoratively, dismissed as a failure of inventiveness, or as evidence of a lack of creative development. In such judgements, however, insufficient attention has been paid to the precise *nature* of what is being repeated.

First, we need to distinguish between the generic borrowings in Wilde's work (which, as we have suggested, may simply be a response to certain kinds of market conditions and transactions with popular literary culture), and the sense of recognition brought about by more direct forms of repetition, such as plagiarism. Second, and more importantly, within the category of plagiarism itself, it is necessary to discriminate between the different units of discourse which are repeated, as well as between the contexts which permit and define such reuse. We will show that, as with his habit of revision, Wilde's writing is characterized by various *types* of repetition, and this complexity is obscured by subsuming them all under the blanket term of plagiarism, carrying, as it does, so many pejorative overtones. There certainly are occasions when the repetition of

---

9 Tensions between the various elements in Wilde's writing practices are discussed by Josephine M. Guy in 'Self-Plagiarism, Creativity and Craftsmanship in Oscar Wilde', *English Literature in Transition*, 41: 1 (1998), 6–23.

lines, phrases, or blocks of dialogue does seem to be the result of straightforward laziness—compensation for a lack of imagination or, more simply, of time. At the other end of the spectrum, however, there are examples of copying that seem almost unconscious, and that appear to be unregistered or unmarked by Wilde. They do not suggest a desire to deceive, but rather indicate the peculiarly atomistic way in which Wilde's creative mind worked—'modular' is the term which we shall use to describe this aspect of his composition. Finally, there are yet other instances (particularly those involving self-plagiarism) where repetition seems to involve an element of calculation, to the extent that it appears strategic. The effect is like that of a carefully contrived signature—an attempt, perhaps, to establish a distinctive but familiar voice in the overcrowded market for popular entertainment. Evidence that such a practice could work can be seen in some of Wilde's Bodley Head books. The exclusivity so carefully cultivated in these publications, and the rarity value which they exploited, may seem at odds with the lack of originality in the works themselves. For example, the publication of *A Woman of No Importance* made explicit how much of it had appeared before as dialogue in *Dorian Gray*, and in ways which the audience at a performance may not have detected. In textual terms, what was the exclusivity for which the reader had to stump up 15s.? As we noted in Chapter 5, initially Wilde was unwilling to have his plays printed as a set, and this reluctance might betray an anxiety about their generic and textual closeness. Mathews and Lane, however, attempted to turn this quality into a positive asset: the decision to produce the plays as a collectable set underlined in a visual and material way, or created a visual and material analogue for, the elements of similarity between them. It attempted, that is, to turn them into the visual equivalent of a literary signature or style. That the books sold out, suggests that some readers at least appreciated this feature of Wilde's dramatic *oeuvre*.

I

We have suggested that the complexity of the cultural environment in which Wilde wrote should alert the modern reader to an equally complex set of motives underlying his composition. His first medium, that of poetry, provides a useful starting-point for understanding that complexity. As we noted in Chapter 3, Wilde valued poetry very highly, and in the early years of his career as a writer he was prepared to commit considerable effort to perfecting individual poems—effort which was not necessarily incompatible with their derivative qualities. A significant number of the pieces collected in *Poems* (1881) had first appeared in periodicals. Where manuscripts for these works survive we see evidence of a process of careful revision from manuscript to periodical to book. On many occasions changes are made to single lexical items. For example, texts of what later became 'By the Arno' see Wilde revising 'golden mist' in line 18 of both the manuscript and *Dublin University Magazine* versions, to 'sea-green mist' in the first edition of *Poems*, to 'sea-green vest' in the 1882 editions. Another early poem, 'Rome Unvisited' shows a similar kind of revision, but in a different direction: here Wilde's final text shows him reverting to his first thoughts. The line in one manuscript 'Is garnered into yellow sheaves' (line 50) becomes 'The reapers garner into yellow sheaves' in a second manuscript version, and is retained in the poem's first publication in the *Month and Catholic Review*. In his revisions for the book publication of the poem, however, Wilde reverted in part to his first thoughts by changing the line to 'Is garnered into dusty sheaves'.

The nature of this kind of literary polishing is perhaps best summed-up in a term adapted by Walter Pater, 'the labour of the file'.[10] We see further evidence of it in the composition of *Reading Gaol*, where Wilde continually requested Smithers to change single words to give a more precise rendering of a mood.[11] Such attention to fine nuances of meaning also occurs at moments in the genesis of the Society Comedies. In an early draft of *Lady Windermere's Fan*, for example, the characterization of Lord Augustus as a society 'masher' is indicated by the prolific use of 'damned' as one of his verbal mannerisms. In later drafts Wilde consistently omitted the word, perhaps because it attributed too great a vulgarity to an aristocratic man-about-town. However in a draft produced much nearer to the time of performance, Wilde reincorporated his first idea, but with a change in spelling (to 'demmed') which softened and made comic the coarseness of the original slang; this change was retained in the 1893 published edition of the play. Revisions of this kind are the easiest to accommodate to a notion of Wilde the

---

[10] Walter Pater, *Marius the Epicurean* (1885; London: Macmillan, 1892), i. 105. The phrase translates Horace's 'limae labor' in *Ars Poetica*, i. 291.

[11] See e.g. *Letters*, 668–9, 671, 676, and 680.

craftsman, as they seem to reveal a refinement of expression consistent with the Paterian idea of literary architectonics, that sense of what Pater later called 'true *composition* and not mere loose accretion'.[12]

However there were other sorts of revisions to poems which appear more contrived in the sense that their effect does not seem to be a wholly aesthetic or expressive one. 'Sonnet on Approaching Italy' in *Poems* (1881) was first published as 'Salve Saturnia Tellus' in the *Irish Monthly* in 1877, with the place and date, 'Genoa, 1877', appended to it. Wilde retitled and slightly revised the piece for the *Biograph and Review* in 1880 as 'Sonnet Written at Turin'. At first sight the occasion of the poem seems (in a quintessentially Romantic way) to be intrinsic to its effect; it suggests that the poem ought to derive some of its power from the specificity of its setting. However the fact that virtually the same lines are seen by Wilde to be equally applicable to more than one location suggests a rather more pragmatic attitude towards writing. Despite the poem's trading on a Romantic response to landscape, Wilde's revisions do not seem to have anything to do with capturing the authenticity of felt experience. While the mechanisms of some of Wilde's revisions seem thoroughly Paterian, the force of Pater's claim (made apropos of Rossetti's poetry) that 'the term was always . . . deliberately chosen from many competitors, as the just transcript of that peculiar phase of soul which he alone knew, precisely as he knew it', is often completely lost in Wilde's work.[13] Moreover, when this pragmatism is set beside forms of rewriting which are more obviously designed to refresh old material, it begins to look as if Wilde's revisions sometimes possess a more calculating and cynical element to them. For example, the poem 'Graffiti d'Italia: I. San Miniato' was originally published as a three-part poem in the *Dublin University Magazine* in 1876. When Wilde recast it for *Poems* (1881) it became two 'new' works. The first part was slightly revised and was entitled 'San Miniato'; the second and third parts of the 1876 poem were also slightly revised and retitled 'By the Arno'. Moreover, Wilde separated these two 'new' works in *Poems* (1881) by some 120 pages: he seems, then, to have been deliberately disguising the fact that they had their origins in a single poem which had already been published.

---

[12] Pater, *Appreciations* (1889; London: Macmillan, 1910), 24.   [13] Ibid. 207.

On the occasions when Wilde revised old material in a way intended to permit its reuse, we can see that the motivation behind revision was more complex than a 'purist' Paterian schema allowed. For Wilde the point of revising individual poems was always for publication or republication. Indeed the limitations of Paterian notions of expressivity, creativity, and revision lie precisely in their inability to take account of the simple exigencies of publication, of the fact that most writing is undertaken with an intention to be published, and that the desire to be published in its turn involves financial imperatives. It is hard to imagine Wilde writing a work such as *Gaston de Latour*, even harder to contemplate that he would have decided not to continue with the half-finished novel (as Pater did), or—again as Pater did—withdraw at his own expense a collection of essays, *Dionysus and Other Studies*, after revising proofs. In addition the development of Wilde's poems from manuscript to periodical to book subjected them to a process of increasing scrutiny: the reader who came across a single poem by Wilde in a literary periodical such as the *Biograph and Review* had more modest expectations than the reader who spent 10s. 6d. on a whole volume of his poetry. It was not just that a collection of poetry made larger claims for itself from a single and occasional poem in a magazine; books and periodicals themselves possessed a different status in the eyes of the Victorian reading public, a fact to which Wilde was alert. We need, then, to be aware that for Wilde the process of revising a work rarely took place in isolation from the desire to sell it, and that desire to sell in its turn inevitably involved a number of non-aesthetic criteria.

We can see exactly these mixed motives in the textual history of Wilde's short fiction, nearly all of which was written initially to be published in periodicals. Wilde produced three volumes of short fiction: *The Happy Prince and Other Tales* (1888), *A House of Pomegranates* (1891), and *Lord Arthur Savile's Crime and Other Stories* (1891). Only the first volume contained material which had not been previously published, although this was because Wilde had tried but failed to place any of the stories in magazines. Two stories from *A House of Pomegranates*, 'The Young King' and 'The Birthday of the Infanta', had appeared in 1888 and 1889 in *The Ladies' Pictorial* and *Paris Illustré*, and all the stories contained in *Lord Arthur Savile's Crime* were first published in the *Court and Society Review* and *World* in 1887. The revisions from periodical to book versions are minor, and some are merely typographical. In

Lord Arthur Savile's Crime, for example, the layout of 'The Canterville Ghost' is altered to divide the story into more sections; likewise the sections of the title story are changed into chapters, and this increases its length, so much so that the story runs to 73 pages in a book of 168 pages. In a similar way, the stories in *The Happy Prince* are set in large type with wide margins; the format could have been designed with the child reader in mind, but it had the serendipitous effect of padding out a small amount of text to fill 116 pages. Those few revisions which were made for book publication tend to be to single lexical items or short phrases. For example, in the fourth section of the book version of 'The Canterville Ghost', 'he took off his boots' becomes 'he removed his boots', and 'the twins' in the same paragraph become 'the insolent young Etonians'. Similarly in 'Lord Arthur Savile's Crime' 'cold metal' is changed to 'wet metal', and 'as if iteration' becomes 'as though iteration'. These sorts of changes do not appear to be very systematic and look to be of the type that might have been made by using the periodical versions as printer's copy. They are certainly not the product of serious rethinking, and do not involve any significant reconceptualizing of the stories. A more substantial, although still minor change concerns the addition of short (and ironic) subtitles to all of the stories in *Lord Arthur Savile's Crime*. Only one of these, the subtitling of 'The Canterville Ghost' as 'A Hylo-Idealist Romance' has a specific referent; on the three other occasions, the change seems to be little more than an afterthought.[14] Similarly, Wilde added dedications to various society women, his wife included, to the stories collected in *A House of Pomegranates*. Part of his intention may have been to signal the adult content of the volume, or to indicate that it was the kind of expensive but elaborate book which a society woman might buy for herself, as much as for her children.

In general terms it seems that Wilde changed his stories very little textually in order to re-present them in book form. Unfortunately we do not have manuscripts for most of them (portions of the manuscript of 'The Fisherman and his Soul' are all that are known to survive), and so it is not possible to discover either the effort that went into their original composition, nor the amount of revision between manuscript and first publication. (It is worth remembering, though, that in the late 1880s, when the stories were being prepared

[14] See Josephine M. Guy, 'An Allusion in Oscar Wilde's "The Canterville Ghost"', *Notes and Queries*, 45 NS: 2 (June 1998), 224–6.

for the periodical press, Wilde was occupied with reviewing for the *Pall Mall Gazette* and with his editorial responsibilities for the *Woman's World*, and would therefore have had relatively little time to devote to them.) All we are entitled to conclude is that Wilde was apparently satisfied with the stories in their first published form or that he did not think that the effort involved in recasting them from periodical to book worthwhile. Textual changes aside, however, we should note that other elements of book publication would inevitably change the presentation of the stories, and perhaps their value. First, and like *Poems* (1881), the very act of collecting occasional pieces conferred a kind of distinction, which Wilde may have thought sufficient to sell works already published individually. Second, there was the issue of illustrations. In *The Happy Prince*, where material appeared for the first time, the stories were accompanied by full-page illustrations by Walter Crane and head-and tail-piece designs by Jacomb Hood (as we have mentioned, illustrations were a *sine qua non* of children's books of this kind). By contrast, there were no illustrations for *Lord Arthur Savile's Crime*, even though some of the stories had been illustrated in their original periodical versions.[15] As we suggested in Chapter 3 the relatively modest sales of that volume may have persuaded Wilde of the benefits of publishing *A House of Pomegranates* with pictures—that is, of selling the artwork as much as the stories. Wilde's attitude towards his short fiction seems pragmatic in that his concern is largely technical, with re-presenting rather than with rewriting old material. It is interesting that a similar set of priorities underlies some of the revisions made to the book version of *Dorian Gray*, even though at first sight these changes do seem to be more thoroughgoing.

The textual history of *Dorian Gray* has been well documented, and reconstructing the way in which the two versions of the novel were composed has been helped by the fact that various manuscript and typescript drafts survive.[16] By his own testimony—and in a pattern repeated with other commissions—Wilde found the work difficult to complete. J. M. Stoddart, an employee of the Philadelphian publisher J. B. Lippincott and Co., commissioned a story from Wilde in late August 1889 and stipulated that it was to be finished by early October. Wilde, following his custom of making

---

[15] The probable reason is that illustrations were too expensive for a 2s. book.

[16] Descriptions of the manuscripts are given by Lawler (ed.), *Dorian Gray*, pp. x–xiii; by Beckson, *Encyclopedia*, 272; and in *OWR*, 107, 116, and 145.

the most of work which was already to hand, originally thought of
offering Stoddart 'The Fisherman and his Soul', a story that was
probably not yet finished. Wilde, however, could not work the story
up into a piece long enough to satisfy the terms of Stoddart's commission.[17] In December he suggested a new subject, which turned
out to be *Dorian Gray*, and which he finished in the spring of 1890,
probably by mid-March because by then Stoddart was commissioning more work, writing to Wilde for a contribution to a projected
publication on the 'ever-important question of Realism and
Idealism'.[18] Wilde sent Stoddart a fair copy of his story, which he
had had typed at Mrs Dickens's Typewriting Office in the Strand.
This typescript has survived, and is interesting because, like the
typescript drafts of many of Wilde's plays, it is marked up in two
hands. One is Wilde's and the other is almost certainly that of
Stoddart. Some of the corrections imposed American usage, but far
from all of the emendations are of this sort. There are also substantial changes, particularly the deletion and insertion of large blocks
of material. The additional material is nearly always in Wilde's
hand, but most of the deletions are by Stoddart; often Stoddart appears to be 'censoring' the text, on occasions striking out Wilde's
later thoughts and corrections. So the tone of the opening of the
typescript of Chapter 3 (folio 44) becomes more muted after
Stoddart's changes. A further example of this sort of editing is to be
found in Chapter 7. The typescript shows that Wilde originally
wrote 'something infinitely tragic in a romance that was at once so
passionate and so sterile'; after Stoddart's editing, this becomes
'something tragic in a friendship so colored by romance'.[19]

We can be fairly certain that Stoddart did not consult Wilde
about these revisions, for he would not have had the time to do so.
Moreover the fact that Stoddart's emendations are on occasions
made to Wilde's own corrections to the typescript shows that it was
his decisions which were final. However it is likely that Wilde had in
any case delegated final responsibility to Stoddart. This possibility
of delegation is borne out by the fact that when Wilde was working
on his revisions for the book version of the novel, he almost

[17] *More Letters*, 87.
[18] Clark Library. Wilde 1890 Mar. 17. ALS J. Alfred Stoddart to Oscar Wilde. These
dates contradict the report in *The Bookman* that Wilde wrote the novel 'in three weeks'; see
Ch. 3, 65.
[19] This typescript (of the first Lippincott edition of *Dorian Gray*) is held at the Clark
Library: W6721M3 P611 [1890] Boxed.

certainly used the Lippincott text and not his original manuscript (which was still in his possession), nor the typescript which had been made from the manuscript. As a result he accepted silently many of Stoddart's suggestions. There is some evidence that Wilde had established a relationship of trust with Stoddart which dated back to their dealings almost a decade earlier; in 1882 Stoddart had published Rennell Rodd's *Rose Leaf and Apple Leaf* which contained an introduction (entitled *L'Envoi*) by Wilde. On that occasion Wilde had entrusted Stoddart with ensuring the correctness of his French.[20]

The changes which Wilde made from the periodical to the book version of *Dorian Gray* were extensive, and are of three different sorts. First, and as we have already noted in Chapter 3, the higher price of the Ward, Lock volume required the addition of further material to give the book some sort of 'added value' above and beyond what was readily available to the purchasers of the periodical. In addition it was put to Wilde by George Lock that he might use this opportunity to change the ending of the novel to make its moral less ambiguous. Wilde's response was to divide chapter 13 into two (becoming chapters 19 and 20 in the book version), and to add six new chapters (3, 5, 15, 16, 17, and 18). These developed the melodramatic elements of the plot; equally importantly Wilde used his new chapters to sharpen his satirical portrait of British aristocratic society, a tactic that would become a hallmark of the Society Comedies, and one that Wilde had already used in a local way in some of the short fiction. The dialogue in these new chapters is notable for its witty urbanity and topical reference to British class obsessions. These sorts of revision give to the book version of *Dorian Gray* precisely that sort of thematic reconceptualization absent from Wilde's local revisions to his short stories: most obviously they change the tone of the novel so that it is less exotic and homoerotic. On the other hand, it is possible to exaggerate the extent of Wilde's structural reworking. Manuscript evidence shows that the new chapters were composed as separate items and more or less 'slotted' into the Lippincott text, in a manner reminiscent of the addition of stanzas to *Reading Gaol*. Moreover for these new chapters Wilde drew on material, particularly jokes, which he already had to hand. So in the new chapter 3 the aside by Mr Erskine that 'Perhaps, after

[20] *More Letters*, 45–6.

all, America has never been discovered . . . I myself would say that it had merely been detected', repeats a sentiment in a notebook jotting which the cataloguers at the Clark Library date from the 1880s: 'It is a vulgar error to suppose that America was ever discovered. It was merely detected.'[21] It is also worth noting that many of the jokes in the new chapters were later reused in *Lady Windermere's Fan* and *A Woman of No Importance*, a strategy which suggests that much of the new material had a free-standing or modular quality to it, and that Wilde did not feel it necessary to tailor it to fit the original Lippincott text.

As well as adding new material, Wilde made a number of substantial but local changes which revised aspects of the novel's tone and characterization. On a few occasions these involved changes in the role and presentation of minor characters. The best-known example is the way in which Mrs Leaf, Dorian's housekeeper, is written down from being a striking comic character (in chapter 8 of the periodical) to that of a faceless servant (in chapter 10 of the book). The most important modulations in the novel's tone are brought about by the addition of short 'purple passages'; for example, the brief description of Dorian's anxiety (as he waits for Alan Campbell) in chapter 12 of the periodical version is elaborated into a melodramatic *tour de force* in chapter 14 of the book:

This was the man that Dorian Gray was waiting for, pacing up and down the room, glancing every moment at the clock, and becoming horribly agitated as the minutes went by. At last the door opened, and his servant entered. (*Periodical*)

This was the man Dorian Gray was waiting for. Every second he kept glancing at the clock. As the minutes went by he became horribly agitated. At last he got up, and began to pace up and down the room, looking like a beautiful caged thing. He took long stealthy strides. His hands were curiously cold.

The suspense became unbearable. Time seemed to him to be crawling with feet of lead, while he by monstrous winds was being swept towards the jagged edge of some black cleft or precipice. He knew what was waiting for him there; saw it indeed, and, shuddering, crushed with dank hands his burning lids as though he would have robbed the very brain of sight, and driven the eyeballs back into their cave. It was useless. The brain had its own food on which it battened, and the imagination, made grotesque by terror, twisted and distorted as a living thing by pain, danced like some foul

---

[21] Clark Library. Wilde W6721M3. P572. [188–?]. See also *OWR*, 141.

puppet on a stand, and grinned through moving masks. Then, suddenly, Time stopped for him. Yes: that blind, slow-breathing thing crawled no more, and horrible thoughts, Time being dead, raced nimbly on in front, and dragged a hideous future from its grave, and showed it to him. He stared at it. Its very horror made him stone.

At last the door opened, and his servant entered. (*Book*)

By far the largest number of changes, however, are those which resemble that polishing 'labour of the file', the alterations to single words and short phrases, a process to which many of the poems were subjected. There is, for example, the series of changes in chapter 8 to a speech by Dorian about the physical weight of his portrait. The typescript produced at Mrs Dickens's Office shows that Wilde's initial thought was to give Dorian a straightforward punning comment: 'there is a good deal of heaviness in modern art'; this was changed for the periodical version to a pun having a thematic significance: the picture is now 'a terrible load to carry'. In the book version neither pun survives: 'I am afraid it is rather heavy' is Dorian's straightforward reply. In a similar way, a description is changed in chapter 2 by just one word: 'he would become ignoble, hideous, and uncouth' in the periodical becomes in the book version: 'he would become dreadful, hideous, and uncouth'.[22]

It is easy to see why these three sorts of revisions—structural, changes to characterization and tone, and to individual lexical items—when taken together, have been seen as evidence of Wilde the craftsman. In the manuscript draft of chapter 3 (for the book version) we see this whole range of rewriting, from the substitution of a word by a synonym, to the more thoroughgoing addition of paradoxical dialogue.[23] It is therefore tempting to conclude that habitual reworking and revising of material was intrinsic to the way in which Wilde composed. However, it is important to register the fact that his revisions are of distinct kinds and often have different motivations. Ironically what appears to be the most substantial recasting, the addition of whole new chapters, may be the most difficult to reconcile with a notion of Wilde the aesthetic purist, because we know that he carried out this work principally in order to sell the book version. The consequence of these added chapters is certainly to change the tone of the novel quite significantly, but it is a moot

---

[22] Lawler (ed.) *Dorian Gray*, 269 and 129; 238; 191 and 25.

[23] See the manuscript draft of ch. 3 held in the Clark Library, particularly fos. 16 and 23. Wilde W6721 M3 P611 [1890] Bound.

point whether the new material is adequately integrated—that is, whether the new tone is successfully sustained. More importantly, and as we have noted, the new material gives evidence of what we can call a 'cut-and-paste' element to Wilde's creativity, and this kind of revision runs counter to notions of the integrity of a literary work. The most dramatic evidence of this mentality exists in the manuscript of Wilde's Chatterton lecture, large parts of which were physically cut out of books written by other hands and pasted together, with only the occasional linking sentence by Wilde.[24] On the other hand, this is not to deny that there are also elements of the 'limae labor' in Wilde's attention to nuances of meaning in *Dorian Gray*. We need to acknowledge that both sorts of revision coexist in Wilde's recasting of his novel, and that they continue to coexist in the drafts of his later work, particularly the plays. This in turn suggests that both methods of writing and revising, however disparate they seem to us, were compatible activities for Wilde. Interestingly, the picture of Wilde which we have described—that of a writer for whom aesthetic and financial imperatives could often pull in opposite directions—does help to explain this tension.

If we turn to the critical writing, we can see exactly the same range of revisions, and exactly the same reasons for them. Wilde left the major part of his contributions to the periodical press uncollected. The essays that he chose to reproduce in book form were, unsurprisingly, those which had appeared in the more 'weighty' periodicals: the *Nineteenth Century*, the *Fortnightly Review*, and *Blackwood's*. His first plan was contained in a proposal to William Blackwood in July 1889 to collect 'a special volume of essays and studies', to include 'The Portrait of Mr W. H.', and 'the things that have appeared in the *Nineteenth Century* and the *Fortnightly*, and that excited much interest'. The essays to which Wilde alludes were 'Pen, Pencil, and Poison' and 'The Decay of Lying'. Blackwood was lukewarm, claiming that 'these volumes are . . . not remunerative to either publisher or author'.[25] A year later the publication of Wilde's longest critical piece, 'The True Function and Value of Criticism', may have revived his interest in bringing out a volume of critical essays. The combination of this piece with 'Pen, Pencil, and Poison',

---

[24] Wilde's AMS notebook lecture on Chatterton contains printed clippings from Daniel Wilson, *Chatterton: A Biography* (1869) and David Masson, *Chatterton: A Story of the Year 1770* (1874). Clark Library. Wilde W6721M3. E78. [1886?].

[25] *Letters*, 246 and note.

and 'The Decay of Lying' (by now there were separate plans for 'The Portrait of Mr W. H.') made a more coherent collection, though the volume would still have been rather slight. In a way which anticipated his attitude towards his theatrical commissions, and to fill out the book, Wilde retrieved an old essay, 'Shakespeare and Stage Costume' which had appeared in the *Nineteenth Century* as long ago as May 1885. In fact that essay in its turn had many similarities to a piece which Wilde had published just two months earlier in March 1885 in the *Dramatic Review* and called 'Shakespeare on Scenery'.[26] It was not simply that the *Nineteenth Century* essay reused Wilde's earlier ideas about archaeological realism on the stage; rather he transposed whole phrases from one essay to the other. There were, then, two problems with reusing 'Shakespeare and Stage Costume' in 1891. Most obviously the reference of the piece was very dated. (It had been written in response to local debates in the periodical press.) In addition that very datedness would have alerted an astute reader to the fact that Wilde had used the material twice before. Aware of these problems, Wilde substantially recast and retitled the essay (as 'The Truth of Masks') in order to disguise its origins and to match its tenor and argument to the other more recent pieces. This tactic is itself confirmation of our earlier assertion that Wilde found sustained original arguments difficult; it is striking that he was willing to take such a risk in a collection intended to substantiate his claim to be taken seriously as a critic.

The collection was the volume which was published as *Intentions* by Osgood, McIlvaine in 1891. There is some evidence, however, that Wilde was not wholly satisfied with it; in particular—and not surprisingly—he seemed to entertain doubts about the value of 'The Truth of Masks'. When he approached William Heinemann in the summer of 1891 with a proposal for a cheaper edition, he suggested that it could be omitted.[27] In a similar way, when discussing the possibility of a French translation with Jules Cantel in the same year, he again suggested omitting the final essay, commenting that 'je ne l'aime plus'. In its place, Wilde offered 'The Soul of Man under Socialism', a substantially longer piece which had recently appeared.[28]

---

[26] Wilde, 'Shakespeare on Scenery', *Dramatic Review*, 1: 7 (14 March 1885), 99; Ross, *Reviews*, 6–10.   [27] *Letters*, 294. See also Danson, *Wilde's Intentions*, 7–9.
[28] *Letters*, 294–5. The translation did not appear until 1914.

All the periodical essays published in *Intentions* underwent substantial revisions. Some were to restore material that had been
deleted by magazine editors for reasons of space.[29] Other revisions
involved the introduction of new material: 'The Decay of Lying'
and 'The Critic as Artist' both had additions made to them, although some were of that 'cut-and-paste' variety which had characterized the new chapters in the book version of *Dorian Gray*. The
best example of this latter sort of revision is the long speech given to
Vivian in 'The Decay of Lying' in *Intentions* about London fogs and
their origins in Impressionist art. It is placed between two of his
other large claims: that 'Life imitates Art far more than Art imitates
Life' and that 'Art never expresses anything but itself'. Taken separately, these two statements are counter-intuitive and seem deliberately contrived to outrage the realist aesthetic which had dominated
Victorian literary and pictorial art. However, the statements themselves are contradicted by other parts of Vivian's argument. First, if
art truly expresses only itself, it can reveal nothing but itself, and
certainly not, as Vivian later suggests that Dutch art should reveal,
'the great soul of Holland'—a kind of spiritual or imaginative truth
that is much more revealing (or that 'interprets' more) than actual
life or 'actual people'. More importantly, if life *does* imitate art, then
why are Japanese people, in Vivian's terms, 'extremely commonplace [with] nothing curious or extraordinary about them', when
Japanese art is the very opposite. As Vivian puts it, '[i]f you set a picture by Hokusai, or Hokkei, or any of the great native painters, beside a real Japanese gentleman or lady, you will see that there is not
the slightest resemblance between them.' But of course there ought
to be, if life really does imitate art. If in England, as Vivian again
claims, the 'mystic eyes of Rossetti's dream, the long ivory throat,
the strange square-cut jaw, the loosened shadowy hair' are to be seen
'wherever one goes to a private view or to an artistic salon', why was
the visitor to Japan 'unable to discover the inhabitants, as [the] delightful exhibition at Messrs Dowdeswell's Gallery showed only too
well'?[30]

These contradictions are not resolved, but reinforced by the additional material about Impressionist art and London fogs, which
gives a further example of life imitating art (but without explaining

[29] See e.g. Wilde's letter to James Knowles, the editor of the *Nineteenth Century*, about
his editorial high-handedness; *Letters*, 274.
[30] Ross, *Intentions and The Soul of Man*, 40–4, 47–8, and 33.

why, on other occasions, this does not hold true). Here it is difficult
to know what precisely Wilde had in mind. There is some evidence
that the inserted passage was included to make the essay more topical, and that this desire for topicality was more urgent than the
need for logic and coherence. Alternatively, it is equally possible
that Wilde was deliberately multiplying the contradictions in the
argument simply to test the boundaries of outrageousness. At the
same time, this last ambition works against another desire (explained to Jules Cantel)—to use the collection to pull occasional
pieces together in order that they might coherently express what
Wilde described as 'mon esthétique'.[31] A simpler explanation is
that, as with *Dorian Gray*, Wilde was under pressure to expand material, and the introduction of a further 'example' to Vivian's list was
the quickest and easiest way, on this occasion, to achieve that goal.

Further revisions to *Intentions* seemed designed to give the essays
a greater elegance of expression. A good example is to be found in
Cyril's opening speech in 'The Decay of Lying'. The periodical version has simply:

My dear Vivian, don't coop yourself up all day in the library. It is a perfectly lovely afternoon. Let us go and lie on the grass and smoke cigarettes
and enjoy nature.

In the book this becomes:

My dear Vivian, don't coop yourself up all day in the library. It is a perfectly lovely afternoon. The air is exquisite. There is a mist upon the
woods, like the purple bloom upon a plum. Let us go and lie on the grass
and smoke cigarettes and enjoy Nature.

Like some of the additions to descriptive passages in *Dorian Gray*,
the extra material alters the tone of the book version: it gives to
Cyril's speeches an element of self-dramatization. Some reviewers
noted the effects of these revisions, describing the style so produced
as 'showy', and possessing a 'plushy lusciousness'.[32]

It is possible to suggest that Wilde's periodical editors had constrained his style, and that some of the revisions to *Intentions* were
intended to re-establish a more distinctive voice. Certainly the elaboration and complexity provided by the revisions result in a rich
if occasionally contradictory verbal texture. Modern critics have
tended to see this texture in terms of a playful subversiveness—that
Wilde's revisions are driven by a conscious desire to intensify the

[31] *Letters*, 295.   [32] *Heritage*, 91–2.

paradoxical nature of his arguments. In the best recent study of the composition of *Intentions*, Lawrence Danson notes that the revisions to 'The Decay of Lying' and to 'Pen, Pencil, and Poison', 'crystallize what had been in suspension in the magazine version'. On another occasion Danson refers to the revisions as 'a fastidious author's stylistic fiddlings'.[33] He implies that the overall effect of the rewriting was to sharpen the polemic of *Intentions*, even if the result was on occasions to expose the tautologies and contradictions of Wilde's case. The problems Danson has in characterizing and evaluating Wilde's revisions are revealing. The critical difficulty of deciding whether revisions produce incoherence or a postmodern *jouissance* may be because they were undertaken for different reasons. Wilde may have wanted to 'crystallize' his arguments, but he was also under a pressing requirement to expand his material, and these demands pulled in different directions. There are reasons to suspect that Wilde did not feel that he had reworked the essays adequately, and his dissatisfaction with 'The Truth of Masks', the essay that required most rewriting, lends some weight to this view. The caveat in the closing paragraph of that piece—'Not that I agree with everything I have said in this essay. There is much with which I disagree'—suggests an attempt to disarm criticism which might draw attention to the volume's inconsistencies.

Of the essays which Wilde originally hoped to reprint, it was 'The Portrait of Mr W. H.' which was most heavily revised, so much so that the essay was doubled in length as Wilde prepared it for book publication. As we argued in Chapter 5, little is known about how Wilde worked on 'Mr W. H.' in the years between its first appearance in *Blackwood's* (1889) and 1895, when plans for its publication as a book were a casualty of his trials. The expanded version of 'Mr W. H.' survives in only one manuscript, which takes the form of new holograph material together with corrected pages from the *Blackwood's* version. Mitchell Kennerley, the discoverer of the enlarged manuscript, claimed in 1921 that it had been retrieved from the house of Frederick Chapman, an office-manager working for Lane at the Bodley Head, who had been asked by Wilde to 'prepare it for the printer'.[34] Horst Schroeder throws doubt on Kennerley's

---

33 Danson, *Wilde's Intentions*, 94 and 43.
34 Quoted in Horst Schroeder, *Oscar Wilde, 'The Portrait of Mr W. H.'—Its Composition, Publication and Reception* (Braunschweig: Technische Universität Carolo-Wilhelmina zu Braunschweig, 1984), 37.

story.[35] Unfortunately there is no way to corroborate Kennerley's account and we cannot be certain whether the manuscript was ever intended as printer's copy. It is worth remembering the frequency with which Wilde used typed (and printed) fair copy as part of his process of composition; consequently it is possible that Kennerley's manuscript was only one of several drafts, and that the 'final' version is lost. These uncertainties limit what conclusions we can draw from the variants between the periodical essay and the longer version. Tantalizingly, 'Mr W. H.' may seem to provide the most substantial evidence for the importance which Wilde placed on revision; on the other hand, the incomplete state of the manuscript and the problems of its provenance, together with the fact that the work remained unpublished during his lifetime, restrict what general lessons can be learned from it. An obvious explanation for its fate is that Wilde was unhappy with the piece, and was not convinced that his rewriting had been successful; moreover these doubts are not necessarily inconsistent with his recriminatory letters to Mathews and Lane over their lack of faith in the work.

Taken together, Wilde's revisions to his poetry, fiction, and criticism show evidence of care and labour, but it is by no means always a Paterian 'limae labor'. Pater employed Horace's trope to imply that a literary work is improved as 'surplusage' is pared away. Pater's frequent use of metaphors from the language of sculpture and metalwork reinforces this idea that literary composition is not 'loose accretion', but its very opposite, a process of deletion or discarding in which the work is enriched 'by far more than the weight of precious metal . . . removed'.[36] However much Wilde celebrated this Paterian artistic singlemindedness, and however much he attended to fine nuances of style, the overall impression his rewriting gives is precisely an impulse towards 'accretion'. As we have shown, Wilde was a writer constantly short of material and all his revisions (certainly those which were made with republication in mind) involved expanding work in hand. Simple expansion of material does not necessarily improve it, and as Pater advised and as Wilde's revisions sometimes demonstrate, expansion could actually threaten a work's integrity. On some occasions (particularly with *Dorian Gray* and some of the criticism) the insertion of long stretches of new text

---

[35] Schroeder, *Oscar Wilde*, 36–9.
[36] *Appreciations*, 19–24; *Marius the Epicurean*, i. 105.

could lead to an inconsistency of tone and occasionally made for incoherence. On other occasions—as with some poems and 'Shakespeare on Scenery'—revisions seem designed to disguise a lack of invention: the same idea or the same piece of work was rewritten so that it could perform different functions in different contexts. Once more, a comparison with Pater is instructive. *Marius the Epicurean*, for example, returns to many of the ideas first formulated in *The Renaissance*; but Pater's revisiting of those ideas was to recast them in a way which explicitly exhibited the development and refinement of his thought. In Wilde's revisiting of old material, it is much harder to distinguish between such creative rethinking and a pragmatic recycling.

It is tempting to explain the details of Wilde's revisions in terms of the institutions of publishing in the 1880s and 1890s, and in terms of the different readerships of books and periodicals which in turn made different demands upon publishers and writers. This explanation would argue that criteria of originality, of topicality, and to a degree of intelligibility, differed between publishing forms. In some ways, these different demands did affect Wilde: he was not infrequently required to omit controversial passages, and to write to a formula in response to the requirements of particular house-styles. Similarly when he was given the opportunity to republish material for a different and at times more sophisticated reader, and with more space at his disposal, he often made attempts to reinstate his original ideas. However, there is one important limitation to using this explanation as the sole framework for understanding Wilde's revisions. The emphasis upon the institutional presupposes a politics of constraint and censorship which in turn assumes an 'ideal' work which Wilde wanted to write, but which he was constantly prevented from so doing. Unfortunately, the evidence fails to support this view. For every occasion on which Wilde was restrained by the medium in which he published, we can find another occasion when he was constrained by his own lack of invention; for every revision in which he restores 'censored' first thoughts, there is another in which he silently accepts the suggestions and corrections of his editor; for every piece of evidence of the 'limae labor', there is further evidence of 'mere loose accretion'. To acknowledge that Wilde's motives for revising his works were mixed, and that the effects so produced were varied, is not necessarily to denigrate him. They speak to the realism and pragmatism of the professional writer's craft; but they are also practices that, as the writing of his plays demonstrates, could produce a masterpiece.

II

The institutions of the commercial theatre in the late nineteenth century, together with the distinctive nature of performance texts, and the simple fact that vastly more information about the composition of Wilde's plays has survived than for any other of his works—these conditions may seem to justify the treatment of his drama as a separate and special case. The strongest evidence for considering Wilde to be a literary craftsman has come from editorial work on his Society Comedies. The sheer number of drafts (over twenty for some acts of a *Woman of No Importance*) and the extent and complexity of the revisions made to them, came as a surprise to modern critics. The temptation was to organize this material into a narrative of development in which the emergence of the final text of a play could be traced through a series of stages. However the construction of stemmata posed a number of practical problems. First, only some drafts of the plays bear dates (and these usually take the form of a stamp from Mrs Marshall's or Mrs Dickens's Typewriting Offices, often made on only the first recto of the typescripts of separate acts, and not on the rest of the folios). Second, the dispersal of the drafts of the plays following Wilde's bankruptcy proceedings led to various errors of collation, in which parts of earlier drafts were bound with parts of later ones. Even when textual features appear to give a clue to dating (with, for example, changes made to characters' names), the editor can be misled, because Wilde often reverted to earlier thoughts in later drafts. In addition, despite the large number of extant documents available, it is clear that many drafts have been lost. The outcome of all this is that, to a considerable extent, the construction of a stemma is in itself largely an interpretative process and therefore cannot be used as evidence to support a larger hypothesis about Wilde's development. So while we can document changes between drafts, we need to be cautious about arranging those changes into a logical progression towards a final text.

These caveats aside, there are many interesting lessons to be learned from a study of the drafts of Wilde's plays. The first concerns the ways in which Wilde began to compose. Very little evidence exists for the initial conception and composition of most of

Wilde's non-dramatic works. However the small number of documents which do survive (for example, notes for a review of Rossetti's poetry, or fragments of the essay on Hellenism, or the manuscript of 'Amiel and Lord Beaconsfield') confirms the evidence we can observe in the play-drafts.[37] It seems that Wilde first drew up a very basic scenario which sketched out the rudimentary structure of the plot and character-types. For plays which were completed (such as *Earnest*) the scenarios which survive often reveal only a passing resemblance to the performed or published work.

The next part of the process of composition (a parallel of which we also see in those manuscripts of non-dramatic works) appears to have been the assembly of discrete blocks of dialogue, often revolving around a particular joke or paradox.[38] These blocks possess a certain free-standing quality that permitted their movement from play to play. But Wilde also appropriated lines from non-dramatic works (most famously, as we have indicated, he incorporated material wholesale from *Dorian Gray* into *A Woman of No Importance*). This suggests that a practice which derives from what we characterized earlier as a pragmatic 'cut-and-paste' mentality almost certainly went much deeper. It is as if Wilde's very creativity itself was manifest via the composition of small, discrete units. The early drafts of the plays are often little more than a profusion of free-standing comic gems. Subsequent drafts show that the most difficult part of writing for Wilde was narrative—that is, the connection of those gems, the discrete comic exchanges or aphorisms, into a dramatic structure, with a coherent exposition of plot and character development. This lack of confidence in handling a long narrative structure is also apparent in *Dorian Gray* and the critical dialogues. Despite Wilde's reputation as a raconteur, the 'stories' of the plays always presented him with his most intractable problems.[39]

At an early stage in his career, Wilde sought advice from Dion Boucicault about *Vera*; he received the reply that the play was 'not *action*—but discussion'. Boucicault went on: 'your action stops for

[37] All these manuscript drafts are in the Clark Library: Wilde W6721M3. D758. [188–?]; Wilde W6721M3. H477. [187–?]; Wilde W6721M3. A516. [1886?].

[38] For example, both the Amiel and Rossetti reviews are structured in terms of a series of comments tied to blocks of quotations. In this sense, and as we describe later, both are reminiscent of the pattern of writing to be found in Wilde's undergraduate commonplace book.

[39] For a discussion of Wilde's reputation as a raconteur, see John Stokes, *Oscar Wilde: Myths, Miracles, and Imitations* (Cambridge: Cambridge University Press, 1996), 23 ff.

dialogue—whereas dialogue should be the necessary outcome of the action exerting an influence on the characters.'[40] There is evidence that some of Wilde's deletions of parts of speeches in the early drafts of the Society Comedies were an attempt to correct this tendency to construct a play around dialogue, even when it meant losing a joke. So at a point halfway through Act II of *A Woman of No Importance* Wilde had to find a witty way to cover the movement of certain characters on and off the stage. He gave this role to Lady Hunstanton who makes a joke about Lord Illingworth at the same time as she orders a servant to fetch Gerald Arbuthnot, and announces to the audience the entrance of a new character, Dr Daubeny. In the published version, Lady Hunstanton makes a simple joke to cover this stage business:

MRS ARBUTHNOT. Lady Hunstanton, I want to speak to Gerald at once. Might I see him? Can he be sent for?

LADY HUNSTANTON. Certainly, dear. I will send one of the servants into the dining-room to fetch him. I don't know what keeps the gentlemen so long. [*Rings bell*] When I knew Lord Illingworth first as plain George Harford, he was simply a very brilliant young man about town, with not a penny of money except what poor dear Lady Cecilia gave him. She was quite devoted to him. Chiefly, I fancy, because he was on bad terms with his father. Oh, here is the Archdeacon. [*To* SERVANT] It doesn't matter.

A very early draft of this exchange is much longer, and has substantially more dialogue, which is in turn prompted by an elaboration of Lady Hunstanton's joke:

MRS ARBUTHNOT. Lady Hunstanton, I want to speak to Gerald at once. Might I see him? Can he be sent for?

LADY HUNSTANTON. Certainly, dear. I will send one of the servants into the dining-room to fetch him. I don't know what keeps the gentlemen so long. [*Rings bell*] When I knew Lord Illingworth first as plain George Harford, he was simply a very brilliant young man about town, with not a penny of money except what poor dear Lady Cecilia gave him. She was quite devoted to him. Chiefly, I fancy, because he was on bad terms with his father. There had been some quarrel—I don't remember about what—some unfortunate connection, I think—but I know they didn't speak, and when they met at the Club, it was said that Sir Thomas always hid himself behind the money article in *The Times*. I am told, by the way, Caroline, that that is quite a common occurrence, nowadays, at London Clubs, and that they have to take in additional copies of *The*

Times at every good Club, there are so many fathers who don't speak to their sons, and so many sons who won't have anything to do with their fathers. I think it is very much to be regretted.[41]

Lady Hunstanton's longer speech was followed by further exchanges between minor characters. This extended dialogue was deleted in a later draft, possibly because the act was too long, or because the speech was more literary than dramatic; but the most likely reason, in Boucicault's terms, was that it was holding up the action. What is more interesting, perhaps, is that Wilde did not discard the material altogether; he merely set it aside, using a condensed and slightly adapted version of it about a year later for a speech for Lady Markby in Act II of *An Ideal Husband*:

> And then the eldest son has quarrelled with his father, and it is said that when they meet at the club Lord Brancaster always hides himself behind the money article in *The Times*. However, I believe that is quite a common occurrence nowadays and that they have to take in extra copies of *The Times* at all the clubs in St James's Street; there are so many sons who won't have anything to do with their fathers, and so many fathers who won't speak to their sons. I think, myself, it is very much to be regretted.[42]

The portable quality of this extended joke perfectly illustrates what we earlier identified as the 'modular' nature of Wilde's composition; but it also confirms Boucicault's observation that dialogue in Wilde's plays tended not to develop from character or action. The disjunction in *Lady Windermere's Fan* and *A Woman of No Importance* between melodramatic moments, where character, plot, and dialogue are integrated, and those set comic pieces (such as the scene in Darlington's rooms in Act III of *Lady Windermere's Fan*) in which character and plot are subordinated to dialogue, suggests that Wilde himself was well aware of this weakness. *The Importance of Being Earnest*, constructed as it is on a series of verbal routines, can be seen as turning that weakness to advantage.

Wilde's difficulties in conceiving the narrative structure of a play as a whole are also evident in errors of stagecraft which the early drafts reveal. It is as if most of his attention is concentrated on the perfecting of the joke, or the paradox, or the elaboration of a purple

[41] This exchange is to be found in the first full manuscript of the play. See British Library, MS Add. 37944. It was carried through to an early typescript draft which is also held in the British Library, MS Add. 37945.

[42] Russell Jackson (ed.), *An Ideal Husband* (1983; London: A & C Black, 1993), II, 643–51.

passage. So in some drafts of the Society Comedies there are more characters than the exposition of the plot demands. In other drafts, the opposite seems to be true; the plot requires the stage to be crowded with characters, but Wilde leaves them with little or nothing to do or to say. A good example is the ballroom scene in Act II of *Lady Windermere's Fan*. Different drafts see different characters, and different numbers of characters, being brought on to the stage; but the same speeches are redistributed among them, with the majority of characters not speaking at all. At these points in the drafts Wilde seems to be careless in his use of minor characters; certainly dramatic characterization and staging are often sacrificed to the local effect of the joke.[43] In an early draft of *A Woman of No Importance* Lord Alfred Rufford (as Lord Arthur) is brought on stage but not given an exit. On yet other occasions, Wilde experienced a great deal of difficulty in handling the machinery of the well-made play, particularly the mechanisms by which important plot-information is disclosed to the audience. So in the early drafts of the last act of *An Ideal Husband*, the use of letters and the handling of overheard conversation are clumsy. The famous necklace/bracelet device, which is so crucial to the plot's resolution, was only fully worked out very near to the time of first performance.[44]

This very unsureness with narrative development and stagecraft may explain another feature of Wilde's writing as it is revealed in the drafts of his plays: the extent to which he collaborated with the managers for whom he worked. A great deal has been made of the uneasy relationship between Wilde and Alexander, particularly regarding changes made after the first night of *Lady Windermere's Fan* and during rehearsals to *The Importance of Being Earnest*. These changes were large-scale and structural, and they fundamentally affected the dramatic impetus of the plays. In the case of *Lady Windermere's Fan*, Alexander wished Mrs Erlynne's identity to be revealed to the audience at the end of the first or second acts rather than during the fourth act. Wilde refused point-blank to accept Alexander's advice, perhaps because he thought the alterations had too profound an impact on the play's tone. Nevertheless after the first night, this change was made and it was retained for the rest of the play's run. Critics have typically seen Alexander's actions in terms of the *realpolitik* of theatre management. The difficulty with

43 See Ian Small (ed.), *Lady Windermere's Fan* (1980; London: A & C Black, 1999), II, 12–13 n.   44 For details, see Jackson (ed.), *An Ideal Husband*, p. xliii.

this line of argument is that Wilde did not revert to his original intentions when he published the play with the Bodley Head. The most obvious explanation for his keeping faith with Alexander's change is that the play's success proved the rightness of his manager's judgement, and that Wilde saw the wisdom of publishing the text of the play to which audiences had responded most favourably. In this explanation Alexander appears not as censor, but simply as a more experienced professional.

On the other hand, what that professionalism actually entailed has only recently been fully understood. Joel H. Kaplan has shown that there was an element of double-dealing in Alexander's relationship with Wilde. Exasperated by Wilde's intransigence, Alexander used his influence to persuade the drama critic Clement Scott to write a review of the first performance of *Lady Windermere's Fan* which reinforced Alexander's own reservations about its shortcomings.[45] This apparently 'independent' opinion was then used by Alexander to bring Wilde to heel, and to enforce the change about the revelation of Mrs Erlynne's identity. Of course it is tempting to see these actions as straightforwardly coercive. However, it should be remembered, as Kaplan points out, that up to February 1892 Wilde did not have a theatrical success to his name in Britain, that Alexander had many reservations about *Lady Windermere's Fan*, and that he had agreed to stage it only under acute pressures of time. Seen in this light, his frustration that someone as inexperienced as Wilde should refuse to take advice is easy to understand, and Wilde's subsequent letters to the press, in which he denied that he had changed the play under pressure, were perhaps an abashed recognition of the reality of the situation.

The manuscript and typescript drafts of *A Woman of No Importance* are more numerous than those of Wilde's first Society Comedy. Taken collectively, this body of material gives the best evidence of collaboration. It seems to indicate that Wilde had learned a lesson from his experience with Alexander at the St James's, for all the indications are that this collaboration was a voluntary one. The drafts of *A Woman of No Importance* are marked up in several hands, often those of Wilde and Herbert Beerbohm Tree, the manager for whom the play was written. Wilde's relationship with Tree was considerably more cordial than with Alexander, but this does not fully

[45] See Joel H. Kaplan, 'A Puppet's Power: George Alexander, Clement Scott, and the Replotting of *Lady Windermere's Fan*', *Theatre Notebook*, 46: 2 (1992), 59–73.

explain the co-creativity to which some of the drafts testify. So one revised typescript of Act III of 'Mrs Arbuthnot' (the working title of *A Woman of No Importance*) contains what is virtually a dialogue between Wilde and Tree about both the length and staging of various scenes.[46] For example, on the verso of folio 15 Tree wrote: 'This is a bombshell/said suddenly'—a comment indicating how he thought the scene should be played. On folio 17, Wilde wrote over a long speech by Mrs Arbuthnot: 'No gesture at chair', a comment which suggests a point of disagreement with Tree's staging.

A more complex example of this co-creativity is to be found in other drafts of the play held in the Herbert Beerbohm Tree Collection. These include actors' parts, a prompt-copy, and a number of typescripts used in rehearsal. Together they show how much of the play's fine detail was not decided until a very late stage, and how much of that detail derived from Tree's sense of what would work in performance. A draft of Act II, for example, gives evidence of copious deletions, which are marked up in a hand other than that of Wilde, and which are almost certainly Tree's. The point of these deletions seems to be to sharpen the action; as with the Texas draft, the effect of the cuts is to reduce the elaboration of jokes, and emphasize the emotional effects of the scene. For example, an exchange in Act II between Mrs Arbuthnot and Lord Illingworth over Gerald's future employment is marked up as follows (deletions are indicated by strikethrough, interpolated material—always in a hand other than Wilde's—in angle brackets):

LORD ILLINGWORTH. [. . .] But don't let us have a scene. ~~Scenes are for the middle classes.~~ <[*Sits*]> Rachel, I want you to look at this matter from the point of view of what is best for our son, leaving you and me out of the question. ~~What is our son at present? The under-paid clerk of a Provincial Bank in a third-rate English town.~~ If you imagine he is happy in ~~such a~~ <his present> position, you are mistaken. He is thoroughly discontented.

MRS ARBUTHNOT. He was not discontented till he met you. You have made him so.

LORD ILLINGWORTH. ~~Of course I made him so. Discontent is the starting point in every young man's career.~~ <Yes, I made him so.> But I did not leave him a mere longing for things he could not get. No! I made him a charming offer. He jumped at it, I need hardly say. Any young man

---

[46] See typescript with manuscript revisions under the title of *Mrs Arbuthnot*, held in the Harry Ransom Humanities Research Center, University of Texas, Austin.

would. And now, simply because it turns out that I am the boy's own father, and he my own son, you propose to practically ruin his future. ~~That is to say, if I were a perfect stranger, you would allow Gerald to go away with me, but as he is my own flesh and blood, you won't. How utterly illogical you are.~~ <Rachel, believe me, you are wrong.>

The same episode in the 1894 book edition reads as follows:

LORD ILLINGWORTH. [. . .] But don't let us have a scene. Rachel, I want you to look at this matter from the common-sense point of view, from the point of view of what is best for our son, leaving you and me out of the question. What is our son at present? An underpaid clerk in a provincial bank in a third-rate English town. If you imagine he is quite happy in such a position, you are mistaken. He is thoroughly discontented.

MRS ARBUTHNOT. He was not discontented till he met you. You have made him so.

LORD ILLINGWORTH. Of course, I made him so. Discontent is the first step in the progress of a man or a nation. But I did not leave him a mere longing for things he could not get. No, I made him a charming offer. He jumped at it, I need hardly say. Any young man would. And now, simply because it turns out that I am the boy's own father and he my own son, you propose practically to ruin his career. That is to say, if I were a perfect stranger, you would allow Gerald to go away with me, but as he is my own flesh and blood, you won't. How utterly illogical you are![47]

We can see that Wilde kept faith with some of the changes made during rehearsal (such as the deletion of 'scenes are for the middle classes'), but that he rejected others. So he reverts to his first phrase, 'such a position', rather than 'his present position'. On other occasions Wilde restores the sense of deleted material, but rephrases it. So 'Discontent is the starting point in every young man's career' becomes 'Discontent is the first step in the progress of a man or a nation'. The most obvious way to understand these sorts of revision is in terms of a collaborative process in which Tree and Wilde co-operated to produce a play which worked on stage.

The most intriguing example of this kind of co-operation concerns the changes made to the end of Act III in a number of typescript drafts housed in the Tree collection. The three most

---

[47] See the typescript entitled *Mrs Arbuthnot* and marked '2nd' held at the Herbert Beerbohm Tree Collection at the University of Bristol. Russell Jackson and Ian Small, the first scholars to see the importance of the collection in establishing a stemma for the play, tentatively identified this typescript as HBT 122. See Jackson and Small, 'Some New Drafts of a Wilde Play', *English Literature in Transition*, 30: 1 (1987), 7–15. See also Ian Small (ed.), *A Woman of No Importance* (1983; London: A & C Black, 1993), II, 580–98.

interesting are given below. We cannot be completely sure of their order, which in itself is evidence of a creative give-and-take. In the first draft changes are marked up in two hands, one of which is Wilde's, and the other (again) almost certainly that of Tree:

GERALD. [*Thrusting her back*] Don't hold me, mother. Don't hold me. ~~I'll kill him!~~

MRS ARBUTHNOT. Gerald!

GERALD. Let me go, I say. <I'll kill him ~~that man~~>

MRS ARBUTHNOT. ~~Don't~~ <Stop>, Gerald, ~~Don't~~ <Stop>! He is your ~~own~~ father.

CURTAIN

What appears to be a later draft reincorporates some of these deletions, but makes some new changes, including the addition of a detailed final stage direction. It is unclear which hand has marked the deletion.

GERALD. [*Thrusting her back*] Don't hold me, mother! Don't hold me! I'll kill him!

MRS ARBUTHNOT. Gerald!

GERALD. Let me go, I say! ~~Don't hold me like that!~~

MRS ARBUTHNOT. Stop, Gerald, stop! He is your own father!

[*MRS ARBUTHNOT sinks on her knees and bows her head. HESTER, with a look of pain, glides from the room. LORD ILLINGWORTH frowns, bites his lip, hesitates for a moment and then goes off. GERALD forces his mother back, and with a look of horror and amazement, gazes into her face*]

CURTAIN

A further draft, which may be later still, incorporates nearly all of the changes made to the version above, but adds instructions for two further melodramatic tableaux:

GERALD. [*Thrusting her back*] Don't hold me, mother! Don't hold me! I'll kill him!

MRS ARBUTHNOT. Gerald! [*Crosses to C., holding* GERALD]

GERALD. Let me go, I say!

MRS ARBUTHNOT. [*Gets to C., with bus*] Stop, Gerald, stop! He is your father.

[*MRS ARBUTHNOT sinks on her knees and bows her head. HESTER, with a look of pain, glides from the room. LORD ILLINGWORTH bites his lip, hesitates for a moment and then goes off. GERALD forces his mother back, and with a look of horror and amazement gazes into her face*]

CURTAIN

[*2nd Tableau:——*GERALD *lifting his mother's head.* HESTER *just at door R.*]

[*3rd Tableau:—Only mother and son on.*]

Finally, in the printed version of the play, the scene appears as follows:

GERALD. [*Thrusting her back*] Don't hold me, mother. Don't hold me—I'll kill him!

MRS ARBUTHNOT. Gerald!

GERALD. Let me go, I say!

MRS ARBUTHNOT. Stop, Gerald, stop! He is your own father!

[GERALD *clutches his mother's hands and looks into her face. She sinks slowly on the ground in shame.* HESTER *steals towards the door.* LORD ILLINGWORTH *frowns and bites his lip. After a time Gerald raises his mother up, puts his arm round her, and leads her from the room*]

ACT DROP[48]

In the published version of the play Wilde rejected the two additional melodramatic tableaux; it is likely that he thought them unnecessary for a text designed for reading rather than performance. On the other hand, the fuller stage directions at the end of the act retain some of the interpretative effects of the deleted material, which again suggests that Wilde was prepared to learn from Tree's theatrical experience. Confirmation that there was a weakness in Wilde's conception of the conclusion of this act is to be found in a speech made by Robert Ross in 1908 in which he discussed various stagings of the play:

I once attended a provincial performance of Wilde's play *A Woman of No Importance*. You may possibly remember from Mr Tree's brilliant revival [in 1907 at His Majesty's] the curtain in Act III, which falls on the exclamation of Mrs Arbuthnot, 'Don't strike him, Gerald, he is your father.' At this performance the manager—he was an actor-manager—fearing that the text was inadequate, fearing that the curtain would not sufficiently impress the house, had instructed the leading artist to turn to the audience with her arms outstretched and to exclaim: 'What a situation!'[49]

It is beyond the scope of this chapter (and perhaps a single book) to give a comprehensive account of Wilde's revisions to all of his plays. Nevertheless, even a snapshot of the evidence, such as that

[48] These typescript drafts were identified by Jackson and Small as HBT 122, HBT 18a, and HBT 129. See Small (ed.), *A Woman of No Importance*, III, 481–5 and sds. For ease of comparison we have italicized all stage directions although they do not always appear in this way in the drafts.

[49] Quoted in Margery Ross, *Robert Ross: Friend of Friends* (London: Jonathan Cape, 1952), 153. See also Joel H. Kaplan, 'Wilde on the Stage', in *The Cambridge Companion*, 257.

given here, requires us to rethink our notions of Wilde as either the 'craftsman-playwright' or the 'political-playwright'. First, there is evidence that, as with his poetry, criticism, and fiction, Wilde was often short of material and inspiration. Kerry Powell has noted the extent to which Wilde's Society Comedies derive their plot situations, character-types, and some of their stage machinery from other contemporary works.[50] The drafts of the plays show us how willingly Wilde would also reuse his own material, importing jokes and exchanges which had already appeared in, or been discarded from, other works. Such a practice suggests that Wilde's creativity was of an unusual kind, what we have called a 'modular' nature. This characteristic in turn is not easy to assimilate to conventional teleological notions of literary creativity. It is also a method not particularly suited to dramatic writing, and it is unsurprising that Wilde found some aspects of playwriting difficult. As Joseph Donohue has noted, Wilde did sometimes write 'swiftly and with great facility'.[51] None the less the drafts of his plays clearly show that the visualization of the stage as a physical space, a sense of the relationship between characterization and dramatic structure, and the conceptualization of dialogue in terms of performance often proved elusive. Moreover it is in precisely these areas that we detect the strongest evidence of that third feature of Wilde's writing, the presence of other hands.

We have already shown that in his critical and fictional writing, Wilde was prepared to accept suggestions made by editors and friends to the extent that he could occasionally cede creative responsibility to others. Furthermore a number of his revisions were driven by pragmatic considerations, such as the need to expand material. We see this same mixture of pragmatism, openness to advice, and the delegation of creativity in the writing of the plays, but in a more pronounced way. The much higher financial risks involved, together with Wilde's unease in the medium, made some forms of 'co-creativity' inevitable. The evidence for collaboration throughout the dramatic *oeuvre* is overwhelming. Wilde revised *Vera* at the behest of Anderson; he made substantial cuts to *The Duchess of Padua* at the insistence of Barrett; many drafts of the Society

[50] See Kerry Powell, *Oscar Wilde and the Theatre of the 1890s* (Cambridge: Cambridge University Press, 1990), *passim*.

[51] See Joseph Donohue (with Ruth Berggren) (ed.), *Oscar Wilde's The Importance of Being Earnest: The First Production* (Gerrards Cross, Bucks: Colin Smythe, 1995), 38.

Comedies show evidence of changes made by more than one hand; and finally, even when there was no sustained rehearsal process to drive textual changes (as with *Salomé*) there are proofs and drafts which show that Wilde actively sought advice from others, such as Adolphe Retté, Pierre Louÿs, and Marcel Schwob.[52] In other words, far from Wilde being censored or constrained by the theatrical institutions of the 1890s, it may be more appropriate to see these institutions being partly responsible for his success: managers such as Alexander, Tree, and Boucicault (like Mathews and Lane at the Bodley Head) helped to create the dramatist which Wilde became. There is no evidence, textual or otherwise, to suggest that Wilde ever had in mind some play that he could have written but was prevented from writing by the power of the West End theatre. His failure to finish plays was his responsibility, not that of any institution. Working in the commercial theatre of the 1890s almost certainly ensured that Wilde's dramatic work had a familiar element to it, but for the most part he was thoroughly complicit in this process. The most intriguing evidence for this complicity is to be seen in the textual history of *The Importance Of Being Earnest*.

Wilde's original conception of the work, and indeed the typescript that he handed over to Alexander late in 1894, was of a four-act play. Donohue has commented on Alexander's dissatisfaction with the piece, describing his sense that *Earnest* 'could not stand by itself as a full-length entertainment in four acts'. The idea of a farce as the main element in a programme was relatively new—a precedent had only been set as late as 1877—and a four-act farce was virtually unheard of. Alexander was determined to reduce the play to what had proved to be a commercially successful if conventional format: he compressed Acts II and III by the elimination of what is known as the 'Gribsby' episode, in which Algy is arrested for debts run up at the Savoy restaurant.[53] Alexander's apparent high-handedness in his treatment of Wilde—he is reported to have ordered Wilde out of rehearsals—has led some critics to detect a kind of censorship at work, similar to his machinations to get his way with *Lady Windermere's Fan*. Donohue suggests that there may have been an element of self-interest as well as business acumen in

[52] See *Letters*, 306; *OWR*, 154; *Encyclopedia*, 324.

[53] See Donohue (with Berggren), *Earnest: The First Production*, 41–2; see also Russell Jackson (ed.), *The Importance of Being Earnest* (1980; London: A & C Black, 1990), pp. xlii–xliii.

Alexander's decision, for the compression would simultaneously save an actor's salary and increase the prominence of his own part in the play. Terence Brown goes further and connects the preparation of the three-act version (made 'at the behest of Wilde's actor manager') with an attempt to reduce the significance of what he identifies as the major theme in the play, the morals of 'a social caste for whom money is the defining element'.[54]

Such arguments omit to note that when Wilde assembled the book version of the play for Smithers, he substantially kept with the structure of the text which Alexander had established, just as he had done with *Lady Windermere's Fan*. If we are disposed to see Wilde's writing as politically motivated then such a decision will seem odd. After all, by 1899 the 'Gribsby' episode had acquired uncanny parallels with Wilde's own life. If Brown is correct in his sense of the power relationship between the Irish outsider and British commercial interests, then one might assume that Wilde would have been more than anxious to restore or reconstruct the deleted material. The play would then have made explicit Wilde's post-prison anger with some elements of British society. Of course there was a powerful practical element in Wilde's decision: in 1899 he did not possess a manuscript of his play—as we have already noted, he had to send to England for a copy of Alexander's prompt-book. He would therefore have had to recover the excised material from memory. On the other hand, Wilde did make many local revisions to Alexander's text, so there was ample opportunity for him to undo some of Alexander's work, yet with the Gribsby episode he chose not to do so. It is impossible to reconstruct precisely Wilde's motives when he revised *Earnest* for publication. Nevertheless it seems that, as with *Lady Windermere's Fan*, he had come to accept that Alexander's judgement was correct. It is reported that on first seeing his cutdown play in rehearsal, Wilde commented to Alexander: 'It is quite a good play. I remember I wrote one very like it myself, but it was even more brilliant than this.'[55] Whatever the authenticity of this anecdote, we can be confident that by 1899 Wilde had come to accept the three-act *Earnest* as fully his own. More significantly, he

54 Terence Brown, 'The Plays', in Holland, *The Complete Works of Oscar Wilde*, 352.

55 Quoted in Ellmann, 406. It is worth noting that Ellmann's source is the often unreliable Hesketh Pearson, *The Life of Oscar Wilde* (London: Methuen, 1946), 257. The origin of the anecdote appears to be A. E. W. Mason, *Sir George Alexander and the St James's Theatre* (London: Macmillan, 1935), 79.

had also recognized its superior theatricality, describing it to Reginald Turner (who had been given a copy of the book version) as 'essentially an acting play' which 'should have been a classic for the English Theatre'.[56] The play might have been ignored in the years immediately following Wilde's imprisonment and then his death, but most judgements made later in the twentieth century endorse its classic status in its three-, rather than four-act form.

III

We have noted that a close examination of Wilde's revisions reveals that he composed partly by manipulating discrete or free-standing units of discourse—by what we have called a kind of modularity. We can see evidence for this quality from Wilde's undergraduate days. His Oxford commonplace book and notebook are filled with brief, cryptic, and disconnected jottings on a variety of authors he had read, including Plato, Hegel, Spencer, and Darwin. There is little evidence from the notebooks that Wilde engaged systematically or in depth with the books he mentions. Alongside the obvious undergraduate *aide-mémoire* (the usual function of commonplace books) he typically records the odd and startling detail shaped into the beginnings of an aphorism or paradox. So, for example, we find:

The condemnation which a great man lays upon the world is to force it to explain him (Hegel).

Or again:

The cognition of sensuous objects may not itself be sensuous.

Or later:

Positivism may be described as catholicism without Christianity as regards it's [*sic*] social aspect, philosophically it is dogmatism without criticism[.]

And again, in what would become a typically Wildeian clausal structure:

The chief moral agent of antiquity was the sense of human dignity, the sense of sin took its place in modern mediaevalism—the first produces the qualities of a patriot, the second of a saint[.][57]

---

[56] *Letters*, 786.
[57] Philip E. Smith and Michael S. Helfand (eds.), *Oscar Wilde's Oxford Notebooks* (New York: Oxford University Press, 1989), 147, 150–1, 156. For examples of 'submerged'

Philip E. Smith's and Michael S. Helfand's edition of the *Oxford Notebooks* makes a Herculean attempt to explain these jottings as 'a carefully reasoned philosophical and political stance, a synthesis of Hegelian idealism and Spencerian evolutionary theory which fundamentally shaped his criticism and fiction'.[58] Although highly ingenious, such an explanation seems totally to misrepresent the nature of Wilde's creativity. Wilde himself acknowledged that his mind was reductive rather than synthetic: in *De Profundis* he boasted, 'I summed up all systems in a phrase, and all existence in an epigram.'[59] The claim is typically extravagant, but the notebooks do reveal a sense that for Wilde taking the measure of an argument depended more on formulating a well-turned, summarizing phrase than on the precision and logic of exposition.

Taken in context—that their function was to record notes, and that such notes are by definition occasional and unsystematic—the gobbet-like character of the notebooks is unremarkable. What has not been recognized is the way the 'magpie' methods of Wilde's undergraduate note-taking (rather than an attention to substantive content) persisted throughout his life. It is evident in many of his recorded conversations, with their *ex-cathedra* tone, as well as in his practice of composing around the polished line or aphorism. It is as if the modular quality that we have observed in Wilde's composition was a pattern laid down very early, to the extent that it appears to represent something fundamental in the way his mind worked. The persistence of that habit helps to explain some of the difficulties which Wilde experienced as a professional writer. The striking absence in the notebooks of sustained argument, detailed exposition, and of logical summary—all find an uncanny equivalent in the problems in organizing his thoughts into coherent narrative structures which Wilde sometimes experienced in his later writing. Such a turn of mind might also explain why Wilde always felt a pressure on his material: discursive prose inevitably generates more text, and generates it much more quickly, than strings of one-liners can ever do. This observation is also helpful in explaining that other feature of Wilde's writing which has by turns puzzled and exasperated critics for over a century: his plagiarism and self-plagiarism.

quotations from Arnold, unnoticed by Smith and Helfand, see Horst Schroeder, 'Matthew Arnold and Oscar Wilde's Commonplace Book', *Notes and Queries*, 40 NS: 3 (Sept 1994), 359–60.

[58] Ibid., p. vii.   [59] *Letters*, 466.

There is no dispute that Wilde's *oeuvre* is marked by a significant amount of repetition, both of his own work and that of others. However, there have been a variety of ways of understanding this phenomenon. Wilde's earliest critics tended to view it simply as unscrupulous plagiarism—as compensation for a lack of originality and inventiveness. Later critics (generally those writing in the last thirty years) have resisted such an argument because it seems to compromise claims for Wilde's seriousness: it conflicts with deeply-held notions of artistic success and artistic integrity. The allegation of plagiarism also seems to run counter to the material assembled by text-editors which, as we have said, has typically (if not always accurately) been interpreted as evidence of Wilde's literary craftsmanship: at first sight 'the revising Wilde' and 'Wilde the plagiarist' seem to be concepts totally at odds with each other. To resolve this contradiction—to understand the elements of repetition in Wilde's work, while at the same time keeping faith with a view of him as a serious artist—modern commentators have found it necessary to exonerate him from the charge of plagiarism; that is, to see in plagiarism something more than simple copying.

Some apologists have invoked the distinction we discussed in Chapter 2—that of an early and a late Wilde—in order to argue that Wilde's reuse of material in the 1880s can be explained in terms of his inexperience. In this view, plagiarism is acknowledged in, say, *Poems* (1881) or the manuscript of the Chatterton lecture, but only to be explained as the understandable response of a writer eager to impress but ill-at-ease with the demands and deadlines of professional authorship. This argument goes on to suggest that the debts in the later works—in *Intentions*, *Dorian Gray*, and the Society Comedies—are of a wholly different order. Here, for Wilde, now a successful author, borrowing has become a knowing game, an act of display rather than disguise, a kind of ironic signature. In its turn this sort of explanation permits Wilde's later works to be aligned with some of the elements held to characterize postmodernism, in which borrowing is redefined as intertextuality, and plagiarism becomes transformed into linguistic *jouissance* or an engagement with textual authority. Apologists less sympathetic to the postmodern turn of contemporary literary criticism have preferred to emphasize the ways in which Wilde's borrowing (again in the late works) transforms or 'subverts' the source material. At the same time, though, there is still the suggestion that some strategy beyond one of simple deceit underlies his plagiarism: so, for example, deliberate repetition is to be explained in terms of a challenge to normative notions of creativity and originality espoused by 'established' critics such as Matthew Arnold.[60]

In these sorts of explanations Wilde's copying is reinterpreted as a sophisticated activity, one which has the apparent advantage of being in line with his own view of himself—that he was, in his words in *De Profundis*, simultaneously a 'born antinomian' and a 'lord of language'.[61] It has a further attraction of reinforcing an interpretative practice which became popular in the 1980s and early 1990s and which involved reading works for their subtexts, or (in the terms of Mikhail Bakhtin's thesis) their polyphonic properties. Reading practices which hypothesize surface versus submerged, or literal versus counter-intuitive meanings inevitably require a certain kind of writing for their substantiation. The doubleness of Wilde's life suggested that his writing might be a perfect subject for such treatment in that it too might have an equally doubled quality. As we suggested in Chapter 1, it was precisely this promise of covert meanings that led critics such as Christopher Craft to read *The Importance of Being Earnest* in terms of the 'flickering presence–absence of the play's homosexual desire' in which 'oppositional meanings . . . are not synthesized or sublated so much as they are exchanged, accelerated, derailed, terminated, cross-switched'.[62] In a similar way, a literal or surface interpretation of Wilde's plagiarism as mere lazy copying could be juxtaposed with a more sophisticated Bakhtinian emphasis on parody and irony. Bakhtin described texts that were 'constructed like mosaics out of the texts of others', and noted the 'complex and ambiguous' nature of the 'relationship to another's word' in which the 'boundary lines between someone else's speech and one's own speech were flexible, ambiguous, often deliberately distorted and confused'.[63] Propositions such as these permitted critics to recognize in Wilde's habit of repetition an element of play, just as they had detected in his conventional heterosexual plots coded references to homosexual desire.

[60] For a discussion of the various explanations of Wilde's plagiarism, see Guy, 'Self-Plagiarism, Creativity and Craftsmanship'.

[61] *Letters*, 468 and 458.

[62] Christopher Craft, *Another Kind of Love: Male Homosexual Desire in English Discourse: 1850–1920* (Berkeley: University of California Press, 1994), 118–19.

[63] Mikhail Bakhtin, 'From the Prehistory of Novelistic Discourse', repr. in David Lodge (ed.), *Modern Criticism and Theory: A Reader* (London: Longman, 1988), 145.

It is tempting to think that if Wilde, or a
existed, postmodernist critics would have i
a way they did, for there are a number of d
which they propose. One of the most (
question of audience—that is, the reader
were directed. The problem is that if cert
came transparent—if, say, the private homoso...
properly public—then the works would inevitably have ...
that they would have offended the majority of their readers. On the
other hand, if other subtextual readings were not sufficiently visible—that is, if copying were to be seen only as copying and not as
an intertextual *jouissance*—then failure would again result. Wilde,
that is, would be condemned for his lack of originality, something to
which Richard Le Gallienne was alert in a review of *Intentions*,
when he observed that Wilde might be seen as a 'damascener', or
decorator, rather than as a 'forger', or inventor, of thought.[64]
Perversely, then, it appears that both literal and subtextual readings
of Wilde's work would have resulted in their rejection by large
groups of contemporary readers. For a writer who desired financial
and cultural success as strongly as Wilde did, and who paid such
close attention to questions of audience and marketability, such
contradictory motives make little sense. In order for postmodern interpretations of Wilde's work to be correct, we must assume that he
was happy to run the risk of offending all but the most unsophisti-
cated of readers—that is, those who possessed insufficient experience and knowledge to recognize and appreciate either his coded
critique of bourgeois sexuality, or his literary debts (that is, the extent, rather than the nature of his copying). Yet all the evidence suggests that it was exactly these sorts of ill-educated 'common' readers
whom Wilde held in the greatest contempt.

A further and related problem with postmodernist interpreta-
tions of Wilde's plagiarism concerns the question of evidence. If we
leave aside the thorny issue of Wilde's motives, it is still necessary to
identify the textual differences between copying that a reader is not
supposed to detect (plagiarism proper) and copying that is self-
consciously and unashamedly exhibited (plagiarism understood as a
game which a reader is necessarily required to detect). In fact this

[64] *Heritage*, 99. Disquiet about subtextual readings of Wilde's work, particularly the
Society Comedies, has also been voiced by Alan Sinfield. See Sinfield, ' "Effeminacy" and
"Femininity": Sexual Politics in Wilde's Comedies,' *Modern Drama*, 37:1 (1994), 34–52.

of attribution is inherent even in Bakhtin's arguments. He
rves that in texts of the Middle Ages 'there were quotations that
ere openly and reverently emphasized as such, or that were half-
hidden, completely hidden, half-conscious, unconscious, correct,
intentionally distorted, unintentionally distorted, deliberately reinterpreted, and so forth'.[65] The list of activities here is complex and
varied, but Bakhtin tells us little about how practically we are to recognize and identify them. We can best see the dimensions of these
difficulties in Wilde's work by taking the most challenging examples
of them first: those of self-plagiarism.

Wilde's joke that 'it was better to be good-looking than good' first
appeared in 1889 in 'The Portrait of Mr W. H.'; it was repeated almost word for word just a year later in *Dorian Gray* as 'it is better to
be beautiful than to be good'. Based on a comparison of the texts
alone, how are we to know whether this is the lazy reuse of a good
joke by a man working to a strict deadline, or whether it is part of an
elaborate intertextual game? The more complex and lengthy the example, the more difficult this judgement becomes. As long ago as
1914 Stuart Mason noted how the line 'Poverty | Creeps through
our sunless lanes' in 'Humanitad' in *Poems* (1881) is repeated almost
verbatim in Act II of *The Duchess of Padua* (1883), verbatim again in
the periodical version of 'The Young King' in *The Lady's Pictorial*
(1888); it is then changed slightly for 'The Critic as Artist' in
Intentions (1891) to 'the poverty that creeps through sunless lanes':
and changed again for the book version of 'The Young King' in *A
House of Pomegranates* (1891), to 'through our sunless lanes creeps
Poverty'.[66] It is just possible to argue that this extended sequence of
repetition is a mischievous example of self-quotation, a kind of signature in the works. However, such an explanation does require
considerable generosity on the reader's behalf. First, we have to explain why Wilde decided to tweak the quotation only on its fourth
outing. If this is *jouissance*, it is not *jouissance* of an obvious or consistent sort. Second, to try to understand the effect of the repetition,
we inevitably have to speculate about Wilde's attitudes towards his
audiences. For intertextuality to operate among dissimilar works,
Wilde must have assumed a consistent group of readers familiar
enough with his *oeuvre* to see the joke. The evidence we possess,
though, flatly contradicts this assumption. Not only were the books

---

[65] Bakhtin, 'From the Prehistory of Novelistic Discourse', 145.
[66] See Mason, 313–14.

in question differently priced and addressed to different sorts of readers, one of the works was never even made available to a British audience.

If we are to use Occam's razor to slice through this problem, then the simple explanation, that repetitions *are* plagiarism, is more likely to be the correct one. Moreover, the fact that Wilde only changed the quotation when he used it twice in the same year (that is, in 1891) might betray an embarrassment about the extent of his recycling of material. There is another way to exonerate Wilde from the accusation of plagiarism, but it rescues him from deceit only by convicting him of carelessness. It is possible that Wilde repeated himself unintentionally—that a well-turned phrase was so deeply lodged in his mind that he simply forgot its source. So it is interesting that this image of poverty reappears in a troping of suffering in *De Profundis* (written in the absence of his own books), as 'there was enough suffering in one narrow London lane to show that God did not love man'.[67] On this occasion Wilde identifies the source of his phrase as an exchange with one of the 'most beautiful personalities I have ever known' (Frances Forbes-Robertson); Wilde suggests, that is, that he is repeating a phrase which originally came to him spontaneously in the course of conversation. It is difficult to see why at this stage in his life Wilde would want to hide the origin of his thought, nor what the point of such deception would have been; but it is equally difficult to explain how the phrase came to mind wrongly attributed, unless we acknowledge that repetition had bred familiarity. The phrase, that is, had become normalized in Wilde's mind, not as part of a verbal game, but simply as a part of a verbal repertoire.

There is a real sense in which none of the explanations of plagiarism and self-plagiarism which we have rehearsed do justice to Wilde's reuse of material. The postmodernist case for a deconstructive *jouissance* seems over-elaborate, impossible to prove, and at odds with Wilde's need to avoid offending his readers. Equally, the suggestion that Wilde was so careless that he either forgot that he had used material previously, or simply did not care that he had done so—this seems to be no explanation at all, weak to the point of banality. Most importantly neither fits with what we know of Wilde's reasons for writing, and of the ways in which he wrote. One of the

[67] *Letters*, 474.

limitations of recent critical debate about Wilde's plagiarism is that it is polarized: either plagiarism is dismissed as totally reprehensible or it is seen as a form of super-sophistication. These, however, are not the only views which the evidence of repetition supports. When we examine it closely, we can see that repetition required a variety of skills, and involved complex motives, ranging from the very calculated to the virtually unconscious. It is also worth bearing in mind that most of Wilde's work is not plagiarized, and that the derivative aspects of a play such as *Earnest* do not diminish our sense of its distinctiveness or of Wilde's comic genius.

The elements of Wilde's writing that he most often repeated are unsurprisingly those he laboured hardest to perfect, and which he presumably required to do the most work for him. These are what we have called the 'well-turned phrases'—the jokes, the one-liners, the aphorisms. A better way to understand *why* Wilde plagiarized might be to look more closely at *what* he plagiarized: at the particular units of discourse that he moved around or repeated. Some examples will be helpful. In the short story, 'The Nightingale and the Rose' (in *The Happy Prince and Other Tales* (1888)), the conventional and ultimately fickle student muses to himself that the nightingale 'is like most artists; she is all style, without any sincerity'. This aphorism underwent many metamorphoses, and finally resurfaced in *Earnest* (1899) as: 'in matters of grave importance, style, not sincerity is the vital thing'. A similar example concerns a paradox in the book version of *Dorian Gray* (1891), 'He atones for being occasionally somewhat over-dressed, by being always absolutely over-educated', which reappeared in 'Phrases and Philosophies For the Use of the Young' (*Chameleon* (1894)) as 'The only way to atone for being occasionally a little over-dressed is by being always absolutely over-educated', and then again in *Earnest*: 'If I am occasionally a little over-dressed, I make up for it by being always immensely over-educated.'

Listing examples of self-quotation may give a falsely simplified view, because the process of transposition in practice involved varying degrees of transformation. In most cases of self-plagiarism the joke is not just retained, it is also tailored to the new occasion. Moreover in this process of tailoring, there appears to be no single strategy at work. So it is possible to construct a spectrum of practices which range from straightforward repetition to complex rewording. At one end of this scale there are examples like the joke first used in 'Lord Arthur Savile's Crime' (in *Lord Arthur Savile's Crime and Other Stories*, (1891))—'My Dear Duchess, surely Providence can resist temptation by this time'—which is reused, word for word, in *An Ideal Husband* (1899): 'LORD GORING: Doesn't that sound rather like tempting Providence? MRS CHEVELEY: Oh! surely Providence can resist temptation by this time.' At the other extreme there is self-plagiarism which required substantial recasting. Hence an aphorism from 'Mr W. H.'—'It is always a silly thing to give advice, but to give good advice is absolutely fatal'—is changed significantly when it is reused in *An Ideal Husband* (1899): 'I always pass on good advice. It is the only thing to do with it. It is never of any use to oneself.' Similarly the comment in 'The Model Millionaire' (in *Lord Arthur Savile's Crime*) that Hughie 'became nothing, a delightful ineffectual young man with a perfect profile and no profession' is fleshed out in 'Phrases and Philosophies' as: 'There is something tragic about the enormous number of young men there are in England at the present moment who start life with a perfect profile, and end by adopting some useful profession.' Finally, there are some examples of condensation: so the familiar epigram from *Dorian Gray* (1891), that 'manners are of more importance than morals', is reduced to the more compact 'manners before morals!' when it is reused in *Lady Windermere's Fan* (1893).

There are a number of points we can make about these instances of self-plagiarism. First, direct or word-for-word transposition is relatively rare. Usually Wilde reworks and refreshes the original joke, sometimes by polishing the aphorism into a tighter verbal construction, and sometimes (as one would expect) by making it more relevant to the narrative into which it has been inserted. Indeed, it seems that it is the generality of this sort of joke—the fact that it answers to general cultural anxieties, rather than to any specific topical concern—which allows for its reuse. That is, the relative freestanding quality of such jokes explains why Wilde might have felt that they would bear repetition, especially if they appeared in different kinds of works. Such an observation, however, is not to undervalue the skill involved in identifying the sorts of one-liners which would sustain such treatment. It is not without significance that Wilde has been the source of more anthologies of 'The wit and wisdom of . . .' variety than any other writer. That these one-liners work a second (or subsequent) time around testifies to a particularly enduring kind of comic genius.

The term 'calculated' is an important one in this context, for it suggests that Wilde was aware that not any kind of joke or aphorism would bear repetition and reworking: in composing his well-turned phrases, he had to keep a careful eye on the cultural context in which they would work, and in which they might continue to work. Put another way, self-plagiarized jokes, when placed alongside the vast majority of one-liners in the *oeuvre* which are not repeated, begin to seem less like the carelessness of a hard-pressed professional, and more like part of a measured strategy. The nature of that strategy can be better seen through a further example. It concerns a running joke about education which is tied to a topical controversy about changes in government policy towards public examinations. The joke first appears, in the form of an aphorism, in *Dorian Gray*:

When I was in the Diplomatic, things were much better. But I hear they let them in now by examination. What can you expect? Examinations, sir, are pure humbug from beginning to end. If a man is a gentleman, he knows quite enough, and if he is not a gentleman, whatever he knows is bad for him.[68]

These lines do not appear in the Lippincott version of the story; they were part of the new material (Ch. 3) which Wilde added when he revised the novel for book publication. The joke is repeated in a slightly different form (but with exactly the same aphorism) in *A Woman of No Importance* (1894):

GERALD. My Mother is awfully conscientious, Lord Illingworth, and I know she doesn't think I am educated enough to be your secretary. She is perfectly right, too. I was fearfully idle when I was at school, and I couldn't pass an examination now to save my life.

LORD ILLINGWORTH. My dear Gerald, examinations are of no value whatsoever. If a man is a gentleman, he knows quite enough, and if he is not a gentleman, whatever he knows is bad for him.[69]

Finally in *Earnest* (1899) we find a vestige of the joke in a more general aphorism about education; that is to say, the specific reference to examinations has been dropped:

LADY BRACKNELL. . . . The whole theory of modern education is radically unsound. Fortunately in England, at any rate, education produces no effect whatsoever. If it did, it would prove a serious danger to the upper classes, and probably lead to acts of violence in Grosvenor Square.[70]

68 Lawler (ed.), *Dorian Gray*, 30–1.
69 Small (ed.), *A Woman of No Importance*, III, 3–10.
70 Jackson (ed.), *The Importance of Being Earnest*, I, 497–502.

At first glance, the joke (in all its versions) appears to belong to an established Victorian controversy about the fitness of a gentleman's education and the value of competitive examinations; both debates can be dated at least as far back as the 1860s.[71] However, at the time when Wilde was writing—the late 1880s—contemporary events had placed a new spin on both topics.

The November 1888 edition of the *Nineteenth Century* published a long article entitled 'The Sacrifice of Education to Examination: A Protest'. Written by Auberon Herbert, it carried the names of over four hundred politicians, churchmen, academics, headmasters of public schools, intellectuals and prominent social reformers, and was followed by three shorter pieces by Max Müller, Frederic Harrison, and Edward Freeman, all of whom supported Herbert's case. The December number of the *Nineteenth Century* printed a response, 'The Protest Against Over-Examination: A Reply'. It comprised three linked essays, each of which defended examinations on the grounds of their 'democratic spirit'. The debate continued the following year in February when two more pieces—'Is Examination a Failure?' and 'The Sacrifice of Education to Examination'—appeared. The first of the essays, by W. Baptiste Scones, attempted to strike a balance between the two sides of the debate by arguing that examinations could be an incentive for the less 'naturally' intelligent type. The second essay restated the original 'Protest' but added the names of another hundred signatories (all Members of Parliament). It was followed by a series of short essays by a number of interested parties, all of whom argued against examinations, and on a variety of grounds, including health, the narrowness of the qualities which examinations tested, the way they disrupted 'proper' learning, the emphasis they gave to rote-learning, and the idea that examinations were simply 'un-English'. Finally a book version of the various 'Protest' materials, again edited by Herbert, appeared in 1889.

The range of topics covered in this debate—the emphasis upon Philistinism, privilege, individualism, and Englishness—would have been irresistibly attractive to Wilde. Moreover he could not have helped but see it, for 'The Decay of Lying' was published in the *Nineteenth Century* in January 1889. It seems likely, then, that a year or so later, when he was casting around for some topical

---

[71] Controversies about the merits of competitive examinations derive in part from the Clarendon and Taunton Commissions of the 1860s. These endorsed their use at public schools and endowed grammar schools; examinations were later adopted by universities.

material to expand and update 'Dorian Gray' for book publication, Wilde remembered the controversy. Furthermore, the issues which the debate had raised were particularly relevant to the themes of that story. Wilde probably began his revisions to the periodical text in late 1890; the book was published in the spring of 1891. That the topic was still current can be seen in the June 1891 number of the *Nineteenth Century* in which another piece on examinations was published. Three years later Wilde would have found in the pages of the *Nineteenth Century* confirmation that the topic was still of interest to the public, for his old Trinity tutor, J. P. Mahaffy, had produced a long article for the periodical entitled 'The Future of Education'. Mahaffy's piece in turn referred back to his earlier article that year entitled, 'Sham Education'. In both essays examinations were once again the central bone of contention. Finally, there was a last piece on examinations early in 1894. Wilde, then, could safely repeat his joke in *A Woman of No Importance*. However it is significant that in the years immediately following, the *Nineteenth Century* lost interest in the debate. These details strongly suggest that Wilde may have been using the pages of that periodical (among others) to gauge public opinion. And they also hint that his decision to drop the specific reference to examinations when he reused the general joke about a gentleman's education for a third time in *Earnest*, may have been prompted by a judgement that the topic was no longer current enough to be funny.[72]

This account of the probable genesis of Wilde's series of jokes about examinations and education indicates that the decision to repeat material may have had a strong element of calculation to it and was the work of an opportunist rather than a lazy writer. It does not seem to have been some form of postmodern game played with a wilful contempt of the reading public. On the contrary, it seems that Wilde first formulated a good line, and then made a careful judgement about how much work that line would to do for him—about what occasions would bear its reuse. Such a creative economy is a form of plagiarism, and it is one almost certainly dictated by Wilde's consciousness that he was short of material. But it is also plagiarism carried out with a skill which is entirely compatible with the pragmatism which we have observed in some of Wilde's revisions.

[72] Details of these debates about education can be found in Guy, 'Self-Plagiarism, Creativity and Craftsmanship', 18–20.

On the other hand, an acknowledgement of the exercise of such skill should not blind us to the fact that there are other instances of self-plagiarism which do seem the product of laziness. So in both the periodical and book versions of *Dorian Gray*, a long purple passage describing Dorian's admiration for needlework and embroidery is lifted almost word for word from a review by Wilde of Alan Cole's translation of Ernest Lefébure's *Embroidery and Lace* (1888) which was published in November 1888 in the *Woman's World*. In the manner of nineteenth-century reviewing Wilde's piece is largely paraphrase, with some direct quotation. For example:

Charles of Orleans had a coat, on the sleeves of which were embroidered the verses of a song beginning '*Madame, je suis tout joyeux,*' the musical accompaniment of the words being wrought in gold thread, and each note, of square shape in those days, formed with four pearls. The room prepared in the palace at Rheims for the use of Queen Joan of Burgundy was decorated with 'thirteen hundred and twenty-one *papegauts* (parrots) made in broidery and blazoned with the King's arms, and five hundred and sixty-one butterflies, whose wings were similarly ornamented with the Queen's arms—the whole worked in fine gold.'[73]

When the material was reused in *Dorian Gray*, Wilde retained (and slightly altered) the quoted material, but did not identify which book Dorian is reading. More interestingly the origins of the paraphrased material were completely obscured through being attributed to the narrative voice of the novel:

. . . and the coat that Charles of Orleans once wore, on the sleeves of which were embroidered the verses of a song beginning '*Madame, je suis tout joyeux,*' the musical accompaniment of the words being wrought in gold thread, and each note, of square shape in those days, formed with four pearls. He read of the room that was prepared at the palace at Rheims for the use of Queen Joan of Burgundy, and was decorated with 'thirteen hundred and twenty-one parrots, made in broidery, and blazoned with the king's arms, and five hundred and sixty-one butterflies, whose wings were similarly ornamented with the arms of the queen, the whole worked in fine gold.'[74]

It is difficult to understand this repetition as anything other than an attempt to pad out the novel from work already to hand.

The examples we have discussed cover only a part of Wilde's plagiarism: they involve the self-plagiarism which appears in published

[73] Ross, *Reviews*, 334–5.   [74] Lawler (ed.), *Dorian Gray*, 107–8.

works. Wilde's writing is also marked by plagiarism from the writing of others, and this kind of plagiarism is not always easy to see because it rarely involves direct or word-for-word copying. Rather, Wilde tends to repeat only half a line or a phrase; or he may borrow another writer's critical vocabulary or stylistic devices and effects. Once again *Dorian Gray* provides some good examples of this kind of indebtedness. The most striking involve Wilde's borrowings from Pater. Lord Henry's advice to Dorian, 'Let nothing be lost upon you. Be always searching for new sensations. Be afraid of nothing', calls to mind the Conclusion to Pater's *Renaissance*: 'What we have to do is to be for ever curiously testing new opinions and courting new impressions.'[75] In this instance, the context of the novel's plotting and characterization suggests that Wilde probably wanted the debt to be recognized—that it is a conscious allusion contrived to signify Lord Henry's allegiance to a Paterian or Oxonian aestheticism. On other occasions, however, it is much less easy to be certain of the effect intended. For example, the following description of Dorian by the third-person narrator echoes (but without precisely copying) a paragraph from the third chapter of Pater's *Gaston de Latour*, which had appeared in *Macmillan's Magazine* from June to October 1889. This is *Dorian Gray*:

Music had stirred him like that. Music had troubled him many times. But music was not articulate. It was not a new world, but rather another chaos, that it created in us. Words! Mere words! How terrible they were! How clear, and vivid, and cruel! One could not escape from them. And yet what a subtle magic there was in them! They seemed to be able to give a plastic form to formless things, and to have a music of their own as sweet as that of viol or of lute. Mere words! Was there anything so real as words?[76]

And this is *Gaston de Latour*:

Yes! that was the reason why visible, audible, sensible things glowed so brightly, why there was such luxury in sounds, words, rhythms, of the new light come on the world, of that wonderful freshness. With a masterly appliance of what was near and familiar, or again in the way of bold innovation, he found new words for perennially new things, and the novel accent awakened long-slumbering associations. Never before had words, single words, meant so much. What expansion, what liberty of heart, in speech: how associable to music, to singing, the written lines![77]

75 Pater, *Studies in the History of the Renaissance* (London: Macmillan, 1873), 211.
76 Lawler (ed.), *Dorian Gray*, 21; the passage occurs in the book and periodical versions.
77 Pater, *Gaston de Latour: An Unfinished Romance* (London: Macmillan, 1897), 70.

In the absence of any obvious narrative clues, it is impossible to know whether this sort of borrowing is straightforward plagiarism, or whether it is playfully allusive. Is the reader meant to identify the narrative voice (along with that of Lord Henry) with the words of Pater? Or did Wilde hope that the debt to *Gaston* would pass unnoticed? Alternatively, it is possible that Wilde was not wholly conscious of what he had borrowed—that the idea and phrasing came into his mind 'detached' (as it were) from their specific origins in his reading of Pater. Such an explanation seems plausible when we remember that *Gaston* was not published in book form during Pater's lifetime, and that Wilde (and his readers) would have had to retain copies of *Macmillan's Magazine* in order to check the derivation. A similar intriguing example is Wilde's famous phrase in *De Profundis*, 'feasting with panthers', which has been traced to Balzac's *Illusions perdues* ('je soupe avec des lions et des panthèrs'). It is impossible to know whether this is a deliberate allusion, an instance of 'creative borrowing', or a phrase so deeply familiarized that Wilde believed it to be his own.[78]

It is important to distinguish the possibility of 'unconscious' indebtedness from psychological theories of influence elaborated by critics such as Harold Bloom.[79] We are not suggesting that through some anxiety to be original Wilde, either consciously or unconsciously, suppressed the extent to which his thoughts had been informed by others. Rather the opposite: Wilde was unusual in being only too ready to acknowledge that all new writing was inevitably dependent upon what had gone before it. For Wilde influence is a reason for celebration not a cause of anxiety. For example, in 1885, he explained that the 'originality . . . which we ask from the artist, is originality of treatment, not of subject. It is only the unimaginative who ever invents. The true artist is known by the use he makes of what he annexes, and he annexes everything.'[80] A year later in his lecture on Chatterton, Wilde went so far as to redefine influence as a form of theft—that is, it was a fully conscious and knowing activity. For Wilde, then, borrowing from others was intrinsic to true creativity; what mattered was the skill and imagination with which a writer used his sources. It may be tempting to dismiss Wilde's

---

[78] See Timothy D'Arch Smith and Horst Schroeder, 'Feasting with Panthers', *Notes and Queries*, 41 NS: 3 (June 1995), 201–2.

[79] See Harold Bloom, *The Anxiety of Influence* (New York: Oxford University Press, 1973).   [80] Ross, *Reviews*, 29.

theory of creativity as little more than naked self-justification designed to divert criticism. However it need not necessarily reflect
badly on him. On the contrary, when viewed in the light of the rest
of our knowledge about his writing practices, it is possible to see in
his theory of creativity an alertness to the particular nature (and
limitations) of his own writing talent.

Throughout this chapter we have frequently drawn attention to
what we have termed the 'modular' nature of Wilde's compositional
practices, and particularly his habit of composing around one-liners, aphorisms, or paradoxes. We have also observed that in his note-
taking Wilde had a tendency to reduce the often complex ideas of
other writers to a single memorable line, to the extent that the imaginative way in which he 'turned' a phrase was more important than
the accuracy of the summary. By putting these two habits together,
we get a sense of an interaction between Wilde's way of reading—of
engaging with the work of others—and his creativity: the reductive
form in which Wilde seems to have assimilated and memorized
ideas may have determined the very 'stuff' out of which he created
his own works. When we add to this our third insight into Wilde's
writing practices—that he was often short of material, and that he
found it difficult to compose sustained pieces of discursive prose—
we can begin to see exactly how the kind of half-conscious or un-
witting plagiarism that we have described might have occurred.

For Wilde, composition seems to have begun with a stock of
ideas, phrases, and vocabulary which had come from his reading.
However, by virtue of the form in which they had been memorized
they had acquired a discrete and relatively free-standing quality.
And this quality in turn ensured that those ideas, phrases, and vocabulary, while always in short supply, were also exceptionally flexible. The special term, the well-turned phrase, the aphorism, the
summarizing quotation—all these units of discourse had uniquely
portable properties which made them capable of adaptation for a
variety of occasions and purposes. Put simply, what we identify as
plagiarism in Wilde's work might sometimes be the trace of the way
his writerly mind worked, of a literary annexing so thoroughgoing
and habitual that the 'theft' was no longer consciously registered; or
evidence that there was no longer a perception that borrowing
needed to be acknowledged. Such a concession does not deny that
on some occasions Wilde's plagiarisms may be, as we have documented, both knowing (in the sense of being playful) or deliberate

(in the sense of being intended to deceive). However, it does explain why on other occasions plagiarism may be unintended in the sense of being unregistered or unmarked by Wilde. Interestingly the strongest evidence for this last kind of plagiarism comes from a text in whose public appeal Wilde probably had the least confidence. It is also a text which depended greatly upon the resources of his memory: *De Profundis*.

Because it was not subject to a process of systematic revision, many of the textual features of the manuscript of *De Profundis* present in a more extreme way the problematic elements of Wilde's composition in general. Readers have noted its rambling structure. It is as if, as Ross realized, that changing the order of particular passages would not have made much difference to its overall effect.[81] The manuscript reads as if it was composed in precisely that modular method we have observed in other works. More significantly there is a considerable amount of repetition of small phrases or particular collocations. Taken in isolation, it is tempting to interpret this repetition in terms of the obsessive quality of Wilde's memories when he was isolated in prison, and in terms of the way in which those memories fuelled his desire for recrimination. However, when the text is examined in relation to Wilde's other writing, that repetition begins look more familiar; it is very like a form of 'semi-conscious', or unmarked self-plagiarism. It may, that is, be further evidence of how Wilde's memory and creativity worked in general.

Some examples will make this point clearer. Early in the manuscript Wilde describes how the news of the death of his mother was broken to him by Constance, and how she 'travelled, ill as she was, all the way from Genoa to England to break to me herself the tidings of so irreparable, so irredeemable a loss'. Later, about halfway through the manuscript, describing what he sees as the responsibility of society towards prisoners, Wilde uses exactly the same collocation, but in a completely different context: '[Society] is really ashamed of its own actions, and shuns those whom it has punished, as people shun a creditor whose debt they cannot pay, or one on whom they have inflicted an irreparable, an irredeemable wrong.'[82]

---

[81] Ross's two editions of *De Profundis* (1905 and 1908) omitted about two-thirds of Wilde's original text. He also reordered some passages, a decision which Hart-Davis (*Letters*, 424) found 'inexplicable'. However, it can be argued that Ross's *De Profundis* is more coherent and less repetitive than the manuscript printed in *Letters*.

[82] *Letters*, 458 and 470.

It does not seem as if the second use of the collocation of 'irreparable' with 'irredeemable' is meant to call to mind the first—it does not seem as if Wilde intends a self-referential effect. After all, to draw attention to the repetition would be to trivialize his grief at his mother's death by making its expression seem formulaic. Rather, it is as if the collocation has simply lodged in Wilde's mind as part of a verbal repertoire which he uses almost intuitively. A more striking example of an unmarked collocation is the way a relationship between human tragedy, the humiliation of his trials, letters, and the Douglas family is troped through the repetition of the word 'revolting'. It occurs some fifteen times in the manuscript:

the mania for writing revolting and loathsome letters;

Monte Carlo, of all revolting places on God's earth;

so revolting had been the scene;

a series of scenes culminating in one more than usually revolting;

so young a life, and one that amidst all its ugly faults had still promise of beauty in it, should come to so revolting an end;

For you to write thus to me, when the very illness and fever from which I was suffering I had caught from tending you, was of course revolting in its coarseness and crudity;

the revolting scenes, and the revolting letter; it is denounced by your father's Counsel as a revolting and insidious attempt;

a revolting and repellent tragedy;

nor to have quoted from your letters the more revolting or heartless passages;

the weight of a terrible, a revolting tragedy, a terrible, a revolting scandal;

When his revolting letters to you were read in open Court he naturally felt ashamed;

notoriety of a second divorce suit, however revolting its details and origin;

transferred to me by revolting malice;

Unfortunately it ended in a very revolting manner.[83]

That the adjective 'revolting' should be repeated so often and so predictably can be explained in part by Wilde's psychological state. Nevertheless, the way in which the adjective seems to structure particular sorts of memories in the form of a particular kind of image recalls that aphoristic and reductive note-taking of his undergraduate days. Rather than seeing the manuscript as the product of unique

[83] *Letters*, 429, 430, 431, 433, 435, 439, 440, 441, 444, 456, 460, 494, 497, 502, and 508.

conditions which produced unique qualities in Wilde's writing, it might be more helpful to acknowledge that it was formed in part by habits of mind of an earlier origin, and of a more fundamental nature. The textual qualities of the manuscript were probably determined as much by Wilde's pre-prison experience as they were by the trials and by Wandsworth and Reading jails.

IV

An account of Wilde's plagiarism would not be complete without mentioning a further form of debt in his work, the more general quality of derivativeness that readers have recognized in the borrowed elements of his plot situations, character-types, themes, and so on. Kerry Powell, Katherine Worth, and Isobel Murray have given us detailed documentation of these kinds of borrowings in Wilde's fiction and drama.[84] Less attention has been given to Wilde's critical writings, in part because the tracing of intertextual links in these works requires a thoroughgoing familiarity with a wide range of Victorian journalism. However, where local studies have been undertaken, critics have discovered a pattern of generalized borrowing similar to the fiction and drama.[85] 'The Soul of Man Under Socialism' provides a particularly startling example of this kind of debt, not least because its paradoxical argument has often been taken to be Wilde's most original social criticism.

Assessments of the originality of Wilde's criticism typically proceed via a process of contextualization where the aim is to discover Wilde's sources or influences, and thereby the nature (and value) of his contribution to contemporary debates—whether and how, that is, his opinions transcend their journalistic occasion. In the case of 'The Soul of Man', critics have drawn attention to Wilde's allusions to the work of writers such as Kropotkin, Shaw, Sidney Webb, William Morris, and (to a lesser extent) to Spencer, Darwin, Engels, and Burke.[86] Like the catholic range of reading indicated by the

[84] See Powell, *Oscar Wilde and The Theatre of the 1890s*; Worth, *Oscar Wilde* (London, Macmillan, 1983); and Murray (ed.), *Oscar Wilde* (Oxford: Oxford University Press, 1989).

[85] See e.g. Danson's account of Wilde's debts in *Intentions* to the work of Pater and of Arnold (Danson, *Wilde's Intentions*).

[86] See e.g. George Woodcock, *Anarchism* (Harmondsworth: Penguin, 1963); J. D. Thomas, ' "The Soul of Man Under Socialism": An Essay in Context', *Rice University Studies*, 51 (1965), 83–95; Isobel Murray (ed.), *Oscar Wilde: The Soul of Man and Prison Writings* (Oxford: Oxford University Press, 1990), pp. vii–xviii.

Oxford notebooks, superficially this list seems to indicate depth and seriousness on Wilde's part. At the same time (and once more like the notebooks), its very eclecticism should give us pause. Wilde's 'use' of such figures is often little more than 'name-dropping': there is no sustained engagement with their positions. Indeed, how could there be? Would it be possible in a short article to synthesize the ideas of Morris and Burke? We should remember that any process of contextualization undertaken by a modern critic is selective and therefore partial. In this respect, it is interesting to see how little consideration has been given to the journalistic context of 'The Soul of Man'. Its relationship with contemporary periodical literature, and thus to what is local and topical, has been consistently marginalized or ignored, despite the fact that the details of its textual history (as we explained in Chapter 6) places it unambiguously within the realm of journalism.

There is clearly no space in the present study to give a full account of that journalistic context. Instead we shall concentrate on one aspect of it, the meaning in contemporary journalism of the term 'Individualism'. Although Individualism is mentioned by Wilde more often than Socialism in the essay, it has been given little attention. Isobel Murray has written of the influence of Emerson on Wilde's understanding of the term.[87] More usually, though, critics simply elide it with anarchism; or they follow Steven Lukes in noting its protean qualities.[88] This notion that the meaning of Individualism cannot be pinned down is seen to fit pleasingly with Wilde's habitual manipulation of linguistic conventions—his allegedly subversive interest in reversal, punning, and in synonyms and antonyms. However, it turns out that Wilde's use of the term Individualism in 'The Soul of Man' is very precise. Of key significance is Wilde's spelling (retained in both versions of the essay) with a capital 'I'. In the late nineteenth century Individualism (with a capital 'I') denoted a specific political ideology, which was routinely identified by journalists with a group of people in Britain who called themselves 'Individualists'. That politics was equally routinely distinguished from the more general methodological atomism implied by the concept of individualism, spelt with a small 'i'. Like the Fabians, the Individualists were prolific writers; they

---

[87] See Murray, ibid.
[88] See Lukes, *Individualism* (Oxford: Blackwell, 1973).

funded their own journals and published in 1889 their own collection of essays in reply to the *Fabian Essays in Socialism* (a work often seen as an influence on Wilde's essay). The Individualists propagandized their activities through a number of pressure groups, most notably The Liberty and Property Defence League, and they were active in Parliament. Understood as a specific politics, Individualism emerged in the mid-1880s, was at its height in the following decade, but had more or less disappeared by 1910.[89]

One consequence of this short lifespan is that, in contrast to Socialism, political historians have generally considered Individualism an irrelevance. Nevertheless, the Individualists were as visible and potent a force in late nineteenth-century politics as Socialists were. Auberon Herbert, Wordsworth Donisthorpe, Lord Elcho, Joseph Levy, and Thomas McKay are names that have been forgotten today, but in the 1880s and 1890s they enjoyed substantial reputations and were as well known to periodical readers as Shaw, Spencer, or Webb were. Moreover, Wilde's theorization of Individualism—particularly his anti-statism—turns out to be indebted to these figures in specific ways. Wilde's idea of voluntaryism, for example, directly invokes the polemic of Auberon Herbert, who founded his own journal (in 1890) to propagandize the merits of voluntary associations, and who also wrote for the *Fortnightly Review*. More generally, Wilde's refiguring of Individualism through a Socialist critique of private property seems much less eccentric and paradoxical when we realize that the typical Individualist polemicist was a high Tory landowner or manufacturer. Furthermore, Wilde's particular way of reconciling Socialism and Individualism did not even originate with him: a remarkably similar position had been argued (and more coherently) in 1889 in the *Contemporary Review* by Grant Allen, a popularizing writer well known to readers of the *Fortnightly* and to Wilde personally.

The occasion of Allen's essay, 'Individualism and Socialism', was the discussion of a pamphlet that he had received from the Liberty and Property Defence League. He claimed that the notion of liberty which it promoted was merely a defence of privilege. More particularly, the landowning Earl of Wemyss (a founder member of the

---

[89] For an account of the politics of the late 19th-cent. Individualists and the pressure group, the Liberty and Property Defence League, see Edward Bristow, 'The Liberty and Property Defence League and Individualism', *Historical Journal*, 18 (1975), 761–89; and M. W. Taylor, *Men Versus the State* (Oxford: Clarendon Press, 1992).

LPDL) represented to Allen an affront to what he termed 'true' or 'thorough-going' Individualism. He defined 'true' Individualism in terms uncannily similar to those of Wilde:

Individualism . . . is only logically and consistently possible if it starts with the postulate that all men must, to begin with, have free and equal access to the common gifts and energies of Nature—soil, water, air, sunshine; and to the common stock of raw material—stone, wood, coal, metal. . . . An Individualist is a man who recognizes without stint the full, free, and equal right of every citizen to the unimpeded use of all his energies, activities and faculties, provided only he does not thereby encroach upon the equal and correlative right of every other citizen.[90]

Allen went on to claim that none of these conditions obtained in Britain because the law protected landowners, whom he called 'the squatting and tabooing class', and compared to 'slave-holders'.[91] Significantly, Allen was careful to distinguish his understanding of Individualism from certain kinds of Socialism. On the one hand, he was prepared to concede that Socialism shared with Individualism 'a strong sense of the injustice and wickedness of the existing system', and an ambition to promote 'a more equitable distribution of the goods of life among those who do most to produce and defend them'. He nevertheless dissented strongly from 'much that the Socialists proclaim as their end and aim'—that is, from what he termed the '*deus ex machina*' role which Socialism gave to the State.[92] Wilde, of course, called this 'authoritarian Socialism'.

Allen's tactic of combining an Individualist anti-statism with a Socialist critique of private property is virtually identical to Wilde's rhetorical strategies in 'The Soul of Man'. The real difference concerns the context and tone of their arguments. Wilde's vision of the future is self-consciously and wittily utopian, one brought about by the mysterious 'law' of evolution. Allen, by contrast, is more concerned with practical politics, such as campaigning for the abolition of monopolies and privileges. To these ends, Allen claims, the 'socalled Socialists and the real Individualists can work in harness side by side most amicably'.[93]

It is impossible to establish with certainty whether Wilde had read Allen's essay. However there is an interesting exchange of letters between the two men which immediately followed the

---

[90] Grant Allen, 'Individualism and Socialism', *Contemporary Review*, 54 (May 1889), 738 and 731–2. [91] Ibid. 732–3. [92] Ibid. 738. [93] Ibid. 739.

publication of 'The Soul of Man'. Wilde's piece had appeared in the *Fortnightly* in the same issue as Allen's essay on 'The Celt in English Art'. On reading it, Wilde wrote to Allen expressing his 'real delight' in the article with its 'superb assertion of that Celtic spirit in Art that Arnold divined, but did not demonstrate'. Wilde went on to propose that Allen join him and some comrades for a celebratory 'Celtic Dinner'. Allen had in the meantime read Wilde's piece and in a letter which crossed in the post commended Wilde on his 'noble and beautiful essay'. 'I would have written every line of it myself', Allen commented, 'if only I had known how'.[94] There may be something a little arch in Allen's response, because, in a sense, he *had* written some of Wilde's essay. At the very least he may have given Wilde the idea about how Individualism and Socialism were to be reconciled. Similarly, the effusiveness of Wilde's praise may have hidden an element of embarrassment and defensiveness.

A contemporary reviewer of 'The Soul of Man' in the *Spectator* found it difficult to believe that Wilde's essay was to be taken seriously; for him, it only made sense as something 'written merely to startle and excite talk'. Certainly Wilde's readers would have found much they recognized. The attack on charity, authoritarianism, and militant Socialism, the advocacy of voluntaryism and the redefinition of Individualism through a Socialist critique of private property—it turns out that none of these arguments was new.[95] Neither were the comments on the role of the artist: these points too had already been rehearsed (although in different ways) in 'The Critic as Artist'. 'The Soul of Man', then, was not distinguished by the originality of its argument, nor indeed by its political sophistication. What is striking is the particular quality of the essay's wit which flatters the reader into thinking that both he (and perhaps Wilde) understand more than is in fact the case. It is once again uncannily reminiscent of the tone recommended by Gissing's Jasper Milvain, when he talks of wanting to write 'for the upper middle-class of

---

94 See *Letters*, 286–7.

95 Strong echoes of Wilde's attack on charity are to be found in a debate in the *Nineteenth Century* over Andrew Carnegie's *Gospel of Wealth*. See, in particular, William Gladstone, 'Mr Carnegie's "Gospel of Wealth": A Review and a Recommendation', *Nineteenth Century*, 28: 165 (Nov. 1890), 677–93, and Card. Archbishop Henry Edward [Manning], Hermann Alder, Hugh Price Hughes, 'Irresponsible Wealth', *Nineteenth Century*, 28: 166 (Dec. 1890), 876–90. Discussions about militant Socialism were also pervasive in late 19th-cent. periodicals; a piece very close to Wilde's argument is T. H. Huxley, 'Government: Anarchy or Regimentation', *Nineteenth Century*, 27: 159 (May 1890), 843–66.

intellect, the people who like to feel that what they are reading has some special cleverness, but who can't distinguish between stones and paste'.[96] On the other hand, the fact that today we are still reading Wilde, whereas the polemic of Grant Allen has been virtually forgotten, says a great deal about the value of that wit, and the skill involved in reducing a complex debate into a series of memorable and thought-provoking aphorisms.

Such a judgement, based on the observation that the essay has many derivative qualities, may disappoint some modern readers. However, we should remember that for the genre in which Wilde was writing originality was not necessarily a *desideratum*; rather repetition may have been intrinsic to the topicality and insistent self-referentiality of the periodical press. The *raison d'être* of the periodical essay was that it formed part of a debate, and consequently it was automatically limited by terms of reference already established. In a similar way, and as we have noted earlier, Wilde's fiction also aligned itself with popular sub-genres which play upon settled expectations of plot, character, and setting. So the very familiarity of its devices may have contributed to the success of the periodical version of *Dorian Gray*. In both criticism and popular fiction, genres in which the skill of the writer consists in an ability to manipulate the familiar and expected, it may be hard (and sometimes pointless) to distinguish between lack of originality and topicality. Many of the generic borrowings in the drama, particularly the Society Comedies, also fall into this category. Thus the generalized, generic indebtedness of Wilde's works, in contrast to the specific borrowing of lines and phrases, might better be explained in terms of Wilde's pursuit of readers and markets.

V

A description of Wilde's writing practices which encompasses the whole of the *oeuvre* proves that any single explanation—that he was driven by a politics, or that he was subject to censorship, or that he was an aesthetic 'purist'—is reductive and distorting. That *oeuvre* is characterized by different sorts of revision and different sorts of plagiarism. As one would expect, the motives behind these practices in their turn vary widely. Some can be seen as purely aesthetic or artistic, that 'limae labor' consistent with notions of literary crafts-manship. However, a considerable number were driven by more pragmatic considerations, often including the simple pressure to expand work. What also emerges from such a survey is the incon-trovertible if uncomfortable fact that Wilde was a writer who did not have an abundance of either intellectual resources or material. There is little sense of that fecund creativity which we associate with the work of Dickens and Balzac. Equally significantly, it ap-pears that Wilde's creative imagination worked best in what was a fairly narrow area, that of the aphorism or polished one-liner.

These conclusions may seem to justify some of the judgements of Wilde made by his contemporaries and by critics in the first half of the twentieth century, that he was a writer of relatively slender tal-ents, whose work was derivative, and who would not stand the test of time. It certainly is true that Wilde was not a writer who pos-sessed the same seriousness and range of Arnold or Shaw, nor the protean inventiveness of Joyce. None the less he did possess quali-ties of genius which although not unique are certainly very rare. In a fittingly paradoxical manner, Wilde's strengths turn out to have derived from what earlier critics judged to be his weakness. The at-tention to the elegance of the well-turned line, and to its portability, made Wilde the most quotable and consistently entertaining writer of the last century. It has been tempting in recent years to denigrate nineteenth-century writers who became involved in consumerism, with commerce and selling; nevertheless, that very attention to what pleased an audience, and the willingness to concede that literature should entertain, have ensured that Wilde's works have succeeded, that—in his words—they have become 'classics'.

APPENDIX A

Wilde's books

June 1878	*Ravenna*. Thomas Shrimpton & Son. 1s. 6d.
? 1880	*Vera; or, The Nihilists. A Drama in Four Acts.* Privately Printed. Acting Edition.
June 1881	*Poems*. David Bogue. 250 copies. 10s. 6d.
July 1881	*Poems*. 2nd. edn. David Bogue. 250 copies. 10s. 6d.
July 1881	*Poems*. Roberts Brothers. $1.25.[a]
Sept. 1881	*Poems*. 3rd. edn. David Bogue. 250 copies. 10s. 6d.
Jan. 1882	*Poems*. 4th. edn. David Bogue. 250 copies. 10s. 6d.
Jan. 1882	*Poems*. 5th. edn. David Bogue. 250 copies. 10s. 6d.
? 1882	*Poems*. 2nd. edn. Roberts Brothers. $1.25.[a]
? 1882	*Vera; or, The Nihilists. A Drama in a Prologue and Four Acts.* Privately Printed (in America).
March 1883	*The Duchess of Padua*. Privately Printed. Acting Edition. 20 copies.
May 1888	*The Happy Prince and Other Tales*. David Nutt. 1,000 copies. 5s. / 65 copies. 21s.
? 1888	*The Happy Prince and Other Tales*. Roberts Brothers. $1.00.[b]
Jan. 1889	*The Happy Prince and Other Tales*. 2nd. edn. David Nutt. 3s. 6d.[c]
? 1890	*The Happy Prince and Other Tales*. 2nd. imp. Roberts Brothers. $1.00.[b]
July 1891	*The Picture of Dorian Gray*. Ward, Lock and Co. 1,000 copies. 6s. / 250 copies. 21s.
May 1891	*Intentions*. Osgood, McIlvaine and Co. 900 copies. 7s. 6d.
May 1891	*Intentions*. Dodd, Mead and Co. 600 copies. $2.25.
July 1891	*Lord Arthur Savile's Crime and Other Stories*. Osgood, McIlvaine and Co. 1,500 copies. 2s.

July 1891	*Lord Arthur Savile's Crime and Other Stories.* Dodd, Mead and Co. 500 copies. $1.00.
Nov. 1891	*A House of Pomegranates.* Osgood, McIlvaine and Co. 1,000 copies. 21s.
Nov. 1891	*A House of Pomegranates.* Dodd, Mead and Co. $5.00.[d]
May 1892	*Poems.* Bodley Head. 220 copies. 15s.
Feb. 1893	*Salomé: Drame en un Acte.* Librairie de L'Art Indépendant / Bodley Head. 500 copies. 10fr. or 5s. / 50 copies. 10s. 6d.[e]
Nov. 1893	*Lady Windermere's Fan.* Bodley Head. 500 copies. 7s. 6d. / 50 copies. 15s.
Feb. 1894	*Salome: A Tragedy in One Act.* Bodley Head / Copeland & Day. 500 copies. 15s. / 100 copies. 30s.
May 1894	*Intentions.* Osgood, McIlvaine and Co. 500 copies. 3s. 6d.
May 1894	*Intentions.* Dodd, Mead and Co. 500 copies. $1.50.
June 1894	*The Sphinx.* Bodley Head. 250 copies. 42s.[f]
June 1894	*The Sphinx.* Bodley Head / Copeland and Day. 25 copies. 105s.
Oct. 1894	*A Woman of No Importance.* Bodley Head. 500 copies. 7s. 6d. / 50 copies. 15s.
? 1894	*The Happy Prince and Other Tales.* 3rd. imp. Roberts Brothers. $1.00.[b]
Jan. 1895	*Oscariana.* Privately Printed. 50 copies. 2s. 6d.[g]
May 1895	*Oscariana.* Privately Printed. 200 copies. 2s. 6d.[g]
May 1895	*The Soul of Man.* Privately Printed. 50 copies. 2s. 6d.[g]
Oct. 1895	*The Picture of Dorian Gray.* Ward, Lock and Co. 6s.[h]
Feb. 1898	*The Ballad of Reading Gaol.* Leonard Smithers. 800 copies. 2s. 6d / 30 copies. 21s.
Feb. 1898	*The Ballad of Reading Gaol.* 2nd. edn. Leonard Smithers. 1,000 copies. 2s. 6d.
March 1898	*The Ballad of Reading Gaol.* 3rd. edn. Leonard Smithers. 99 copies. 10s. 6d.
March 1898	*The Ballad of Reading Gaol.* 4th. edn. Leonard Smithers. 1,200 copies. 2s. 6d.
March 1898	*The Ballad of Reading Gaol.* 5th. edn. Leonard Smithers. 1,000 copies. 2s. 6d.
March 1898	*The Ballad of Reading Gaol.* 6th. edn. Leonard Smithers. 1,000 copies. 2s. 6d.

Feb. 1899   *The Importance of Being Earnest*. Leonard Smithers. 1,000
                   copies. 7s. 6d. / 100 copies. 21s.

June 1899   *The Ballad of Reading Gaol*. 7th. edn. Leonard Smithers.
                   2,000 copies. 2s. 6d.

July 1899   *An Ideal Husband*. Leonard Smithers. 1,000 copies. 7s. 6d
                   / 100 copies. 21s.

Notes:
   [a] Mason reports that the 'first impression' of the American edition of *Poems* (1881) sold
out 'within a few days of its appearance' (Mason, 324). It is not known how many copies of
either *Poems* (1881) or *Poems* (1882) were printed for the American market.
   [b] It is not known how many copies of *The Happy Prince* were printed for the American
market; the issuing of a second and third impression in 1890 and 1894 suggest that demand
may have been stronger there than in Britain.
   [c] The print-run of Nutt's second edition of *The Happy Prince* is not known; however, it
is unlikely to have been much larger than the first. Significantly, Nutt refused Wilde's suggestion in 1891 for a special Christmas edition.
   [d] It is not known exactly how many of the 1,000 copies printed were issued for sale in
America.
   [e] Correspondence between Wilde and John Lane suggests that only 25 of the large paper
copies were actually released for sale (of these, 15 were intended for sale in Britain; the price
of those sold in France is not known.)
   [f] Of these 250 copies, 200 were printed for sale in Britain and 50 for sale in America with
a special insertion carrying the imprint of Copeland & Day. It is not known how the print-
run of the large paper edition was divided between the British and American markets.
   [g] These books were all printed by Arthur Humphreys. The price at which they were sold
is not known for certain; however, evidence from correspondence between Humphreys and
Wilde together with their material qualities suggest 2s. 6d. as the most likely figure.
   [h] It is not known how many copies of this edition were printed; however, it was remaindered only a year later.

APPENDIX B

Wilde's Journalism

This appendix lists Wilde's known work as a critic and reviewer. It excludes the poems in prose and the poetry first published in periodicals. It also omits all of Wilde's correspondence published in the press. This last body of material is easily accessible in the *Miscellanies* volume in Ross's 1908 edition and in Hart-Davis's editions of the *Letters*. It includes: a letter to the (New York) *World* in 1882 about the audience for one of Wilde's lectures; a letter of 1883 on *Vera* to the *New York Herald*; public letters from Wilde to Whistler printed in the *World* in 1883, 1885, and 1886, and in *Truth* in 1890; a letter on Swinburne to the *Pall Mall Gazette* (repr. in the *Pall Mall Budget*) in 1886; letters to the *St James's Gazette*, the *Daily Chronicle*, the *Scots Observer* in 1890 over *The Picture of Dorian Gray*; a letter to *The Times* ('An Anglo–Indian's Complaint') in 1891; letters to the *Speaker* and the *Pall Mall Gazette* about *A House of Pomegranates* also in 1891; letters of 1892 to the *Daily Telegraph* about contemporary drama and to the *St James's Gazette* about *Lady Windermere's Fan*; letters of 1893 and 1894 to *The Times* about *Salomé* and the 'Thirteen Club'; three letters written to the *Pall Mall Gazette* in 1894 about 'the Ethics of Journalism' and the authorship of *The Green Carnation*; a letter to the *Evening News and Post* in 1895 over the Queensberry libel case; and letters to the *Daily Chronicle* in 1897 over prison life.

The principal sources of information are Stuart Mason, *Bibliography of Oscar Wilde* (London: T. Werner Laurie Ltd., 1914) and the bibliography in Ross's *Miscellanies*. In his corrected proof copy of his *Bibliography*, now held at the William Andrews Clark Memorial Library, University of California, Los Angeles, Stuart Mason identifies Wilde as the author of two further reviews in the *Pall Mall Gazette*: 'Various Versifiers' (28 April 1887) and 'A Batch of Books' (26 July 1888). John Stokes has also identified Wilde as the author of another review in the *Pall Mall Gazette*—'A Russian Realistic Romance' (28 May 1886). More recently Oskar Wellens has identified Wilde as the reviewer of J. A. Symonds's *Sketches and Studies in*

Italy in the *Athenaeum* (1879). The following list is almost certainly not comprehensive. In his introduction to *Miscellanies*, Ross acknowledged 'there must be buried in the contemporary press many anonymous reviews which I have failed to identify' (p. xiv). A full scholarly edition of Wilde's journalism is currently being prepared by Russell Jackson and John Stokes for the Oxford English Texts Edition of Wilde's *Complete Works*. It will attempt to identify the extent of Wilde's writing for the periodical press. Though the list below is probably incomplete, it nevertheless bears testimony to the amount of work expected of the professional reviewer in the 1880s. It is also interesting to see the range of titles in which Wilde published at any one time.

Finally, we should note that modern journals give volume numbers and part numbers. Nineteenth-century publishers tended to follow volume numbers by an issue number reckoned from the beginning of the journal's run (a practice usual today in newspapers). We have kept to the nineteenth-century system rather than imposing the volume and part numbers used by modern libraries.

1877

'The Grosvenor Gallery', *Dublin University Magazine*, 90, no. 535 (July 1877), 118–26.

1879

'The Grosvenor Gallery', *Saunders' Irish Daily News*, 190, no. 42,886 (5 May 1879), 5.
[Anon.] Review of J. A. Symonds, *Sketches and Studies in Italy*, *Athenaeum*, no. 2694 (June 1879), 754–5.

1882

'Mrs Langtry' [review of *An Unequal Match*], *World* [New York], 23, no. 7749 (7 Nov. 1882), 5.

1884

'Mr Oscar Wilde on Woman's Dress', *Pall Mall Gazette*, 40, no. 6114 (14 Oct. 1884), 6.
'Mr Oscar Wilde on Woman's Dress', [repr.] *Pall Mall Budget*, 32, no. 838 (17 Oct. 1884), 12.
'More Radical Ideas upon Dress Reform', *Pall Mall Gazette*, 40, no. 6138 (11 Nov. 1884), 11–12.
'More Radical Ideas upon Dress Reform', [repr.] *Pall Mall Budget*, 32, no. 842 (14 Nov. 1884), 22–3.

1885

'Mr Whistler's Ten O'Clock', *Pall Mall Gazette*, 41, no. 6224 (21 Feb. 1885), 1–2.

'Mr Whistler's Ten O'Clock', [repr.] *Pall Mall Budget*, 33, no. 857 (27 Feb. 1885), 16.

'The Relation of Dress to Art. A Note in Black and White on Mr Whistler's Lecture', *Pall Mall Gazette*, 41, no. 6230 (28 Feb. 1885), 4.

'The Relation of Dress to Art. A Note in Black and White on Mr Whistler's Lecture', [repr.] *Pall Mall Budget*, 33, no. 858 (6 March 1885), 11.

[Anon.] 'Dinners and Dishes', *Pall Mall Gazette*, 41, no. 6236 (7 March 1885), 5.

[Anon.] 'Dinners and Dishes', [repr.] *Pall Mall Budget*, 33, no. 859 (13 March 1885), 29–30.

[Anon.] 'A Modern Epic', *Pall Mall Gazette*, 41, no. 6241 (13 March 1885), 11–12.

'Shakespeare on Scenery', *Dramatic Review*, 1, no. 7 (14 March 1885), 99. [Under signature in facsimile.]

[Anon.] 'A Modern Epic', [repr.] *Pall Mall Budget*, 33, no. 860 (20 March 1885), 27.

[Anon.] 'A Bevy of Poets', *Pall Mall Gazette*, 41, no. 6253 (27 March 1885), 5.

[Anon.] 'Parnassus versus Philology', *Pall Mall Gazette*, 41, no. 6257 (1 April 1885), 6.

[Anon.] 'A Bevy of Poets', [repr.] *Pall Mall Budget*, 33, no. 862 (3 April 1885), 29–30.

'Shakespeare and Stage Costume', *Nineteenth Century*, 17, no. 99 (May 1885), 800–18.

' "Hamlet" at the Lyceum', *Dramatic Review*, 1, no. 15 (9 May 1885), 227. [Under signature in facsimile.]

[Anon.] 'Two New Novels', *Pall Mall Gazette*, 41, no. 6293 (15 May 1885), 5.

[Anon.] 'Two New Novels', [repr.] *Pall Mall Budget*, 33, no. 869 (22 May 1885), 4.

' "Henry the Fourth" at Oxford', *Dramatic Review*, 1, no. 17 (23 May 1885), 264–5. [Under signature in facsimile.]

[Anon.] 'Modern Greek Poetry', *Pall Mall Gazette*, 41, no. 6302 (27 May 1885), 5.

[Anon.] 'Modern Greek Poetry', [repr.] *Pall Mall Budget*, 33, no. 870 (29 May 1885), 26.

' "Olivia" at the Lyceum', *Dramatic Review*, 1, no. 18 (30 May 1885), 278. [Under signature in facsimile.]

' "As You Like It" at Coombe House', *Dramatic Review*, 1, no. 19 (6 June 1885), 296–7. [Under signature in facsimile.]

[Anon.] 'A Handbook to Marriage', *Pall Mall Gazette*, 42, no. 6452 (18 Nov. 1885), 6.

1886

[Oxoniensis] 'Half Hours with the Worst Authors', *Pall Mall Gazette*, 43, no. 6501 (15 Jan. 1886), 4.

'Half Hours with the Worst Authors', [repr.] *Pall Mall Budget*, 34, no. 904 (21 Jan. 1886), 21.

[Anon.] 'One of Mr Conway's Remainders', *Pall Mall Gazette*, 43, no. 6515 (1 Feb. 1886), 5.

[Anon.] 'One of Mr Conway's Remainders', [repr.] *Pall Mall Budget*, 34, no. 906 (4 Feb. 1886), 27.

'To Read or Not to Read', *Pall Mall Gazette*, 43, no. 6521 (8 Feb. 1886), 11.

'The Best Hundred Books' [repr. of 'To Read or Not to Read'], *Pall Mall Budget*, 34, no. 907 (11 Feb. 1886), 11.

' "Twelfth Night" at Oxford', *Dramatic Review*, 3, no. 56 (20 Feb. 1886), 34–5. [Under signature in facsimile.]

[Anon.] 'The Letters of a Great Woman', *Pall Mall Gazette*, 43, no. 6544 (6 March 1886), 4–5.

[Anon.] 'The Letters of a Great Woman', [repr.] *Pall Mall Budget*, 34, no. 911 (11 March 1886), 27–8.

[Anon.] 'News from Parnassus', *Pall Mall Gazette*, 43, no. 6575 (12 April 1886), 5.

[Anon.] 'Some Novels', *Pall Mall Gazette*, 43, no. 6577 (14 April 1886), 5.

[Anon.] 'News from Parnassus', [repr.] *Pall Mall Budget*, 34, no. 916 (15 April 1886), 29.

[Anon.] 'Some Novels', [repr.] *Pall Mall Budget*, 34, no. 916 (15 April 1886), 29–30.

[Anon.] 'A Literary Pilgrim', *Pall Mall Gazette*, 43, no. 6580 (17 April 1886), 5.

[Anon.] 'Béranger in England', *Pall Mall Gazette*, 43, no. 6583 (21 April 1886), 5.

[Anon.] 'A Literary Pilgrim', [repr.] *Pall Mall Budget*, 34, no. 917 (22 April 1886), 28–9.

[Anon.] 'Béranger in England', [repr.] *Pall Mall Budget*, 34, no. 917 (22 April 1886), 29–30.

[Anon.] 'A Fire at Sea' [trans. of Ivan Turgenev's 'Un incendie en mer'] *Macmillan's Magazine*, 54, no. 319 (May 1886), 39–44.

[Anon.] 'The Poetry of the People', *Pall Mall Gazette*, 43, no. 6601 (13 May 1886), 5.

' "The Cenci" ', *Dramatic Review*, 3, no. 68 (15 May 1886), 151. [Under signature in facsimile.]

' "Helena in Troas" ', *Dramatic Review*, 3, no. 69 (22 May 1886), 161–2. [Under signature in facsimile.]

[Anon.] 'A Russian Realistic Romance', *Pall Mall Gazette*, 43, no. 6614 (28 May 1886), 5.

[Anon.] 'Pleasing and Prattling', *Pall Mall Gazette*, 44, no. 6672 (4 Aug. 1886), 5.

[Anon.] 'Pleasing and Prattling', [repr.] *Pall Mall Budget*, 34, no. 932 (5 Aug. 1886), 30.

[Anon.] 'Balzac in English', *Pall Mall Gazette*, 44, no. 6706 (13 Sept. 1886), 5.

[Anon.] 'Balzac in English', [repr.] *Pall Mall Budget*, 34, no. 938 (16 Sept. 1886), 29–30.

[Anon.] 'Two New Novels,' *Pall Mall Gazette*, 44, no. 6709 (16 Sept. 1886), 5.

[Anon.] 'Ben Jonson', *Pall Mall Gazette*, 44, no. 6712 (20 Sept. 1886), 6.

[Anon.] 'Ben Jonson', [repr.] *Pall Mall Budget*, 34, no. 939 (23 Sept. 1886), 29.

[Anon.] 'The Poets' Corner,' *Pall Mall Gazette*, 44, no. 6718 (27 Sept. 1886), 5.

[Anon.] 'The Poets' Corner,' [repr.] *Pall Mall Budget*, 34, no. 940 (30 Sept. 1886), 29.

[Anon.] 'A Ride through Morocco', *Pall Mall Gazette*, 44, no. 6728 (8 Oct. 1886), 5.

[Anon.] 'A Ride through Morocco', [repr.] *Pall Mall Budget*, 34, no. 942 (14 Oct. 1886), 31.

[Anon.] 'The Children of the Poets', *Pall Mall Gazette*, 44, no. 6733 (14 Oct. 1886), 5.

[Anon.] 'The Children of the Poets', [repr.] *Pall Mall Budget*, 34, no. 943 (21 Oct. 1886), 30–1.

[Anon.] 'New Novels', *Pall Mall Gazette*, 44, no. 6745 (28 Oct. 1886), 4–5.

[Anon.] 'A Politician's Poetry', *Pall Mall Gazette*, 44, no. 6750 (3 Nov. 1886), 4–5.

[Anon.] 'Lord Carnavon's "Odyssey" ' [repr. of 'A Politician's Poetry'], *Pall Mall Budget*, 34, no. 945 (4 Nov. 1886), 28.

[Anon.] 'Mr Symonds' History of the Renaissance', *Pall Mall Gazette*, 44, no. 6756 (10 Nov. 1886), 5.

[Anon.] 'A "Jolly" Art Critic', *Pall Mall Gazette*, 44, no. 6763 (18 Nov. 1886), 6.

[Anon.] 'A "Sentimental Journey" Through Literature', *Pall Mall Gazette*, 44, no. 6774 (1 Dec. 1886), 5.

[Anon.] 'Two Biographies of Sir Philip Sidney', *Pall Mall Gazette*, 44, no. 6783 (11 Dec. 1886), 5.

1887

[Anon.] 'Common Sense in Art', *Pall Mall Gazette*, 45, no. 6806 (8 Jan. 1887), 5.

[Anon.] 'Miner and Minor Poets', *Pall Mall Gazette*, 45, no. 6826 (1 Feb. 1887), 5.

[Anon.] 'A Miner Poet' [repr. of 'Miner and Minor Poets'], *Pall Mall Budget*, 35, no. 958 (3 Feb. 1887), 31.

[Anon.] 'The Poets and the People. By One of the Latter', *Pall Mall Gazette*, 45, no. 6840 (17 Feb. 1887), 4.

[Anon.] 'A New Calendar', *Pall Mall Gazette*, 45, no. 6840 (17 Feb. 1887), 5.

'The Canterville Ghost' [part I], *Court and Society Review*, 4, no. 138 (23 Feb. 1887), 183–6.

[Anon.] 'A New Calendar', [repr.] *Pall Mall Budget*, 35, no. 961 (24 Feb. 1887), 29.

'The Canterville Ghost' [parts II, III, and IV], *Court and Society Review*, 4, no. 139 (2 March 1887), 207–11.

[Anon.] 'The Poets' Corner', *Pall Mall Gazette*, 45, no. 6856 (8 March 1887), 5.

[Anon.] 'The American Invasion', *Court and Society Review*, 4, no. 142 (23 March 1887), 270–1.

[Anon.] 'Great Writers by Little Men', *Pall Mall Gazette*, 45, no. 6873 (28 March 1887), 5.

[Anon.] 'Great Writers by Little Men', [repr.] *Pall Mall Budget*, 35, no. 966 (31 March 1887), 29–30.

[Anon.] 'A New Book on Dickens', *Pall Mall Gazette*, 45, no. 6876 (31 March 1887), 5.

[Anon.] 'A New Book on Dickens', [repr.] *Pall Mall Budget*, 35, no. 967 (7 April 1887), 30–1.

[Anon.] 'Our Book Shelf', *Pall Mall Gazette*, 45, no. 6885 (12 April 1887), 5.

[Anon.] ['The Great Ormond Street Child's Hospital'], *Court and Society Review*, 4, no. 145 (13 April 1887), 337.

[Anon.] 'The American Man', *Court and Society Review*, 4, no. 145 (13 April 1887), 341–3.

[Anon.] 'The New Play', *Court and Society Review*, 4, no. 145 (13 April 1887), 357.

[Anon.] 'Our Book Shelf', [repr.] *Pall Mall Budget*, 35, no. 968 (14 April 1887), 30.

[Anon.] 'A Cheap Edition of a Great Man', *Pall Mall Gazette*, 45, no. 6890 (18 April 1887), 5.

[Anon.] 'The Butterfly's Boswell', *Court and Society Review*, 4, no. 146 (20 April 1887), 378.

[Anon.] 'The Child-Philosopher', *Court and Society Review*, 4, no. 146 (20 April 1887), 379–80.

[Anon.] 'Mr Morris's Odyssey', *Pall Mall Gazette*, 45, no. 6897 (26 April 1887), 5.

[Anon.] 'The Rout of the R. A.', *Court and Society Review*, 4, no. 147 (27 April 1887), 390.

[Anon.] 'Various Versifiers', *Pall Mall Gazette*, 45, no. 6899 (28 April 1887).

[Anon.] 'Mr Morris's Odyssey', [repr.] *Pall Mall Budget*, 35, no. 970 (28 April 1887), 30–1.

[Anon.] 'A Batch of Novels', *Pall Mall Gazette*, 45, no. 6902 (2 May 1887), 11.

[Anon.] 'Should Geniuses Meet?', *Court and Society Review*, 4, no. 148 (4 May 1887), 413–14.

[Anon.] 'A Batch of Novels', [repr.] *Pall Mall Budget*, 35, no. 971 (5 May 1887), 29–30.

[Anon.] 'Some Novels', *Saturday Review*, 63, no. 1645 (7 May 1887), 663.

'Lord Arthur Savile's Crime. A Story of Cheiromancy' [parts I and II], *Court and Society Review*, 4, no. 149 (11 May 1887), 447–50.

'Lord Arthur Savile's Crime. A Story of Cheiromancy' [parts III and IV], *Court and Society Review*, 4, no. 150 (18 May 1887), 471–3.

'Lord Arthur Savile's Crime. A Story of Cheiromancy' [parts V and VI], *Court and Society Review*, 4, no. 151 (25 May 1887), 495–7.

' "Town and Country Tales": Lady Alroy', *World*, 26, no. 673 (25 May 1887), 18–19.

[Anon.] 'The Poets' Corner', *Pall Mall Gazette*, 45, no. 6926 (30 May 1887), 5.

[Anon.] 'Mr Pater's Imaginary Portraits', *Pall Mall Gazette*, 45, no. 6937 (11 June 1887), 2–3.

' "Town and Country Tales": The Model Millionaire', *World*, 26, no. 677 (22 June 1887), 18–19.

[Anon.] 'A Good Historical Novel', *Pall Mall Gazette*, 46, no. 6986 (8 Aug. 1887), 3.

[Anon.] 'A Good Historical Novel', [repr.] *Pall Mall Budget*, 35, no. 985 (11 Aug. 1887), 29.

[Anon.] 'New Novels', *Saturday Review*, 64, no. 1660 (20 Aug. 1887), 264.

[Anon.] 'The Lorgnette', *Court and Society Review*, 5, no. 167 (14 Sept. 1887), 249–50.

[Anon.] 'Two Biographies of Keats', *Pall Mall Gazette*, 46, no. 7029 (27 Sept. 1887), 3.

[Anon.] 'Two Biographies of Keats', [repr.] *Pall Mall Budget*, 35, no. 992 (29 Sept. 1887), 29–30.

[Anon.] ' "Sermons in Stones" at Bloomsbury. The New Sculpture Room at the British Museum', *Pall Mall Gazette*, 46, no. 7045 (15 Oct. 1887), 5.

[Anon.] ' "Sermons in Stones" at Bloomsbury. The New Sculpture Room at the British Museum', [repr.] *Pall Mall Budget*, 35, no. 995 (20 Oct. 1887), 8–9.

[Anon.] 'A Scotchman on Scottish Poetry', *Pall Mall Gazette*, 46, no. 7052 (24 Oct. 1887), 3.

[Anon.] 'A Scotchman on Scottish Poetry', [repr.] *Pall Mall Budget*, 35, no. 996 (27 Oct. 1887), 30–1.

'Literary and Other Notes. By the Editor', *Woman's World*, 1, no. 1 (Nov. 1887), 36–40.

[Anon.] 'Mr Mahaffy's New Book', *Pall Mall Gazette*, 46, no. 7066 (9 Nov. 1887), 3.

[Anon.] 'Mr Mahaffy's New Book', [repr.] *Pall Mall Budget*, 35, no. 999 (17 Nov. 1887), 28.

[Anon.] 'Mr Morris's Completion of the Odyssey', *Pall Mall Gazette*, 46, no. 7079 (24 Nov. 1887), 3.

[Anon.] 'Sir Charles Bowen's Virgil', *Pall Mall Gazette*, 46, no. 7084 (30 Nov. 1887), 3.

'Literary and Other Notes. By the Editor', *Woman's World*, 1, no. 2 (Dec. 1887), 81–5.

[Anon.] 'Mr Morris's Completion of the Odyssey', [repr.] *Pall Mall Budget*, 35, no. 1001 (1 Dec. 1887), 27–8.

[Anon.] 'Sir Charles Bowen's Virgil', [repr.] *Pall Mall Budget*, 35, no. 1001 (1 Dec. 1887), 29–30.

[Anon.] 'The Unity of the Arts. A Lecture and "A Five O'Clock" ', *Pall Mall Gazette*, 46, no. 7094 (12 Dec. 1887), 13.

[Anon.] 'Aristotle at Afternoon Tea', *Pall Mall Gazette*, 46, no. 7098 (16 Dec. 1887), 3.

[Anon.] 'Early Christian Art in Ireland', *Pall Mall Gazette*, 46, no. 7099 (17 Dec. 1887), 3.

[Anon.] 'Aristotle at Afternoon Tea', [repr.] *Pall Mall Budget*, 35, no. 1004 (22 Dec. 1887), 29–30.

[Anon.] 'Art at Willis's Rooms', *Sunday Times* no. 3376 (25 Dec. 1887), 7.

1888

'Literary and Other Notes. By the Editor', *Woman's World*, 1, no. 3 (Jan. 1888), 132–6.

[Anon.] 'The Poets' Corner', *Pall Mall Gazette*, 47, no. 7128 (20 Jan. 1888), 3.

'Literary and Other Notes. By the Editor', *Woman's World*, 1, no. 4 (Feb. 1888), 180–4.

[Anon.] 'The Poets' Corner', *Pall Mall Gazette*, 47, no. 7150 (15 Feb. 1888), 2–3.

[Anon.] 'Concerning Nine Poets' [repr. of 'The Poets' Corner'], *Pall Mall Budget*, 36, no. 1012 (16 Feb. 1888), 30.

[Anon.] 'Venus or Victory?', *Pall Mall Gazette*, 47, no. 7158 (24 Feb. 1888), 2–3.

'Literary and Other Notes. By the Editor', *Woman's World*, 1, no. 5 (March 1888), 229–32.

[Anon.] 'The Poets' Corner', *Pall Mall Gazette*, 47, no. 7193 (6 April 1888), 3.

[Anon.] 'M. Caro on George Sand', *Pall Mall Gazette*, 47, no. 7200 (14 April 1888), 3.

[Anon.] 'A Batch of Books', *Pall Mall Gazette*, 48, no. 7288 (26 July 1888).

[Anon.] 'The Poets' Corner', *Pall Mall Gazette*, 48, no. 7365 (24 Oct. 1888), 5.

'A Fascinating Book. A Note by the Editor', *Woman's World*, 2, no. 13 (Nov. 1888), 53–6.

[Anon.] 'Mr Morris on Tapestry', *Pall Mall Gazette*, 48, no. 7373 (2 Nov. 1888), 6.

[Anon.] 'Sculpture at the "Arts and Crafts" ', *Pall Mall Gazette*, 48, no. 7379 (9 Nov. 1888), 3.

[Anon.] 'The Poets' Corner', *Pall Mall Gazette*, 48, no. 7385 (16 Nov. 1888), 2–3.

[Anon.] 'Printing and Printers. Lecture at the Arts and Crafts', *Pall Mall Gazette*, 48, no. 7385 (16 Nov. 1888), 5.

[Anon.] 'The Beauties of Bookbinding. Mr Cobden-Sanderson at the Arts and Crafts', *Pall Mall Gazette*, 48, no. 7391 (23 Nov. 1888), 3.

[Anon.] 'The Beauties of Bookbinding. Mr Cobden-Sanderson at the Arts and Crafts', [repr.] *Pall Mall Budget*, 36, no. 1053 (29 Nov. 1888), 22.

[Anon.] 'The Close of the "Arts and Crafts." Mr Walter Crane's Lecture on Design', *Pall Mall Gazette*, 48, no. 7397 (30 Nov. 1888), 3.

'A Note on Some Modern Poets. By the Editor', *Woman's World*, 2, no. 14 (Dec. 1888), 108–12.

'English Poetesses', *The Queen*, 84, no. 2189 (8 Dec. 1888), 742–3.

[Anon.] 'Sir Edwin Arnold's Last Volume', *Pall Mall Gazette*, 48, no. 7406 (11 Dec. 1888), 3.

[Anon.] 'Australian Poets', *Pall Mall Gazette*, 48, no. 7409 (14 Dec. 1888), 2–3.

[Anon.] 'Australian Poets', [repr.] *Pall Mall Budget*, 36, no. 1056 (20 Dec. 1888), 29.

'The Young King', *Lady's Pictorial*, Christmas Number (1888), 1–5.

1889

'The Decay of Lying: A Dialogue', *Nineteenth Century*, 25, no. 143 (Jan. 1889), 35–56.

'Pen, Pencil, and Poison: A Study', *Fortnightly Review*, 45, no. 265 (Jan. 1889), 41–54.

'London Models', *English Illustrated Magazine*, 6, no. 64 (Jan. 1889), 313–19.

'Some Literary Notes. By the Editor', *Woman's World*, 2, no. 15 (Jan. 1889), 164–8.

[Anon.] 'Poetry and Prison. Mr Wilfrid Blunt's "In Vinculis" ', *Pall Mall Gazette*, 49, no. 7425 (3 Jan. 1889), 3.

[Anon.] 'Mr Andrew Lang's "Grass of Parnassus" ', *Pall Mall Gazette*, 49, no. 7425 (3 Jan. 1889), 5.

[Anon.] 'The Gospel According to Walt Whitman', *Pall Mall Gazette*, 49, no. 7444 (25 Jan. 1889), 3.

[Anon.] 'The New President', *Pall Mall Gazette*, 49, no. 7445 (26 Jan. 1889), 3.

'Some Literary Notes. By the Editor', *Woman's World*, 2, no. 16 (Feb. 1889), 221–4.

'The Decay of Lying: A Dialogue', [repr.] *Eclectic Magazine* [New York], 49, no. 2 (Feb. 1889), 184–98.

[Anon.] 'One of the Bibles of the World', *Pall Mall Gazette*, 49, no. 7459 (12 Feb. 1889), 3.

[Anon.] 'One of the Bibles of the World', [repr.] *Pall Mall Budget*, [37], no. 1064 (14 Feb. 1889), 222.

[Anon.] 'Poetical Socialists', *Pall Mall Gazette*, 49, no. 7462 (15 Feb. 1889), 3.

[Anon.] 'Mr Brander Matthews's Essays', *Pall Mall Gazette*, 49, no. 7472 (27 Feb. 1889), 3.

'Some Literary Notes. By the Editor', *Woman's World*, 2, no. 17 (March 1889), 277–80.

[Anon.] 'Mr William Morris's Last Book', *Pall Mall Gazette*, 49, no. 7475 (2 March 1889), 3.

[Anon.] 'Adam Lindsay Gordon', *Pall Mall Gazette*, 49, no. 7494 (25 March 1889), 3.

[Anon.] 'Adam Lindsay Gordon', [repr.] *Pall Mall Budget*, [37], no. 1070 (28 March 1889), 414.

[Anon.] 'The Poets' Corner', *Pall Mall Gazette*, 49, no. 7499 (30 March 1889), 3.

'The Birthday of the Little Princess', *Paris Illustré* [New York and London], 2, no. 65 (30 March 1889), 203, 206–7, 209.

'L'Anniversaire de la Naissance de la Petite Princesse', *Paris Illustré* [Paris], 2, no. 65 (30 March 1889), 203, 206–7, 209.

'Some Literary Notes. By the Editor', *Woman's World*, 2, no. 18 (April 1889), 333–6.

[O. W.] 'Mr Froude's Blue Book', *Pall Mall Gazette*, 49, no. 7511 (13 April 1889), 3.

[O. W.] 'Mr Froude's Blue Book', [repr.] *Pall Mall Budget*, [37], no. 1073 (18 April 1889), 507.

'Some Literary Notes. By the Editor', *Woman's World*, 2, no. 19 (May 1889), 389–92.

[Anon.] 'Ouida's New Novel', *Pall Mall Gazette*, 49, no. 7539 (17 May 1889), 3.

[Anon.] 'Ouida's New Novel', [repr.] *Pall Mall Budget*, [37], no. 1078 (23 May 1889), 670.

'Some Literary Notes. By the Editor', *Woman's World*, 2, no. 20 (June 1889), 446–8.

[Anon.] 'A Thought-Reader's Novel', *Pall Mall Gazette*, 49, no. 7555 (5 June 1889), 2.

[Anon.] 'The Poets' Corner', *Pall Mall Gazette*, 49, no. 7571 (24 June 1889), 3.

[Anon.] 'Mr Swinburne's Last Volume', *Pall Mall Gazette*, 49, no. 7574 (27 June 1889), 3.

'The Portrait of Mr W. H.', *Blackwood's Edinburgh Magazine*, 146, no. 885 (July 1889), 1–21.

[Anon.] 'Mr Swinburne's Last Volume', [repr.] *Pall Mall Budget*, [37], no. 1084 (4 July 1889), 862.

[Anon.] 'Three New Poets', *Pall Mall Gazette*, 49, no. 7587 (12 July 1889), 3.

'The Portrait of Mr W. H.', [repr.] *Eclectic Magazine* [New York], 50, no. 2 (Aug. 1889), 236–50.

1890

'A Chinese Sage', *Speaker*, 1, no. 6 (8 Feb. 1890), 144–6.

'Mr Pater's Last Volume', *Speaker*, 1, no. 12 (22 March 1890), 319–20.

[Anon.] 'Primavera', *Pall Mall Gazette*, 50, no. 7856 (24 May 1890), 3.

'The Picture of Dorian Gray', *Lippincott's Monthly Magazine*, 46, no. 271 (July [20 June] 1890), 3–100.

'The True Function and Value of Criticism; With some Remarks on the Importance of Doing Nothing: A Dialogue' [part I], *Nineteenth Century*, 28, no. 161 (July 1890), 123–47.

'The True Function and Value of Criticism; With some Remarks on the Importance of Doing Nothing: A Dialogue' [part II], *Nineteenth Century*, 28, no. 163 (Sept. 1890), 435–59.

1891

'The Soul of Man Under Socialism', *Fortnightly Review*, 49, no. 290 (Feb. 1891), 292–319.

'A Preface to "Dorian Gray" ', *Fortnightly Review*, 49, no. 291 (March 1891), 480–1.

'The Soul of Man Under Socialism', [repr.] *Eclectic Magazine* [New York], 53, no. 4 (April 1891), 465–83.

1894

'Phrases and Philosophies for the Use of the Young', *The Chameleon*, 1, no. 1 (Dec. 1894), 1–3.

1895

'Who Should be Laureate?', *Idler Magazine*, 7, no. 39 (April 1895), 403.

Select Bibliography

ALLEN, GRANT, 'Individualism and Socialism', *Contemporary Review*, 54 (May 1889), 730–41.

AMOR, ANNE CLARK, *Mrs Oscar Wilde: A Woman of Some Importance* (London: Sidgwick and Jackson, 1983).

AUERBACH, NINA, and U. C. KNOEPFLMACHER (eds.), *Forbidden Journeys: Fairy Tales and Fantasies by Victorian Women Writers* (London: University of Chicago Press, 1992).

BAKHTIN, MIKHAIL, 'From the Prehistory of Novelistic Discourse', in David Lodge (ed.), *Modern Criticism and Theory: A Reader* (London: Longman, 1988), 124–56.

BECKSON, KARL (ed.), *Oscar Wilde: The Critical Heritage* (1970; London: Routledge, 1997).

—— *The Oscar Wilde Encyclopedia* (New York: AMS Press, 1998).

BLACK, MICHAEL, 'Editing a Constantly-Revising Author: the Cambridge Edition of Lawrence in Historical Context', in Mara Kalnins (ed.), *D. H. Lawrence: Centenary Essays* (Bristol: Bristol Classical Press, 1986), 191–210.

BLOOM, HAROLD, *The Anxiety of Influence* (New York: Oxford University Press, 1973).

BORNSTEIN, GEORGE, and RALPH G. WILLIAMS (eds.), *Palimpsest: Editorial Theory in the Humanities* (Ann Arbor: University of Michigan Press, 1993).

BRISTOW, EDWARD, 'The Liberty and Property Defence League and Individualism', *Historical Journal*, 18 (1975), 761–89.

BRISTOW, JOSEPH, '"A complex multiform creature": Wilde's sexual identities', in Peter Raby (ed.), *The Cambridge Companion to Oscar Wilde* (Cambridge: Cambridge University Press, 1997), 195–218.

—— *Sexuality* (London: Routledge, 1997).

BROWN, JULIA PREWITT, *Cosmopolitan Criticism: Oscar Wilde's Philosophy of Art* (London: University Press of Virginia, 1997).

BURNS, SARAH, *Inventing the Modern Artist* (New Haven: Yale University Press, 1996).

CALLOWAY, STEPHEN, 'Wilde and the Dandyism of the Senses', in Peter Raby (ed.), *The Cambridge Companion to Oscar Wilde* (Cambridge: Cambridge University Press, 1997), 34–54.

CAREY, JOHN, *The Intellectuals and the Masses* (London: Faber, 1992).

CLAYWORTH, ANYA, '"Laurels Don't Come For the Asking": Oscar Wilde's Career as a Professional Journalist'. Unpublished Ph.D. thesis (University of Birmingham, 1996).

COAKLEY, DAVIS, *Oscar Wilde: The Importance of Being Irish* (Dublin: Town House, 1994).

COHEN, ED, *Talk on the Wilde Side* (New York: Routledge, 1993).

CRAFT, CHRISTOPHER, *Another Kind of Love: Male Homosexual Desire in English Discourse: 1850–1920* (Berkeley: University of California Press, 1994).

DANSON, LAWRENCE, *Wilde's Intentions: The Artist in his Criticism* (Oxford: Clarendon Press, 1997).

DAVIDSON, JOHN, *Fleet Street Eclogues* (London: The Bodley Head, 1893).

DELLAMORA, RICHARD, *Masculine Desire: The Politics of Victorian Aestheticism* (Chapel Hill: University of North Carolina Press, 1990).

DOLLIMORE, JONATHAN, 'Different Desires: Subjectivity and Transgression in Wilde and Gide', *Textual Practice*, 1: 1 (1987), 48–67.

—— *Sexual Dissidence* (Oxford: Clarendon Press, 1991).

DONOHUE, JOSEPH (with RUTH BERGGREN) (ed.), *Oscar Wilde's The Importance of Being Earnest: The First Production* (Gerrards Cross, Bucks: Colin Smythe, 1995).

DOOLEY, ALLAN C., *Author and Printer in Victorian England* (London: University Press of Virginia, 1992).

DOUGLAS, ALFRED, *Autobiography* (1929; London: Martin Secker, 1931).

ELIOT, SIMON, *Some Patterns and Trends in British Publishing: 1880–1919* (London: Bibliographical Society Occasional Papers, 1993).

ELLMANN, RICHARD (ed.), *The Artist as Critic: Critical Writings of Oscar Wilde* (London: W. H. Allen, 1970).

—— *Oscar Wilde* (London: Hamish Hamilton, 1987).

ELTIS, SOS, *Revising Wilde: Society and Subversion in the Plays of Oscar Wilde* (Oxford: Clarendon Press, 1996).

FELTES, NORMAN, *Literary Capital and the Late Victorian Novel* (London: University of Wisconsin Press, 1993).

FONG, BOBBY, 'The Poetry of Oscar Wilde: A Critical Edition.' Unpublished Ph.D. thesis (University of California, Los Angeles, 1978).

—— and KARL BECKSON (eds.), *Oscar Wilde: Poems and Poems in Prose* (Oxford: Oxford University Press, 2000).

FOTHERGILL, ANTHONY (ed.), *Oscar Wilde: Plays, Prose Writings and Poems* (London: J. M. Dent, 1996).

FREEDMAN, JONATHAN, *Professions of Taste: Henry James, British Aestheticism and Commodity Culture* (Stanford: Stanford University Press, 1990).

GAGNIER, REGENIA, *Idylls of the Marketplace* (Stanford: Stanford University Press, 1986).

GISSING, GEORGE, *New Grub Street* (1891; Harmondsworth: Penguin, 1987).

GOULD, WARWICK, 'The Crucifixion of the Outcasts: Yeats and Wilde in the Nineties', in George Sandulescu (ed.), *Rediscovering Oscar Wilde* (Gerrards Cross, Bucks: Colin Smythe, 1994).

GREGOR, IAN, 'Comedy and Oscar Wilde', *Sewanee Review*, 74: 2 (1966), 501–21.

GUY, JOSEPHINE M., *The British Avant-Garde: The Theory and Politics of Tradition* (Hemel Hempstead: Harvester-Wheatsheaf, 1991).

—— 'Self-Plagiarism, Creativity and Craftsmanship in Oscar Wilde', *English Literature in Transition*, 41: 1 (1998), 6–23.

—— 'An Allusion in Oscar Wilde's "The Canterville Ghost"', *Notes and Queries*, 45 NS: 2 (June 1998), 224–6.

—— 'Aesthetics, Economics and Commodity Culture: Theorizing Value in Late Nineteenth-Century Britain', *English Literature in Transition*, 42: 2 (1999), 143–71.

—— '"Trafficking With Merchants for His Soul": Dante Gabriel Rossetti Among the Aesthetes', *Proceedings of the British Academy* (forthcoming).

—— and IAN SMALL, *Politics and Value in English Studies* (Cambridge: Cambridge University Press, 1993).

———— 'How Many "Bags of Red Gold"?: The Extent of Wilde's Success as a Dramatist', *English Literature in Transition*, 42: 3 (1999), 283–97.

———— 'The British "Man of Letters" and the Rise of the Professional', in Lawrence Rainey (ed.), *The Cambridge History of Literary Criticism*, vii (forthcoming).

HART-DAVIS, RUPERT (ed.), *The Letters of Oscar Wilde*, (1962; London: Hart-Davis, 1963).

—— (ed.), *More Letters of Oscar Wilde* (London: John Murray, 1985).

HOLLAND, MERLIN (ed.), *The Complete Works of Oscar Wilde* (Glasgow: HarperCollins, 1994).

HYDER, CLYDE K. (ed.), *Swinburne as Critic* (London: Routledge and Kegan Paul, 1972).

INMAN, BILLIE ANDREW, 'Estrangement and Connection: Walter Pater, Benjamin Jowett, and William M. Hardinge', in Laurel Brake and Ian Small (eds.), *Pater in the 1990s* (Greensboro, NC: ELT Press, 1991), 1–20.

JACKSON, JOHN WYSE (ed.), *Aristotle at Afternoon Tea: The Rare Oscar Wilde* (London: Fourth Estate, 1991).

JACKSON, RUSSELL (ed.), *Oscar Wilde, The Importance of Being Earnest* (1980; London: A & C Black, 1990).

—— (ed.), *Oscar Wilde: An Ideal Husband* (1983; London: A & C Black, 1993),

—— 'Oscar Wilde's Contract for a New Play', *Theatre Notebook*, 50 (1996), 113–14.

—— and IAN SMALL, 'Some New Drafts of a Wilde Play', *English Literature in Transition*, 30: 1 (1987), 7–15.

JOHNSON, LIONEL, 'For a Little Clan', *Academy*, 59 (13 Oct. 1900), 314–15.

JONES, KATHLEEN, *Learning not to be First: The Life of Christina Rossetti* (Windrush Press: Gloucestershire, 1991).

KAPLAN, JOEL H., 'A Puppet's Power: George Alexander, Clement Scott, and the Replotting of *Lady Windermere's Fan*', *Theatre Notebook*, 46: 2 (1992), 59–73.

—— 'Oscar Wilde's contract for *A Woman of No Importance*', *Theatre Notebook*, 48: 1 (1994), 46–8.

—— 'Wilde on the Stage', in Peter Raby (ed.), *The Cambridge Companion to Oscar Wilde* (Cambridge: Cambridge University Press, 1997), 249–75.

KENNELLY, BRENDAN (ed.), *The Penguin Book of Irish Verse* (Harmondsworth: Penguin Books, 1970).

KIBERD, DECLAN, *Inventing Ireland* (1995; London: Vintage, 1996).

—— 'Oscar Wilde: The Resurgence of Lying', in Peter Raby (ed.), *The Cambridge Companion to Oscar Wilde* (Cambridge: Cambridge University Press, 1997), 276–94.

KNOX, MELISSA, *Oscar Wilde: A Long and Lovely Suicide* (London: Yale University Press, 1994).

KOHL, NORBERT, *Oscar Wilde: The Works of a Conformist Rebel* (Cambridge: Cambridge University Press, 1988).

KSINAN, CATHERINE, 'Wilde as Editor of *Woman's World*', *English Literature in Transition*, 41: 4 (1998), 408–26.

LANDON, H. C. ROBBINS, *1791: Mozart's Last Year* (London: Thames and Hudson, 1988).

LANG, CECIL Y. (ed.), *The Letters of Matthew Arnold*, ii (London: University Press of Virginia, 1997).

—— (ed.), *The Letters of Matthew Arnold*, iii (London: University Press of Virginia, 1998).

LAWLER, DONALD (ed.), *Oscar Wilde: The Picture of Dorian Gray* (New York: W. W. Norton, 1988).

LEVEY, MICHAEL, *The Case of Walter Pater* (London: Thames and Hudson, 1978).

LEWIS, LLOYD, and HENRY JUSTIN SMITH, *Oscar Wilde Discovers America* (New York: Harcourt Brace, 1936).

LUKES, STEVEN, *Individualism* (Oxford: Blackwell, 1973).

MCCORMACK, JERUSHA (ed.), *Wilde the Irishman* (London: Yale University Press, 1998).

McDonald, Peter D., *British Literary Culture and Publishing Practice: 1880–1914* (Cambridge: Cambridge University Press, 1997).

McGann, Jerome J., *The Textual Condition* (Princeton: Princeton University Press, 1991).

Maguire, J. Robert, 'Oscar Wilde and the Dreyfus Affair', *Victorian Studies*, 41: 1 (Autumn 1997), 1–29.

Mander, Raymond, and Joe Mitchenson, *The Lost Theatres of London* (London: Rupert Hart-Davis, 1968).

—— —— *The Theatres of London* (London: New English Library, 1975).

Martin, Robert K., 'Oscar Wilde and the Fairy Tale: "The Happy Prince" as Self-Dramatization', *Studies in Short Fiction*, 16 (1979), 74–7.

Mason, A. E. W., *Sir George Alexander and the St James's Theatre* (London: Macmillan, 1935).

Mason, Stuart [Christopher Millard], *Oscar Wilde: Art and Morality: A Defence of 'The Picture of Dorian Gray'* (London: J. Jacobs, 1908).

—— *A Bibliography of Oscar Wilde* (London: T. Werner Laurie, 1914).

Melville, Joy, *Mother of Oscar* (London: John Murray, 1994).

Moore, George, *Literature at Nurse, Or Circulating Morals* (London: Vizetelly and Co., 1885).

Morgan, Charles, *The House of Macmillan* (London: Macmillan, 1943).

Muir, Percy, *English Children's Books: 1600 to 1900* (London: B. T. Batsford Ltd., 1954).

Murray, Isobel (ed.), *The Oxford Authors: Oscar Wilde* (Oxford: Oxford University Press, 1989).

—— (ed.), *Oscar Wilde: The Soul of Man and Prison Writings* (Oxford: Oxford University Press, 1990).

Nelson, James G., *The Early Nineties: A View from the Bodley Head* (Cambridge, Mass.: Harvard University Press, 1971).

Nowell-Smith, Simon (ed.), *Letters to Macmillan* (London: Macmillan, 1976).

O'Toole, Fintan, 'Venus in Blue Jeans: Oscar Wilde, Jesse James, Crime and Fame', in Jerusah McCormack (ed.), *Wilde the Irishman* (London: Yale University Press, 1998), 71–81.

Pater, Walter, *Studies in the History of the Renaissance* (London: Macmillan, 1873).

—— *Marius the Epicurean* (2 vols. London: Macmillan, 1885).

—— *Appreciations* (London: Macmillan, 1889).

—— *Gaston de Latour: An Unfinished Romance* (London: Macmillan, 1897).

Pearson, Hesketh, *The Life of Oscar Wilde* (London: Methuen, 1946).

—— *The Last Actor-Managers* (London: Methuen, 1950).

Pine, Richard, *The Thief of Reason: Oscar Wilde and Modern Ireland* (Dublin: Gill and Macmillan, 1995).

POWELL, KERRY, *Oscar Wilde and the Theatre of the 1890s* (Cambridge: Cambridge University Press, 1990).

RABY, PETER, *Oscar Wilde* (Cambridge: Cambridge University Press, 1988).

—— 'The Origins of *The Importance of Being Earnest*', *Modern Drama*, 37: 1 (1994), 139–47.

—— 'The Making of *The Importance of Being Earnest*', *Times Literary Supplement*, no. 4629 (20 Dec. 1991), 13.

—— *The Importance of Being Earnest; A Reader's Companion* (New York: Twayne, 1995).

—— 'Wilde's Comedies of Society', in Peter Raby (ed.), *The Cambridge Companion to Oscar Wilde* (Cambridge: Cambridge University Press, 1997), 143–60.

REED, FRANCES MIRIAM (ed.), *Oscar Wilde's Vera; or, the Nihilist* (Lampeter, Dyfed: Edwin Mellen Press, 1989).

ROBERTS, WILLIAM, 'The First Edition Mania', *Fortnightly Review*, 55 NS (Jan.–June 1894), 347–54.

ROBERTSON, W. GRAHAM, *Time Was* (London: Hamish Hamilton, 1931).

ROSS, MARGERY, *Robert Ross, Friend of Friends* (London: Jonathan Cape, 1952).

ROSSETTI, DANTE GABRIEL, 'Madeline with other Poems and Parables. By Thomas Gordon Hake, M.D.', *Academy*, 2 (1 Feb. 1871), 105–7.

ROWELL, GEORGE, 'The Truth About *Vera*', *Nineteenth Century Theatre*, 21: 2 (Winter 1993), 94–100.

SANDULESCU, GEORGE (ed.), *Rediscovering Oscar Wilde* (Gerrards Cross, Bucks: Colin Smythe, 1994).

SCHROEDER, HORST, *Oscar Wilde, 'The Portrait of Mr W. H.'—Its Composition, Publication and Reception* (Braunschweig: Technische Universität Carolo-Wilhelmina zu Braunschweig, 1984).

—— 'A Printing Error in "The Soul of Man Under Socialism"', *Notes and Queries*, 43 NS: 1 (March 1996), 49–51.

SEILER, ROBERT M., *The Book Beautiful: Walter Pater and the House of Macmillan* (London: Athlone Press, 1999).

SHEWAN, RODNEY (ed.), '*A Wife's Tragedy*: An Unpublished Sketch for a Play by Oscar Wilde', *Theatre Research International*, 7: 2 (1982), 75–131.

SIEGEL, SANDRA, 'Oscar Wilde's Gift and Oxford's "Coarse Impertinence"', in Tadhg Foley and Seán Ryder (eds.), *Ideology and Ireland in the Nineteenth Century* (Dublin: Four Courts Press, 1998), 69–78.

SINFIELD, ALAN, *The Wilde Century: Effeminacy, Oscar Wilde and the Queer Moment* (London: Cassell, 1994).

—— '"Effeminacy" and "Femininity": Sexual Politics in Wilde's Comedies', *Modern Drama*, 37: 1 (1994), 34–52.

SLOAN, JOHN, 'In a Music Hall', *Review of English Studies*, 46 (1995), 435–7.

SMALL, IAN, *Conditions for Criticism* (Oxford: Clarendon Press, 1991).

—— (ed.), *Oscar Wilde: A Woman of No Importance* (1983; London: A & C Black, 1993).

—— *Oscar Wilde Revalued* (Greensboro, NC: ELT Press, 1993).

—— (ed.), *Oscar Wilde: Complete Short Fiction* (Harmondsworth: Penguin, 1994).

—— (ed.), *Oscar Wilde: Lady Windermere's Fan*, (1980; London: A & C Black, 1999).

SMITH, PHILIP E., and MICHAEL S. HELFAND (eds.), *Oscar Wilde's Oxford Notebooks* (New York: Oxford University Press, 1989).

SMITH, TIMOTHY D'ARCH, and HORST SCHROEDER, 'Feasting with Panthers', *Notes and Queries*, 41 NS: 3 (June 1995), 201–2.

SNIDER, CLIFTON, 'Eros and Logos in Some Fairy Tales by Oscar Wilde: A Jungian Interpretation', *Victorian Newsletter*, 84 (Fall 1993), 1–8.

STEPHENS, JOHN RUSSELL, *The Profession of the Playwright* (Cambridge: Cambridge University Press, 1992).

STOKES, JOHN, 'Wilde on Dostoevsky', *Notes and Queries*, 27 NS : 3 (June 1980), 215–16.

—— *In the Nineties* (Hemel Hempstead: Harvester-Wheatsheaf, 1989).

—— *Oscar Wilde: Myths, Miracles, and Imitations* (Cambridge: Cambridge University Press, 1996).

—— 'Wilde the Journalist', in Peter Raby (ed.), *The Cambridge Companion to Oscar Wilde*, (Cambridge: Cambridge University Press, 1997), 69–79.

SUTHERLAND, JOHN, *Mrs Humphry Ward: Eminent Victorian, Pre-Eminent Edwardian* (Oxford: Clarendon Press, 1990).

—— *Victorian Fiction: Writers, Publishers, Readers* (London: Macmillan, 1995).

SWINBURNE, ALGERNON, *George Chapman* (London: Macmillan, 1875).

TAYLOR, M. W., *Men Versus the State* (Oxford: Clarendon Press, 1992).

THOMAS, J. D., '"The Soul of Man Under Socialism": An Essay in Context', *Rice University Studies*, 51 (1965), 83–95.

WEBER, CARL J., *The Rise and Fall of James Ripley Osgood* (Waterville, Maine: Colby College Press, 1959).

WELLENS, OSKAR, 'A Hitherto Unnoticed Review by Wilde', *Notes and Queries*, 40 NS: 3 (Sept. 1994), 364.

WHITE, ALLON, *The Uses of Obscurity* (London: Routledge and Kegan Paul, 1981).

WHITE, VICTORIA, 'Women of No Importance: Misogyny in the Work of Oscar Wilde', in Jerusha McCormack (ed.), *Wilde the Irishman* (London: Yale University Press, 1998), 158–65.

WOODCOCK, GEORGE, *Anarchism* (Harmondsworth: Penguin, 1963).

Worth, Katherine, *Oscar Wilde* (London, Macmillan, 1983).
Worthen, John, 'D. H. Lawrence: Problems with Multiple Texts', in Ian Small and Marcus Walsh (eds.), *The Theory and Practice of Text-Editing* (Cambridge: Cambridge University Press, 1991), 14–34.
—— 'Lawrence and the "Expensive Edition Business"', in Ian Willison, Warwick Gould, and Warren Chernaik (eds.), *Modern Writers and the Market Place* (Basingstoke: Macmillan, 1996), 105–32.

Index